Chess: Man vs Machine

Bradley Ewart

San Diego • New York
A. S. Barnes & Company, Inc.
In London:
The Tantivy Press

A. S. Barnes and Co., Inc.

The Tantivy Press
Magdalen House
136-148 Tooley Street
London, SE1 2TT, England

First Edition
Manufactured in the United States of America
For information write to A. S. Barnes and Company, Inc., P.O.
Box 3051, San Diego, CA 92038

Library of Congress Cataloging in Publication Data

Ewart, Bradley, 1932-
    Chess: Man vs. Machine

    Bibliography: p.
    Includes index.
    1. Chess — Data processing — History.   2.   Chess —
Miscellanea.   I.   Title.
GV1447.E93   794.1'7   77-84566
ISBN 0-498-02167-X

1 2 3 4 5 6 7 8 9   84 83 82 81 80

To Bethy

Abbreviations Used in Illustration Credits

AC   Author's collection.
AH   American Heritage Publishing Company.
BB   Beethoven-Haus, Bonn.
BC   Bapst Library, Boston College, Chestnut Hill, Massachusetts.
BL   British Library, London.
BN   Bibliothèque Nationale, Paris.
CPL   Cleveland Public Library, collections other than those of the John G. White Department.
DM   Deutsches Museum, Munich.
EPFL   Maryland Department, Enoch Pratt Free Library, Baltimore.
FLP   Print and Picture Department, Free Library of Philadelphia.
GRH   General Research and Humanities Division, The New York Public Library, Astor, Lenox, and Tilden Foundations.
HM   *Harper's New Monthly Magazine.*
HW   *Harper's Weekly.*
ILN   *Illustrated London News.*
INPS   I. N. Phelps Stokes Collection, Prints Division, The New York Public Library, Astor, Lenox, and Tilden Foundations.

JGW   John G. White Department, Cleveland Public Library.
JM   John Mulholland Collection in the Walter Hampden-Edwin Booth Theatre Collection and Library at The Players.
JTW   James T. White and Company.
KB   Koninklijke Bibliotheek, The Hague.
KCPL   Kansas City Public Library, Kansas City, Missouri.
MCF   Medical and Chirurgical Faculty of the State of Maryland.
NMU   Collection of the National Museum from Music Box to Barrel Organ, Utrecht, Holland.
NPG   National Portrait Gallery, London.
NYPL   Picture Collection, The New York Public Library.
ON   Österreichische Nationalbibliothek, Vienna.
SA   Scientific American, Inc.
SH   Schloss Heinsheim.
SS   Schlosshauptmannschaft Schönbrunn, Schloss Schönbrunn, Vienna.
TM   Technisches Museum für Industrie und Gewerbe, Vienna.

International Federation for Information

Haines Photographic Services
Kansas Missouri Chess League

For translating the book on the chess automaton by Racknitz, I am deeply indebted to Elizabeth Somer Färber of Graz, Austria. I also thank Martin Kunze, Sherri Remmick, and Michael Magoon for additional German-English translations.

I gratefully acknowledge all those who have contributed support and encouragement, particularly the John Heim and Sam Ewart families.

Finally, I especially appreciate the aid of my dear wife Mary Beth Heim Ewart. She read the manuscript at several stages, and her suggestions have been a helpful influence throughout the preparation of the book.

1
"An Illusion Which Does Honor to the Human Mind":
Kempelen's Automaton Chess Player

1.

"What do you think of these supernatural phenomena?" asked the Empress Maria Theresa, as she sat, like the common parent of a large family, amid a crowd composed of her own children, the upper nobility, and foreign ambassadors. The year was 1769 and the Empress had gathered the spectators to watch a Frenchman named Pelletier perform magnetic tricks which, although new to the Viennese court, were commonly seen in exhibitions on the boulevards of Paris.

Maria Theresa was extremely fond of all sorts of entertainments. In her youth, she had thought nothing of staying up all night dancing and playing cards. She had sung in elaborately staged operas with members of the court and imperial family. Indeed, had she not been destined to rule the Habsburg empire, her voice might have assured her of a successful operatic career. In her later years—she was then fifty-two—she had become an enthusiastic spectator.

The Empress had directed her question to Baron Wolfgang von Kempelen, the Hungarian gentleman sitting at her side. He was counselor to the Royal Chamber of the Empress in Hungary and a celebrated mechanical genius. For that reason, Maria Theresa had summoned him to Vienna from

The Empress Maria Theresa started a conversation and ended by commissioning the building of a chess automaton. BY PERMISSION OF ON.

Baron Wolfgang von Kempelen began constructing his famous Turk in 1769. COURTESY OF JGW.

his home in Pressburg (Bratislava) to sit next to her at the performance and advise her.

"It's nothing which should surprise you," replied the thirty-five-year-old Kempelen. "Nothing is simpler. Anyone can do those experiments which seem to you so extraordinary."

"If it weren't for your reputation as a learned man, I would doubt what you say. But I'd be more willing to believe all this is a mere trifle if you yourself would show us something more marvelous, more incredible."

"I accept your majesty's challenge, and I dare hope to make you forget that French charlatan forever. However, I beg of you, Madam, at least one year's time before presenting myself before you."

"One year!" exclaimed the Empress.

"One year!" repeated Kempelen in a low voice, and he retired.

With the performance at an end, Maria Theresa returned to her principal preoccupation that year: the program of instruction to prepare her youngest daughter, Marie Antoinette, for her future role as

For Marie Antoinette it was good-bye Schönbrunn, hello Versailles. Later the Turk would make the same trip. BY PERMISSION OF ON.

In the 1926 French film *Le Joueur d'Échecs*, Charles Dullin played Baron von Kempelen. COURTESY OF KB.

Queen of France, an effort doomed to failure. Kempelen, meanwhile, returned to Pressburg to begin the project which had no doubt been forming for some time in his mind. The challenge by his Empress had been all that was needed to get it under way.

Born at Pressburg on January 23, 1734, Kempelen at 35 could claim a remarkable variety of achievements. Since childhood he had excelled in mechanics and engineering to such an extent that he sometimes nearly impoverished himself through his flair for invention, which consumed his spare funds and the time he might have devoted to more profitable pursuits. He was an expert on hydraulics and mechanics, a good naturalist, and an excellent artist and architect. His talents were employed in designing the cascades at Schönbrunn Palace and in supervising the construction of the Royal Palace at Budapest. He later studied the human voice and constructed a mechanical speaking machine capable of imitating human speech. He held high government offices both at the imperial court in Vienna and at Pressburg, which was then the capital of Hungary. He also served as director general of the state-owned salt mines in Hungary. In later years, he even wrote for the theater.

Kempelen, with his wife and children, lived on the first floor of his Pressburg residence. On the second floor, he had a small workshop which served as an anteroom to his study. The benches in the workshop were strewn with the tools of a carpenter, locksmith, and watchmaker, all resting in apparent disarray. To a casual observer there was little to suggest the nature of the work in progress. Only the inventor's mechanical mind could visualize what might be forthcoming.

Passing from the workshop into the study, the visitor found himself in a room nearly surrounded by large oak shelves and cabinets containing books, antiques, and a small collection of objects of natural history. Spaces of wall between the cabinets were decorated with paintings and prints executed by Kempelen himself.

For six months after his return to Pressburg, the Baron spent most of his time in the workshop. His new invention was completed in the early spring of 1770, in only half the time he had promised. After trying it out a few times, he partly disassembled it, carefully loaded it into a carriage, and set out, accompanied by several assistants, for Vienna.

2.

When Maria Theresa learned that Baron von Kempelen's masterpiece was finished and ready to be displayed, she assembled her family, the court, and many scientists and scholars to see the promised exhibition. Among the spectators was her son and

At **Schönbrunn Palace in 1770 Kempelen first exhibited the Turk.** FROM AC.

co-regent, the Emperor Joseph II. It is likely that the debut of the Baron's invention took place at Schönbrunn Palace, since the Empress spent much of her time there after the death, in 1765, of her husband, Francis Stephen of Lorraine.

As soon as the spectators had assembled, an announcement rang out above the buzz of conversation. Baron Wolfgang von Kempelen, counselor to the Royal Chamber of the Kingdom of Hungary, celebrated mechanician and inventor, would for the first time in history present a mechanical device that rivaled, even surpassed, the human brain in the intricacies of its organization. He would demonstrate the greatest mechanical achievement of all time, his remarkable automaton chess player. A startled silence fell over the guests as an assistant wheeled the machine into the room. They saw a slightly larger than life-size figure dressed in Turkish costume and seated behind a maple cabinet 3½ feet long, 2 feet wide, and 2½ feet high. The Turk's chair was attached to the cabinet, which could be rolled about on four castors. His right arm lay extended upon the top of the cabinet, while his left arm held a long Turkish pipe, as if he had just been smoking. The mustached Turk wore a turban and a long fur-lined cloak. His features were just human enough to convey an unearthly supernatural feeling without leaving any doubt that he was an artificial being of wood and metal. The eyes of the figure appeared to be gazing upon an 18-inch-square chessboard, which was permanently fixed to the surface of the cabinet.

The first idea which occurred to many of the spectators was that the cabinet was large enough to conceal a human player, who would somehow direct the Turk's game from within. One eyewitness, Karl Gottlieb von Windisch, reported that he, along with most of the crowd, could not help suspecting at first that a child was contained in the cabinet. From its dimensions, Windisch guessed that a ten- or twelve-year-old might have been hidden inside.

Many of the audience began to voice such opinions and they derided Kempelen for thinking them so gullible as to be taken in by so obvious a deception. Would the good Baron be so kind as to allow them to inspect the cabinet?

Kempelen seemed not the least dismayed by the outcry. He had, in fact, hoped for just such a reaction. Holding up his hands for silence, he announced that he would open each and every door of the cabinet and also the body of the Turk for as thorough an inspection as anyone wished to make. He would not only open all of the doors in the cabinet, but would move the machine around the room, turn it in any direction, and allow each spectator to examine it as he pleased.

He then began the demonstration that would be repeated each time the Turk was displayed. Though countless thousands were to witness the routine during the next eighty-five years, few would be less mystified than Windisch, who stated, "I was not backward in my scrutiny. I searched into its darkest corners; and finding no possibility of its concealing any object of even the size of my hat, my vanity was terribly mortified at seeing my ingenious conjecture put totally to flight."

To begin the demonstration, Kempelen opened the door of a compartment on the Turk's right-hand side. It occupied slightly less than one third the length of the cabinet and appeared to be completely filled with wheels, levers, cylinders, and other pieces of clockwork. Kempelen then opened a smaller door in the rear of the cabinet to allow spectators to see through the spaces between the machinery. In order to show that no person was hiding behind the tangle of wheelwork, Kempelen called for an attendant to bring a lighted candle, which he held just inside the rear door.

Closing that rear door, the Baron came around to the front and pulled out the single long drawer at the bottom of the cabinet. From it he took a set of chessmen of red and white ivory, set in a wooden block, and placed it next to the Turk's chessboard. Also in the drawer was a small elongated box containing six miniature chessboards, each of which

Before each game Kempelen displayed the Turk with all doors open. COURTESY OF JGW.

16

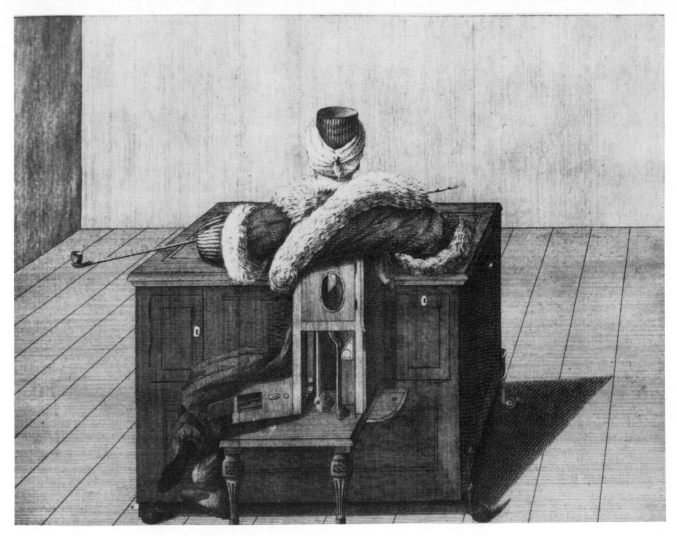

The Turk was wheeled around to show the doors in the rear of the figure. COURTESY OF JGW.

presented an endgame situation. The endgames could be set up on the automaton's board and played out when time did not permit the playing of full-length games.

The large compartment under the Turk's left hand occupied two thirds the length of the cabinet and had two doors in front and a smaller one in the rear to show that there was no false back to the compartment. The space within, as was next demonstrated, was nearly empty except for two pieces of machinery which looked like quadrants. On the floor of the large compartment were a small oblong wooden box or casket, a cushion, and a small board inscribed with golden letters. Kempelen removed the casket and board and set them on a side table. The pillow would be used to support the Turk's arm between moves. The Baron again called for the candle, which he thrust through the open rear door of the compartment to throw light into its remotest corners.

Finally Kempelen wheeled the Turk around, lifted his robes, and threw them over his head,

exposing the back of the figure. There, more doors were opened, revealing, as promised, the complete structure of the automaton's interior, which seemed to contain only more wheels and levers. There was even a small door in the Turk's trousers to show that his legs were hollow.

Then, with garments still turned up and with all doors flapping loosely, Kempelen wheeled the automaton around the room for a thorough inspection by all present. When the spectators had satisfied themselves completely as to the machine's anatomy and lack of human occupant, Kempelen shut all doors and placed the apparatus behind a railing or balustrade, the purpose of which, he announced, was to prevent anyone from shaking, touching, or leaning upon the machine, and to allow himself a space to walk between the crowd and the front of the cabinet. Next Kempelen reached into the interior of the machine and appeared to make some adjustment. He then removed the pipe and placed the Turk's left arm on the cushion.

At that point the inventor directed everyone's attention to the small cabinet or casket that he had placed upon a little table nearby. The casket's door faced away from the audience, so that Kempelen could open it and peer in from time to time during the game that followed, without exposing its mysterious contents to view. It was the casket, he declared, that contained the secret directing force which controlled the Turk's arm, causing it to select the logical move in response to any move by a human opponent.

There remained only to select an opponent for the Turk. If anyone thought the adversary was to be Kempelen or a confederate planted in the crowd, such ideas were quickly dispelled when the inventor announced that the Turk would challenge each and every person who wanted to test the machine. Several volunteers stepped forward from among the scholars and scientific advisers the Empress had assembled and, though one was selected to be first, each would get his turn.

It is interesting to note at this point that the Turk had played a few games in Pressburg before he was taken to Vienna. The man who had been chosen for the honor of being the automaton's first opponent was Herr Matthias, a friend of Kempelen and a counselor of the empire. One day late in 1769, Matthias had been invited to Kempelen's house for a game of chess with "an unusual opponent."

When Matthias arrived, he found that a kind of tent had been erected in Kempelen's drawing room. Then the silken curtains of the tent were drawn aside, revealing the inventor with his newly constructed automaton. Kempelen demonstrated the Turk in the same manner as he later did in Vienna and allowed Matthias, a player of some ability, to match himself against the machine. The test was quite effective, assuring the inventor that his automaton was ready to be shown before the Empress and her court.

Before the beginning of the first game for the Empress, Kempelen announced that the first move would always be reserved for the automaton and that no move, once made, could be retracted. Moreover, if either opponent made a false move, the piece making the move would be removed from the board and the move would be forfeited. Also he requested all adversaries to take care in placing each piece exactly in the center of a square. That, he assured them, was necessary to prevent damage to the Turk's fingers.

Up to that time, the Baron had cleverly convinced everyone that the machine could hold no human director and that its sole motive power was the machinery just demonstrated, but the greatest test of the automaton was yet to come. Could the Turk really play a game of chess? As if in reply to that unspoken question in the minds of all assembled, the slow whir of clockwork machinery was heard and the automaton moved his head from side to side, as if contemplating the board before him. Seeming to make a decision quickly, he slowly raised his left arm from the cushion and moved his hand, with astonishing precision, into position over a pawn. Then, after hovering a moment, the hand descended by a movement of the wrist, the fingers spread, grasped the pawn, and moved it forward two squares. The hand then returned to its place on the cushion and the sounds of machinery died out.

The Empress and the whole assemblage followed those events with a mixture of admiration and great astonishment, but one old woman, who surely remembered the tales she had been told in her childhood, crossed herself with a heavy and devout sigh and, according to Windisch, hid herself in a window seat, as distant as she could be from the evil spirit which she firmly believed possessed the automaton.

No doubt thinking he could beat any machine at chess, the opponent made his move. The automaton responded as before by surveying the board and making a move, and the game proceeded. When the Turk captured a piece, he first removed it from the board and then replaced it with his own chessman. It soon became apparent that the automaton was not only playing chess, but was playing it exceptionally well. He made his moves without any apparent aid from Kempelen, who did nothing but noisily wind up the Turk's machinery every ten or twelve moves. At other times, the inventor sat among the spectators or strolled about the room, never touching the automaton. He would, during the course of several moves, stand with his back toward the chessboard and converse with some member of the audience. At other times he would go to the small table, open the door of the casket, and gaze inside, as if to reassure himself that everything was in order, insisting that the little box was necessary for the automaton's operation. Though twenty or thirty persons kept their eyes on Kempelen at all times, he never betrayed by the slightest movement any possible means of communication with the machine other than those mentioned.

When attacking his opponent's Queen, the Turk politely signaled the threat by nodding his head twice. When the adversary's King was endangered, the automaton announced the check with three nods. Soon the figure was nodding his head quite frequently. Finally, after the opponent had made a move, the Turk shook his head, indicating his refusal to continue. Kempelen stepped forward and explained that the gentleman had just been checkmated and that the automaton had won the game. Then the inventor again demonstrated the interior of the cabinet by opening its doors and lifting the Turk's robes as before.

The Baron kept his invention in Vienna for a time, while many games were played with the automaton, who won most, if not all, his contests. To test the Turk's powers of discrimination, adver-

The automaton always moved with his left hand, resting it on a pillow between moves. COURTESY OF JGW.

Transporting a chess automaton was always a problem. COURTESY OF JGW.

saries frequently made false moves contrary to the rules of chess. Whenever that occurred, the Turk, seemingly outraged, indignantly shook his head from side to side in disapproval. He then snatched up the offending piece and took a move himself, thus depriving his opponent of both piece and move, a situation which nearly always assured the Turk a victory. The automaton himself never made illegal moves, thus avoiding the penalty of his own rule.

3.

Eventually business obligations called Kempelen back to Pressburg. Meanwhile, news of the marvelous automaton chess player had spread throughout most of Europe. With each retelling, the story, which was quickly picked up by the newspapers and journals, became more exaggerated and distorted. The modest Kempelen had built the Turk simply to provide a few days' entertainment for the Empress and the imperial court and had thus expected, upon his return home, to put the automaton aside and resume his work, which had been neglected somewhat during the time he had spent working on the chess player. He was, however, greatly mistaken in that expectation. As word of the automaton spread, visitors to his dwelling in Pressburg formed first a small stream, then a steady flow, and finally a mighty torrent, interrupting him day and night and preventing any thoughts other than those of the automaton from entering his mind. He was also inundated with letters demanding that he explain the automaton or begging his permission to inspect the mechanism.

Kempelen installed the Turk in his upstairs study. Visitors were received in an apartment downstairs, then led up through the workshop and into the study, where the automaton, placed opposite the doorway, first struck the view of visitors. There the Baron exhibited the Turk before groups of twenty to thirty persons and allowed the visitors to engage the automaton in games of chess.

When time did not permit the playing of full games, the Baron got out the small box from the drawer of the Turk's cabinet. The box contained six miniature chessboards, each of which showed a different endgame position. Kempelen allowed a guest to select any endgame and to choose to play either side. The trick was that each endgame was designed so that the winner would be the player who played first and the Turk was always given the honor of the first move. His opponent usually chose the side that had the most or the strongest pieces. Some tried to outguess the machine by picking the side that looked weaker, but it made no difference. With the first move, the automaton almost always won.

The Turk also performed what is known as the Knight's Tour. After the chessmen were removed from the board, a spectator was allowed to place a Knight upon any of the squares and, from there, the Turk moved it successively over the sixty-four squares in just sixty-four moves, without stopping on any square more than once.

The one final trick in the Turk's repertoire involved the board with golden letters, which was placed on the automaton's chessboard at the completion of all chess activity. Kempelen then pretended to adjust some interior mechanism which seemingly enabled the Turk to answer any question

19

Presburg, Posonium.

In Pressburg, Kempelen's home soon became the center of much unwelcome attention. BY PERMISSION OF BL.

The Reverend Mr. Louis Dutens wrote perhaps the first English account of the automaton. BY PERMISSION OF BL.

from the audience by pointing successively to letters making up the reply. To indicate the end of each word, the automaton returned his arm to the cushion. An assistant usually repeated each letter and word in a loud voice, for the benefit of persons in the rear of the room.

One of the many groups of visitors to Kempelen's house included the English ambassador, several English lords, Prince Guistiniani, and the Reverend Mr. Dutens. Louis Dutens was an English clergyman of French Huguenot ancestry who had received his clerical post at Elsdon as a favor from his friend and patron the Duke of Northumberland. When Dutens first arrived at Elsdon, his appearance, manners, and foreign accent excited considerable surprise among his parishioners, but his professional duties, they soon discovered, consisted chiefly of escorting the Duke's son, Lord Percy Algernon, around the capitals of Europe.

After trying the automaton's skill in a game, Dutens wrote the first English report of the Turk in a letter to the *Gentleman's Magazine*, datelined Pressburg, July 24, 1770. A French version of the same letter appeared in the *Mercure de France*. Like many others, Dutens tried to deceive the Turk by making a false move. At one point in the game he moved his Queen like a Knight. Instead of removing the Queen and taking a move, the automaton merely replaced the impertinent piece on the square from which it had made the illegal Knight move and allowed Dutens to continue.

A frequent visitor to Kempelen's study was the aforementioned Karl Gottlieb von Windisch, who was personally acquainted with Kempelen and who often played chess with the automaton. In 1773, Windisch published some accounts of the Turk in several provincial German journals and later included them in his *Georgraphy of the Kingdom of Hungary*. Windisch wrote some letters about the automaton to his friend Chrétien de Mechel in Basel and, in 1783, Mechel published the letters in a pamphlet, with three plates carefully engraved from Kempelen's own drawings of the automaton. Apparently neither Windisch nor Dutens learned

Karl Gottlieb von Windisch, who witnessed the Turk's debut, later provided the most complete description of the automaton. BY PERMISSION OF ON.

the secrets of how the Turk played chess. "Is it an illusion?" asked Windisch, "So be it. But it is, then, an illusion which does honor to the human mind; an illusion more surprising, more inconceivable, than all those which are to be found in the different collections of mathematical recreations." Dutens, who appeared even more mystified than Windisch, wrote, "You will perhaps expect me to propose some conjectures as to the means employed to direct this machine in its movements. I wish I could form any that were reasonable and well founded; but notwithstanding the minute attention with which I have repeatedly observed it, I have not been able in the least degree to form any hypothesis which could satisfy myself."

Kempelen himself was the first to admit the automaton was an illusion. To a group of friends, including Windisch, he declared, "It is a mere trifle, not without merit as to its mechanism; but those effects, which to the spectator appear so wonderful, arise merely from the boldness of the conception, and the fortunate choice of the means employed by me to carry out the illusion."

While not attempting to pass off the automaton as a pure machine, the Baron never revealed in public just what the illusion was or what means he used to carry it out. Yet he did not want the fame and applause the automaton had suddenly thrust upon him. "Torn to pieces by the crowd, who eagerly rushed to view the phenomenon," wrote chess journalist George Walker, "Kempelen found it was easier to raise a spirit than to lay him again. Pestered with letters demanding explanation, from all the savants of Europe; annoyed at the absurdities . . . by the public press; and called upon morning, noon, and night to set up [the automaton], poor Kempelen

began to find that fame, however glittering, has its drawbacks. Many years of time, and the greater part of his fortune, had he lavished in improving the science of hydraulics. These efforts were before the public; but, although deservedly of merit, his improved fire-engines and water-pumps were altogether pushed into the shade, in favor of the automaton chess player!"

Kempelen perhaps could have quelled the interest in his automaton by simply exposing the Turk's secrets to the public, but he could not bring himself to do that. Though he thought them "a mere trifle," he could not give up so easily the secrets which had baffled the best scientific minds of all Europe. The Baron had several offers to purchase the automaton and the secrets for large sums of money from persons hoping to profit by exhibiting the Turk. Kempelen, however, had not created the automaton to make money and he had not charged visitors to view the automaton, since his sense of honor prevented him from taking profits from an invention he regarded as a trick. It was for him a mere

George Walker, author of "Anatomy of the Chess Automaton," spread the Turk's fame. COURTESY OF JGW.

recreation; he considered his profession was science, not magic tricks and conjuring.

Finally Kempelen hit upon an idea to unburden himself of the tiresome duties thrust upon him by the Turk. He partly dismantled the automaton, stowed him away, and let it be known that the mechanism had been damaged by frequent moving from place to place. As a result, he said, the machine could no longer be exhibited. Thus he was able to resume work on the mechanical devices which he believed to be his life's work.

In the story "Enoch Soames" by Max Beerbohm, Soames, who fancied himself a writer destined for literary immortality, sold his soul to the devil in exchange for a chance to visit the reading room of the British Museum one hundred years in the future to savor the acclaim denied him in the present. Had Kempelen made a similar deal for a two-hundred-year time trip, he would have found a few scattered references to himself as a hydraulic engineer and inventor of a speaking machine. However, he would have found that he was chiefly remembered for a feat he considered a mere trifle, a trick, a bagatelle: the invention of the famous automaton chess player.

ON THE CHESSBOARD
The Knight's Tour

When Windisch witnessed the first public exhibition of Kempelen's chess automaton, he was, of course, amazed by the Turk's ability to conduct a game of chess, but in addition he added, "The moving of the Knight successively over the sixty-four squares of the board, in as many leaps, is also a feat too remarkable to be passed over. As soon as the chessmen are taken off, one of the bystanders places a Knight on any square of the board he chooses. The Automaton lifts up the Knight, and beginning at the square on which he stands, causes it to cover the sixty-four squares in the same number of moves, without missing one, and without touching one

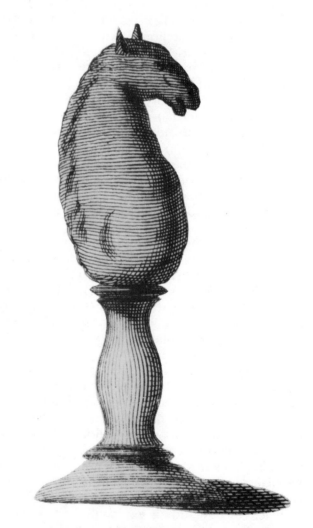

A Knight's Tour adorned the title page of Racknitz's book on the automaton. COURTESY OF JGW.

The Knight's Tour began by allowing a spectator to place the piece on any square of the chessboard. COURTESY OF JGW.

22

The Swiss mathematician Leonard Euler solved the Knight's Tour algebraically. BY PERMISSION OF ON.

square twice over. The spectator marks the squares in the progress of this difficult calculation, by placing a counter on each square to which the Knight is played. No matter what square you first seat the Knight upon, he never misses the performance of his task."

The Knight's Tour, which was often performed by the Turk throughout his career, was nothing new in Kempelen's day. A complete tour of the chessboard probably had been known to al-Adli, a ninth-century Moslem composer of chess problems. Even before that time, early Moslem and Indian manuscripts had described half-board tours of thirty-two squares.

About 1759, the great Swiss mathematician, Leonard Euler, worked out general principles for calculating the Knight's Tour and composed a number of beautifully symmetrical tours. Further methods for composing tours were later described by Vandermonde, Moon, De Moivre, and Roget.

Despite the difficulty of composing Knight's Tours, there are considerably more possible tours of the sixty-four squares than one might suppose. Estimates have ranged from the conservative "exceeds thirty-one million" to the not-so-ridiculous "zillions."

The most interesting routes are the reentrant or closed tours, in which it is possible to start on any square and return to that same square on the sixty-fourth move. The Turk always performed that type of tour, in which, as Windisch reported, a spectator was allowed to begin the demonstration by placing the Knight on any one of the sixty-four squares. The most interesting of the closed tours display some form of symmetry.

Knight's Tour 1

When Kempelen exhibited the Turk, the automaton may have executed the following fascinating symmetrical design. It is almost certain that this Knight's Tour was used at a later period of the automaton's career. The tour was composed by Euler around 1759 and undoubtedly would have been available to Kempelen.

Euler also composed tours comprising half the board. Two such pathways, when combined, form a complete tour, provided it is possible to jump from one half to the other. In the following example, the series 1...32, when inverted, is identical with 33...64. As pointed out in *Le Palamede,* 1842, other tours may be constructed by making transformations in the original route 1...32, such as:

I. 7...1, 8...32.
II. 7...1, 8...25, 32...26.
III. 15...10, 7...1, 8, 9, 16...21, 24...32, 23, 22.

One of the most fascinating of the symmetrical Knight's Tours was first published in the *Schach Zeitung,* 1849. As in many other symmetrical tours, any two squares on the opposite side of the center, and equidistant from it, have numbers with a difference of thirty-two. But in addition, this tour forms a magic square. The numbers in each rank and file add up to 260. Surprisingly, this is not the only Knight's Tour discovered which forms a magic square.

37	62	43	56	35	60	41	50
44	55	36	61	42	49	34	59
63	38	53	46	57	40	51	48
54	45	64	39	52	47	58	33
♞	26	15	20	7	32	13	22
16	19	8	25	14	21	6	31
27	2	17	10	29	4	23	12
18	9	28	3	24	11	30	5

2	11	58	51	30	39	54	15
59	50	3	12	53	14	31	38
10	♞	52	57	40	29	16	55
49	60	9	4	13	56	37	32
64	5	24	45	36	41	28	17
23	48	61	8	25	20	33	42
6	63	46	21	44	35	18	27
47	22	7	62	19	26	43	34

2
Cashing Coin from Base Metal: Travels with the Turk

1.

In the fall of 1781, nearly a year after the death of Maria Theresa, her son and heir the Emperor Joseph II interrupted the work of his counselor Baron von Kempelen with a summons to appear at court. When the inventor arrived in Vienna, Joseph told him that he remembered the automaton chess player, which had excited so much interest a decade earlier, and wondered if Kempelen could again present the marvelous Turk at court for the forthcoming visit of the Grand Duke and Duchess of Russia. The Baron was gratified to have a chance to please his sovereign and immediately consented to begin the task of rehabilitating the automaton.

Joseph liked the Grand Duke Paul and especially favored his consort, the Grand Duchess Marya Fyodorovna. He had met the royal couple the year before, when he had visited Russia, and had praised them in a letter to Maria Theresa, saying, "The Grand Duke is greatly undervalued abroad. His wife is very beautiful and seems created for her position. They understand each other perfectly. They are clever and vivacious and very well educated, as well as high-principled, open and just. The happiness of others is more to them than wealth."

Paul, however, had been greatly ill at ease with his mother, the Empress Catherine II; and thus, in September 1781, he and the Grand Duchess began an extended visit to the capitals of Europe. Traveling as the Count and Countess du Nord, they

The Emperor Joseph II, a devotee of chess, did not forget Kempelen's Turk. BY PERMISSION OF ON.

planned to stop first at Vienna, where Joseph wished to do everything he could to make their visit a pleasant one. The Emperor thought Kempelen's automaton might amuse his royal guests, who fancied chess.

The Grand Duke Paul was responsible for the Turk's resurrection. BY PERMISSION OF ON.

2.

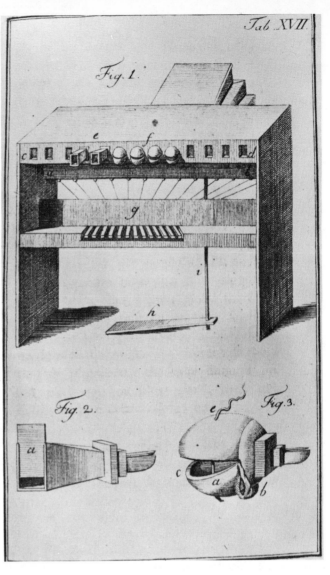

Progress was slow on this early-model speaking machine, so Kempelen abandoned it and started over. COURTESY OF JGW.

Kempelen, since 1769, had been experimenting with speaking machines, artificial devices patterned after the human voice and capable of imitating it to some extent. He hoped that after the machines were perfected they might enable mute persons to speak.

At first the inventor tried to produce vowel sounds by positioning his hand in various ways inside a funnel-shaped device fitted with a tube, but that attempt proved unsatisfactory. Then after a detailed study of the human vocal organs, he constructed a jawlike mechanism consisting of a two-part, hinged, hollow, oval box fitted with a sound tube powered by a bellows. The sounds *a, o,* and *u* could be produced with the jaws in various positions, but the *e* sound was faulty, while *i* was impossible to produce.

Further experiments with the device enabled Kempelen to add the consonant sounds *l, m, n,* and *p* and to combine them with vowels to create syllables and words, such as *maman, papa, aula, lama,* and *mulo.* He built the vowel and consonant elements into a keyboard instrument resembling a small organ, but the sounds did not come out just right, so

that *papa* sounded like *phaa-ph-a.*

After working on the machine for two years he was so dissatisfied that he abandoned it completely and began work on a new speaking machine. The new device, more like a human speech organ, had an elastic, funnel-shaped rubber mouth and two tubes of tin to represent a nose. By shutting the mouth and opening both nasal tubes, he could produce a perfect *m* sound, which could be changed to *n* by simply closing one of the tubes. He soon discovered a way to make a *p* sound which, when modified, sounded something like the consonants *d, g, k,* and *t.* By further manipulations and combinations he was able to produce about thirty words and a few phrases. The machine's vocabulary included utterances such as *astronomie, chapeau, opera, comédie, pantomime;* and even *Constantinopolis, Mississippi,* and *Josephus Secundus Romanorum Imperator.*

Eventually Kempelen refined the machine to the

26

Kempelen operated this speaking machine, now at the Deutches Museum, Munich, as a musician plays a fine instrument. COURTESY OF DM.

point where it could pronounce any word in Latin, French, or Italian. It was capable of speaking complex sentences such as "*Ma chère Mama, aimé moi; je vous aime de tout mon coeur—Oh, ma chère Mere, on m'a fait du ma-a-a-al.*"

When Kempelen exhibited the machine, spectators saw a cloth-covered box sitting on a table. While pumping a bellows apparatus on the side, the inventor would slip his hand under the cloth to form words requested by the audience.

Once a young lady found Kempelen alone in the room where he was exhibiting the speaking machine. As she approached, the Baron bowed and addressed her by name while, at the same time, a second voice joined him in the greeting. Kempelen could hardly keep the poor girl from running out of the room in terror, but finally reassured her by explaining the invention.

The speaking machine also answered questions from spectators. When Windisch heard the device, he said it answered "clearly and distinctly" in a "sweet and agreeable" voice, but that it pronounced the letter *r* "lispingly and with a certain harshness." He added, "When its answer is not perfectly understood, it repeats it slower, and if required to speak a third time, it repeats it again, but with a tone of impatience and vexation." Goethe once heard the machine and commented that it could produce some childish words very nicely.

Kempelen had intended to dress the machine in the form of a human child of the age of five or six. He thought the voice sounded like that of a child of that age, and, in addition, he wanted to show that the machine was not yet perfected but was in a state

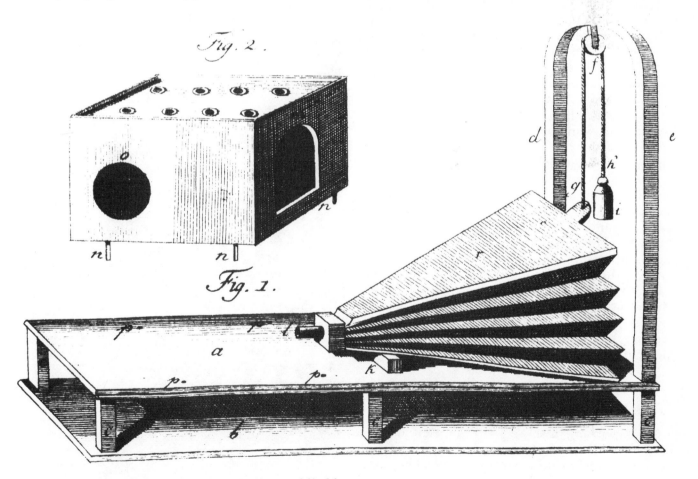

Kempelen's right elbow operated the bellows while his hands entered the two holes in the box. COURTESY OF JGW.

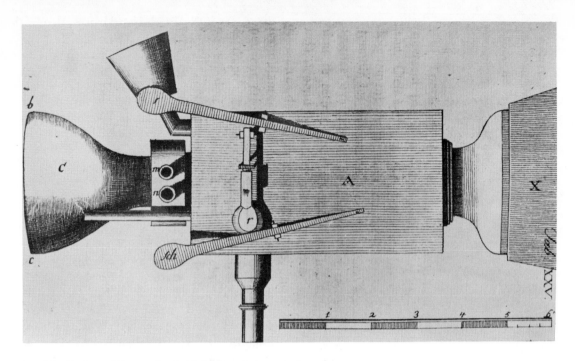

Inside the box, Kempelen's right hand operated various levers and keys while his left hand manipulated the flexible mouth, *C*. COURTESY OF JGW.

of childhood. However, the inventor probably never carried out his plans to dress the machine.

Kempelen realized his speaking machines were not faultless, but hoped that in the future some inventor would be able to perfect them. He thus described the machines fully in his book *The Mechanism of Human Speech*. Many years later, a copy of the book fell into the hands of Sir Charles Wheatstone, who decided to reconstruct one of the machines from the descriptions and diagrams. A friend of Wheatstone heard of the experiments and came to see the machine and hear it talk. The friend's young son, who accompanied his father, later wrote, "I saw Sir Charles manipulate the machine, and heard it speak; and although the articulation was disappointingly crude, it made a great impression on my mind. Sir Charles very kindly loaned my father Baron von Kempelen's book, and I devoured it when we reached home." Thus it was not Wheatstone who fulfilled Kempelen's hopes for the perfection of the speaking machine, but rather that young lad, whose name was Alexander Graham Bell.

3.

After working five weeks, Kempelen had the Turk ready to perform for the visit of the Grand Duke and Duchess in November 1781. The Baron had completely refurbished the automaton with new clothing and decorations in preparations for the court appearance, which took place as planned.

Sir Charles Wheatstone reconstructed Kempelen's speaking machine. BY PERMISSION OF NPG.

Although the royal pair had been lavished with every entertainment that human talent and ingenuity of the day could provide, they were struck with surprise and admiration when the Turk was exhibited for their amusement. They, along with others of the nobility present, urged Kempelen to take the automaton on a tour of the European capitals so that others might see the amazing invention.

That suggestion must have caused some conflict within the inventor's conscience, for he still felt that it was wrong to profit from an invention he knew to be a deception. As George Walker put it, "His nice sense of honor prevented him from stooping to coin cash, from metal so intrinsically base, as he felt the ore in question really to be."

But on the other hand, Kempelen's fortunes had been badly depleted by several years of incessant work on the speaking machines, from which he had not yet gained any profits. Many of the courtiers advised him that he owed it to his family to take advantage of the money-making potential of the chess automaton.

It would have mortified Kempelen to have been discovered in a deception before the public, but he no longer feared that the secrets of the Turk's operation would be exposed. He had exhibited the automaton often enough to be confident of success. Furthermore, the inventor wanted an excuse to travel and exhibit his speaking machines publicly, for he felt that the inventions were not fully appreciated at home.

Perhaps the deciding factor in favor of the tour was provided by the Emperor Joseph, who joined the others in being delighted and astonished by the feats of the Turk. The Emperor was eager for the rest of Europe to see such a marvel, which had arisen in the Habsburg realms. Thus Joseph liberally rewarded Kempelen for his performance and offered to allow the inventor a leave of absence for two years, during which time his salary as counselor of finances would continue. The Baron agreed to take the automaton chess player on a journey through France, England, and Germany, where the Turk had become something of a legend since his first appearance at the Viennese court in 1770.

Travel in the eighteenth century was anything but pleasant. To get anywhere, it was necessary to spend many days bumping along over rough roads in a horse-drawn carriage. Kempelen at first considered sending the automaton on tour with an exhibitor while he himself remained at home. The inventor, however, rejected that plan because he feared the Turk might require repairs, which would have to be entrusted to some foreign workman. If that failed, the profits from the tour might be lost. Thus Kempelen decided to go along to supervise repairs, but he did not wish to have to exhibit the machine himself. For that purpose he hired an assistant known as Herr Anthon to officiate at the exhibitions.

The Baron hired another assistant, a strong chess player whose name may never have been revealed, to act as the automaton's concealed director. There are several possible clues to that director's identity, but none is completely satisfactory. The French conjurer, Robert-Houdin, revealed in his memoirs that the Turk's secret director was a legless Polish patriot named Worousky. The rest of Robert-Houdin's story, however, seems at great variance with the true history of the Turk and will be quoted in a later chapter on fictional automatons, not so much because it is fiction, which it may be, but because many pieces of fiction have been based upon the account. It is just possible, however, that there might have been a real director named Worousky.

Edgar Allan Poe thought that in Kempelen's time the secret director of the Turk had been an Italian who traveled with the Baron but was never seen during exhibitions of the automaton. Mrs. Rivardi, a friend of the Kempelen family, once reported that the director (or directress) was Kempelen's own twelve-year-old daughter, who eventually had to give up her duties for reasons of health. Kempelen evidently kept the secret identity of his director carefully hidden, since it is not known which, if any, of the above reports are true.

The Turk himself required some modifications to facilitate packing him for journeys from one city to another. Eventually all preparations were completed, so that early in the year 1783 Kempelen set out for Paris, accompanied not only by his assistants, but by his wife, his two daughters, and his two sons.

4.

Kempelen arrived at the French capital about the middle of April, 1783. He planned to exhibit the Turk at a theater there beginning Monday, the twenty-first. Before he could begin, however, he was summoned to give an exhibition for the royal court at Versailles. Interest there was so great that it was not until May that he was able to show the automaton in Paris. At Versailles the automaton was

At Versailles the Duke beat the Turk. FROM AC.

29

occasionally outplayed, once by the Duc de Bouillon. The Duke then asked the Turk if he would play the great Francois André Danican Philidor, but the automaton answered, by means of his alphabet board, that he was unworthy of such competition.

Eventually Kempelen moved into Paris and made his headquarters at the Hotel d'Aligne, rue d'Orléans St. Honore. At that time the center of chess in Paris, and in fact the world, was the Café de la Régence. After moving to Paris, Kempelen matched his automaton against the best of the players at the famous café. The Régence had been built on the location of Henry IV's victorious entry into Paris and so it was said to be natural that it became the perpetual battleground of kings. It was frequented by the foremost chess players of the day, such as Verdoni, Léger, Carlier, and Bernard; but the greatest among them was the nearly legendary Philidor, unequaled in his time at chess and also a noted musician.

The Turk was no match for the players at the Régence; yet he put up such a good fight that he always won a round of applause for his efforts. Kempelen never claimed that his chess player was invincible and it seemed only natural that the world's best flesh-and-blood players could beat a machine. It almost seemed as if the defeats actually enhanced the Turk's popularity. There were in Paris, however, only seven or eight persons who could beat the Automaton.

Bernard, although he had beaten the automaton,

Against the Turk, Philidor failed by winning. COURTESY OF JGW.

was convinced that his adversary had displayed great resources. Thus there was a great demand for a game between the Turk and Philidor. Interest in viewing the wondrous machine was especially high at the Académie des Sciences and a performance was organized before that body, in which the Turk was to compete with Philidor. The game proved to be a very difficult ordeal for Philidor and one in which he failed, but not in the ordinary way.

While preparations for the match were in progress, Kempelen went to the great French master with an unusual request: "I am not a sorcerer, as you well know, and my automaton is no stronger than I. It is my last resource and my only livelihood now. Think, sir, what it would mean to me if I could announce at the exhibitions and proclaim in the newspapers that my automaton had beaten you."

Philidor, with his usual benevolence and lack of vanity, replied, "Sir, I would be glad to do it."

Then, after a moment's reflection, he added, "But you must admit that, in your own interest, we must not appear to conspire. I must defend myself and it must not seem that I am demonstrating any negligence, but I shall do all I can, I promise you, to be beaten by your automaton."

His good wishes were in vain, however, and all his efforts to succumb were futile. Philidor found it more difficult to lose under such conditions than to win and finally had to beat the Turk. All those who witnessed the contest agreed that Philidor had hardly played his best game; yet the great master himself often said that the chess game with the automaton was the most fatiguing of any that he had ever played. It was because he had failed to achieve his goal: defeat!

Before Kempelen left Vienna, he had asked M. Valltravers to write a letter introducing him to Benjamin Franklin, who was then American Ambassador to France.

The occasion of this letter is furnished me [wrote Valltravers on December 12, 1782], by a very ingenious gentleman, Monsieur Kempelen, Counsellor of his Imperial Majesty's Finances for the Kingdom of Hungary who, on a furlough obtained for two years, is ready to set out for Paris, Brussels, and England, attended by his whole family; not only to satisfy his own curiosity, but also in a great measure, that of the public. Endowed with peculiar taste and genius for mechanical inventions and improvements for which he sees no manner of encouragement in these parts, he means to import several of his most important discoveries and experiments wherever they shall be best received and rewarded. As an amusing specimen of his skill in mechanics, and as a means at the same time of supporting his traveling charges, he intends to exhibit the figure of a Turk playing at chess with any player, and answering, by pointing at the letters of an alphabet, any question made to him. I saw him play

At the time Kempelen's Turk visited Paris, Franklin lived in this residence at Passy. In one wing he kept the press on which he printed his *Morals of Chess*. COURTESY OF JGW.

twice without discovering his intelligent director anywhere in or about him. If there were nothing but the organization of his arm, hand and fingers, besides the motions of his head, that alone would entitle him to no small admiration. Besides his chess player, Monsieur Kempelen has amused himself with forming the figure of a child, uttering the first articulate sound of elocution. Of these I have heard it pronounce distinctly upwards of thirty words and phrases. There remain but five or six letters of the alphabet, the expression of which he intends to complete in Paris.

Franklin was at that time residing at Passy, now a fashionable section of Paris but then a village half a mile from the city. He was an avid chess enthusiast and often played the game at Passy with his intimate friend Mme. d'Hardancourt Brillon. Franklin and another chess companion, Louis Le Veillard, once entered the room where Mme. Brillon was taking a bath behind a screen. The gentlemen began playing chess and thus kept the poor woman waiting uncomfortably for hours while the game continued. "Never hereafter shall I consent to begin a game in your bathroom," wrote Franklin upon reaching home. "Can you forgive me this indiscretion?"

It was Mme. Brillon who inspired Franklin to write his famous *Morals of Chess*. Franklin's own manners at the chessboard, however, were not beyond reproach. He seems to have been a poor loser and he made a great show of impatience with opponents who moved too slowly to suit him. At such times, Franklin would rudely drum upon the table with his fingers. Once, when his chess opponent Chaumont tactfully pointed out that he was violating one of the rules in his own *Morals of Chess*,

Franklin replied, "Nonsense, it is a trifle, not worth speaking about."

Franklin sometimes played chess at the Café de la Régence when he was negotiating in Paris. As his fame grew among the French, he usually attracted a crowd that was more interested in seeing the man than the game. One contest that is supposed to have taken place at the Régence was reported by Franklin's grandson and, in a slightly different version, by Lafayette. Franklin's King was in check and he was about to lose the game but, had that not been the case, he himself could have checkmated his adversary on the move. Choosing to ignore the threatened King, Franklin dispensed with the rules of chess and made his move.

"Sir," protested his antagonist, "you cannot leave your King in check like that."

"I see he is in check," replied Franklin, "but I shall not defend him. If he was a good king like yours, he would deserve the protection of his subjects, but he is a tyrant and has cost them already more than he is worth. Take him, if you please. I can do without him, and will fight out the rest of the battle *en Republicain*."

Franklin was at Passy when, on May 28, 1783, Kempelen wrote him from Paris, saying:

If I have not, immediately on my return from Versailles, renewed my request that you will be present at a performance of my automaton chess player, it was only to gain a few days in which I might make some progress in another very interesting machine, upon which I have been employed and which I wish you to see at the same time. Please, sir, have the kindness to inform me of the day and hour when I shall have the honor of receiving you in my rooms.

Dr. Franklin accepted the Baron's invitation and played against the Turk. As Franklin's grandson

later attested, the ambassador was "pleased with the Automaton." Franklin's interest in the chess automaton is further evidenced by the presence in his library of a copy of Philip Thicknesse's book on the automaton, which was published the following year in London. Before Kempelen left Paris, Franklin gave him a letter of introduction to a fellow chess enthusiast, Hans, Count von Brühl, who represented Saxony at the London court and who sometimes played Philidor.

Many persons who saw the Turk in Paris suspected some sort of trickery, but they were mystified as to just what it was. Windisch's letters describing the automaton's first appearance at the Viennese court were published in Paris during the Turk's visit there and were subsequently made available in various translations at nearly every major stop on Kempelen's route. The Baron often handed out copies of the pamphlet to interested persons at the exhibitions. While Windisch had minutely detailed the appearance and the method of presentation of the chess automaton, he had not been very helpful in explaining the Turk's inner secrets. At least one Frenchman, Henri Decremps, attempted to fill that gap by including an explanation of the automaton in

The American Ambassador was more diplomatic at court than at the chessboard. FROM HM.

LETTRES

DE M.

CHARLES GOTTLIEB DE WINDISCH

SUR

LE JOUEUR D'ECHECS

DE M. DE KEMPELEN.

TRADUCTION LIBRE DE L'ALLEMAND,

*Accompagnée de trois Gravures en taille-douce
qui repréfentent ce fameux Automate,
& publiée*

PAR CHRÉTIEN DE MECHEL,

Membre de l'Académie Impériale & Royale
de Vienne & de plufieurs autres.

A BASLE CHEZ L'EDITEUR.
MDCCLXXXIII.

Avec Privilège de S. M. Impériale & Royale.

Windisch's book was available in several languages.
COURTESY OF JGW.

Karl Gottlieb von Windisch's

Briefe

über den

Schachspieler

des

Hrn. von Kempelen,

nebst drey Kupferstichen
die diese berühmte Maschine vorstellen,

herausgegeben

von Chr. von Mechel

der K. K. und anderer Akademien Mitglied.

Mit allergnädigstem K. K. Privilegio.

Basel in dem von Mechel'schen Kunstverlage.
1783.

Henri Decremps thought a dwarf was the answer to the mystery of the Turk. COURTESY OF JGW.

his book *La Magie Blanche Dévoilée* (White Magic Exposed). The book, which appeared about a year after Kempelen's visit, consisted mostly of explanations of the tricks of Giovanni Giuseppe Pinetti, a noted magician of the day. Among Pinetti's attractions was a Turkish automaton known as the Grand Sultan. The Sultan did not play chess, but answered questions by nodding his head to signify "yes" or "no." The automaton could also count by striking a bell with a hammer held in his hand.

Decremps was incorrect in many of his efforts to solve Pinetti's tricks, but publication of the book by Decremps resulted in a loss of interest in the magician's performances so that he left Paris for a time. The explanation of the chess automaton was also erroneous, but it took a somewhat peculiar form. The automaton Decremps pretended to describe was not Kempelen's Turk, but a similar mechanism supposedly built by an inventor called Van-Estin, who reportedly revealed much to Decremps but would not "tear entirely the veil" which covered his secrets. Van-Estin explained, wrote

Decremps, that the chess automaton was controlled by a dwarf hidden in the cabinet. When the cabinet doors were opened, he revealed, the dwarf was outside the cabinet, except for his legs and thighs which were hidden in "hollow cylinders which seemed designed to move wheels and levers."

Van-Estin, it was said, would not disclose how the dwarf hidden in the cabinet knew the moves of his adversary, but offered three possible solutions: (1) Compass needles under the squares of the board were acted upon by magnets in the chessmen. (2) The exhibitor signaled the dwarf by means of code words or hand signals. (3) The chessboard was partly transparent.

As will be explained in Chapter Eight, the solution for the Van-Estin automaton was not the correct explanation for the secrets of Kempelen's Turk but it was one of the earliest of many attempts to solve the mystery. Kempelen continually refused to disclose the secrets; yet he maintained that the explanation was very simple. When one French nobleman asked him about it, Kempelen replied, "If you knew it, my Prince, it would seem as nothing." The inventor knew that as soon as the truth was out the public would quickly lose interest, but that as long as he guarded the secrets he would continue to make money.

In a picture from a book by Decremps, the chess automaton was surrounded by various magical paraphernalia, including Vaucanson's automaton ducks. COURTESY OF KB.

In London, Philidor stirred up interest in chess by playing blindfolded. COURTESY OF JGW.

The FAMOUS
Chefs-Player,

No. 14, *St. James's-Street*, next BROOKS's.

THE famous Automaton, which plays at Chefs with every Body, who chufes to play againft it, is to be feen every Day at One o'Clock, (Sundays excepted.) Its Figure and Drefs reprefent a Turk, with a Pipe in his Hand, fitting by a neat Counter or Table, upon which the Chefs-Board is placed.——Previous to the Performance, Mr. ANTHON, who always attends the Exhibition, opens the Doors of the Counter, that the Company prefent may have a View of the interior Machinery, by which the Motions are executed. This being done, and the Doors fhut up, the Automaton begins the Game by making the firft Move, handing the Piece to a proper Place by Motions refembling thofe of a living Perfon; after which, it refts its Hand upon a Cufhion, when that Perfon of the Company, who plays againft it, has made his Move, the Automaton moves in its Turn, and fo on alternately as the Laws of the Game require. When the Automaton gives Check to the Queen, it is announced to the Antagonift by Two Nods of its Head; if the Check be given to the King, it nods Three Times; but if a Piece be moved to the wrong Square, either by Defign or Inadvertence, the Automaton fhakes its Head, takes the Piece, replaces it in its former Place, and takes the Advantage of then playing its own, becaufe the Antagonift has loft the Move by his Mif-play. And laftly, when the Check-mate is given on either Side, if the Oppofer attempts to purfue the Game, the Automaton refufes by fhaking its Head.

The Game being over, and the Pieces all taken off, except one of the Knights, which may be fet at Pleafure on any one of the Sixty-four Squares, the Automaton moves it fucceffively, by its proper Move, into every Square of the Board, without ever bringing it twice into the fame Square.

Finally, this Automaton gives Anfwers to any Queftion propofed by the Spectators. This is accomplifhed by fhewing with its Fingers on an Alphabet-Table, the Letters, which compofe the Words neceffary for that Purpofe.

Befides this Automaton, there is another Machine to be feen, not lefs wonderful and new. Such a Contrivance was attempted in feveral Ages, without any Succefs, and its Performance reputed quite impoffible. This Machine now is brought into Execution, confifting in a fmall Organ, which having the Voice of a Child between five and fix Years of Age, fpeaks a great many Words very diftinctly, when played by its Inventor.

Admittance FIVE SHILLINGS.

Parties of at leaft Eight Perfons, may have a private Exhibition to themfelves, at any other Hour of their own Choice, on giving previous Notice to Mr. ANTHON, at the above-mentioned Place, and fending for Tickets.

Printed by H. REYNELL, (No. 21,) Piccadilly, near the Hay-Market.

A 1784 advertisement for the London exhibitions of the chess automaton told of Anthon but not Kempelen.
COURTESY OF JGW.

Philip Thicknesse, usually described as an eccentric, "Exposed and Detected" Kempelen's Turk. BY PERMISSION OF BL.

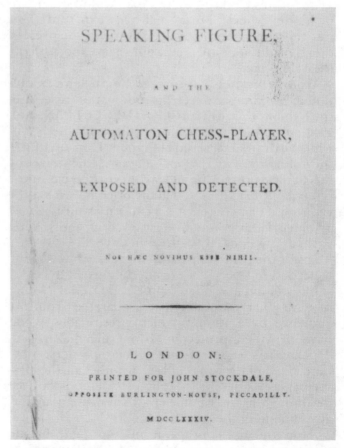

COURTESY OF JGW.

5.

As originally planned, Kempelen and his entourage left Paris and, crossing the English Channel, arrived in London in time for the exhibition season which began in the fall of 1783. There was in London at that time a growing interest in chess, especially among the aristocracy. That enthusiasm was due primarily to the influence of Philidor, who was engaged by the prestigious Chess Club for a stay of four months in the English capital every winter.

At first, the Turk was exhibited at No. 8 Saville Row, Burlington Gardens, but was later moved to No. 14 St. James's Street. At both locations, the chess automaton was shown from one to two o'clock every afternoon except Sundays at an admission price of five shillings. "Hundreds and thousands of persons," wrote the exuberant Walker, "flocked to the show; and the silver crowns rained down on the ingenious inventor, till he was knee-deep in the argent stream."

One of the most interesting visitors to the exhibition was Philip Thicknesse, an elderly gentleman who had been quite an adventurer in his youth. He had served with Oglethorpe in Georgia and as a soldier of fortune in Jamaica. Later he had become lieutenant-governor of Languard Fort and was the self-styled patron of the artist Thomas Gainsborough, until their friendship was broken by a "wretched squabble." Thicknesse had, said one writer, "in a remarkable degree the faculty of lessening the number of his friends and increasing the number of his enemies."

Thicknesse was outraged at having had to pay fifteen shillings to admit his family to see the Turk, but his character was such that he probably wouldn't have missed the performance at any price. Forty years earlier Thicknesse had been one of three hundred spectators who had gathered to witness a coach move without horses. "Many persons present were angry with me," explained Thicknesse, "for saying it was trod round by a man within the hoop, or hinder wheels; but a small paper of snuff, put into the wheel, soon convinced every person present that it could not only move, but sneeze too, *perfectly like a Christian*."

When Thicknesse discovered Kempelen's exhibition in St. James's Street, his indignation rose. "Let the Exhibitor . . . call it a GOOD DECEPTION, and, I will subscribe to the truth of it," he exclaimed; "but while he draws a large sum of money from us, under the *assurances of its being an Automaton* that moves by mechanical powers, he endeavours to deceive, and it is fair game to expose it, that the price at least may be reduced. For I confess it is a curiosity, and I believe as much money would be received at one shilling each, as is gained, by demanding five."

Inside the exhibition hall, Thicknesse saw what he conceded to be "a well-executed figure of a Turk," sitting behind a wooden cabinet, and under "a kind of tent." The automaton was separated from the audience by a railing, which presumably would have provided protection from such hazards as Thicknesse's paper of snuff. The only person behind the railing was Anthon, who began the performance by opening the cabinet to demonstrate the machinery inside. Kempelen, when present, generally sat among the spectators.

After the usual preparations the game began, during which Anthon stood next to the Turk's right elbow. Before each move, Thicknesse noted, the exhibitor would put his left hand into his pocket and make a great show of moving his hand and fingers back and forth, as if he were thus influencing the automaton's movements. Occasionally Anthon would unlock and lock the little cabinet on a side table or wind up the automaton with a key. Thicknesse was deceived by none of those actions, which he judged were "merely to puzzle the spectators." He remarked that Anthon was a good chess player, to which the exhibitor instantly replied, "*La, la; so, so.*" Thicknesse, however, did not really think that Anthon was the Turk's director but suspected instead "*an invisible Agent,*" a child, in fact, "of ten, twelve, or fourteen years of age," who was concealed inside the automaton's cabinet. To support that argument, Thicknesse noted that the automaton was exhibited only from one to two o'clock, when longer performances would have allowed more profits. He reasoned that the hidden player could not have endured longer confinements.

At first Thicknesse guessed that the concealed director "may probably see the moves, by a looking-glass fixed to the ceiling," but he soon changed his mind, conjecturing, "I rather think the invisible player sees all the moves through the hair trimmings of the Turk's habit." He was certain that the director moved the automaton's hand by putting his own arm into the sleeve of the Turk. As evidence, he noticed one or two movements in the ermine trimmings of the Turk's cloak at a time when the automaton should have been completely at rest. Thicknesse was undoubtedly correct in that observation since Edgar Allan Poe saw a similar motion while observing the Turk more than fifty years later. Thicknesse was quite close to the truth about the chess automaton and published his ideas in a pamphlet in 1784, but since he did not support his theories with drawings or a more detailed explanation, his exposé was regarded by many as mere rhetoric.

Although the chess player was an enormous success in London, it must have been a great disappointment to Kempelen that his speaking machine was all but ignored. The inventor advertised the contrivance along with the chess automaton and he himself demonstrated its ability to reproduce any word that a spectator might call for; but there was good reason for the public apathy. Less than a hundred yards from Kempelen's hall, a Frenchman was exhibiting, for half a crown admittance, a rival attraction known as the "Speaking Figure." It consisted of a doll "about the size of a very young child," suspended by a ribbon around its waist in the doorway of a room. The doll had in its mouth a tin horn about a foot in length, into which spectators could whisper questions in French, English, German, or Italian.

"*Quelle age avez vous?* How old are you?" asked

The Speaking Figure, a fraudulent rival of Kempelen's speaking machine, was exhibited just down the street. COURTESY OF JGW.

Kempelen's visit to London was a financial success but the Baron had hoped that somehow his inventions would be received with more enthusiasm among scientists. He probably never realized what a profound effect one of his machines had upon the Reverend Edmund Cartwright and upon the course of the Industrial Revolution. Had Cartwright not visited Kempelen's exhibition in London, he probably would have remained an obscure country clergyman and poet. The events which resulted from that visit were described by Cartwright himself:

Happening to be at Matlock in the summer of 1784, I fell in company with some gentlemen of Manchester, when the conversation turned to Arkwright's spinning machinery. One of the company observed that as soon as Arkwright's patent expired, so many mills would be erected and so much cotton spun that hands never could be found to weave it. . . . I replied that Arkwright must set his wits to work to invent a weaving mill. . . . The Manchester gentlemen unanimously agreed that the thing was impracticable; and, in defence of their opinion, they adduced arguments which I certainly was incompetent to answer, . . . having never at the time seen a person weave. I controverted, however, the impracticability of the thing by remarking that there had lately been exhibited in London an automaton figure which played chess. "Now you will not assert, gentlemen," said I, "that it is more difficult to construct a machine that shall weave than one which shall make all the variety of moves required in that complicated game."

Thicknesse, who naturally intended to expose the fraud.

"J'ai dix-huit. I am eighteen," replied the Speaking Figure in a faint whisper.

After a bit of investigation, Thicknesse explained that a "prostrate confederate" was concealed over the doorway and spoke or listened through a trumpet mounted in a hole in the ceiling. A third trumpet, hidden in the doll's feathered headdress, transmitted sounds between the other two trumpets. To prove his point, Thicknesse installed a similar Speaking Figure in his own home.

Although the Speaking Figure was a fake, it must have appeared to many gullible spectators a more remarkable invention than Kempelen's genuine speaking machine. The Speaking Figure had also been exhibited in Paris, which probably explains the apparent lack of interest there in Kempelen's speaking machine. Moreover, Kempelen had not perfected all the details of construction of his device until several months after his arrival in Paris. In 1784, while Kempelen was still in London, Thicknesse anonymously published his ideas in a booklet, *The Speaking Figure, and the Automaton Chess-player, Exposed and Detected.*

Shortly thereafter Cartwright remembered the conversation and began to solve the problem of constructing a power loom. He immediately employed workmen to put his plans into effect. His first invention, which he patented in 1785, was, in his own words, "a most rude piece of machinery." He soon found, upon inspecting some ordinary looms then in use, that they were actually easier to operate than his invention. In 1787, however, he patented a much improved power loom, which was eventually refined further. By 1833, more than 100,000 of the machines were in operation, changing the clothing industry forever. Ironically, Cartwright probably never realized that Kempelen's automaton, the inspiration for it all, was only a deception; but that, of course, did not make Cartwright's inventions any less real.

6.

Kempelen remained in London for nearly a year but left in time to reach Leipzig in September 1784 for the Michaelmas Fair. Along the way he stopped for brief exhibitions at cities such as Frankfurt am Main and Gotha. In Leipzig, the Turk and even the speaking machine were soon attracting enthusiastic audiences. They were, in fact, the two most remarkable attractions at the fair. Kempelen demonstrated the speaking machine, which was greatly admired, while Anthon officiated when the chess automaton was exhibited.

In Leipzig the Turk's adversaries were not permitted to make their moves on the same chessboard as the automaton, but rather on another board placed at a table outside the railing and to one side. That arrangement, it was claimed, allowed the spectators a better view, and possibly it prevented the opponents from hearing the movements of the concealed director.

Kempelen, as before, sat among the spectators and sometimes seemed to take no interest in the games. Occasionally, however, he spoke to Anthon

in a coded language which none of the audience could understand. If a game lasted too long, Kempelen would suggest that it be speeded up or perhaps terminated.

There seems to have been at Leipzig more interest in the Turk's ability to answer questions than there had been in London. After a game had been concluded and the Knight's Tour had been performed, Anthon brought out the board with golden letters, placed it on the cabinet, adjusted the machinery, and wound up the automaton as he did during a game. At one of the Leipzig performances the questioning session began with a spectator asking, "Turk, what do you think of the women in Leipzig?"

The automaton appeared to reflect for a moment, and then began to point at letters on the board, pausing to place his arm on the cushion between words. Although he had formed his replies in French when in Paris, he now answered in German. Anthon loudly pronounced each word for the benefit of persons standing at a distance.

"THEY ARE EXCEEDINGLY BEAUTIFUL," spelled out the Turk with laborious precision.

The audience was greatly amused, and soon another onlooker inquired, "How does this machine work?"

"HAVEN'T YOU SEEN IT?"

"What is in that small box over there?" asked another.

"A PART OF THE SECRET."

"How is the Emperor in Vienna?"

"VERY WELL."

"How did your last opponent play?"

"AS WELL AS PHILIDOR."

"Turk, are you married?"

"I HAVE MANY WIVES."

"How old are you?"

"192 MONTHS."

"How do you like Leipzig?"

"IT IS A SMALL PARADISE."

"How many variations are there in the game of chess?"

In response to the last question the Turk first pointed to the one, then many times to the zero, indicating an inconceivably large number.

The Turk lost only two games in Leipzig and thus excited great curiosity as to how a machine could play chess so well. Two of the spectators, Carl Friedrich Hindenburg and Johann Jakob Ebert, each wrote booklets detailing the visit and attempting to explain the mystery. Neither writer, however, suspected that a concealed player was responsible for the automaton's operation. They seemed to be convinced that much of what they had observed was purely mechanical, influenced perhaps by Anthon through magnetism or some other force. It was exactly the impression that Kempelen and Anthon had hoped to convey.

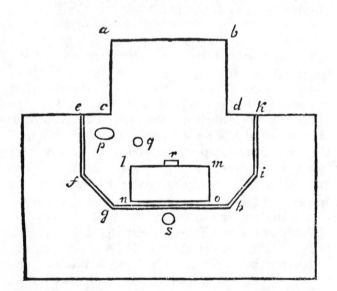

The automaton's exhibition area in Frankfurt featured the Turk, *r*, behind his cabinet, *lmno*. He faced the audience with his back to a recess in the wall, *abcd*. A railing, *efghik*, separated the automaton from his opponent, *s*, and the spectators. Anthon usually stood at *q*, between the Turk's cabinet and the small cabinet, *p*. In Frankfurt, the automaton played about thirty games, losing only two. COURTESY OF JGW.

Joseph Friedrich, Freyherr zu Racknitz, was a model automaton builder. COURTESY OF SH.

Schloss Heinsheim, now a hotel, was the home of Racknitz. FROM AC.

Colored plates of Racknitz's models illustrated his book. COURTESY OF JGW.

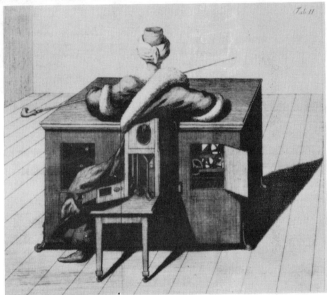

This Racknitz plate showed the Turk as viewed from behind. COURTESY OF JGW.

At Dresden a much more fascinating and original attempt to probe the Turk's secrets was undertaken by Joseph Friedrich, Freyherr zu Racknitz. Kempelen arrived in Dresden toward the end of 1784 and began a series of exhibitions similar to those in Leipzig. Racknitz often visited the exhibition hall, where he became acquainted with Kempelen and discussed the chess automaton with him. The inventor, however, would not reveal the automaton's secrets, so Racknitz set out to solve the enigma for himself. He began his observations by watching the automaton as a whole, and then by scrutinizing one part of the machine at a time. At the same time, he collected, compared, and examined the remarks and speculations of other observers. He also studied a copy of Windisch's letters describing the automaton.

After systematically rejecting several suggested solutions, Racknitz finally concluded that a person hidden in the machine itself moved the Turk and directed his games. He was uncertain just how Kempelen had accomplished the trick but he felt that he himself at least might be able to duplicate the automaton. At a social gathering Racknitz explained his ideas to some friends, who encouraged him to explore the matter further. He therefore began to

39

According to some stories, the Turk's tour ended in a storeroom at Potsdam. FROM HM.

construct two small models of the automaton, not over a foot in length, the first to demonstrate how the hidden director conducted a game, and the second to show the whole machine. To complete the models, Racknitz enlisted the aid of Lieutenant Honig, his former mathematics teacher, who corrected some details in the plans and built many of the interior parts.

It took Racknitz nearly five years from the date of Kempelen's Dresden visit to complete his models, have drawings made of them, and publish his booklet, *Ueber den Schachspieler des Herrn von Kempelen und dessen Nachbildung* (On Kempelen's Chess Player and Its Imitation). The work appeared quite impressive, especially its seven colored plates showing every detail of Racknitz's models. Unfortunately, many persons did not look far beyond the plates and failed to realize that they portrayed only the models Racknitz had made and not Kempelen's original automaton. No doubt the most notorious example of such a person was Thomas Collinson, an Englishman who toured the continent shortly after the publication of Racknitz's book. Mr. Eden, the English envoy in Dresden, had introduced Collinson to Racknitz, who presented the visitor with a copy of his book on the automaton. Collinson greatly admired the work and, not being able to read German, hoped to get it translated but, without waiting for the translation, he examined the "curi-ous plates neatly coloured" and distilled the entire work into one sentence. "A well-taught boy, very thin and small of his age (sufficiently so that he could be concealed in a drawer almost immediately under the chess-board), agitated the whole." Thus was born the famous thin, small boy, who figured in nearly every subsequent work on the chess automaton and, through a further compounding of errors, later became a thin, *tall* boy. Collinson also originated the legendary "Mr. Freyhere" through his ignorance of the title of his host, Joseph Friedrich, Freyherr zu Racknitz (roughly equivalent to Baron von Racknitz). Both "Mr. Freyhere" and the thin, small boy first made their appearances in a letter from Collinson, quoted in the 1796 supplement to Hutton's *Philosophical and Mathematical Dictionary*.

Before going to Dresden, Collinson had visited Kempelen in Vienna and had noticed that "not a word passed about the chess-player." He then concluded, "This discovery at Dresden accounts for the silence about it at Vienna." Actually, Racknitz discovered very little that had not been suggested previously. Decremps in 1784 and Johann Lorenz Boeckmann in 1785 had already published explanations which contained essentially the same elements Racknitz proposed in 1789. Racknitz was aware of the two earlier works, but claimed he had not seen them until his models were completed. As will be explained in Chapter Eight, all three solutions were probably incorrect except for the fact that a human director was concealed in the cabinet.

After Dresden, Kempelen visited some other German cities and then exhibited his machines in Amsterdam in 1785. According to some accounts, the tour ended that same year in Berlin after Frederick the Great sent word that his court would welcome a chance to see and play against the famous automaton chess player.

Although Frederick was probably not a strong chess player, his name has sometimes been linked with the game. When Philidor visited the Prussian court at Potsdam in 1750, the King watched the Frenchman play but did not himself participate. Frederick was thought to have once carried on a correspondence game with Voltaire. The King supposedly sent his moves by royal courier to his old teacher, who often contemplated the position at the Café de la Régence before dispatching a reply.

The story of Frederick and the chess automaton borders on the legendary but has found its way, in some form, into nearly every account of the Turk. According to most of the tales, Frederick was no match for the Turk, who defeated the King and his entire court. The monarch, however, was unwilling to let Kempelen depart without revealing the automaton's inner workings, and he thus offered the inventor an enormous sum of money for the secrets of the machine. Some stories claim that Frederick purchased the automaton and kept the invention for many years in a storeroom at Potsdam; but later versions held that Frederick merely paid for the Turk's secrets, allowing Kempelen to keep the machine. In either case, it was said that the price was paid and the courtiers were dismissed, after which Kempelen revealed to Frederick alone the secrets which had so greatly mystified the world. As the inventor had often predicted, when the solution was disclosed its fascination was lost, and Frederick was completely disillusioned. "The spell was dissolved," added Walker, "the charm broken." Though the monarch must have felt humiliated to have been deceived, he never divulged the secret for which he had paid so dearly.

In 1785, at the end of his two-year leave, Baron

Frederick the Great, it was said, paid a handsome price for the automaton's secret. FROM HM.

von Kempelen returned to Vienna, where he experimented with fire-fighting equipment and hydraulic systems and tried to improve upon Arkwright's cotton mill and upon the steam engine of Boulton and Watt. He not only wrote *The Mechanism of Human Speech* but even composed works for the theater. Despite some reports that Anthon continued to exhibit the Turk, it seems more likely that the chess automaton remained dormant for a period of about twenty years, a time marked by the revolutions and wars that ushered out the eighteenth century and began the nineteenth. On March 26, 1804, Kempelen died at the age of seventy but his automaton chess player was destined for a career of fifty more years—a career filled with fantastic adventures the Baron could scarcely have imagined.

tion, had persuaded Josephine to intercede with Napoleon on the Duke's behalf. Josephine's efforts, however, had not succeeded, and as the chess game began Mme. de Rémusat dared not lift her eyes to Napoleon. After several moves Napoleon took his turn and then murmured, almost to himself, a verse of Corneille:

> He who pardons easily invites offenses;
> Punish the assassin, pursue his accomplices.
> But then! always blood, always torture.
> And the blood spread upon a thousand
>   conspirators
> Makes my days more accursed, and not more
>   assured.

The game continued, and Mme. de Rémusat rejoiced momentarily in the hope that the Duke might be pardoned. She noticed, however, that her position on the board was beyond remedy, and after a few more moves Napoleon rose and declared, "You are checked and mated. Tomorrow I shall give you your revenge. Today let us speak of other things."

But their faces were grave and they hardly dared speak. The only sound heard was Napoleon muttering under his breath as he paced quickly back and forth in the room, his hands behind his back. As he reconsidered over and over to himself the possibility of a pardon, he quoted Voltaire:

> You know the difference in the Gods we serve:
> Your gods have counselled murder and vengeance,
> Mine, when your arm is raised against me,
> Command that I should pity and forgive.

Mme. de Rémusat believed the Duke was saved, but it was not to be, for at daybreak he was shot. Josephine cried upon learning the news, and Mme. de Rémusat did not think of demanding her revenge of Napoleon.

2.

All during Napoleon's spectactular rise to First Consul and then, in 1804, to Emperor of the French, Kempelen's chess automaton remained in Vienna, inactive and almost forgotten. Kempelen, in his later years, sought to dispose of the automaton and tried to make a bargain with the inventor and musician Johann Nepomuk Maelzel, who had taken a fancy to the machine. The Baron repeatedly offered to sell the automaton, but demanded 20,000 francs, a price Maelzel thought excessive, so the bargain was not made. About two years after Kempelen's death in 1804, the Baron's son approached Maelzel and renewed the offer to sell the chess player. The younger Kempelen, who did not share his father's fondness for mechanics, had no

interest in the automaton and had not even been entrusted with the secrets of the Turk's operation. He was therefore happy to allow Maelzel to purchase the apparatus for 10,000 francs, half the price the Baron had asked.

The automaton's new owner was a large, phlegmatic man whose sandy hair and whiskers framed a ruddy visage set with heavy-lidded blue eyes, a wide but pleasant mouth, and a Roman nose. Although irritable at times, he was very kind, especially with children, and he had a great capacity for making friends.

Maelzel was thirty-four years old at the time he purchased the chess automaton, having been born August 15, 1772, at Regensburg (Ratisbon), Bavaria. He was the son of an organ builder and thus had an opportunity to study the piano and musical theory, as well as the mechanical aspects of his father's trade. By the age of fourteen Maelzel was already considered one of Regensburg's best pianists, and from 1788 to 1792 he gave lessons on the instrument. His principal interest, however, was in the field of mechanical inventions, so he jour-

This nineteenth-century cylinder orchestration, now in the collection of the National Museum from Music Box to Barrel Organ, Utrecht, Holland, is a cousin of Maelzel's panharmonicon. COURTESY OF NMU.

neyed to Paris and London to study applied mathematics.

After settling in Vienna in 1792, Maelzel combined his knowledge of music and mechanics to construct a sort of mechanical military band, consisting of automatic instruments such as flutes, trumpets, drums, triangle, and strings which were struck by hammers, all contained within a ten-foot-high cabinet. A descending weight, housed in a fourteen-foot structure at the instrument's right, turned the main cyclinder, which set the whole device in motion. Maelzel sold the instrument, which played works by Haydn, Mozart, and Crescentini, for 3000 florins to the Archduke Charles of Austria. That prince allegedly purchased it solely for the purpose of annoying his friends, a fact which, if true, seems to indicate not only that Charles had a rather strange sense of humor, but that the instrument had not exactly attained musical perfection.

Maelzel then set to work on a new mechanical orchestra, supporting himself meanwhile by performing on the piano and giving lessons. Maelzel's musical talents were such that he earned the praises of even Beethoven, who in 1795 wrote that he "possesses a considerable knowledge of music and plays with good technique."

The new mechanical instrument, known as the panharmonicon, was much improved and contained, in addition to the instruments of its predecessor, clarinets, recorders, oboes, horns, bassoons, a serpent, and a big bass drum, all worked by weights acting upon cylinders. The wind instruments, arranged in two rows, were somewhat comparable to organ pipes. By means of reeds, Maelzel had approximated the sounds produced by the action of the lips and tongues of human players. The whole assemblage was housed in a glass cabinet six-feet square at the base and pyramidal in shape, rising to a height of five feet.

The panharmonicon was first exhibited in Vienna in 1804, to the great delight, it was reported, of all who heard it. The instrument had a powerful sound but was also capable of executing the piano passages perfectly.

In 1807 Maelzel took the panharmonicon to Paris, where it performed outdoors on the Champs de Mars, causing as much astonishment as pleasure. After that introduction, Maelzel announced that there would be daily panharmonicon concerts at two in the afternoon and at eight o'clock in the evening at the Hotel de Montmorency, Rue du Mont-Blanc, chaussée d'Antin, beginning the eighth of March.

The concerts were so popular that in July, Maelzel opened, due to "public demand," a second concert at each performance. The admission was three francs for one show, six francs for two. Later in the year the concerts were moved to a new location at

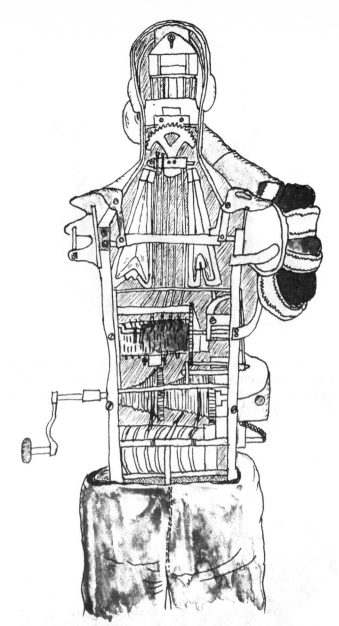

The Kaufman Trumpeter, like that of Maelzel, had leather bellows for lungs and reeds which imitated the sound of a brass instrument. FROM AC.

No. 1, Cour des Fontainnes. Opening there December 12th, the panharmonicon featured a new work by Daniel Steibelt which depicted the four turning points of the day.

After the concerts were well under way, Maelzel returned to Vienna, leaving the panharmonicon under the care of a manager. In October 1808 he returned to Paris to unveil his newest invention, the Automaton Trumpeter, a life-size figure that was to share the program with the panharmonicon. The Trumpeter was wound up with a key and usually performed to the accompaniment of Maelzel on the piano, but on special occasions the automaton was soloist with a real live band or orchestra. In either case, the program usually consisted of a French or Austrian cavalry maneuver, followed by a specially

45

The Emperor Franz I of Austria spent much of his time fighting Napoleon. BY PERMISSION OF ON.

It was the Battle of Wagrum that brought Napoleon to Schönbrunn in 1809. FROM AC.

Vienna, where his reputation as a skilled inventor had earned him the appointment of Mechanician to the Royal and Imperial Court, a post similar to the one Kempelen had held. The Emperor at that time was Franz I, who had become Holy Roman Emperor after the two-year reign of his father, Leopold II, the younger brother of Joseph II. After the dissolution of the Holy Roman Empire, Franz had become Emperor of Austria.

On February 8, 1809, Franz declared war on France. At first it seemed that Austria might be victorious, but by May things had gone so well for Napoleon that his army was on the outskirts of Vienna. As court mechanician, Maelzel had been summoned to Schönbrunn to execute some work for the Empress. When Napoleon arrived at Schönbrunn in July, after his victory at the Battle of Wagrum, the imperial family and most of the court had fled, but the court mechanician remained in the rooms assigned him.

Visitors to Schönbrunn can view the room where Napoleon stayed. COURTESY OF SS.

The Great Gallery of Schönbrunn was the site of Napoleon's escapade with the Turk. COURTESY OF SS.

Napoleon left these two eagles at the gates of Schönbrunn as a reminder of his visit. COURTESY OF SS.

Schönbrunn when Napoleon strode into the room. Maelzel stepped forward to greet the great general, but Napoleon's interest was riveted on a figure in the center of the gallery behind the mechanician. There, separated from the spectators by a rope barrier, sat the automaton chess player, looking much as he had when Kempelen first introduced him forty years earlier. The Turk was, in fact, the same age as Napoleon himself.

Although Napoleon was eager to begin a game with the automaton, Maelzel first produced a set of keys from his pocket to open the cabinet and demonstrate that nobody was concealed inside. He performed the demonstration in the same manner Kempelen had, opening each door in succession until it appeared that the whole interior of both the cabinet and figure was open to the view of Napoleon and the entire assemblage.

While a peace treaty with Austria was negotiated, Napoleon remained at Schönbrunn until October, residing in the same study and adjoining bedroom he had chosen during his first occupation of the palace in 1805. Sometime during his stay, probably late in July, Maelzel let it be known that he had something that might interest Napoleon, and an exhibition was arranged.

A crowd had gathered in the Great Gallery at

Maelzel had discarded the little casket which Kempelen or Anthon had placed on a table nearby when the Turk was exhibited. Some years later, when asked why he had done away with the casket, Maelzel explained that he did not believe the audiences were as gullible as they had been in Kempelen's day. Maelzel also dispensed with the board inscribed with golden letters, which the Turk had used to answer questions. George Walker

The Turk appeared much as he had in Kempelen's time.
COURTESY OF JGW.

49

Napoleon's chessboard was the map of Europe, upon which, observed George Walker, "he could afford odds to Julius Caesar." COURTESY OF JGW.

Napoleon was supposed to have played chess on this table. COURTESY OF NYPL.

games, the one with Mme. de Rémusat is probably intermediate in believability. In 1880 *The Chess Player's Chronicle* noted that "Napoleon had really at that time an *accès* or fit of Chess upon him, and played every night," but concluded that "it is altogether improbable that, at a period when the preservation of games was almost unknown, and there were no Chess organs, a game at court should have been taken down."

Nevertheless, the game did appear in the French chess journal *Le Palamède*, July 15, 1845. At the time the game was supposedly played, the rules of chess had not become well standardized; therefore, it is not surprising that Mme. de Rémusat, though she played the black pieces, had the first move. In most subsequent reprintings of the game, the colors have been reversed, giving Mme. de Rémusat White. Here, however, the game is presented in its original form, except that modern chess notation is used.

The opening was described in *Palamède* as "a woman's opening: reserved and timid." It soon transposed into something resembling Alekhine's Defense, which of course had not been invented at the time.

Irregular Opening

Malmaison, March 20, 1804

	White	Black
	Napoleon Bonaparte	Madame de Rémusat
1	———	P–Q3
2	N–KB3	P–K4
3	N–B3	P–KB4
4	P–K4	P×P
5	QN×P	N–QB3
6	KN–N5	P–Q4
7	Q–R5ch	P–N3
8	Q–B3	N–R3
9	N–B6ch	K–K2
10	N×Pch	K–Q3
11	N–K4ch	K×N
12	B–B4ch	K×B
13	Q–N3ch	K–Q5
14	Q–Q3 mate	

Game 2

The game between Napoleon and the Turk was probably first published in the chess column of the *Illustrated London News*, November 30, 1844. Although the source of the game was not specified, *The Chess Player's Chronicle*, 1880, thought it "by no means unlikely that the moves were taken down at the time by Maelzel's direction: while the game is not, like the others, too good for a confessedly bad player." Napoleon played miserably, it is true, but we may pardon him for that. What seems really inexcusable is the performance of Allgaier, who was directing the Turk. On move 15, he missed a brilliant combination and the chance to create a beautiful game. Of course, capturing Napoleon's Queen can hardly be considered a blunder, but it is a pity he did not see the mate in two moves.

As recorded in the *Illustrated London News* and later in many chess journals, the game ended with "Mate in four moves." Such a mate could have been accomplished, however, only with the cooperation of Napoleon; actually six moves were required to force mate. The game was accompanied by the remark, "Napoleon, who played with the black pieces, insisted on having the first move."

Irregular Opening

Schönbrunn Palace, Vienna, July, 1809

	White	Black
	The Turk (Allgaier)	Napoleon Bonaparte
1	———	P–K4
2	P–K4	Q–B3
3	N–QB3	B–B4
4	N–B3	N–K2
5	B–B4	P–QR3

6	P–Q3	O–O
7	B–KN5	Q–Q3
8	N–KR4	P–R3
9	B×N	Q×B
10	N–B5	Q–K1
11	N–Q5	B–N3
12	N×Pch	K–R2
13	Q–R5	P–KN3
14	N–B6ch	K–N2
15	N×Qch?	

15 N–B5ch! would have forced a pretty mate in two. Napoleon might have chosen to capture either Knight, but if 15...K×N, 16 Q–R4ch, P–N4, 17 Q–R6 mate. Or if 15...P×N, 16 Q–N5ch, K–R1, 17 Q–R6 mate.

15		R×N
16	Q–N5? (N–B5ch!)	P–Q3
17	B×BP	R–R1
18	Q×NPch	K–B1
19	B–Q5	K–K2

Here "Mate in four" was erroneously announced for White, but could have been accomplished only with the aid of Black:

20	Q–B7ch	K–Q1
21	Q–B6ch	K–Q2? (K–K1!)
22	Q–K6ch	K–Q1
23	N–B7 mate	

To avoid extensive analysis, the real mate is left to the reader to find.

A Tale and a *Fantaisie*

Napoleon participated in many games of chess with Berthier, Bourrienne, Murat, the Duc de Bassano, and others during the armistice of Vienna and later in the Polish and Russian campaigns, but apparently none of the games were preserved. There was apparently a great desire among early nineteenth-century chess enthusiasts to hear of Napoleon's exploits in connection with their favorite game. To satisfy that hunger, Louis Charles Mahé de Labourdonnais, chess champion and editor of *Le Palamède*, collected from Napoleon's associates any stories which centered around the chessboard. He received one such anecdote verbally from Count Merlin, the Duc de Bassano, and the interpreter Amedèe Jaubert, with whom Napoleon played constantly in Egypt.

During the Polish campaign, the Persian ambassador was announced before the Emperor in Paris. Napoleon was absorbed in a game of chess with Berthier, but ordered the ambassador to be shown in anyway. While Jaubert interpreted, Napoleon questioned the ambassador about many civil and

"Ah! my poor Louis XVIII," Napoleon was reported to have said, "you have fallen." COURTESY OF JGW.

lished as authentic, a fact which undoubtedly would have greatly pleased Napoleon.

Scotch Game

St. Helena, 1820 (supposedly)

White	*Black*
Napoleon (actually Capt. Kennedy)	Count Bertrand (actually Rev. Owen)
1 P–K4	P–K4
2 N–KB3	N–QB3
3 P–Q4	N×P
4 N×N	P×N
5 B–QB4	B–B4
6 P–QB3	Q–K2

7 O–O	Q–K4
8 P–KB4	P×P dis ch
9 K–R1	P×P
10 B×Pch	K–Q1
11 P×Q	P×R(Q)
12 B×N	B–K2
13 Q–N3	P–QR4

Here Napoleon announced mate in five moves as follows:

14 R–B8ch!	B×R
15 B–N5ch	B–K2
16 B×Bch	K×B
17 Q–B7ch	K–Q1
18 Q–B8 mate	

4

A Quarrel Between Friends: Maelzel and Beethoven

1.

Had not the ingenious and quick-witted Maelzel sold the Chess Automaton, . . . there is every probability that several things of importance in the world's history would not have occurred. Notably, Beethoven would never have been recognized as a great musician, his life would have been still further stunted by poverty and neglect, and specifically, he would not have composed one of his best known works.

Can that be true? Whether or not one agrees completely with that evaluation from the 1917 article "Beethoven and Chess" by Charles Willing, it must at least be admitted that Maelzel greatly influenced Beethoven at a very critical point in the great composer's life. Although the chess automaton played a passive role during that time, it was a very important period in shaping the future career of Maelzel, the Turk's proprietor. In tracing the story, we shall have the opportunity of becoming better acquainted with the Prince of Entertainers.

The episode began during the latter half of 1809, shortly after the game between Napoleon and the automaton, at which time Maelzel left his apartment in Schönbrunn Palace and moved to rooms in Stein's pianoforte factory in Vienna. Sometime between then and 1812 Maelzel was invited to demonstrate the automaton chess player in Milan at the court of the Viceroy of Italy. Since Napoleon's relatives were

Eugène Beauharnais was the new owner of the chess automaton. FROM AC.

sitting at that time on many of the thrones of Europe, it is not surprising that the Viceroy was Eugène Beauharnais, the son of the Empress Josephine and the adopted stepson of Napoleon. Eugène had followed Napoleon in the campaigns of Italy and Egypt and was a general of brigade by 1804. When Napoleon established the empire that year, he named Eugène successively Prince of the Empire, Arch-chancellor of State, and then Viceroy of Italy. Governing from Milan, the Viceroy was Napoleon's most loyal lieutenant. He raised an 80,000-man army of Italy, which fought in the campaigns of Austria, Spain, and Russia.

Eugène was an avid chess player and had, during the Austrian campaign, occupied his leisure by playing chess with Triaire, one of his adjutants. After the Battle of Wagrum, the Viceroy had been sent to Pressburg, where he remained until July twenty-second, getting the city's bombed-out Danube bridge back into operation. He thus may have missed witnessing Napoleon's encounter with the Turk, but he evidently at least had heard about the automaton. When Eugène saw the mechanical chess player demonstrated in Milan, he would not be satisfied until he knew the automaton's secrets, and thus he offered to purchase the Turk for the princely sum of 30,000 francs.

Maelzel, though reluctant to part with the automaton, was too astute a businessman to refuse a price three times what he had paid for the machine. Thus the bargain was made, the courtiers were dismissed, and the doors locked to assure that the secret would not pass beyond the automaton's new master. Then Maelzel threw open all the doors of the cabinet and Eugène Beauharnais joined the very select group of perhaps a dozen persons who knew how the chess player was operated. For now it will suffice to say that he saw a man, a real human chess player, looking somewhat uncomfortable in his newly revealed hiding place.

How did Eugène react to the astonishing revelation he had just witnessed? According to Walker, "He shrugged up his shoulders, took a pinch of snuff, laughed at the joke, and though he probably thought his purchase *rather dear at the price,* expressed much gratification at inspecting the figure in all its parts. He even subsequently placed himself in the necessary relation with the automaton, and giving it the invisible impulse, conducted it during several games against some of his most intimate friends."

Soon, however, the novelty wore off and the automaton became little more than a museum piece. The Turk was at his best only when functioning, and he did not function well without someone like Maelzel. To operate the automaton properly, Eugène would have had to employ a strong chess master as director, and that he apparently never did, since the followers of Napoleon had little time

The conflagration of Moscow, a tragedy for Napoleon, was for Maelzel a brilliant inspiration. COURTESY OF NYPL.

for such diversions. The chess historian George Allen reported that the Duke of Saxe-Weimar saw the automaton in 1812 "abandoned to inglorious repose" in the Casa Buonaparte, Eugène's viceregal palace at Milan. Millin, in his *Voyage dans le Milanais,* said Allen, also recalled seeing the Turk there in about the same time.

2.

After having disposed of the automaton chess player in Milan, Maelzel returned to Vienna, where he kept himself busy with his other mechanical devices. In 1810, when Napoleon married the Habsburg princess Maria Louisa, Maelzel installed upon the balcony of his own home in Vienna an automaton that sang nuptial hymns in honor of the bridal couple. The imperial pair, who were actually in Paris at the time, seemed miraculously to appear at a window of Maelzel's dwelling to acknowledge the tribute. Before departing within, they bowed to the wildly cheering crowd below who scarcely suspected that Maelzel had achieved the effect with a pair of lifelike automatons.

If Maelzel took the opportunity to celebrate Napoleon's good fortunes, he was equally quick to profit from his bad ones. The Viennese, who had been twice invaded and occupied by Napoleon's armies, were elated to hear of the Emperor's disastrous Russian campaign of 1812. Maelzel, hardly failing to notice that fact, constructed an elaborate mechanical diorama, which he called the *Conflagration of Moscow*. During the next thirty-five years Moscow would endlessly burn and reburn, accompanied by somber music and by the jingle of coins at the box office. An eyewitness at a performance of the diorama once wrote,

> When the curtain rose, last night, Moscow lay before us in miniature. There was the "Holy City" with its churches, palaces, bridges, houses, etc., and with its towering minarets bathed in the silvery light of the full moon. Across a bridge, near the foreground, the French army was advancing; while in front were crowds of citizens, bearing upon their backs such valuables as they could carry away. Anon a bright flame shot up

from the heart of the city, and the great conflagration had commenced. The fire spread slowly on all sides, sending up tongues of flames and clouds of smoke, until nearly the entire city was involved, and the lurid glare of burning churches and houses had drowned out the moonbeams and spread the red pall of ruin and devastation over everything. The strains of martial music, the booming of artillery, the rattle of musketry, and crushing of falling walls added to the deception and carried the spectator back to those dread nights in September, 1812, when the most heroic sacrifice of modern times was made by a patriotic people.

Maelzel planned to feature the *Conflagration of Moscow* at his Künstkabinett, an exhibition hall which he opened in Vienna in 1812. Visitors to the Künstkabinett could view such attractions as statues, paintings, and various scientific wonders, among which were "a large electrical machine with apparatus for popular experiments" and probably at least one model of Kempelen's speaking machine. There were performances by the automaton trumpeter and later by the new panharmonicon. One could also witness a mechanical diorama known as *Haydn's Seasons* "in a sensational décor with appropriate transformations. In winter, the snow fell, and the shepherds' huts were buried by avalanches; in summer the rain streamed down, the thunder rumbled . . ."

3.

I. 1812 Maelzel was principally employed in the construction of the *Conflagration of Moscow* and of his new improved panharmonicon, which was seven feet long, six feet wide, and six feet high and contained mechanical violins, cellos, trumpets, flutes, clarinets, drums, cymbals, and a triangle. Its clockwork machinery was operated by weights acting on cylinders, each of which produced a different musical composition.

Beethoven, who was fascinated by Maelzel's mechanical curiosities, frequently visited the mechanician in his workshop in the pianoforte factory. The two were intimate friends and had probably known each other as early as 1795, when Beethoven had written a letter of introduction for a "Herr Menzel," evidently a misspelling of "Maelzel." In the letter, Beethoven, who was less than two years older than Maelzel, praised his friend's abilities at the piano. Both musicians had come, in 1792, to make their fortunes in Vienna, drawn from their respective homes in Bonn and Regensburg to the musical capital of the world.

In the spring of 1812 Beethoven and Maelzel, along with other companions, gathered for a sort of

Maelzel's *Conflagration of Moscow* was undoubtedly the model for this later version, which was complete with fireworks. COURTESY OF CPL.

Beethoven often visited Maelzel's workshop. BY PERMISSION OF ON.

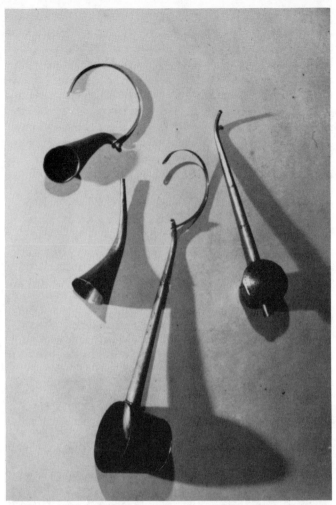

For Beethoven, Maelzel constructed these ear trumpets on display at Beethoven-Haus, Bonn. BY PERMISSION OF BB.

farewell dinner. Beethoven, on the advice of his physician, was going for the summer to the baths at Teplitz, Karlsbad, and Franzenbrunn and then to visit his brother Johann in Linz. Maelzel planned a trip to London to exhibit the mechanical trumpeter, a journey, however, which he had to postpone indefinitely. According to Beethoven's biographer Anton Schindler, "Beethoven, who was in the company of his intimate friends was, as usual, cheerful, witty, satirical—'unbuttoned' as he called it— improvised at this farewell dinner" the canon to the words *"Ta, ta, ta, lieber, lieber, Maelzel."*

The "ta, ta, ta" represented the strokes of the musical chronometer, an improvement by Maelzel of a similar device by Stöckel. Maelzel's instrument, the forerunner of his more famous metronome, consisted of a small lever, which was set in motion by a toothed wheel, and which kept time by beating on a small wooden anvil. Stöckel's chronometer had worked upon similar principles, but had been too large for practical use. There had been for some years a need for such a machine to mark time in music, and the composers Salieri, Beethoven, Weigl, Gyrowetz, and Hummel had enthusiastically praised Maelzel's invention in a public testimonial.

Schindler claimed that the "ta, ta, ta" cannon was the basis for the *Allegretto* of Beethoven's *Eighth Symphony,* but later scholars disputed the idea, since the *Eighth Symphony* was probably sketched out before the cannon was written. However, the cannon does show Beethoven's high esteem for Maelzel at the time.

As Beethoven's hearing became progressively worse, Maelzel spent much time in an effort to construct an ear trumpet that might be of some benefit to the composer. The mechanician eventually completed at least six instruments, but only the smallest and simplest appeared to be of any practical use. However, Beethoven used the device for a period of eight or ten years.

By the winter of 1812-1813 Maelzel had completed work on the new panharmonicon and was busy placing musical compositions on its cylinders in preparation for the trip to London, which he still hoped to make. He had even by that time persuaded Beethoven to accompany him on the proposed journey.

The first cylinders which Maelzel prepared contained Cherubini's *Lodoiska Overture,* Haydn's *"Military" Symphony,* and the overture and chorus from Handel's *Timotheus,* and by late January he had

60

Ignaz Moscheles wrote marches for Maelzel's panharmonicon. FROM HM.

The Duke of Wellington scored a victory and another inspiration for Maelzel. FROM AC.

begun to record an echo piece composed for him by Cherubini. The following summer he added some marches by the popular young pianist Ignaz Moscheles, who often visited the workshop during construction of the cylinders. It is interesting to note that those cylinders, which were stored in the basement of a museum in Stuttgart, still exist, although the panharmonicon was destroyed when the museum was bombed during World War II.

4.

The trip to England was further postponed until the late autumn of 1813, because Beethoven's brother Carl was in ill health. Maelzel, moreover, wanted to remain in Vienna to complete some work on the *Conflagration of Moscow,* which he hoped to exhibit in England. By the end of the year, Carl was in better condition and the *Conflagration* was complete, so it appeared that nothing remained to delay the much-postponed journey. However, Maelzel had been turning over an idea in his mind as suggested in Thayer's *Life of Beethoven:*

> He knew by experience the principal cities of the Continent, and London well enough to forsee, that the noble compositions of Handel, Haydn, and Cherubini secured the success of his panharmonicon there; but that if he could add to its repertory some new, striking and popular

piece, bearing the now great name of Beethoven, he would increase both its attractiveness and the public interest and curiosity in the composer.

Thanks again to Napoleon, Maelzel had just the inspiration he needed for the new panharmonicon piece. After Napoleon had fled from Moscow, he had partly recovered from the Russian defeat, raised a new army, and even won some new victories. The Viennese and others who had grown weary of Napoleon had, in fact, viewed the Russian campaign with mixed feelings; after all, who but the Russians wanted to win by burning their own capital city? Then on June 21, 1813, Arthur Wellesley, the Duke of Wellington, won a magnificent victory over Napoleon at Vittoria, Spain. Here was a new hero who could stand up to the tyrant and beat him on the battlefield. When news of the victory reached Vienna, Maelzel immediately recognized the subject of the new panharmonicon piece, and he easily persuaded Beethoven to write the *Battle of Vittoria* or *Wellington's Victory* for the mechanical instrument. Battle pieces were very popular at that time. Beginning with Frederick the Great's victory at the *Battaille de Prague,* nearly every battle or siege of any importance in the past fifty years had been the subject of an orchestral refighting of some sort. A *Battle of Vittoria* would be very popular in Vienna and would be guaranteed instant success on the

The large University Hall or Redoutensale was obtained for the 1813 concerts. FROM AC.

Trumpeter, with full orchestral accompaniment—one by Dussek, the other by Pleyel.

3. *Wellington's Victory.*

By writing the Archduke Rudolph, Beethoven was able to influence university officials to allow him the use of the large University Hall for the concerts. Thus the arrangements for the concerts were well under way, and Beethoven began the task of rehearsing the orchestra.

Although Beethoven was unmatched as a composer, his style of conducting was somewhat ludicrous. Spohr recalled that "at *piano* he crouched down lower and lower as he desired the degree of softness. If a *crescendo* then entered he gradually rose again and at the entrance of the *forte* jumped into the air." His exaggerated style became particularly pathetic at one rehearsal session when he lost his place and skipped ten or twelve measures ahead of the orchestra. That caused him to prematurely leap up, then stare in bewilderment at the orchestra, which was still playing *pianissimo*. Later, during one of the concerts, the same thing happened. The singer Franz Wild noted that a disaster was prevented when "at the critical moment Kapellmeister Umlauf took the commander's staff and it was indicated to the orchestra that he alone was to be obeyed. For a long time Beethoven noticed nothing of the change; when he finally observed it, a smile came to his lips . . ."

At one point in rehearsing the symphony, the violin players refused to continue, exclaiming that the passage was impossible to play. Beethoven patiently begged them to take the music home and practice it. When the passage went smoothly at rehearsal next day, the musicians rejoiced at being able to please the composer.

While Beethoven rehearsed the orchestra, Maelzel had some posters printed, announcing the first concert. On these he made the mistake of speaking of the battle piece as his own property. Maelzel believed that to be true, because he had shared in the composition of the work, and Beethoven had undoubtedly given him the panharmonicon version, which had preceeded it. Beethoven, however, objected to what he considered usurpation of his property, and although Maelzel, at some expense, had the posters changed to say the piece was composed "out of friendship and for his journey to London," there were violent arguments, the beginning of a long, bitter dispute.

Despite the altercation, the two charity concerts were performed as scheduled, and they were a tremendous success. Spohr commented, "They were masterly, in spite of Beethoven's eccentric, and at times absurd, conducting. The Battle Piece or Military Symphony, created such a furor that Beethoven found himself suddenly and overwhelmingly popular. This popularity extended even to the humblest of Viennese. That the unlet-

work. It seems likely that most of the performers viewed the concert as a gigantic musical joke and none wanted to be left out. Schuppanzigh would be concertmaster, while Spohr and Mayseder would take second and third places in the violins. The famous Dragonetti would play double bass. Meyerbeer and Hummel would play drums, while Moscheles would be on cymbals. Salieri would beat time for the drummers and salvos. Everyone wanted to take part in the huge professional frolic, which Beethoven himself would conduct.

Besides *Wellington's Victory,* on which Beethoven was working diligently, Maelzel knew the composer had completed a new symphony, the *Seventh,* in A major. As an interlude between those longer works, Moscheles would be on cymbals. Salieri would beat than the battle piece. His own automaton trumpeter would play two of his programmed marches, accompanied by full orchestra. Thus the complete program for the two charity concerts scheduled for the eight and twelfth of December, 1813, was:

1. "An entirely new symphony," by Beethoven (the *Seventh,* in A major).

2. Two marches played by Maelzel's Mechanical

64

The Automaton Trumpeter of Friedrich Kaufman, built shortly after Maelzel's Trumpeter, may be seen today at the Deutsches Museum, Munich. BY PERMISSION OF DM.

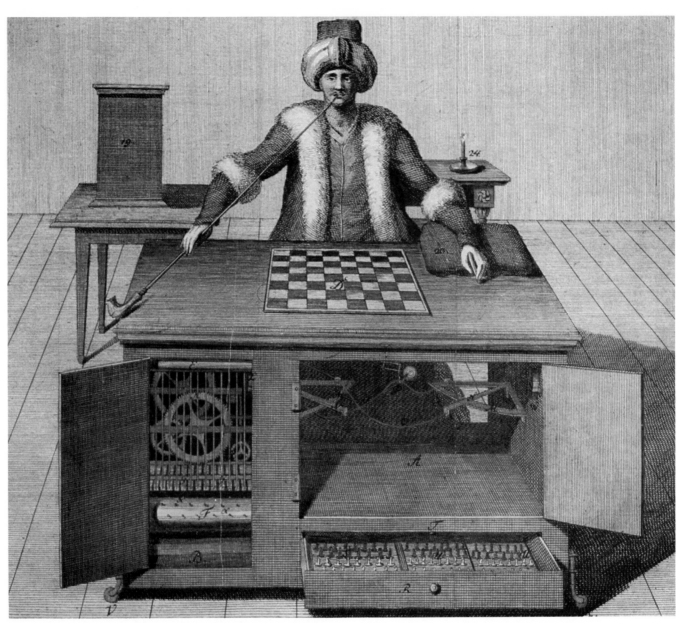

Racknitz's book was illustrated with colored engravings of small models he had constructed to show how the Turk might have operated. COURTESY OF JGW.

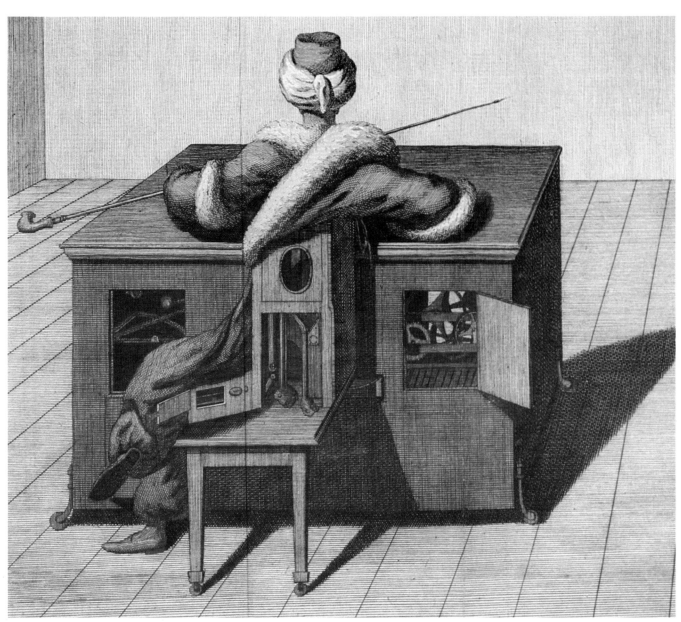

This rear view of the Turk by Racknitz was nearly identical to a similar drawing by Windisch. COURTESY OF JGW.

The Great Gallery at Schonbrunn. COURTESY OF SS.

tered should respond to his music was in Beethoven's eyes his greatest triumph."

5.

After the concerts, Beethoven prepared a "Note of Thanks," expressing his appreciation to all who had donated their services and concluding with, "But our greatest thanks are due to Herr Maelzel, since it was he who first conceived the idea of this concert and there fell to him afterwards the management, care and arrangement—the most arduous labors of all." The tribute was never published, however, since the dispute between the two former companions continued to worsen.

In the lawsuit resulting from that quarrel, only the documents presenting Beethoven's side of the argument have been preserved. As Thayer pointed out, "Maelzel's contra-suit to his lawyer is lost. He had no young disciple planning with zeal to preserve it and give it, with his version of the story, to posterity." The "young disciple" was Schindler, author of one of the earliest Beethoven biographies. Thayer, in his own biography, presented Maelzel's side more fairly. He challenged many of the inaccuracies in Schindler's version of the events and in Beethoven's own statements. Thayer's analysis along with that of subsequent Beethoven biographers seems to indicate that, while neither party in the quarrel was beyond reproach, most of the discredit falls upon Beethoven.

Immediately after the first concert on December eighth, Beethoven returned the fifty ducats he had borrowed from Maelzel and declared that he would never travel with the mechanician, since he had learned of his character. In Beethoven's "Deposition" to his lawyer, he called Maelzel "an ill-bred fellow, quite uneducated and without refinement." As proof of Maelzel's "low and disloyal character," Beethoven quoted his former friend as having said, "I shit on Vienna. . . ; I did not do this for the sake of the wounded but for the money." Beethoven also claimed that Maelzel had spread a rumor that the composer owed him four hundred gold ducats.

Beethoven nevertheless claimed he had been willing to allow Maelzel to take *Wellington's Victory* to London, but "only on certain conditions," of which the composer would inform him. Maelzel, however, maintained the battle piece was his own property, a "friendly gift," to which Beethoven replied, "who would allow himself to be compelled to give a friendly present to such a man?" To emphasize that he could no longer give the work unconditionally to Maelzel, Beethoven prepared an elaborate copy of the battle piece and sent it to the Prince Regent of England. That monarch, however, took no notice of the score; it was filed away in his library and not performed in England until several years later. If

Maelzel had complied with Beethoven's wishes, he might have obtained some sort of conditional rights to perform *Wellington's Victory*, but the mechanician continued to believe, with considerable justification, that the work was his property.

Maelzel had delayed his journey for many precious weeks while laboring to make a success of the two charity concerts, which had so aroused public interest that further concerts were demanded. Beethoven, in fact, arranged for his own benefit two more concerts on January second and February twenty-seventh, but he completely ignored Maelzel and denied him any share in the profits from those successful events. Beethoven deleted Maelzel's Trumpeter from the programs of the concerts and substituted selections of his own. He lengthened the February concert by introducing for the first time his *Eighth Symphony* in addition to the *Seventh* and the battle symphony.

Although extremely disappointed with Beethoven's behavior, Maelzel remained for several weeks in Vienna, hoping perhaps that some sort of friendly agreement could be reached. He met several times with Beethoven at the office of Dr.

During most of his association with Maelzel, Beethoven resided in a flat on the top floor of the Pasqualati House, now Wein 1, Mölkerbastei 8. The *Seventh Symphony* was written here. FROM AC.

At Leuchtenberg Palace, Munich, Maelzel again took possession of the Turk. BY PERMISSION OF ON.

lated, according to Schmidt, that Maelzel was not to leave the Continent to exhibit the automaton. In a letter Maelzel later wrote, he referred to the Turk as "the automaton chess player entrusted to me by H.R.H. Prince Eugène," but in the same letter he offered to sell the Turk as if the automaton were his own property. In any case, we know that Maelzel took and retained possession of the Turk, made some payments to Eugène, and later left the Continent. With the chess automaton again under his control, Maelzel returned to Paris to begin a new series of European exhibitions that would equal, and perhaps even surpass, the success of the earlier tour under Baron von Kempelen.

5

How to Operate a Chess Automaton for Fun and Profit: The Turk's Second Tour of Europe

1.

Europe in 1818 must have been one of the most pleasant of places and times. Napoleon was safely confined on St. Helena, and gone were the wars, the suffering, and the enmity among nations. It was a world of little interest to historians, but a world safe for the exhibitors of chess automatons. The Turk was nearly fifty years old by then, and the mysteries of his chess-playing mechanism had not yet been fully revealed to the public. Most spectators could not even remember the previous exhibitions of the chess automaton, while those few old enough to recall his visits welcomed him as an old friend and spread his fame among younger persons.

When Maelzel arrived in Paris with the automaton again in his possession, he went to the Café de la Régence, still the world center of chess. Unlike Kempelen, however, he did not challenge the strongest players at the Régence to public chess matches. Instead he enlisted the services of those heirs of Philidor as secret directors of the Turk. Boncourt, one of the chess professors Maelzel recruited, seemed the most unlikely possible candidate for the job. Although an excellent chess player, he was a strapping fellow six feet tall. The French journalist Depping, who was acquainted with Boncourt, commented, "It is almost impossible to believe that a man of his large dimensions could, by any manner of means, ensconce himself within a box of four feet in length, three in height, and two in

width, and yet be able to play a skillful game of Chess." Maelzel may have chosen Boncourt for that very reason. Who would have suspected that a man of such proportions was the secret director? In Kempelen's day many spectators suspected that a child or a dwarf directed the Turk. Windisch, Dutens, Racknitz, Decremps, and Thicknesse had all expressed such opinions in their works, and Maelzel probably reasoned that if he could get the giant Boncourt into the automaton, the secret would be safe. Maelzel once said that he had made several alterations in the Turk's mechanism "calculated to render its action of more difficult explanation." Could one of those have been a modification to allow the automaton to accommodate a larger operator?

Boncourt, however, did not long remain the Turk's director. Besides the disadvantage of his large size, he was about fifty years old. Furthermore, Boncourt was a slow player, a decided drawback for a director of the automaton, since spectators tended to lose interest if a game became prolonged. After all, the Turk was supposed to be a calculating machine able to outpace the fastest human minds. Although Maelzel may not have voiced that claim, it was certainly implied, and his most successful operators were rapid players.

One incident which occurred during a performance of the Turk in Paris nearly resulted in Boncourt's exposure, but it was due to neither his large size nor his slowness of play. One day Maelzel had

The Café de la Régence was still the world center of chess. COURTESY OF JGW.

just wheeled out the automaton to begin a demonstration when a strangely human noise seemed to issue from somewhere within the mechanism. Embarrassed by what he immediately recognized as a poorly muffled sneeze, the mechanician quickly pushed the Turk behind the nearest curtain and did not return until he was certain that Boncourt had recovered. After several such perilous mishaps, Maelzel solved the problem by installing a clamorous spring mechanism, which the concealed director could activate by merely pushing an interior button at the first sign of symptomatic tickling. He could then relieve himself by sneezing or coughing as loudly as he wished without any danger of revealing his presence.

One of the recurring themes in the history of chess automatons is that the persons who directed them were nearly—but not quite—world champion chess players. Boncourt, for example, was always overshadowed by the powerful Labourdonnais, who was recognized as the best player in Europe

from 1820 until his untimely death in 1840. When Labourdonnais died, Pierre de Saint-Amant was generally considered the top player. Boncourt had defeated Saint-Amant in a match by a score of 19–16 while Labourdonnais was champion, but by the time Labourdonnais died, Boncourt was in his seventies and was no longer able to defeat Saint-Amant. Boncourt was strongest in the complicated positions of the middle game of chess. "In the twenty-five years I have played chess," Labourdonnais once remarked, "never did I see Boncourt commit an error in a crowded situation."

Besides Boncourt, Maelzel also employed Weyle and Alexandre to direct the Turk in Paris. Aaron Alexandre, a native of Germany, was about fifty-two years old but was a small man and could therefore fit into the automaton more easily than Boncourt. Alexandre presided over his own Paris chess club at the Café de l'Échiquier and was the author of the *Encyclopédie des Échecs,* which covered all chess openings known at the time. Weyle, also a German, for many years made his living by playing for stakes at the Régence.

Although the chess automaton was Maelzel's main

attraction, he also exhibited the mechanical trumpeter and the panharmonicon. They were nearly as popular with audiences as was the Turk, and the Paris exhibitions were successful, but Maelzel, who had always felt that the English would appreciate his shows, decided to visit London in the autumn of 1818.

2.

In London Maelzel spent several weeks searching for a suitable place to exhibit his machines and finally selected a house at No. 4, Spring Gardens.

Since Maelzel had not brought with him from Paris a director for the Turk, he contacted J. H. Sarratt, then the foremost chess player in England. Sarratt himself was too ill to consider anything so strenuous as directing the automaton, but he recommended for the job his student and assistant, William Lewis. Sarratt had been revising some of his works on chess, and Lewis was aiding him by doing

Boncourt, who directed the Turk in Paris, was second in chess only to Labourdonnais, shown here. COURTESY OF JGW.

One of the Turk's Paris directors was Aaron Alexandre, author of the *Encyclopédie des Échecs*. COURTESY OF JGW.

William Lewis, pictured here in his later years, directed the Turk in London. COURTESY OF JGW.

71

Maelzel on the piano, executed on the slack rope "the most surprising feats with the greatest agility, and without any apparent mechanism." While on the rope or in the hand, one of the rope dancers was heard to exclaim, with a French accent, "Oh! La! La!"

Maelzel also exhibited some speaking figures that, when an arm was moved, said "Maman" and "Papa." The principle employed in the figures was probably similar to that used in Kempelen's speaking machines. Later, of course, there were many talking dolls, but in Maelzel's time they were unique. Professor Jones of the Franklin Institute once said he would have rather tried to make the chess player than one of the speaking figures, which he claimed had "frequently baffled the skill of the most ingenious mechanicians." Jones also greatly admired the performance of the rope dancers, stating that it very much surpassed all that he had seen before.

When some of the London gentlemen heard the voices of the rope dancers and the speaking figures, they suggested to Maelzel that it would be an improvement if he could make the Turk say "check" instead of nodding his head to warn his opponent. The idea appealed to Maelzel, and he constructed and installed the Turk's new voice apparatus during the London visit. Some have claimed that the Turk's voice was introduced by Kempelen on his visit to London in 1784 or by Maelzel at the time of his trip to America, but Maelzel himself said the alteration was made during his London exhibitions. On a later visit to Paris Maelzel modified the mechanical voice to utter something like the French word *échec*, which the automaton continued to exclaim during the rest of his chess career.

As part of the publicity surrounding the Turk's visit to London, there was published in 1819 a book entitled *Letters on the Automaton Chess-player of De Kampelen*. That was simply a new English translation of Windisch's letters, originally published in 1783. The Windisch account was soon followed by a new book, *Observations on the Automaton Chess Player, Now Exhibited at 4, Spring Gardens*, by "An Oxford Graduate." The anonymous Oxford graduate was widely quoted, but his *Observations* added little to Windisch's earlier description of the automaton. The Oxonian could not explain how the Turk was operated, dismissing the enigma, in Walker's words, "with a parcel of 'probablys,' leading to no conclusion whatever."

Lewis once related that while he directed the Turk one evening "a gentleman came fully determined to win and accompanied by several friends who believed that he would." Lewis opened the game with his usual King's Gambit but soon found that his opponent knew all the correct moves. Thinking he recognized Peter Unger Williams, a

In London, Maelzel exhibited the Turk at 29, St. James's Street, SW1, in the building seen here at the left. Kempelen had exhibited the automaton at No. 14. At the end of the street is St. James's Palace. FROM AC.

some of the analytical tasks. Lewis thus had a vast theoretical knowledge of chess and great skill as a player, and he directed the play of the Turk with much success. Soon the automaton was winning nearly every game and was attracting widespread praise by the London press. As a result of the publicity there was no longer enough room for the crowds at Spring Gardens, so Maelzel moved his exhibition to a larger hall at No. 29, St. James's Street.

In addition to the Turk and the Trumpeter, Maelzel had room in the new hall to exhibit his orchestrion, a mechanical orchestra patterned after the panharmonicon. Eventually Maelzel enlarged his presentation to include his popular diorama the *Conflagration of Moscow* and an attraction billed as the automaton slack rope dancers. The rope dancers were small figures which, accompanied by

Maelzel's automaton slack rope dancers, like those seen here, were motivated from backstage by thin wires inside the rope itself, which was really a hollow tube.
COURTESY OF JGW.

strong player who had for some time been absent from London chess circles, Lewis realized he had to play with great care. The game lasted an hour and a half, but Lewis was able to win back his gambit pawn with a good position, and he then forced his adversary to resign. The visitor, as Lewis had guessed, was indeed Williams, one of Sarratt's pupils, who had become a top English player only eighteen months after he learned the moves. Lewis informed Maelzel that Williams was a quick and brilliant player with great genius for chess, so the mechanician, with his usual good judgment, called

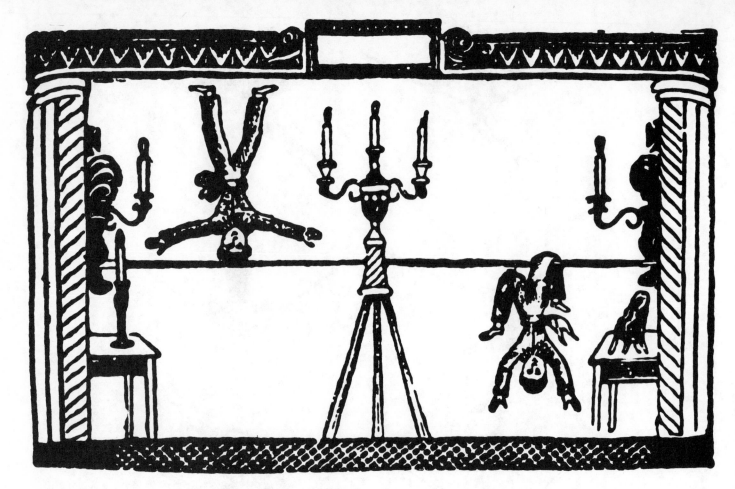

There were many automaton rope dancers exhibited throughout the nineteenth century.

upon Williams and enlisted his aid to occasionally direct the automaton. Thus, rather than opposing the Turk, Williams became the assistant director, an arrangement which suited Lewis very well. To further relieve Lewis, Maelzel also obtained the services of W. J. Hunneman, who in 1820 recorded and published *A Selection of Fifty Games from Those Played by the Automaton Chess Player in London.* Hunneman played endgames, while Lewis or Williams directed the automaton in complete games.

From November 1818 until the following February, Maelzel limited his exhibitions to three days a week, but beginning in February he increased their frequency to six days a week, resting only on Sundays. Each day would begin with afternoon performances at one and three o'clock, during which the Turk, directed by Hunneman, played only endgames. There was scarcely any danger of the automaton's losing an endgame. To assure success, Lewis made up a little booklet bound in green morocco, which contained endgame studies. From those Maelzel chose the endgames to be played by the Turk each day. Lewis had carefully selected each endgame position so that it could always be won by the player who moved first. Maelzel generously allowed the challenger to play

whichever side he wished, but always reserved the first move for the automaton.

The afternoon sessions were usually followed by evening performances at eight, when complete games were played. Since confinement within the automaton was always a strain upon the director, exhibitions were limited whenever possible to an hour. Short presentations by the Trumpeter and other attractions were included in both the afternoon and evening performances, for which Maelzel charged an admission of two and a half shillings for adults and only one and half for children.

The London exhibitions continued into 1819 until the beginning of summer, when the season ended. Maelzel planned to visit other cities in England and Scotland during that summer, but Lewis did not wish to leave London. Thus it was necessary to seek another director, and except for an occasional substitution at later periods Lewis ended his association with the Turk.

Like Boncourt, Lewis might have been the foremost player of his day had it not been for Labourdonnais. After the death of Sarratt in 1821, Lewis was generally regarded as the best English player, and he went that year to France to play against Deschapelles, whom many considered Europe's strongest player. Deschapelles, however, refused to meet the Englishman without giving him odds of pawn and move, a practice the French

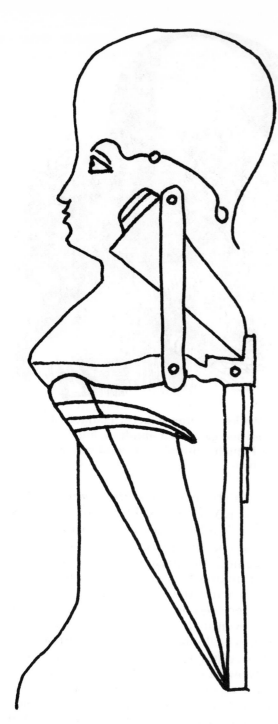

Maelzel's speaking figures were genuine but had a limited vocabulary. When the arms were moved, a bellows mechanism was activated. The speaking figures were exhibited at the Paris Exposition of 1823. FROM AC.

Paul Morphy was greatly influenced by the writings of Lewis. COURTESY OF JGW.

Although Lewis had shown there was little, if any, difference in strength between Deschapelles and himself, Labourdonnais was a different matter. Labourdonnais went to England in 1823 and defeated Lewis in a match by a score of 5-2, ending any doubt about who was champion. In 1834 the two adversaries met again for a match of about seventy games, and although the score is not known, Labourdonnais was again the victor.

Lewis's fame, however, rests more on his ability as a chess writer than as a player. In 1825 he opened a chess school in London but went bankrupt two years later. He closed the chess rooms but in 1832 published his lessons in the form of a book, *Progressive Lessons of the Game of Chess,* which Murray called a "landmark in the history of the game." That and later works established the Lewis or English school of chess, which replaced the school of Philidor and governed the style of all English and German players for the following fifty years. The greatest practitioner of the Lewis school was the American Paul Morphy, perhaps the strongest player of all time.

3.

Jacques-François Mouret, who in 1819 replaced Lewis as the Turk's director, was probably nearly the equal of Boncourt and Lewis on the chessboard and possessed several other qualities that made him one of the most successful of the automaton's operators. Mouret, a man of wit and humor, was a

master employed to show his disdain for all challengers. Under those conditions Lewis won one game and drew two, but since the games were played at odds nothing was decided. In the opinion of chess historian H. J. R. Murray, "Had they played on even terms, there can be no doubt that Lewis's knowledge of the openings would have made him the more successful player." Deschapelles did not even play his own pupil Labourdonnais on even terms and retired from chess when his protégé surpassed him.

confederate, whose well-acted affectation of astonishment was to heighten the effect and character of the exhibition.

This incredulity was, however, soon to be removed, the scene to take a change which none expected and few who witnessed it will forget. A false move was made (inadvertently, as we were afterwards informed) which the figure instantly rectified in its usual manner; at the unexpected outstretch of its arm to replace the piece on which the mistake had occurred, our friend, who was not forewarned of this piece of its practice, started with evident tokens of amazement; but when it proceeded, without giving him time to recollect himself from his surprise, to make *its own move*, he half rose in his seat, stared incredulously in the face of the automaton, expecting to detect at once some living agency, and on the quiet mechanical settling of the playing arm on its cushion, actually sank back on the chair and FAINTED! nor was he sufficiently recovered for removal, without medical assistance.

Mouret's skill and cunning, combined with the overconfidence, slowness, and superstition of the automaton's adversaries, resulted in an overwhelming advantage for the Turk. On those rare occasions when, to Maelzel's great distress, he found his automaton in a losing position, the mechanician had certain ways of rescuing the game or, at least, of making the defeat seem less conspicuous. We have seen that, either by intention or accident, the Turk's antagonists sometimes made false moves, to which the automaton replied by removing the offending piece and taking a move of his own. Sometimes when defeat appeared imminent, Maelzel would step forward and blandly request the near-victorious adversary to make a false move. With that invitation Maelzel cleverly implied that the spectators anxiously desired to see how the Turk might answer such a provocation. The hapless opponent usually complied, only to find that the resulting loss of his piece was enough to reverse the contest in favor of the automaton.

On the occasion of other impending losses, Maelzel was known to adjourn the game, claiming there was no more time to continue. He then courteously invited the player to return and resume the game at a later time, almost always at an hour when no spectators would be present. Therefore, when the fatal "checkmate" finally rang out, it fell only upon the ears of Maelzel and the hidden director. Thus the public seldom witnessed the Turk's defeat.

The rare defeats that could not be avoided or concealed did little to mar the reputation of the automaton. The success of the exhibitions may have been due as much to the character and reputation of Maelzel as to any other factor. To illustrate that point, George Allen explained:

He stood before the visitors of his room, by no means as a showman, but as a great inventor. Such he had proved himself to be by his panharmonicon, his rope dancers, his metronome, and his Trumpeter; and a genius that could do so much was half-believed to be capable of inventing a machine that could calculate the combinations of chess. And not his talent alone—his appearance and manners attracted the applause of his visitors. He was the perfection of politeness and amiability; he was passionately fond of children, and invariably reserved for them his front seats and distributed sweetmeats among them; and occasionally gave a benefit to orphans, or widows, or some other charity, in a way that evinced real benevolence of disposition.

From 1818 to 1821 Maelzel toured successfully in England, Scotland, and nearby cities on the Continent, spending most of his time in London and visiting other cities during the summer months. He found that short exhibitions in several different cities were very profitable. Maelzel once claimed that a two-week stay in Liverpool had brought in more receipts than six months in London.

The mechanician might have become wealthy from his exhibitions, but he lived very extravagantly, often spending money as fast as he made it. He was a perfectionist and would spare no expense to maintain his exhibits in faultless condition, even if he had to tear them apart and rebuild them completely. In addition, he was making payments, though often irregularly, to Eugène Beauharnais. Perhaps to solve his financial problems, Maelzel offered to sell some of his machines. An 1820 handbill of his London exhibitions announced that the panharmonicon, the Trumpeter, the *Conflagration of Moscow*, and his metronome patent were all to be disposed of.

Because of Maelzel's shaky financial situation, his directors often found him in arrears. At one time he owed Lewis fifty pounds, of which he paid back twenty-five, perhaps in the hope of persuading Lewis to accompany him on a proposed trip to Russia. Maelzel, it seems, was also slow in paying Mouret. Once during an exhibition of the automaton in Amsterdam, the King of Holland sent Maelzel three thousand francs and reserved most of the exhibition hall for himself and his retinue. On receiving the money, the mechanician ran to announce the good news to Mouret over lunch. Maelzel rejoiced at the opportunity to match his Turk against the monarch and immediately began preparations for a grand exhibition.

The King was expected to arrive at 12:30, and Maelzel anxiously awaited his arrival, but at noon Mouret had not yet arrived to take up his post inside the automaton. Maelzel, in great panic, went to search for his associate and finally found him in bed, trembling convulsively.

"What's the meaning of this?" demanded Maelzel.

"What's wrong with you?"

"I have a fever," moaned Mouret.

"What do you mean? There was nothing wrong with you at lunch a little while ago."

"True. I was stricken quite suddenly."

"The King will soon arrive."

"Let him go back again."

"But what can I tell him?"

"Just say the automaton has a fever."

"How can you joke at a time like this?"

"Who's laughing?"

"But we've never made so much money."

"You can give it back."

"I beg of you, get up."

"Impossible."

"I'll get a doctor."

"Useless."

"Isn't there anything that will help?"

"Now that you mention it, I can think of just one thing."

"Name it."

"You can give me the fifteen hundred francs you owe me."

"Yes, I will . . . this evening."

"No, no, right now."

Realizing there was only one thing to do, Maelzel went to get the money, which, as Mouret had predicted, proved an excellent cure: the automaton had never played such an inspired game. The King himself did not play against the Turk but was represented instead by his Minister of War, whom

When King William I of the Netherlands arrived, Mouret knew it was payday. BY PERMISSION OF ON.

he advised from nearby. When the automaton soundly defeated the partnership, the loss was blamed entirely upon the poor Minister.

After the adventure in Amsterdam Maelzel returned to London in the fall of 1820 for his third season of exhibitions in the English capital. Early the following year the Turk became the subject of a new book entitled *An Attempt to Analyse the Automaton Chess Player of Mr. de Kempelen. With an Easy Method of Imitating the Movements of That Celebrated Figure.* Many books and journals had dealt with the automaton since Maelzel's arrival in London in 1818, but none had shown much original thinking. Most had, in fact, merely quoted parts of *Observations on the Automaton Chess Player,* which was itself a superficial work. The new book, about forty pages long, contained a clearly illustrated explanation of how a fully grown man could have concealed himself within the automaton and directed from there a game of chess.

Robert Willis, who had modestly omitted his name from the title page but was soon recognized as the book's author, had solved the mysteries of the automaton solely through his powers of observation and reasoning. Accompanied by his sister, Willis had repeatedly visited the Turk's exhibitions in London and had eventually pieced together his analysis. His conclusions were similar to those of Thicknesse in 1774, but, unlike Thicknesse, Willis rested his conclusions on a carefully constructed framework of illustrated explanations, clearly demonstrating how the Turk might have been constructed. Willis thought the automaton's director occupied three positions, the first two while the cabinet was opened and the third while conducting a game.

The book on the automaton was for the twenty-one-year-old Willis a prelude to a distinguished career as a scholar and lecturer. In 1837 he was named Jacksonian professor of mechanics at Cambridge, and he was noted for his work in architecture and archeology. Willis was in many ways curiously like Kempelen; he even modified and improved the Baron's speaking machine.

Maelzel, it was claimed, admitted that Willis's explanation of the automaton was true. Even if it was not entirely accurate in every detail, as some have maintained, it was essentially correct. Thus it is tempting to conclude that the publication of the book hastened Maelzel's departure from London in the spring of 1821, but of course he usually left the city at that time of year anyway. From London the mechanician proceeded to Paris, which became his base of operations for the next several years.

Later in 1821 Maelzel again visited Amsterdam to exhibit the chess automaton. There he was confronted by the angry Winkel, from whom, on a previous visit, he had usurped the plans for the metronome. The Dutchman had soon learned of

The Count de Rechberg was interested, but no sale was made. BY PERMISSION OF ON.

According to Willis's drawing the Turk had grown a beard. BY PERMISSION OF GRH.

New York aboard the Havre packet ship *Howard* on December 20, 1825, leaving Mouret in Paris, where a secure position as a postal employee undoubtedly provided him a welcome relief from the hazards of travel with the Prince of Entertainers.

interest in the machine quickly faded. Maelzel even wrote to London in an attempt to make a deal, but he did not receive any satisfactory offers. He arranged for two exhibitions of the automaton, along with other pieces of his machinery, before the whole French court at the house of the Duchess de Berry, hoping that someone among the guests might want to buy the Turk. The Count de Rechberg and other foreign ambassadors twice visited Maelzel in his Paris exhibition hall at Boutique No. 9, Nouvelle Galerie des Panoramas, but though they displayed a great interest in the automaton, none of them expressed any desire to acquire the machine, nor did anyone else.

Maelzel had hoped that the festivities accompanying the coronation of King Charles X might bring to Paris some foreigners who would wish to purchase the automaton, but still no buyer appeared. Having failed in all his attempts to dispose of the Turk, Maelzel planned to take the automaton on a tour of Germany. While in Munich he hoped to exhibit the Turk for Eugène's widow, the Duchess of Leuchtenberg. It is not clear whether Maelzel ever made that trip, but it is certain that at some time after April 1825 he decided to take the chess automaton to America. Maelzel may have fled from Europe to avoid the lawsuit, and he may have taken the automaton against the wishes of his creditors. On the other hand, he may have partly settled the suit, agreed to pay a balance of four thousand francs, and taken the Turk with the full consent of the Duchess. In either case, Maelzel embarked for

ON THE CHESSBOARD
The Turk's London Games

Game 4

When Maelzel was touring Europe with the Turk from 1818 to 1825, systems for recording games of chess were just becoming popular. Before that period there is hardly any record of games with the chess automaton. Most of the contests which follow demonstrate how the Turk played under the direction of William Lewis or Jean-Jacques Mouret, but the first shows the style of Boncourt, one of the Turk's directors in Paris. Boncourt played the game as himself, not as the Turk. His opponent, who was forced to agree to a draw after forty moves, was Labourdonnais, the foremost player of his time. Although resourcefully played by both sides, it by no means proved Boncourt the equal of the great master, since Labourdonnais played the game without seeing the chessboard. It was first published in *The Chess Player's Chronicle*.

Philidor's Defense

Café de la Régence, Paris

White	*Black*
Labourdonnais	Boncourt
1 P–K4	P–K4

2	N–KB3	P–Q3	
3	B–QB4	P–KB4	
4	P–Q3	P–QB3	
5	N–QB3	B–K2	
6	O–O	N–B3	
7	Q–K2	P–QN4	
8	B–N3	P–N5	
9	N–Q1	P×P	
10	P×P	B–R3	
11	B–QB4	B×B	
12	Q×B	P–Q4	
13	P×P	P×P	
14	Q–K2	P–K5	
15	N–Q4	Q–Q2	
16	N–K3	N–B3	
17	N×N	Q×N	
18	N–B5	B–B1	
19	B–K3	Q–Q2	
20	N–Q4	B–Q3	
21	P–KB4	O–O	
22	P–KR3	P–KR4	
23	QR–Q1	B–B4	
24	P–B5	QR–K1	
25	P–B4	P×P e.p.	
26	P×P	R–K4	
27	P–B4	B×N	
28	B×B	R×P	
29	R×R	Q×R	
30	B×N	Q×B	
31	P×P	Q–K4	
32	P–Q6	P–K6	
33	P–Q7	R–Q1	
34	Q–B4ch	K–R2	
35	R–Q5	Q–R8ch	
36	K–R2	P–N3	
37	Q–B5	Q–B3	
38	Q×KP	R–KB1	
39	R–K5	Q–Q3	
40	P–N3	R–B2	

Draw

Game 5

Lewis directed the Turk in this game played at Spring Gardens on New Year's Eve, 1818, shortly after Maelzel first opened his exhibitions in London. Opening with his usual King's Gambit, Lewis had little difficult forcing the exchange of his Rook for the Black Queen with an easy win over a weak adversary.

King's Gambit

No. 4, Spring Gardens, London, December 31, 1818

White		Black	
The Turk (Lewis)		Simons	
1	P–K4	P–K4	
2	P–KB4	P×P	
3	B–B4	Q–R5ch	

4	K–B1	P–Q3	
5	P–QB3	N–QB3	
6	P–Q4	Q–K2	
7	N–B3	N–B3	
8	B×P	N×KP	
9	QN–Q2	B–B4	
10	N×N	B×N	
11	Q–N3	N–Q1	
12	R–K1	P–KB4	
13	N–N5	P–QN3	
14	B–Q5	P–B3	
15	B×B	P×B	
16	R×P	Q×R	
17	N×Q	B–K2	
18	N×Pch	K–Q2	
19	Q–Q1	P–KR4	
20	N–B5	P–NK3	
21	N×B	K×N	
22	B–N5ch	K–Q2	
23	P–Q5	P–B4	
24	P–KN3	P–N4	
25	Q–Q3	P–B5	
26	Q×NP	R–B1ch	
27	K–N2	K–B2	
28	Q–N7ch	N–B2	
29	R–KB1	K–N3	
30	R×N	R×R	
31	Q×R	Resigns	

Game 6

"One of the most skilful amateurs of the time" was the Turk's adversary in this game, which, like the previous one, was first published in *The Chess Player's Chronicle,* 1841.

Sicilian Defense

No. 29 St. James's Street, London, 1819

White		Black	
The Turk (Lewis)		Amateur	
1	P–K4	P–QB4	
2	P–KB4	P–K3	
3	N–KB3	P–Q4	
4	B–N5ch	B–Q2	
5	B×Bch	N×B	
6	P–K5	N–R3	
7	P–QB3	B–K2	
8	P–Q4	P–B5	
9	O–O	P–QN4	
10	B–K3	N–KB4	
11	Q–K2	N×B	
12	Q×N	P–KR3	
13	QN–Q2	P–QR4	
14	P–KR3	N–B1	
15	N–R2	N–R2	
16	Q–K2	P–N4	
17	P–B5	P×P	
18	R×P	O–O	
19	Q–R5	R–R3	
20	N–N4	Q–N3	

83

24	P–KR5	B–Q2
25	Q–KB3	P–K5
26	Q–N4	Q–Q4
27	P–N6	P–KR3
28	B–N4	R×P
29	R×R	B×R
30	Q–B4	P–R4
31	B–Q6	P–Q6
32	R–Q2	P–K6

Black won.

Game 11

Mouret knew how to turn the supposed disadvantage of his missing King Bishop Pawn into a powerful asset. The Turk's unidentified opponent in this game decided to allow the automaton to win back his pawn in exchange for rapid development. White even threatened mate, but the Turk found a mate of his own on the open King Bishop file.

French Defense

London, 1820

White	Black
Amateur	The Turk (Mouret)

Remove Black's King Bishop Pawn.

1	P–K4	P–K3
2	P–Q4	P–QB3
3	Q–B3	P–Q4
4	B–Q3	P–KN3
5	N–KR3	P×P
6	B×P	Q×P
7	O–O	N–B3
8	N–N5	B–N2
9	R–Q1	Q–N3
10	Q–KR3	O–O
11	N×RP	N×N
12	B×NP	

Black mates in three moves.

		Q×Pch
13	K–R1	Q–B8ch
14	R×Q	R×R mate

Game 12

Here Baron Sturmer set up a pawn blockade to keep the Turk's pieces from penetrating his position, but under Mouret's guidance the automaton broke through the King Bishop file for another spectacular mate.

French Defense

London, 1820

White	Black
Baron Sturmer	The Turk (Mouret)

Remove Black's King Bishop Pawn.

1	P–K4	P–K3
2	P–Q4	P–QB3
3	B–K3	P–Q4
4	P–K5	P–KN3
5	B–K2	N–KR3
6	B×N	B×B
7	P–KN3	Q–N3
8	P–QN3	P–QB4
9	P×P	Q×BP
10	P–KB4	N–B3
11	N–KB3	O–O
12	P–B3	P–R4
13	N–Q4	B–Q2
14	B–N5	QR–B1
15	Q–Q3	KR–B2
16	N–K2	N×KP!
17	P×N	B×B
18	Q–B2	

Black mates in three moves.

		Q–B7ch
19	K–Q1	Q–B8ch
20	R×Q	R×R mate

Game 13

Unfortunately for Mouret the Turk's games were not always short. Mercier, one of the top London players, held the automaton to a draw in this extended contest. Mouret must have grown weary after so long a confinement; he could have won, but perhaps he just wanted to end the ordeal.

French Defense

London, 1820

White	Black
Mercier	The Turk (Mouret)

Remove Black's King Bishop Pawn.

1	P–K4	P–K3
2	P–Q4	P–QB3
3	P–KB4	P–Q4
4	P–K5	P–QB4
5	P–QB3	N–QB3
6	N–B3	Q–N3
7	Q–N3	Q–B2
8	B–N5	B–Q2
9	B–K3	P×P
10	P×P	N–R3
11	O–O	N–KN5
12	QN–Q2	N×B
13	Q×N	B–K2
14	QR–B1	O–O
15	B–Q3	P–KN3
16	P–QR3	Q–N3
17	P–QN4	P–QR4
18	P–N5	N–Q1
19	P–QR4	N–B2
20	N–N3	N–R3

	White	Black
21	P-KR3	N-B4
22	B×N	NP×B
23	N-B5	B-K1
24	Q-B2	K-R1
25	P-R4	P-R3
26	R-B2	KR-N1
27	R/1-B1	R-N5
28	P-N3	B-R4
29	K-R2	R/1-KN1
30	R-KN1	R/1-N3
31	R/2-B1	K-R2
32	N-Q2	Q-R2
33	P-N6	Q×P
34	R-N1	Q-B3
35	R×P	R-N2
36	N/2-N3	B×N
37	R×Rch	R×R
38	N×B	Q-N3
39	Q-Q2	B-B6
40	Q-B3	B-K5
41	Q-N3	Q×Q
42	N×Q	R-N2
43	N-B5	R-N7ch
44	K-R3	B-B6
45	P-N4	B×Pch
46	R×B	P×Rch
47	K×P	K-N3
48	N×P	P-R4ch
49	K-N3	R-N6ch
50	K-R2	K-B4
51	N-B5	R-K6
52	N-N7	K×P
53	N×P	R-K7ch
54	K-R3	R-K6ch
55	K-R2	K-N5
56	N-B6	R-K7ch
57	K-N1	K×P
58	P-R5	R-QB7
59	N-N4	R-Q7
60	P-R6	K-N6
61	K-B1	R×P
62	P-R7	R-B5ch
63	K-K2	R-B1
64	N×P	R-QR1
65	P-K6	R×P
66	P-K7	R-R1
67	N-B6	P-R5
68	P-K8(Q)	R×Q
69	N×R	K-N7? (P-R6!)
70	N-B6	P-R6
71	N-N4	Draw

Game 14

Brand, another strong London player, played the Turk to at least two draws, of which the following is an example.

French Defense

London, 1820

	White	Black
	Brand	The Turk (Mouret)

Remove Black's King Bishop Pawn.

	White	Black
1	P-K4	P-K3
2	P-Q4	P-QB3
3	P-QB4	P-Q3
4	N-KB3	P-KN3
5	B-K3	B-N2
6	P-K5	P-Q4
7	P-B5	P-N3
8	B-Q3	P×P
9	P×P	N-Q2
10	Q-B2	N-K2
11	B-Q4	Q-B2
12	Q-B3	O-O
13	O-O	N-B4
14	B×N	R×B
15	R-K1	P-QR4
16	P-QR3	P-R5
17	QN-Q2	B-QR3
18	P-QN3	P×P
19	N×P	B-N4
20	QN-Q2	B-KR3
21	N-B1	R-R5
22	N-K3	R-B1
23	KR-N1	R/1-R1
24	R-N4	Q-R4
25	R×R	Q×R
26	N-N4	B-N2
27	N-B6ch	B×N
28	P×B	P-R3
29	P-B7ch? (Q-K3!)	K×P
30	N-K5ch	N×N
31	B×N	Q-K5
32	B-R8	P-K4
33	B×P	R-R5
34	R-K1	Q-Q6
	Draw	

Game 15

Perhaps to avoid the French Defense, Brand tried the English Opening, probably not yet known by that name. The Turk managed to win two pawns, but again the result was a draw.

English Opening

London, 1820

	White	Black
	Brand	The Turk (Mouret)

Remove Black's King Bishop Pawn.

	White	Black
1	P-QB4	P-K4
2	P-Q3	N-KB3
3	N-QB3	P-QB3
4	P-K3	P-Q4
5	P×P	P×P
6	B-Q2	N-B3
7	P-QR3	B-Q3
8	Q-N3	B-B2

8	QN–Q2	P–Q4	16	P–KN4	N×B
9	P–K5	B–QR3	17	P×N	P×P
10	B–B2	QN–B3	18	B–Q3	B–N6ch
11	N–N5	Q–Q2	19	K–Q2	B×B
12	N/2–B3	N×P	20	K×B	Q–N4ch
13	N×N	B×N	21	K–B2	R–B7ch
14	P–Q4	B–Q3	22	K–B1	Q×P mate
15	P–KR4	N–B4			

6

A Tale of Four Cities: Maelzel and the Turk in America

1.

New Yorkers who followed the "Ship's News" would have noted the arrival on February 3, 1826, of a certain "Mr. Maelzel, Professor of Music and Mechanics, inventor of the Panharmonicon, the Musical Time-Keeper, etc." That announcement was followed shortly by an attractive editorial in the *Evening Post,* introducing to the public the automaton chess player. Soon after disembarking, Maelzel had called upon the *Post*'s editor, William Coleman, to present him with letters of introduction and to enlist his editorial support.

Maelzel and the Turk had clearly arrived in the New World, but it would be two months before the citizens of New York would have the privilege of witnessing a performance of the famous automaton, for, as usual, Maelzel was in no rush to open his exhibitions. He rented a suitable hall at the National Hotel, 112 Broadway, just across from City Hall, and began the unhurried task of unpacking his boxes and assembling his exhibits. As he liked to keep a close watch over his machinery and those who assisted him, Maelzel made his own lodgings in the hotel.

One possible cause for delay in opening the exhibitions was that Maelzel had not brought with him a director for the Turk. To fill that vacancy, the mechanician had to enlist the services of a French woman, the wife of a man he had engaged to manipulate the slack rope dancers. Although the new directress would conduct only endgame play, it undoubtedly required some time for Maelzel to instruct her in her duties.

George Allen suggested that another possible cause for delay might have been the renewal of legal proceedings with the Leuchtenberg family. At that time, it was thought, Maelzel owed them about eight hundred dollars, a sum he was not yet prepared to pay. However, the executors probably realized that Maelzel would be able to pay more promptly if he were allowed to keep the automaton, and they thus postponed their demands for payment.

On Thursday, April 13, 1826, about one hundred persons, responding to an advertisement in the papers, gathered at the National Hotel to witness Maelzel's first American exhibition of the chess automaton and other attractions. Although the attendance was disappointing, those present quickly spread the news of the wonders they had seen, so that it soon became necessary at each performance to turn away scores who could not be seated.

After that Maelzel no longer had to publicize the chess automaton; the newspapers did it for him. One editor, in fact, felt obliged to apologize to his readers for "permitting the Automaton to occupy so much of his columns," explaining that "persons at a distance can form no idea how much the attention of our citizens is occupied by it."

Régence, sending him the money he would need for his passage to New York. It is likely that before leaving France Maelzel had made arrangements for the first-rate player to join him in America as soon as possible, but travel by sea was so slow that it would be at least three months from the time he sent for the new director until his arrival. Maelzel, increasingly anxious to present the Turk in complete games in New York, awaited the time when a ship from France would bring the new director. By June first, however, he had seen no sign of his new associate and had reluctantly closed the New York exhibitions with the intention of moving to Boston.

Five days later Maelzel changed his mind and announced that he would open again in New York after unpacking, which would take a week or two. Maelzel may have simply wished to remain in New York to take advantage, on July fourth, of the celebration of the fiftieth anniversary of the signing of the Declaration of Independence. On the other hand, he might have delayed his departure in the hope that the foreign director would finally arrive in time to give some New York performances, but if that was the case, Maelzel was disappointed.

Another possible cause for the postponement of the Boston trip was that Maelzel was detained by an agent of the Leuchtenberg family, who demanded the final payment of eight hundred dollars before they would release the automaton for further travel. By that time Maelzel was able to pay the sum, and he at last resumed full title to the chess automaton.

Finally, on July fifth, Maelzel again closed his exhibitions. That time he really left for Boston, without having presented the Turk in any complete games.

2.

On Wednesday evening, September 13, 1826, Maelzel opened his exhibition season in Boston. After that, he held performances twice daily, as in New York. For the Boston exhibitions, Maelzel had rented rooms in Julien Hall, at the corner of Milk and Congress streets. Those quarters provided an exhibition hall, as well as the usual chambers for lodging and eating near his exhibits.

To direct the Turk, Maelzel had brought with him to Boston a young New Yorker. The Bostonians loudly demanded the opportunity to play the automaton in complete games, but Maelzel still would not entrust his youthful director with anything but endgames. Even in the endgames, however, the Turk was beaten three times, once because of a blunder by the director, and twice because Maelzel gallantly allowed the antagonist the first move.

After about two weeks in Boston, Maelzel was beginning to realize that the endgames would not continue to satisfy his audiences. He had therefore

At Julien Hall, Boston, the new director joined Maelzel just in time. COURTESY OF BC.

nearly decided to initiate one of the top Boston players as his director. The chess players of Boston, it should be noted, considered Maelzel a talented artist rather than a mere showman, and they treated him with great respect and friendliness. Thus he soon became well acquainted with many of the city's leading players, from among whom he might have selected a director, but before that happened word reached Maelzel that his new, foreign director had finally arrived in New York.

William Schlumberger, a young man in his early twenties, stepped off the packet *Howard* in New York on the twenty-seventh of September. From his appearance one might not have judged him a likely candidate to direct the chess automaton. He was, like Boncourt, a full six feet in height. Nevertheless, he became one of the Turk's most competent directors, as well as Maelzel's good friend and loyal companion.

As Allen pictured Schlumberger, "his manners were gentlemanly, and his conduct every way respectable. His countenance was remarkably agreeable in expression; his features well-defined and handsome; his nose well-formed and prominent. The admirable formation of his head, with its dark brown hair, and his beautiful chestnut eyes, are always dwelt upon by those who had known him. His figure was muscular and well-proportioned, with the drawback which Poe has commemorated, of 'a remarkable stoop in the shoulders.' When visiting gentlemen's houses, he was always neatly and respectably dressed; but at all other times he . . . was by no means careful of his personal appearance."

Schlumberger, who was known at the Café de la Régence as Mulhouse after his place of birth, belonged to a wealthy manufacturing family of that city. After receiving a good education, especially in

94

Had it not been for Labourdonnais, playing on the right side of the chessboard at left, one of the Turk's directors might have been the champion of Europe. Before going to America, Schlumberger often played Labourdonnais at the Café de la Régence. COURTESY OF JGW.

mathematics and languages, he and his brother had been placed in charge of the Paris branch of the family business. Eventually a commercial misfortune had ruined the firm and caused him to turn for his livelihood to chess, which probably was his primary interest anyway. As a professor of chess he had supported himself by giving chess lessons at the Café de la Régence. At the chessboard he was fully the equal of Boncourt, Alexandre, and Mouret, and second only, as they all were, to Labourdonnais. Had it not been for Labourdonnais, who could give even the strongest players odds of pawn and move, it is interesting to speculate that one of the Turk's directors would probably have been chess champion of Europe. By enlisting the aid of directors such as Allgaier, Boncourt, Alexandre, Lewis, Mouret, and Schlumberger, Maelzel was guaranteed that the automaton was virtually unbeatable.

Perhaps Schlumberger's most famous pupil at the Café de la Régence was Saint-Amant, who succeeded Labourdonnais as editor of the chess journal *Palamède*. In 1842, at the height of his career, Saint-Amant praised his former teacher, who had first initiated him in the intricacies of combinational play through repeated practical examples. At the same time, however, Saint-Amant pointed out that Schlumberger had been barely existing upon three or four francs a day, which he earned as a chess instructor. There were then few opportunities for a professional chess player to earn a living. Therefore, Schlumberger, whom Allen called a striking example of a perfect chess enthusiast, welcomed the chance to become permanently employed as Maelzel's director at a salary of fifty dollars a month plus traveling expenses.

When Schlumberger arrived in Boston about October first, it was impossible to hide himself from

Pierre de Saint-Amant, seen here, was Schlumberger's most illustrious pupil. COURTESY OF JGW.

the top chess devotees. One of those gentlemen, Samuel Dexter, had visited the Café de la Régence on a recent trip to Paris and had seen Schlumberger playing there with Labourdonnais. Therefore, Maelzel made no attempt to conceal the identity of his new director from the Boston chess circle, as he did from the general public. For them, the secret was *how* Schlumberger controlled the automaton. Maelzel, in fact, encouraged his new director, whose good manners made a favorable impression wherever he visited, to play privately at the homes of the

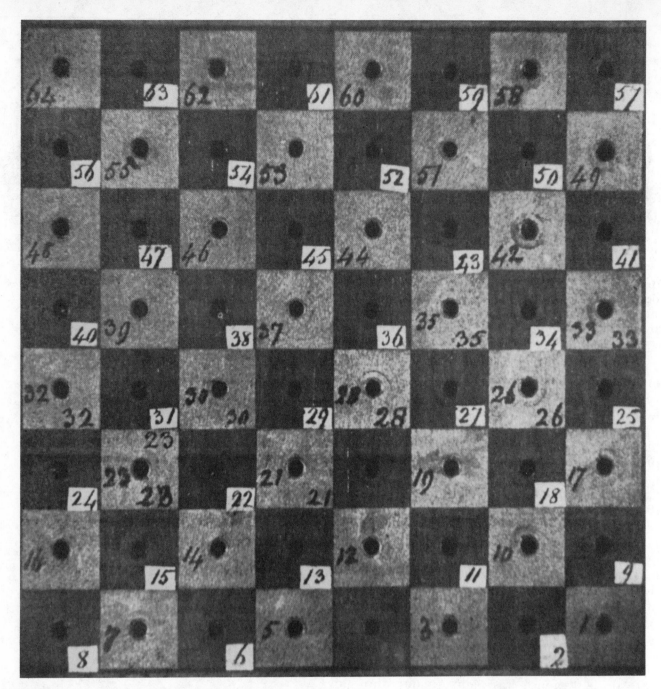

Maelzel's traveling chessboard with holes for pegged pieces was probably the one he used in games with Schlumberger. COURTESY OF JGW.

Boston players. By that means, it was soon established that none of them was a match for Schlumberger.

Schlumberger required about two weeks' practice to learn to conduct a game from within the Turk's mechanism. The director took a room in a boarding-house adjoining Julien Hall, so that he could dine with Maelzel while the two played chess. That agreeable habit became a permanent feature of their relationship as long as they were together.

On such occasions [wrote Allen] they had . . . a most amusing way of keeping the chessboard *en*

permanence between them, while making a deliberate and gentle progress through the pleasant stages of the savory meal. Attacks and counterattacks were vehemently carried on, fork in hand. Maelzel would meditate a move as he masticated; and Schlumberger, always rapid at chess, would reply without the loss of a mouthful. The severity of desperate situations was softened to the German's heart by copious draughts of claret; and his French antagonist, in the keen pursuit of victory, put the glass often unconsciously to his lips. Neither of them was by any means deliberately disposed to intemperance; yet if the game happened to be protracted to an extraordinary number of moves, Maelzel, to be sure, would be steady as a rock, but Schlumberger might,

As satirized in Cruikshank's 1819 print, the Londoners were fascinated with the game of chess and were thus a ready audience for Maelzel's automaton. COURTESY OF JGW.

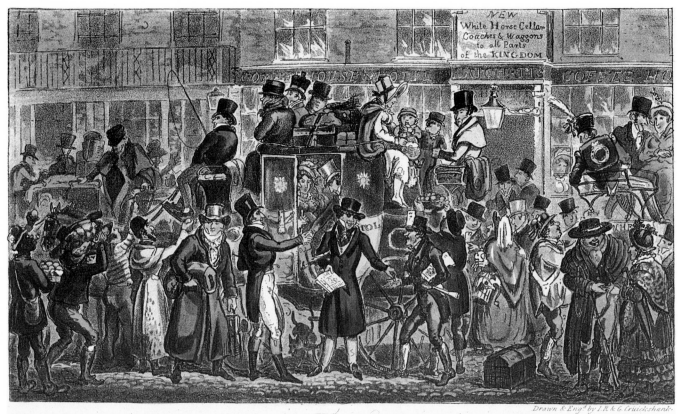

Drawn & Eng.d by I.R & G Cruickshank.

WHITE HORSE CELLAR, PICCADILLY. — *Tom and Logic bidding "Jerry "good bye", upon his going into training, & his return to Hawthorn Hall.*

Pub.d for Sherwood, Neely & Jones July 1 18 1

Maelzel and Mouret undoubtedly started many of their tours aboard a carriage such as this one drawn by Cruikshank for Pierce Egan's *Life in London.* BY PERMISSION OF BL.

In New York Maelzel opened on Broadway at the
National Hotel, one of the buildings in the row at the
right of this print by John William Hill. BY PERMISSION
OF INPS.

Grandville's fanciful *"orchestre a la vapeur,"* **or steam orchestra, caricatured the mechanical music Maelzel was noted for.** BY PERMISSION OF BL.

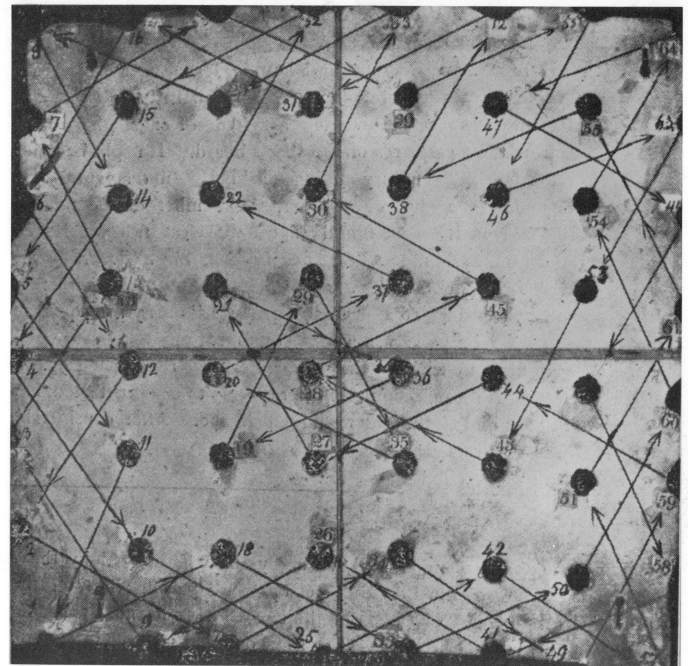

This diagram was evidently laid over the traveling chessboard so that Schlumberger or other directors could practice the Knight's Tour. COURTESY OF JGW.

perhaps, murmur his "*Échec et mat!*" with the least sign of a hiccup upon him.

On October thirteenth Maelzel felt that Schlumberger was ready, and he informed the Boston players they would soon have the opportunity of playing full games with his automaton at private exhibitions, which would be held, for a short time, at noon daily. The first such session was held on the sixteenth and it was the first time Schlumberger ever directed the automaton. As expected, Schlumberger performed brilliantly, and Maelzel was delighted that the automaton could finally perform

full games. But that very same evening a youthful challenger defeated the Turk—in an endgame.

Later in the week the automaton suffered a second defeat, this time in a full game. Evidently Schlumberger was having some difficulties getting used to his duties, but in the process he made a minor celebrity of his adversary Dr. Benjamin Green, who from that time on was known in Boston chess circles as "the man who beat the automaton."

Perhaps those two losses shook Maelzel's confidence in his new associate, so that during another game the exhibitor questioned the wisdom of a move his automaton had just made. Instead of repeating the move on the opponent's board, Maelzel went over to the Turk's board and nonchalantly replaced the piece where it had been. Immediately the automaton repeated the move, but Maelzel again vetoed it. A third time the Turk made the same move, but with such vehemence that Maelzel reluctantly relayed it to the adversary's board. The result of the game proved Schlumberger had been correct.

On another occasion Schlumberger nearly revealed himself by emitting a loud sneeze just as Maelzel was bringing the automaton from behind the curtain. The startled Maelzel quickly wheeled the noisy mechanism backstage, but soon returned and carried on as if nothing had happened. Since a similar incident had occurred once when Boncourt was directing the automaton in Paris, Maelzel again resolved to install a noisy spring which Schlumberger could activate during such crises.

While the Turk was in Boston or shortly thereafter, there was published a pamphlet entitled *The History and Analysis of the Supposed Automaton Chess Player*, by Dr. Gamaliel Bradford, a physician who served for several years as Superintendent of the Massachusetts General Hospital. Bradford's account, like several others, drew mainly upon Willis's booklet for both explanation and diagrams, but the doctor added several original ideas based upon his own observations. He even timed the intervals between an opponent's moves and the automaton's replies, finding that they varied from only ten seconds to three minutes. He thus concluded it was unlikely that Maelzel initiated the moves at the times he relayed the adversary's moves to the Turk's board.

Maelzel did not give Bradford much time to observe the automaton, since the inventor left Boston only two weeks after Schlumberger began directing. He headed for Philadelphia on October twenty-eighth, stopping for a short stay in New York in response to a challenge which had appeared in the *New York American*. A man calling himself "Greco" had declared that he would represent New York chess in a three-game match with the automaton "for love or money," and he would thus prove the superiority of New York players over those of Boston. Maelzel, upon arriving in New York, answered the challenge on November seventh, saying that a number of Boston gentlemen had authorized him to defend their reputation by accepting Greco's challenge at stakes of $1,000, or up to $5,000 if he preferred. Soon Maelzel was visited by two New York players who, according to Greco, were capable of playing "with a degree of skill inferior to no champion whatever, either American or European." When they arrived at Maelzel's lodgings, the two players discovered that Maelzel's troupe had a new member, a Mr. Schlumberger, who would enjoy playing a few private games. A few days after those encounters Greco humbly reported in the *American*, "I am sorry to state that both the American chess players on whose skill I relied so arrogantly

have been beaten with ease by a foreigner. I must therefore back out from my challenge, as better men have done before me, and subscribe to the automaton's superiority without a trial."

3.

Maelzel apparently had a greater affinity for Philadelphia than for any other American city, and thus he made that city a center for his travels and established many lasting friendships there. Before beginning exhibitions in Philadelphia he rented an old building on Fifth Street below Walnut and spent a considerable sum in remodeling the second floor to provide both an exhibition hall and his own private rooms, where he and Schlumberger could dine. In addition, he widened the stairway and rented out the lower floor of the building, which came to be known as Maelzel Hall. Maelzel also rented a storeroom from John F. Ohl, a friend who often advised him on business matters. During Maelzel's travels the old storeroom provided a convenient place to deposit some of his exhibits, safe from persons who might wish to pry into their

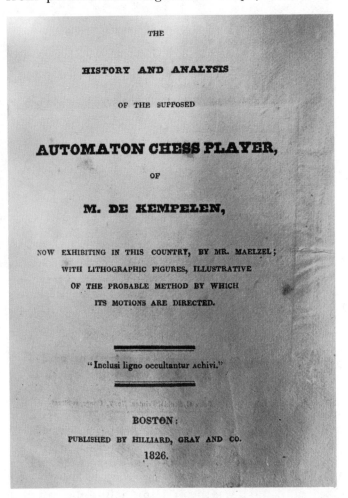

THE

HISTORY AND ANALYSIS

OF THE SUPPOSED

AUTOMATON CHESS PLAYER,

OF

M. DE KEMPELEN,

NOW EXHIBITING IN THIS COUNTRY, BY MR. MAELZEL;
WITH LITHOGRAPHIC FIGURES, ILLUSTRATIVE
OF THE PROBABLE METHOD BY WHICH
ITS MOTIONS ARE DIRECTED.

"Inclusi ligno occultantur achivi."

BOSTON:
PUBLISHED BY HILLIARD, GRAY AND CO.
1826.

Dr. Gamaliel Bradford's booklet on the Turk contained some original observations, but his pictures were copied from Willis. COURTESY OF JGW.

secrets. Even the automaton chess player spent some time in storage there.

The newspapers did not announce Maelzel's arrival in Philadelphia until December 22, 1826, although he had been in the city about a month arranging for his exhibitions. During preparations for his opening he kept a crew of workmen busy on various parts of his attractions. Most had little understanding of what they were doing, since Maelzel kept to himself the overall plan of each mechanism, entrusting them to nobody. One of the workmen called to assist in the final preparations gained more of Maelzel's trust than usual. He was Joseph J. Mickley, a young piano manufacturer who was summoned in late December to make some minor repairs on the piano Maelzel used to accompany the Trumpeter and the rope dancers. Maelzel took an immediate liking for the friendly young Mickley, who was a native of the Moravian settlement at Bethlehem, Pennsylvania, and spoke fluent German.

When Mickley arrived at Maelzel Hall, he found the inventor busily training someone hidden behind the curtains in the proper manipulation of the rope dancers. Speaking emphatically in French, the teacher ordered, fretted, admonished, and scolded his unseen pupil, who mildly and good-naturedly interjected his protests. Maelzel paused in his tirade to apologize to Mickley for his awkward disciple, saying pleasantly, "He is a novice: he has been only a little while with me." From behind the curtains there emerged a tall stooping young man, whom Maelzel introduced to Mickley as "Monsieur Schlumberger." The man who had formerly worked the rope dancers had long since departed along with his wife, the Turk's French directress. Schlumberger had thus inherited the duties of both Maelzel's former associates. In addition, he had become a sort of confidential secretary and clerk, writing letters for Maelzel and supervising the men who worked on the exhibits. Above all, Schlumberger was Maelzel's best friend and companion, and a ready opponent at chess, which occupied many spare hours at the exhibition hall.

When not otherwise occupied, Schlumberger

of the best chess players in each city.

In return, the Turk was of incalculable value in

promoting chess in Philadelphia and in other American cities. News of the automaton's exploits were carried in all the papers, generating a lively interest in chess and causing a great demand for the books of Philidor, Sarratt, Cochrane, and Lewis. Even before the Turk arrived in Philadelphia, the news of his coming had excited so much enthusiasm for the game that the city's first chess club was formed and had enrolled over one hundred members in early 1826. Vezin, the leading spirit of chess in Philadelphia in those days, often said in later years that he knew nothing of real chess until he began to play with the director of the automaton.

The day after Christmas 1826 Maelzel opened his first Philadelphia exhibition season, which lasted nearly three months. The Turk, along with the Trumpeter and the rope dancers, performed each day at noon and again in the evening. Schlumberger directed the Turk in both endgames and full games, losing only one of each during that visit to Philadephia. The endgame, lost to Daniel Smith, was the same three-pawn position responsible for one of the automaton's defeats in New York. The winner of the full game was a certain Mrs. Fisher, who, being a woman, was gallantly given the first move. It was rumored, in fact, that Maelzel gave her the whole game by ordering Schlumberger to allow her to win. The contest was begun on January thirtieth but could not be completed, so was continued the following day. After Mrs. Fisher's thirty-ninth move, Maelzel, realizing the game was lost, politely thanked the lady and observed that his automaton was fairly beaten. The *Philadelphia Gazette* printed the game, which appears to be the only example of Schlumberger's play ever recorded.

Full games were rarely played, but in one of them, lasting five hours and played in three sittings, the Turk fought an eminent Philadelphia player to a draw. The automaton, it was noted, appeared very hard pushed, pausing up to seven and a half minutes between the more difficult moves.

The February 1827 issue of *The Franklin Journal and American Mechanic's Magazine* contained an article, "Observations upon the Automaton Chess Player, now exhibiting in this city, by Mr. Maelzel, and upon various Automata and Androides." The journal's editor and author of the article, Dr. [Jo]nes, included in it some elements of [exposure] but added interesting observations of [th]e Turk. He also commented briefly on [the Trumpe]ter and the rope dancers. Although [his observa]tions did not seem to damage the [popularity] of the Turk, they probably irritated [Maelzel, and] Jones's article may have hastened his [decision to] leave Philadelphia. Besides, he knew [this was the] fourth American city whose inhabitants [had had th]eir curiosity aroused by the chess au[tomaton.] He therefore closed his exhibitions at Maelzel Hall on March twentieth and proceeded to Baltimore.

When Maelzel arrived in Baltimore he began there his customary preparations for exhibitions. He selected a hall at the Fountain Inn, on Light Street, and as usual remodeled it to provide himself living quarters adjoining his exhibition room.

Schlumberger, who took a room elsewhere, spent much of his time playing chess with Maelzel or with the leading players of the city, among which a Mr. Amelung was considered the strongest. Schlumberger soon found he could give odds to all who challenged him.

One day the director was playing with Dr. Joshua Cohen, to whom he regularly gave odds of a Knight, when a friend of Dr. Cohen came in. The doctor offered the visitor his seat at the board and a chance to test his skill against the "soul of the automaton." Since the new adversary asked no odds, Schlumberger played him even and after a hard contest was defeated.

"I cannot play even with you," said Schlumberger, "I must give you a piece."

In the ensuing game, Schlumberger gave Knight odds and won. In the first game he had not been able to arouse in himself sufficient interest to play his best, while in the second the Knight handicap had challenged him to play more strongly.

Public exhibitions at Fountain Inn began Monday evening, April 30, 1827, and according to Maelzel's advertisements they commenced with perform-

In Baltimore, Maelzel exhibited the Turk at the Fountain Inn, shown here as it appeared just before it was torn down in 1871. COURTESY OF EPFL.

ances by "the amusing little Bass Fiddler, Automaton Trumpeter, and Automaton Slack Rope Dancers." The automaton chess player was to be exhibited "only to private parties on application to Mr. Maelzel," but it seems likely that the Turk was called upon to perform nearly every evening. The automaton was seldon challenged to play full games, but in those few that were called for he was unbeaten. In endgames, however, he suffered a few defeats.

One of the successful endgame challengers was that same Dr. Cohen who had received Knight odds in private games with Schlumberger. The doctor was a constant spectator at exhibitions but had never himself taken part in the play. One evening before a large audience Maelzel challenged the spectators to play the automaton, but no one stepped forward. Spotting Dr. Cohen among the company, Maelzel invited the physician to come forward and oppose the Turk. Dr. Cohen was at first reluctant, but, urged by his friends and noting Maelzel's plight, he seated himself at the opponent's table and began to study the endgame diagram he was given. He shrewdly chose the side which he suspected had been made to appear weaker, reasoning that it was really meant to win. Schlumberger, of course, could have easily won either side with the first move, but Maelzel, as an inducement to play, had allowed the doctor to begin the game.

Dr. Cohen, playing merely to oblige Maelzel and expecting to be speedily checkmated, at first moved perfunctorily. He soon observed, however, that his position grew steadily stronger, and, encouraged by the excitement of the audience, he began to play with great care. Eventually Maelzel noted, to his great dismay, that the physician would win the contest. With checkmate just a few moves away, Maelzel cunningly resorted to one of his old tricks. As if merely to demonstrate an interesting feature of the automaton, he calmly asked Dr. Cohen to make a false move. When the physician amiably complied, the Turk angrily shook his head, rapped sharply on the table, and removed the offending piece. Then, amid great applause and laughter, the automaton made his own move on the board. "But how about the game?" exclaimed a few of Dr. Cohen's supporters, but their cries were drowned out by the amusement over the Turk's antics.

Nevertheless, the next morning's papers carried the news of Dr. Cohen's triumph. The good-natured physician, who knew Maelzel was always angry with Schlumberger for losing a game, was really sorry about his victory. On those rare occasions when Schlumberger lost, Maelzel used to swear horribly at his meek and penitent director. Dr. Cohen, despite the advantage of the first move, had not played accurately and should have lost, but Schlumberger, who had perhaps taken a bit too much wine with his dinner, had also played badly.

Dr. Joshua Cohen apologized for beating the Turk.
COURTESY OF MCF.

Charles Carroll, last surviving signer of the Declaration of Independence, also survived a game with the Turk.
COURTESY OF NYPL.

The next day, Dr. Cohen called upon Maelzel and apologized for beating the automaton. Maelzel, who complained that the game had been poorly played, promptly challenged his friend to play the same position at the next exhibition, but Dr. Cohen politely declined, protesting that he had gained enough notoriety.

Not all of the Turk's defeats were Schlumberger's fault. Occasionally, out of courtesy, Maelzel allowed a distinguished adversary to beat the automaton. Such was almost certainly the case when, on June second, the *New York Mirror,* in a story "The Automaton Beat Again," reported "The venerable Charles Carroll of Carrollton, the only surviving signer of the Declaration of Independence, now in his eighty-ninth year, beat his Turkish majesty in a game of chess, on Wednesday week, in the city of Baltimore, to the great delight of a crowded audience." There was more to the story, however, than the brief news item conveyed.

Carroll, a slight, affable old gentleman, arrived by carriage at the Fountain Inn exhibition hall at about noon on Wednesday, May twenty-third, accompanied by his daughter and son-in-law, the Catons, and by Robert Gilmor, a leading Baltimore merchant and patron of arts and letters. Gilmor had already attended several performances of the chess automaton and had become quite interested in solving the mystery of the machine.

As soon as Maelzel discovered that a Founding Father of the Republic was present, he displayed a great deal of attention and requested that his distinguished visitor play the automaton. Carroll, who had once been a good chess player, readily consented to a game with the Turk.

The contest began, and it quickly became evident that Maelzel had every intention of allowing the old gentleman to win. But, since Carroll had lost much of his playing ability, Schlumberger found the task of losing was not an easy one. At one point the Turk could have checkmated his elderly adversary by simply moving in his Queen, which was supported by a Bishop. Before the fatal blow could be delivered, however, Maelzel announced that he had to make an adjustment in the automaton's machinery. He took a light and went behind the Turk "to examine and put to rights the interior."

Maelzel's repair work was so effective that, instead of administering the checkmate, the automaton placed his Queen in the path of Carroll's Rook, which of course captured the piece. Even without his Queen it was no easy matter for Schlumberger to force his adversary to win the game, and the deception fooled hardly anybody. Carroll himself said, "I think you have favored me in this game." But in spite of the whole conspiracy, he seemed satisfied with his victory.

and waited. At the end of the first hour's performance, Maelzel wheeled the chess automaton behind the curtain. The excessive heat of that southern spring evening left poor Schlumberger, in the depths of his confinement, gasping for relief. To aid his friend, Maelzel stepped to the window, opened wide the shutters, and then returned to open up the machine. As the two youths stared in amazement, the tall, sweating, shirt-sleeved figure of Schlumberger emerged from within the mysterious contrivance.

One of the boys told his father what he had seen and a few days later, on Friday, June first, the Baltimore *Federal Gazette* recorded the revelation under the headline "The Chess Player Discovered." That same day Gilmor, in his own words, "called in for a moment at Meredith's to talk of the recent discovery by a boy, of the secret of Maelzell's [sic] Automaton Chess Player; which was, as we all suspected, moved by a man concealed in the machine."

When some of Maelzel's friends heard the news, they rushed to tell him of the exposure, but they found the exhibitor quite calm. He was used to such pretended discoveries, he said disdainfully, and he

Robert Gilmor was a disillusioned supporter of Maelzel. COURTESY OF JTW.

Up to that time Gilmor had been convinced that Maelzel himself conducted the Turk's games by touching certain combinations of keys concealed on the automaton's cabinet, and he had defended that theory against the opinions expressed by several of his friends that there was someone hidden in the cabinet. "I cannot conceive the possibility," Gilmor had declared, "of a man being concealed within the desk at which the figure sits and plays. It would be a contemptible trick, and unworthy of the ingenuity of the inventor of the machine." Maelzel's adjustment of the automaton for the benefit of Carroll, however, was too transparent for even Gilmor.

Maelzel had been exhibiting in Baltimore only a few weeks when a series of disturbing events began. The first was the publication on May nineteenth of an article, "The Automaton Chess Player," in the *North American*, a Baltimore weekly paper. That piece borrowed both text and diagram from the story in the *Franklin Journal*, which had claimed that the Turk was directed by "a concealed intelligent agent."

The *North American* article was merely speculative, but a more direct exposure soon occurred. During the last week in May two boys, one fifteen and the other nineteen, resolved to discover the secrets of the automaton. Having failed to solve the mystery in the exhibition hall, they decided upon another approach, and so they climbed to the roof of a shed adjoining the backstage area of the exhibition room

Chess historian George Allen was the author of "The History of the Automaton Chess Player in America," a source for much of the information in this chapter and the next. COURTESY OF JTW.

would pay no hush money. Several of his companions, however, warned him of the gravity of the situation and convinced him he should take steps to discredit the discovery. Maelzel therefore began to consider plans for repeating the trick he had staged in New York. He thought perhaps he might teach one of his young friends to direct the automaton so that Schlumberger could dramatically appear and act as the Turk's adversary, just as the French woman had done.

Before he could put the plan into operation, however, Maelzel was saved by a remarkable piece of luck. On June fifth the *Federal Gazette* carried another article casting some doubt upon its original story of the discovery. The reason for the sudden change of opinion was that some of the other American papers had contested the truth of the exposure. A rival Baltimore paper, the *Republican*, even asserted that one of the boys who had made the discovery had "demanded money for disclosing it." The *National Intelligencer* of Washington, then the most prestigious journal in America, treated the *Gazette* article as "a clever device by the proprietor to keep alive the interest of the community in his exhibition." After that, the other newspapers would not repeat the story of the discovery and the *Gazette's* editor, looking somewhat foolish, was forced to defend his stand in several issues. Moreover, the general public refused to believe the truth of the discovery. "Thus it was," concluded Allen, "that a revelation, which might have been expected to spread over all the country like wildfire, did nothing but raise a slight smoke in one city, and even there, as if fairly ashamed of itself, it soon vanished into air."

At that time the hot summer weather in Baltimore made exhibitions of any sort unbearable, so it was not surprising that Maelzel closed his hall on June second. Three days later, thanking the people of Baltimore for their kind patronage, he announced that in a short time he would exhibit, in addition to the chess player and other attractions, his famed *Conflagration of Moscow*. The magnificent diorama, which had just arrived from Paris, he hoped would divert the public's attention from further speculation about the Turk's secrets.

Having thus temporarily closed his Baltimore exhibitions, Maelzel hurried off to New York to investigate first-hand still another disturbing new development. He had heard reports that someone there had been exhibiting a rival automaton chess player.

ON THE CHESSBOARD
Foregone Conclusions: Some Endgames Played by the Turk and a Game with Mrs. Fisher

In America the Turk played endgames more often than full games. At first that was due to the lack of a competent director. The endgames seemed to satisfy most audiences, but the New York player who called himself "Greco" saw through the deception and wrote, "The ends of games played by the machine . . . are of the most subtle construction. Few players, even of the highest order, are able to seize the solution of these different situations on viewing them set up for the first time. On the other hand, the individual who governs the automaton's board, being fully possessed, by constant practice and experience, of every possible move which can occur, engages in contest with charmed strength and unfair advantage unless the opponent happened to have seen and studied the situation. The only fair test of skill would be full games."

After Schlumberger became the Turk's director, Maelzel allowed the automaton to play complete games, but they were not often called for. Endgames continued to satisfy most of the automaton's adversaries in America. At each performance, Maelzel presented the challenger with an endgame diagram printed on a card and allowed him to choose the side he would play. His choice made little difference, since, as shown by the following examples, all could be won by the player having the first move. Except on a few rare occasions, it was always the Turk who had the deadly first move.

Endgame 1

At the first exhibition in America, [wrote Allen] the position set up was the forty-first of Stamma (in Lewis's *Oriental Chess* the sixty-eighth), wherein Black, who was bound to lose, had the advantage of a pawn, and that too a *passed* pawn, within one step of the royal line. The adversary of course chose the side of Black, and lost (say the newspapers) in five moves. Against such an adversary, even the female Director could be safely risked with a change of sides. The pieces were set up again; the automaton took the Black—with the first move—and won again in about the same number of moves. "The figure was then removed amid great and deserved plaudits."

The following endgame position is the one Allen described, although it appears that Black has a two-pawn advantage rather than only one.

	If White moves first:	
1	R–K1ch	R–N8
2	R–QB1	R×Rch
	If 2...P–R4, then P×P etc.	
3	K×R	P–R4
4	P×P	P–N5
5	P–R6	P–N6
6	P–R7	P–N7
7	P–R8(Q or B) mate	

BLACK

WHITE

BLACK

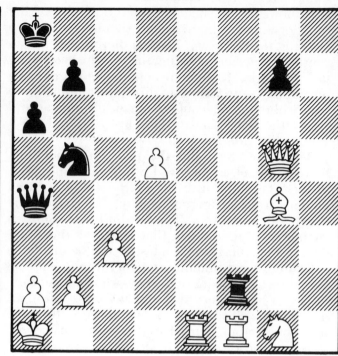

WHITE

If Black moves first:

1		R–B2ch
2	K–N3	K–N8
3	R–K1ch	R–B1
4	R×Rch	K×R
5	K×P	K–Q7 wins
	Or if	
2	K–Q1	K–N7
3	R–N4ch	K–R6 wins
	If 3 R–K7ch, K–N8 wins	
	Or if	
2	K–Q2	K–N7
3	R–N4ch	K–R6
4	R–N6	R–B5
5	R–R6ch	R–R5 wins

Endgame 2

Even when guided by the most inexperienced directors, it is easy to see how the Turk could have won the following two endgame positions, as long as the automaton was allowed the first move.

If White moves first:

1	R–K8ch	K–R2
2	Q–K3ch	P–N3
3	Q–K7ch	N–B2
4	Q×N mate	

If Black moves first:

1		N×P
2	Q–Q5ch	K–R2
3	P–R3	Q×Pch
4	P×Q	R–R2 mate

Endgame 3

In the unlikely event his opponent chose Black in the following example, the Turk, with White, simply captured the enemy Queen with an easy win.

BLACK

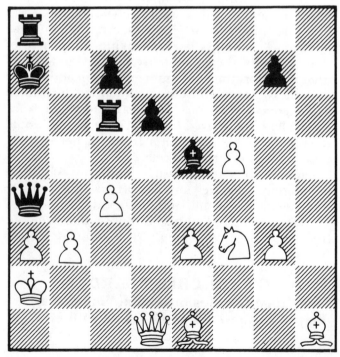

WHITE

104

If White moves first:
1 P×Q wins

If Black moves first:

1	Q×RPch
2 K×Q	K–N2ch
3 B–R5	

If 3 K–N4, R–N3 mate

	R×Bch
4 K–N4	R–N3ch
5 K×R	B–B6ch mate in two moves

If 6 P–N4, R–R3ch; 7 K–N5, P–B3 mate
or 6 K–R4, R–R3ch; 7 K–N5, P–B3 or R–R4
mate

Endgame 4

The difficult position of three pawns against three pawns was the cause of at least two of the Turk's defeats in endgame play. One of Maelzel's directors in New York lost the position, and even Schlumberger fell victim to the intricate formation, losing to Daniel Smith in Philadelphia. The position formed the frontispiece of John Cochrane's *Treatise on the Game of Chess,* 1822. The caption read, "The party moving first will win."

The following solution is adapted from Cochrane's *Treatise:*

1 P–B5	K–N4
2 K–R2! (K–N2? loses)	P–N5
3 K–N2	P–B5
4 K–N1	

White must now play opposite the pawn that moves.

	P–R6
5 K–R2	

If now 5...P–B6, 6 K–N3 stops the advance, therefore,

	K–R3
6 P–B6	K–R2
7 P–N5	K–N1
8 P–R6	K–R1 or R2
9 P–B7 Queens next move and wins	

Cochrane then gave eight additional variations. The player moving first, White in this case, can lose if he does not play accurately, as illustrated by the following variation.

1 P–B5	K–N4
2 K–N2? (K–R2!)	P–B5! (P–N5? loses)
3 K–R2	

If 3 K–R3, P–B6! wins

	P–B6! (P–N5? still loses)
4 K–R1	

If 4 K–N1, P–R6! wins without the NP

	P–R6
5 K–N1	P–N5
6 K–R1 or R2	P–B7 Queens next move and wins

Endgame 5

In Baltimore the Turk, directed by Schlum-

BLACK

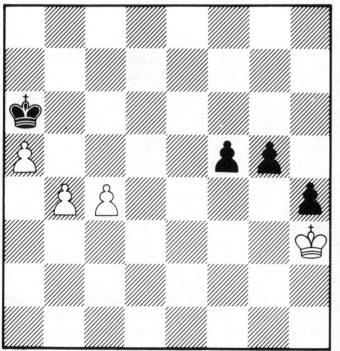

WHITE

BLACK

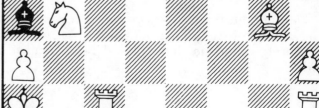

WHITE

berger, lost this position to Dr. Joshua Cohen, who played White. In addition to allowing the physician his choice of sides, Maelzel graciously granted him the honor of moving first. Dr. Cohen played inaccurately, giving up his advantage, but Schlumberger too played carelessly, and thus the automaton was defeated.

If White moves first:

1 QR–K1	Q–KN7

Lewis gave this move, but 1...Q×R; 2 R×Q, R–B1 seems to give Black better chances.

2 R–R8ch	N–N1
3 R×Nch	K×N
4 P–Q7 dis ch	Q×B
5 P–Q8(Q)ch	R–B1
6 Q×Rch	K×Q
7 P×Q wins	

If Black moves first:

1	N×P
2 QR–K1	

If 2 N×N, B×N wins

	N×Nch
3 P×N	Q–Q5ch
4 K moves	Q–N7 mate

Game 21

In Philadelphia on January 30 and 31, 1827, the Turk was beaten by Mrs. Fisher in a game played at two different sittings. Out of "devotion to the fair sex" Maelzel allowed Mrs. Fisher the first move and probably ordered Schlumberger to lose. Unfortunately, this may be the only surviving example of Schlumberger's play.

The *American Chess Magazine* reprinted the game in 1847. The notes, some of which are quoted below, were probably written by Charles H. Stanley, the magazine's editor.

French Defense

Philadephia, January 30–31, 1827

White	Black
Mrs. Fisher	The Turk (Schlumberger)
1 P–K4	P–K3

"Most of our readers, we presume, are aware that the automaton was a Turk; had he been a Christian, he surely would not have played P–K3 against a lady."

2 N–QB3	P–Q4
3 Q–B3	N–KB3
4 B–Q3	P–QB4
5 P–QN3	B–Q3

"His 'Turkship' has not yet discovered the dexterity of his fair antagonist; expecting to achieve an easy victory, he considers it beneath his dignity to take care of his pawns." Or is this part of his plan to allow the lady to win?

6 P×P	P×P
7 N×P	N×N
8 Q×N	O–O
9 B–N2	N–B3
10 P–QR3	B–K3
11 Q–K4	P–KN3
12 O–O–O	Q–Q2
13 P–KR3	B–B4
14 Q–B3	B×B
15 Q×B	QR–K1
16 N–B3	P–QR3
17 P–KN4	P–QN4
18 P–QB4	

"We like the boldness and decision of Mrs. F.'s style of play; this is true chess."

	P×P
19 Q×P	R–N1
20 K–N1	Q–N2
21 Q–B3	N–Q5? (P–B3)

"Badly played." Schlumberger does indeed seem to be trying to lose.

22 N×N	B–K4
23 Q×P	B×N
24 Q×B	P–B3
25 Q–B4ch	K–N2
26 K–R2	KR–QB1
27 Q–R4	R–B7
28 P–N4	Q–Q4ch
29 Q–N3	

"The hour having passed by," reported the *Philadelphia Gazette,* "Mr. Maelzel politely requested the lady to continue the game on the following day."

	Q–K5
30 KR–K1	Q–B3
31 R–QB1	R×R
32 R×R	Q–Q3
33 R–Q1	P–QR4
34 P–QN5	P–R5
35 Q×P	Q–Q4ch
36 Q–N3	Q–QB4
37 P–Q4	Q–N4
38 P–QR4	Q–B5
39 Q–N3	Resigns

"Never was better account rendered of Infidel and Saracen, on the sandy desert of his own soil, than is now given by the fair champion of Christendom of her unbelieving foe, on the chequered field of his own battleground."

7

"A Sublime Departure": Last Days of the Turk

1.

While conversing pleasantly with a friend, Maelzel once said, "You Americans are a very singular people. I went with my automaton all over my own country—the Germans wondered and said nothing. In France, they exclaimed, *Magnifique! Merveilleux! Superbe!* The English set themselves to prove—one that it could be, and another that it could not be, a mere mechanism acting without a man inside. But I had not been long in your country, before a Yankee came to see me and asked, 'Mr. Maelzel, would you like another thing like that? I can make you one for five hundred dollars.' I laughed at his proposition. A few months afterwards, the same Yankee came to see me again, and this time he said, 'Mr. Maelzel, would you like to buy another thing like that? I have one ready made for you.' "

The Yankee in Maelzel's story was one of the two brothers, J. and D. Walker, who, with the aid of a mechanic named Bennet, constructed the American Automaton Chess Player at Ithica, New York. They had evidently patterned their imitation after the original Turk, which they had seen at exhibitions.

As Maelzel explained in his story, he laughingly spurned the first two offers, but when he learned that the counterfeit Turk was actually being displayed in New York, he was forced to take the matter seriously. Newspaper accounts proclaimed the Walker automaton as good as the Turk in all respects, except that he was by no means as strong a player. When Maelzel heard that, he immediately wrote to his friend William Coleman, asking his

opinion of the rival automaton. Coleman sent back the dismaying response that the Walker automaton was decidedly the better of the two. Thus after closing the Baltimore exhibitions for the summer of 1827, Maelzel hastened to New York to see for himself.

When he arrived there, Coleman took him to an exhibition hall at the corner of Reade Street and Broadway, a place known principally as the home of the Boisseaux Dancing Academy. There, since May, the Walker brothers had been showing their automaton, which they billed as the American Automaton Chess Player. Seated next to Coleman, Maelzel fidgeted as he noted that the cabinet of the American Automaton was several inches shorter than that of the Turk, and the height and depth were also proportionally less. Furthermore, the American apparatus appeared to contain more machinery. When the Walkers exhibited the interior of their machine, they opened all the front doors and brought out the drawer to its utmost extent. They even opened front and back doors in the body of the figure and held a light behind it, so that the spectators sitting in front could see all of the machinery within. The three back doors, the front doors, and the drawer, were all open at the same time, and none was locked until every one had been opened. Although the workmanship of the American Automaton was less elegant than that of the Turk, the American moved his arm more gracefully and naturally than the original and uttered the English "Check!" rather than its French equivalent.

After the performance Maelzel approached the

two brothers and, exuding an air of affected slyness, said to them, "Your automaton is very good, but then you know it is very different from mine. There is no use of us having two automatons in the field. I will give you a thousand dollars for your machine, just to tear it up; and you shall become my cashiers."

Rejecting the offer, the Walkers proceeded to exhibit their automaton in Saratoga, Ballston Spa, and other places, while Maelzel returned to Baltimore, hoping the new rival would not pose a serious threat to his own machine. He had noted that the two Yankees were no match for himself as showmen and that their automaton could be beaten by anyone, which he judged would soon prove fatal to the success of the venture.

Back in Baltimore, Maelzel spent several months preparing for his new exhibitions of the *Conflagration of Moscow*, which opened on Monday, October 8, 1827, about four months after he had closed his doors for the summer. Due perhaps to the recent near exposure of the Turk and the appearance of a rival, Maelzel decided it would be prudent for the Turk to affect a graceful but temporary retreat from public attention. Therefore, in his exhibitions the spectacular *Conflagration* supplanted the chess automaton. An inconspicuous note at the foot of his advertisements had often announced, "The automaton chess player will be exhibited only to private parties, on application to Mr. Maelzel." Now Maelzel used that proclamation as an excuse to virtually withdraw the Turk from public view. Although Schlumberger's services were no longer required in his role as director of the Turk, he was kept busy with the more prosaic duties connected with performances of the slack rope dancers, the *Conflagration of Moscow*, and other exhibits requiring his assistance.

The Baltimore exhibitions lasted until November sixteenth. A few weeks later Maelzel returned to Philadelphia, apparently planning to proceed soon to New York, but on January 5, 1828, he opened a season in Philadelphia which lasted until April nineteenth. In December, shortly after his arrival, he had been irked by the discovery that the American Automaton Chess Player was being exhibited in Philadelphia. Perhaps for that reason, he did not exhibit his own chess automaton during his engagement in that city, and he probably relegated the Turk to the old storeroom he rented from Mr. Ohl.

After closing in Philadelphia, Maelzel moved his exhibitions to Boston, pausing in New York on May ninth to caution the public against the Walker automaton, then exhibiting there. "The impostor," he admonished them in an *Evening Post* advertisement, "was not the automaton *he* had exhibited in New York two years before, nor had it any real pretentions to the skill and power of that celebrated chess player." John Scudder, who was at that time managing the American Chess Player, replied in the *Post* on May twelfth, that his chess player was "at least the equal" of Maelzel's automaton, "if not superior."

Maelzel's warning, however, may have had the desired effect, since the American Automaton Chess Player was advertised for sale several weeks later, and one of the Walker brothers actually did become Maelzel's cashier.

According to one account, Maelzel himself bought the automaton "for five thousand dollars, and most ruthlessly consigned him to the flames." In fact, no such heavy-handed dealings were necessary, since fate again intervened in Maelzel's favor, producing a solution more satisfying to him than any he might have engineered himself.

It happened that at the time the American Automaton Chess Player was placed on the market, the French aeronaut Eugène Robertson was in New York arranging to make some balloon ascensions there. Robertson, a showman of the caliber of Maelzel himself, purchased the automaton, evidently planning to exhibit the mechanism in conjunction with his aeronautical performances.

Eugène Robertson was one of a remarkable family of early-eighteenth-century aeronauts, headed by the father Etienne Gaspard Robertson. The elder Robertson, born at Liége, Belgium, in 1763, had been a professor of physics there at the outbreak of the French Revolution. During that turbulent period he went to Paris to propose that the government construct a huge Archimedean mirror to concentrate the rays of the sun and thus burn up the British Navy. A commission was organized to study the invention, and they even gave it a favorable report, but for some reason the plan was never put into effect. Robertson, however, remained in Paris and was the first person in France to experiment with electric batteries, but it was as a balloonist that he chiefly left his mark.

Eugène Robertson was born in Paris in 1799, and a second son, Dmitri, was sired in St. Petersburg, Russia, eight years later. The elder Robertson had no taste for family life and as a result had never married. "It was one of those bastard congregations that one sees springing up during revolutionary times," wrote Jules Francois Dupuis-Delacourt, a fellow aeronaut and friend of the family.

Although both sons followed their father's profession, there were scarcely any family ties among the three, each going his own way and pursuing his own aeronautical career. Dmitri's home base was St. Petersburg from whence his aerostatic ventures took him to Germany and India. Eugène made ascensions in Lisbon, Oporto, Madrid, and Paris. He is noted for having made at Lisbon a spectacular pioneer parachute descent from a balloon at a height of 15,000 feet.

Eventually, however, spectators in the European cities became so accustomed to seeing balloon ascensions that it was necessary to seek new audiences in remoter areas, and thus Eugène had toured New York, Philadelphia, New Orleans, and Havana.

At the time he purchased the American Automaton Chess Player in 1828, he was back in New York, where he made ascensions on September 18 and October 22 at Castle-Garden. The first of those nearly ended in tragedy when a sudden gust of wind swept the rising balloon against a tall mast, which had earlier been erected in honor of the visit of General Lafayette. Robertson, saluting the cheering spectators with his back to the mast, suddenly found himself falling from the overturned gondola. Fortunately, Robertson managed to grasp the gondola, and, after dangling for ten desperate minutes a hundred feet above the screaming spectators, he was able to grab the mast rope and pull himself down. In the process, however, he broke several teeth with which he had been clinging to the rope. He even succeeded in preventing the balloon from escaping, but he was unable to keep a number of ladies from fainting.

Such was the new proprietor of the American Automaton Chess Player. Robertson returned for a short visit to Paris, where, on August 3, 1829, he made an ascension in the Tivoli Garden. He then took his balloon and chess automaton to Mexico, where he died in Mexico City in 1836, or, according to another account, in Vera Cruz in 1838. By a strange coincidence both his father and brother died during that two-year period; one in Paris, the other in Calcutta. The Walker Brothers never again heard of the American Automaton Chess Player— and neither, one may presume, did Maelzel.

On June 4, 1828, Maelzel opened his exhibitions in Boston but closed after about three weeks, announcing that he had to make a short visit to New York. Earlier, in Philadelphia, he had similarly interrupted his engagement for an urgent trip to New York. Apparently, the object of those New York excursions was to negotiate with the builder of still another rival attraction, the Automaton Whist Player. Since May 14 the whist player had been showing his skill at the National Hotel in New York, and Maelzel may have discovered that the machine was there when he went to New York to see the American Automaton Chess Player. The whist player's inventor, Mr. Balcom, had also exhibited the automaton at a museum in Rochester, New York.

After several trips to New York, Maelzel was finally successful in coming to terms with Balcom, who for a considerable sum was persuaded to part with the machine. Later the whist player made his debut as a part of Maelzel's own growing exhibition, but evidently the new attraction never became very popular with audiences. The reason may have been Schlumberger, who once vehemently objected, "I do not like whist, but I *do* like chess."

In addition to the automatons of Walker and Balcom, there was to be yet another chess automaton built in America in Maelzel's time. That model was primarily destined for the title role in the three-act comedy *The Automaton Chess Player*, by none other than J. Walker. The play opened July 8, 1831, at New York's Bowery Theatre, where it shared billing with Eagleston, the American Hercules, on the Corde Volante. The Walker production did not enjoy a long run, and the Thespian automaton was soon retired. He was, however, exhibited in New York for many years afterward.

2.

On July 15, 1828, Maelzel announced in Boston that he wished to sell the *Conflagration of Moscow*, and about a month later a group of three Bostonians purchased the diorama for $6,000, along with the Trumpeter, the rope dancers, and the speaking figures. The company hired as an exhibitor William F. Kummer, a traveling jewelry salesman whom Maelzel had recommended.

After closing his exhibitions on September 6, Maelzel disassembled the Turk, packed him in boxes, and sent him to be stored in Ohl's storeroom. A week later it was announced that Mr. Maelzel would reopen his Boston exhibitions in compliance with numerous requests. In fact, the real Maelzel was at that time on board a ship bound for Europe. The Boston Company, which had bought Maelzel's name as well as his exhibits, presented the *Conflagration of Moscow*, the Trumpeter, the rope dancers, the speaking figures, and the automaton violoncellist, all under the supervision of Kummer, who was ably assisted by Schlumberger. After an engagement at Julien Hall in Boston, Kummer and Schlumberger took the exhibition on a long tour, beginning with Providence, Baltimore, Richmond, and New York—and some time afterward continuing on to New Orleans, Nashville, Louisville, and Cincinnati.

On April 13, 1829, while preparing for exhibitions at Tammany Hall in New York, Maelzel's exhibition was suddenly joined by the Prince of Entertainers himself, who had just disembarked from the Havre packet. An agreement was quickly negotiated under the terms of which Maelzel and the Boston company would jointly exhibit their respective attractions, and the partnership remained in New York from the opening of exhibitions on May eighteenth until May twenty-fourth the following year.

In addition to the Turk, who was brought out of retirement, Maelzel exhibited several new attractions which he had brought with him from Paris. One of them, the *Mechanical Theatre*, was specifically designed to capture the interest of children in the audience. Maelzel, who loved children, admitted them for half price and reserved the two front benches exclusively for them. The *Mechanical Theatre* featured small mechanical figures such as the Bass Fiddler, the French Oyster Woman, the Old French Gentleman, the Chinese Dancer, the Little Troubadour, and Punchinello.

Another mechanical exhibit was the *Grand Tournament* or *Grand Carrousel,* which consisted of eight horses and twenty human figures displaying feats of horsemanship before the illuminated background of a landscape and fountain. Maelzel also brought from Europe the *Cathedral of Rheims,* a spectacular diorama depicting the interior of the edifice. In addition to the splendors of the cathedral, painted by the artist Ciceri, spectators could view a mechanical congregation "walking to and fro, and moving about in all directions." During the showing of the diorama, bells rang and compositions by Rossini, Mercandante, and Auber were played on the "melodium," a musical instrument of Maelzel's invention, "never heard in America." Maelzel's melodium was evidently a new form of the panharmonicon.

The Maelzel exhibition had grown so large that it was divided and exhibited at two different locations in New York. At Tammany Hall every evening the program consisted of the Turk, the Trumpeter, the speaking figures, the slack rope dancers, and the *Conflagration of Moscow.* The other dioramas were exhibited at 223 Broadway and were accompanied by the melodium.

In Boston that summer Maelzel reportedly staged an impressive mechanical concert, which consisted of "a set of musical automata, no less than 42 in number, which compose a complete orchestra, and execute several of the most difficult pieces of music in the most perfect manner." The program included overtures to *Don Giovanni, La Vestale,* and *Iphigénie.* If we may believe reports in the London *Times* and the Vienna *Theater Zeitung,* the automatons executed the music by movements of their fingers, "precisely as if they were living performers." It was alleged that an American company offered Maelzel $300,000 for the whole mechanism, but the inventor held out for $500,000 and eventually got $400,000. It seems unlikely, however, that Maelzel ever received such an incredible sum or anything near it.

On September 26, 1829, Maelzel advertised for sale the *Mechanical Theatre* and the *Cathedral of Rheims* as well as the automaton whist player and other items, but apparently no buyers were found at that time. Maelzel frequently offered to dispose of parts of his exhibitions, planning either to rebuild them or replace them with new exhibits. Although he had attempted to sell the Turk in Europe in the 1820s, he had evidently decided to retain the

ADMIT

TO ALL THE EXHIBITIONS

OF THE

AUTOMATON

CHESS PLAYER.

NOT TRANSFERABLE.

A season ticket to the Turk's exhibitions! What more could anyone ask for? COURTESY OF JGW.

automaton by the time he reached America, or perhaps he simply could not locate a suitable purchaser.

From 1830 to 1834 Maelzel continued to exhibit in Philadelphia, New York, and Boston. During that period there were probably times when he did not exhibit at all, or during which he kept his doors open but did not need to advertise. Although records are inconclusive, he may have taken his exhibition down the Ohio and Mississippi to New Orleans, or perhaps into Canada. There is also some evidence that he made a second voyage to Europe. At Philadelphia late in 1831 he advertised his intention to abandon public exhibitions and again offered to sell his *Conflagration of Moscow* and other exhibition items, perhaps as a prelude to a European visit.

Maelzel exhibited in New York from May 14, 1832, and far into that summer, the time of the dreaded cholera epidemic, about which Poe wrote, "The very air . . . seemed to us redolent with death." Although many New Yorkers fled the city in fear of the terrifying disease, Maelzel remained at Masonic Hall showing the Turk, the Trumpeter, the slack rope dancers, and the *Conflagration of Moscow* for the entertainment of those who dared remain.

The following summer Maelzel was in Boston, but he probably spent most of his time in Philadelphia, exhibiting at Maelzel Hall or at other locations there. An exhibition in May 1834 at Masonic Hall, on Chestnut Street in Philadelphia, was probably typical of the period. The first part began with a performance by the automaton chess player, followed by the Trumpeter, the *Mechanical Theatre*, the speaking figures, and the rope dancers. The *Grand Tournament* began the second part of the exhibition, which concluded with the *Cathedral of Rheims*. At other times the *Conflagration of Moscow* was featured on the program.

Dr. Silas Weir Mitchell, a Philadelphia physician and author, fondly remembered first visiting Maelzel's exhibition as a child, and in 1857 he wrote a nostalgic recollection of those performances:

There is a long row of wide-awake little faces on the front bench. The wild eyes of childhood are watching the nimble puppets. A paynim-puppet cuts deftly off a puppet's head, and tiny tumblers leap and bound, and Lilliputians ride more desperately than bigger men, and fight and quarrel in similar fashion. You will remember, also, the little oyster woman, with her sugar bivalves, which none but the little girls got; and how you wished you, too, were a girl, for the nonce, all for the love of sugar-oysters. Then Moscow burned for the thousandth time, and while Napoleon fled, and Frank and Cossack rode and ran, you avowed to your big brother that it was great fun, and you'd just like to come every night, always. And then, those babies whose squeezed stomachs gutturally groaned, *ma ma, pa pa,* you can buy them in any toy-shop, now-a-days. That stalwart trumpeter, so

An 1834 showbill detailed Maelzel's program in Philadelphia. COURTESY OF JGW.

gifted with unbounded lungs, we shall not soon forget him; and last, and, perhaps, least for you, that joy of your elders—the automaton chess player, the Turk—even he, with his oriental silence and rolling eyes, would haunt your nightly visions for many an evening after.

111

While in Philadelphia, Maelzel sometimes rented the Masonic Hall on Chestnut Street for his exhibitions. COURTESY OF FLP.

In Richmond, a young editor named Edgar Allan Poe visited Maelzel's exhibition. COURTESY OF NYPL.

During the 1834 season at Masonic Hall in Philadelphia, the Turk was beaten by Samuel Smyth, a handsome youth of eighteen. Smyth's game began during a public exhibition, but because of the time limit imposed by Maelzel, the game could not be completed. Smyth, accompanied by a friend, called at the exhibition room the next morning, where Maelzel greeted him with great courtesy and invited him to sit down and play out the game with Schlumberger. When Smyth won the game, his friend was so excited that he rushed from the room without his hat and ran up Chestnut Street to report the news to the local paper. Schlumberger showed no sign of ill humor at his loss, but instead displayed a great interest in the youth's talent for chess and encouraged him to come frequently to play in private.

3.

During the period from 1834 to 1836 Maelzel's exhibition appeared in Richmond, Charleston, and Washington, D.C. For those visits Maelzel sometimes divided his exhibits, showing the *Conflagration of Moscow* in one city, while at the same time the automaton chess player was featured in another. The *Conflagration* was probably a duplicate, or perhaps an improvement, of the diorama which Maelzel had sold to the Boston company in 1828. The original *Conflagration,* or perhaps still another copy of it, was exhibited in New York and Philadelphia in 1834. Thus several exhibitions bore the name of Maelzel, giving the impression that the great exhibitor was in several places at once.

When Maelzel brought the Turk to Richmond in December 1835, the editor of the *Southern Literary Messenger* came around to write a story on the automaton. That editor, who had just been appointed to the position with the December issue of the magazine, was Edgar Allan Poe. With his salary of about eight hundred dollars a year, Poe, who was twenty-six, was supporting himself, his Aunt Maria Clemm, and his thirteen-year-old cousin Virginia Clemm, to whom he had been secretly married the previous year. All three were living in the boardinghouse of Mrs. Yarrington.

During Poe's two years with the *Messenger* its circulation rose from 500 to 3,500 due mainly to his own efforts. He was not only the journal's editor but also its principal contributor. Poe wrote for the *Messenger* eighty-five reviews, six poems, three stories, and four essays, including "Maelzel's Chess-Player," which appeared in the issue of April 1836. "Maelzel's Chess-Player," which may be found in nearly every library as part of some collection of Poe's works, is undoubtedly the most widely read publication on the Turk. Poe's biographers have often commented on the essay, usually agreeing with Joseph Wood Krutch, who wrote that it "furnishes the first extended example of the author's skill in what he called ratiocination and which is marked by the most elaborately methodical exposition. It may well be considered as the first of his writings which bases itself not upon dreams nor upon pseudo-science but upon the logical faculty alone."

As an exposure of the Turk, the essay may be classified among the many descendants of Robert Willis's *Attempt to Analyse the Automaton Chess Player.* Poe inherited Willis's explanation through Sir David Brewster's *Letters on Natural Magic,* first published in

112

Although critical of the placement of the right arm, Poe felt this illustration was a "tolerable representation" of the Turk. COURTESY OF JGW.

was *not* the illness of *Schlumberger*. The inferences from all of this we leave, without further comment, to the reader.

The incident of Schlumberger's illness had happened during Maelzel's first visit to Richmond in the fall of 1834, at which time Poe was living in Baltimore. There, it has been suggested, he may have come across the *Federal Gazette* article telling of Schlumberger's exposure by two boys in May 1827 and also the *North American* article, both of which he may have used in writing his essay. It matters little, however, how he gathered his data, or even if his facts were entirely correct. As Hervey Allen wrote in *Israfel, the Life and Times of Edgar Allan Poe,*

> Out of a dead book or a banal news-sheet, Poe developed the habit of culling the one living incident, the pertinent fact, or the picturesque scene. That the French of obscure titles, the original sources, and the precise wording of quotations were somewhat garbled, is of importance only in the cemetery of the scholastic mind, for, by the living use of such matter, Poe frequently conferred upon it the only gleam of vitality which it ever possessed.

Although some of the other writings on the Turk are not entirely devoid of any "gleam of vitality," few if any approach the literary brilliance of "Maelzel's Chess-Player."

4.

After the Richmond engagement Maelzel returned to Philadelphia, where on April 26, 1836, he

1832. Brewster, the distinguished author of over three hundred scientific papers, probably became aware of the chess automaton while editing the *Edinburgh Philosophical Journal,* in which he reviewed and quoted Willis's pamphlet. Poe based his explanation of the automaton on Brewster's book, and he may also have seen the *North American* article of May 1827, which he mistakenly thought was the origin of Brewster's account. Despite a few inaccuracies in his essay, Poe made some valuable observations, which were, in his own words "taken during frequent visits to the exhibition of Maelzel." Some of them, which may help to show how the Turk was directed, will be explained in the next chapter.

Maelzel did not take Poe into his confidence as he often did the leading chess players in the cities he visited. When asked, "Is the automaton a pure machine or not?" Maelzel replied, "I will say nothing about it." He did not inform Poe that Schlumberger was the "soul of the automaton," but Poe managed to identify the director by means of his own.

> There is a man, *Schlumberger* [wrote Poe] who attends [Maelzel] wherever he goes. . . . Moreover, some years ago Maelzel visited Richmond with his automaton. . . . *Schlumberger* was suddenly taken ill, and during his illness there was no exhibition of the Chess-Player. The reason assigned for the suspension of . . . performances

Signor Antonio Blitz received advice from Maelzel on the subject of audience control. COURTESY OF CPL.

113

association with Signor Blitz. By that time many people had read Poe's essay on the chess automaton, and according to one paper Poe had even challenged "a reply from Maelzel himself." Instead of answering the challenge, the restless Maelzel headed west, taking with him the Turk, the Trumpeter, the melodium, the rope dancers, the speaking figures, the *Mechanical Theatre,* and *The Pyric Fires,* another of his dioramas.

By September or October Maelzel was in Pittsburgh, and from there he traveled by steamboat down the Ohio and Mississippi during the fall of 1836 and the following winter. After visiting Cincinnati and Louisville, he arrived in New Orleans, where on Monday, January ninth, he opened his exhibition in a hall on Poydras Street at the corner of Camp. For the evening's entertainment, which began each weekday at seven, he charged an admission of one dollar, but as usual children were admitted for half price. The performances continued until Saturday, February 25, 1837.

Instead of retracing his path up the great rivers, Maelzel decided to return to Philadelphia by sea, a plan which allowed him to stop for a short exhibition season in Havana. The engagement in Havana was greeted with great applause, but the Cubans were disappointed to learn that Maelzel had not brought with him the famous *Conflagration of Moscow.* In preparation for the long riverboat journey, he had again sold the huge diorama. Before leaving Havana, however, Maelzel promised to return soon with a new, far more beautiful *Conflagration,* built just for them.

Returning to Philadelphia in the spring of 1837, Maelzel discovered that a new attempt to expose the Turk had been published in his absence. In the *National Gazette* of February sixth, he found a copy of an article from a recent issue of the Parisian chess journal *Palamède.* The piece, by Mathieu De Tournay, was entitled *"La Vie et Les Aventures de L'Automate Joueur D'Échecs"* (The Life and Adventures of the Automaton Chess Player). It differed from most previous publications on the chess automaton in that it did not borrow the ideas of Willis. De Tournay had instead adopted the explanation proposed in a one-page story that had appeared in the *Magazin Pittoresque* in 1834. The anonymous author of the *Pittoresque* article had supposed that the Turk was operated with the aid of an elaborate magnetic chessboard, somewhat like the one Racknitz had detailed. George Walker thought the source of the explanation in *Pittoresque* had been none other than Jacques Mouret, Maelzel's former director. Mouret, according to Walker, had "burnt out his brain with brandy" and had "sold the secrets of his prison-house to the French penny magazine." There is, however, some cause to doubt that Mouret was the source of the *Pittoresque* article.

It is known, however, that in May 1837 Mouret died in Paris after having been for several years paralyzed in all his limbs and in a great state of suffering. He had been a postal employee and had a small pension, but during his final days he had been dependent upon the Paris chess community, which generously came to his aid.

Maelzel saved a copy of De Tournay's article, but at the time he was less interested in the Turk than in his plans for the new *Conflagration of Moscow,* which he intended to construct on a grand scale. For that purpose he rented the Adelphi Buildings on Fifth Street near Walnut, where, during the summer and autumn of 1837, he kept a large crew of mechanics at work. In order to personally superintend and expedite the construction, he moved into private rooms on the premises.

Maelzel hoped to exhibit the new *Conflagration* in Havana and then in all the principal cities of South America. In anticipation of the tour, Maelzel employed a Mr. and Mrs. Fischer in Philadelphia. Mr. Fischer, an experienced exhibitor, would relieve Schlumberger of some of his duties, while Mrs. Fischer would act as cook and housekeeper for the whole company. To ensure that everything would run smoothly when they reached Cuba, Maelzel tried out the new living arrangements at the Adelphi Buildings for some time before their departure.

Displaying an excess of his usual perfectionism, Maelzel badgered his workmen incessantly, insisting

One of Schlumberger's Philadelphia chess companions was Henry Vethake, who later became Provost of the University of Pennsylvania. COURTESY OF FLP.

116

that they redo any work inconsistent with his high expectations. He was so absorbed with the construction of the new diorama that he gave no exhibitions during the entire summer and autumn.

As a result, Schlumberger was free to accept the invitations of the Philadelphia chess amateurs to play at their homes. Among those who frequently played with the director at that time was Henry Vethake, who later became Provost of the University of Pennsylvania. By that time Schlumberger had visited nearly all the principal cities of the United States and had played with the leading chess players wherever he went. No one had come close to beating him on a regular basis. There was at that time no United States Chess Championship, but it seems very likely that, as William Kummer later asserted, Schlumberger was then the strongest player in the country.

Schlumberger had grown more and more into the confidence and affection of Maelzel. "Their connection," wrote George Allen, "had lasted so long, they were always so much together, their manner towards each other was such, that an opinion grew up, among our German citizens, at least, that Schlumberger was a near relation, or an adopted son, of Maelzel's; nay, some thought him to be actually his son."

With November came the time scheduled for their departure for Havana, but the new *Conflagration of Moscow* was not yet completed. Maelzel delayed the vessel a week but still had to sail with some of the details of the diorama only partly finished. Finally he embarked with his entourage on November 9, 1837, aboard the brig *Lancet* under the command of Captain Young. The *Lancet* belonged to Maelzel's friend John Ohl, who had connections in Havana through his shipping business. Maelzel knew the best time for his exhibitions in Havana would be during the carnival season from Christmas to Ash Wednesday, which in 1838 fell upon the last day of February. He had therefore timed his departure so as to arrive in late November with four or five weeks to prepare for the holiday season.

A few days after Maelzel disembarked in Havana, a ship arrived from New York, bringing the indefatigable Signor Blitz, who had himself decided to bring his show to the Cuban capital for the season of festivity. The magician rented a hall nearby for his performances and was a frequent and welcome visitor in Maelzel's rooms.

Maelzel was ready to open his doors in time to take full advantage of the Christmas merrymaking, and the season began with great success. The splendid new diorama of Moscow, it appeared, fully justified the time and attention to detail that its creator had lavished upon it. Soon the exhibition drew crowds of festive Cubans and there was an air of great optimism. It seemed a most propitious start for a successful South American tour. However, the Havana exhibition was to be, not a beginning, but an ending, a most disastrous ending for those most closely associated with the Turk.

One morning, while busy in his own exhibition hall, Signor Blitz was surprised by the sudden appearance of Maelzel. The normally convivial showman was evidently in a state of extreme agitation. "Schlumberger is dead!" he blurted out abruptly. Maelzel's dear companion had died quite suddenly of yellow fever. Blitz, who often visited his two friends, had not even known that poor Schlumberger was ill.

Maelzel at first took great pains to keep the death of Schlumberger as secret as possible, hoping to save the Havana exhibitions from ruin. "He undoubtedly calculated upon providing himself with some other director," wrote Allen, "and upon continuing his exhibitions with the same alacrity and success as before. If so, he was deplorably mistaken—and that too from a cause, which he could not have taken into account, namely, the sudden and absolute prostration of his own spirit, hitherto so hopeful and so indomitable, consequent upon the loss of one, who had been for so many years his devoted and efficient ally."

Schlumberger's untimely death marked the beginning of a dismal decline for Maelzel's Havana exhibitions, which dragged on miserably for several months after the fatal event. Moscow still burned brightly, but it must have been somehow evident that the soul of its exhibitor had been nearly extinguished, and the performances were poorly attended. Sensing the impending failure, the Fischers abandoned Maelzel to his melancholy fate, thus adding the blow of desertion to the one inflicted by death. Nearly sixty-six years old, Maelzel found himself alone in a strange land, reduced in circumstances, and involved in debt. In the darkened and empty exhibition hall, the enormous panorama of Moscow must have seemed more desolate than Moscow itself had ever appeared to Napoleon—as wretched and forlorn as Maelzel's own spirit.

"His pride and spirit could not battle with the change," commented Blitz. There was nothing to do but close the exhibitions and return to Philadelphia, the plans for South America having vanished completely. Maelzel wrote a pathetic letter to William Kummer in Philadelphia, requesting him to engage an exhibition hall for him there and recounting his misfortunes in Havana. According to Allen, "the letter was gloomy in its backward view of the past—gloomy in its prospect of the future—ominous signs, in the case of a man naturally so cheerful and so hopeful as Maelzel."

Captain Nobre, master of Ohl's brig the *Otis*, greeted his friend Maelzel, who boarded the ship in Havana on Saturday, July fourteenth, for the voyage back to Philadelphia. The Captain could hardly ited at various locations in New York from October 1837 until about the same time the following year. Assuming it was Maelzel's original Trumpeter, the inventor must have sold the mechanism before leaving Havana. Eventually, the Trumpeter found a home with a Philadelphia family. He was last heard publicly when in 1871 Signor Blitz exhibited him in Philadelphia at the Great Central Fair in Logan Square. As late as March 1863, a humorist named Gallagher was exhibiting Maelzel's *Conflagration of Moscow* at the Spring Garden Institute Hall, Philadelphia, along with dioptic paintings and a ventriloquism act. It is difficult to trace further the destinies of the various pieces of Maelzel's exhibition, but the fate of the automaton chess player is known.

For over a year the Turk remained in the possession of Ohl, stored in a warehouse at Lombard Street Wharf in Philadelphia. The hoped-for buyer had not appeared, so that by the spring of 1840 Ohl was willing to part with the automaton for the same four hundred dollars he had paid at auction. Dr. John Kearsley Mitchell, a prominent physician and lecturer from Philadelphia, and an acquaintance of Maelzel, had long been fascinated by the elusive secrets of the Turk's operation. He thus resolved to purchase the automaton, but not for himself. Instead, he organized a club composed of seventy-five gentlemen, each of whom would subscribe five or ten dollars to become joint owners of the chess player. Mitchell authorized James Gibson to collect a total of five hundred dollars in dues, which would pay the price Ohl was asking and allow an additional hundred for "contingent expenses." The automaton thus became the property of a club, the members of which would be privileged to share the secrets of the famous machine.

It is interesting to note that the author of "Maelzel's Chess-Player" had been living in Philadelphia since 1838, writing for various magazines and trying to launch a literary journal of his own. In fact, Dr. Mitchell was the personal physician of Poe and his wife Virginia, and Mitchell had on the evening of February 29 invited Poe to his home. Poe's name,

The Turk's new owners were listed and their dues collected. COURTESY OF JGW.

During the summer, Dr. Mitchell worked on the automaton in his home, at the left of this photo, at the corner of eighteenth and Locust streets, Philadelphia. COURTESY OF FLP.

however, was not listed among the seventy-five who purchased the Turk.

After the four hundred dollars were paid to Ohl, the boxes containing the dismembered Turk were brought to Dr. Mitchell's office and eagerly opened. "A perfect chaos was disclosed," reported Allen, "and the work of restoring the mechanism to its pristine integrity and efficiency was found to be no slight one." Maelzel, following his usual precautions to discourage snoopers from prying into his secrets, had mixed with the contents of the boxes pieces of other exhibits, particularly the *Carrousel*. In addition, parts of the Turk were missing and had to be searched for in other boxes still in Ohl's warehouse. A list of "things not found and to be looked for," in Dr. Mitchell's handwriting, listed "doors of the boxes, castors, dress, top of head, rod for neck, chessmen, pipe, seat of Turk, and legs of Turk." Presumably most of the missing parts were found, and Dr. Mitchell, often consulting William Kummer, amused himself during the summer of 1840 in the "pleasant labors of restoration." With the help of Willis's drawings, the *Palamède* article of De Tournay, the plates in Racknitz's book, and suggestions from "ingenious friends," the Turk was finally reassembled, but only "after many amusing failures."

In the first week of September Dr. Mitchell invited the club members to his office, where he first displayed the restored automaton and what he claimed to be the Turk's mode of operation. The director on that occasion was Kummer, who later explained, "I took my seat in the mysterious chess-table, practiced repeatedly, and then animated the head, arms, fingers, and voice (Echec!) of the Grand Turk, and at an exhibition in his office to a large private assemblage, astonished and amused them." Later the Turk was made available for private exhibitions for the families of club members.

Librarian Lloyd P. Smith was, in his youth, the Turk's last director. COURTESY OF FLP.

The Chinese Museum, Philadelphia, was the Turk's home for nearly fourteen years. COURTESY OF FLP.

Kummer was soon replaced as director by Lloyd P. Smith, a young amateur chess player who later became librarian of the Library Company of Philadelphia. Smith was calling one evening at the home of a young lady friend, when a message arrived suggesting that he go at once to relieve Kummer, who was ill. He left at once for the scene of action, leaving the poor girl without a beau for the evening.

Kummer wrote an article for the newspapers

121

13	Q–B7	B–R5ch
14	K–N1	P–B6
15	R×P	Q–K8ch
16	R–B1	B–B7ch
17	Q×B	R×Bch
18	K–R1	Q–K5ch
19	Q–B3	B–B4
20	N–Q2	Q×Qch
21	N×Q	B–K5
22	R–B2	N–Q2
23	B–B4	R–KB1
24	B–N5ch	K–B2
25	QR–KB1	R–KN1
26	B–R4	QR–KB1
27	B–N3	R×N
28	R×R	R–KB1
29	K–N2	R×R
30	R×R	N–B3
31	K–B2	B×R
32	K×B	K–Q2
33	B–R4	K–K3
34	B×N	K×B
35	K–B4	P–Q4
36	P–KR4	P–KR4
37	P–QR4	P–QR4
38	P–QN3	P–QN4
39	K–N3	K–B4
40	K–B3	Draw

Game 23

In the next game the automaton employed a few simple tactics to win a piece from A. Zerega of the New York Chess Club. The director was Stanley.

Petroff's Defense

Private Exhibition, New York, October 31, 1845

	White	*Black*
	Automaton (Stanley)	Zerega
1	P–K4	P–K4
2	N–KB3	N–KB3
3	N×P	P–Q3
4	N–KB3	N×P
5	P–Q3	N–KB3
6	B–K2	B–K2
7	O–O	O–O
8	N–B3	P–QB3
9	P–KR3	P–KR3
10	N–R2	N–R2
11	P–B4	P–B4
12	B–B3	N–Q2
13	N–K2	QN–B3
14	N–N3	P–Q4
15	B–R5	Q–B2
16	B–N6	B–Q3
17	Q–B3	B–K3
18	B–Q2	Q–Q2
19	P–QB3	B–KB2
20	B×P	Q–B2
21	P–KR4	P–KN4
22	RP×P	P×P
23	N–N4	P×P
24	B×P	B×B
25	Q×B	Q×Q
26	R×Q	N–R4
27	B×Nch	K×B
28	R×Bch	R×R
29	N×N	QR–KB1
30	R–K1	R–B4
31	R–K7ch	K–N3
32	N–K5ch	K×N
33	P–N4ch	K–N4
34	P×R	R×P
35	P–Q4	Resigns

8

An Automaton of the Third Class: Secrets of the Turk

1.

Anyone who has followed the exploits of the Turk throughout the preceding seven chapters must surely have already learned some of the automaton's secrets. It is obvious, for instance, that a director was regulary employed to accompany the exhibition, and we have seen that at least sixteen persons served in that capacity during the eighty-five years of the automaton's existence. If further proof is required, Maelzel himself once admitted in a letter that the automaton "has to be directed."

But there were other mysteries to be solved besides the question of a director, and thus we have spoken of the automaton's secrets in the plural. As soon as one question is correctly answered it leads to another, resulting in something like the following series of problems:

(1) Was the Turk a true machine or was a human director required?

(2) Did the person who exhibited the Turk direct the games or was it done by a concealed person?

(3) Where and how was the concealed director hidden?

(4) How exactly did the concealed director operate the Turk?

The first three questions may be correctly resolved with little difficulty. In 1836 De Tournay observed that they had become like a "comedy," yet in earlier days that comedy had puzzled even the

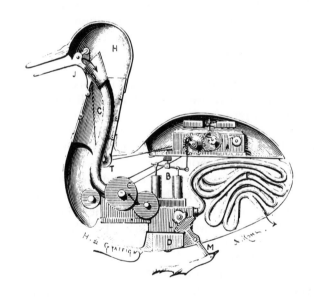

Vaucanson's duck was an example of an automaton of the first class, because it acted solely from the effects of machinery. A clockwork movement at A operated the moving parts, including a mill for grinding grain, C; a pump, B, for moving the grain through the intestines, F; and a gear, L, for motivating the feet. BY PERMISSION OF BL.

most erudite scholars. However, only the fourth question offers any real challenge today. It is the real mystery, which has never really been satisfactorily solved, but before examining that problem it is first necessary to dispose of the comedy.

Was the Turk a true machine? Willis defined

Kempelen wanted people to think the secret of the Turk's operation lay in this small box, but Maelzel managed to exhibit the automaton perfectly well without it. COURTESY OF JGW.

accept Willis's classification scheme, it becomes clear that the Turk really was an automaton—an automaton of the third class, operating entirely under the control of a director concealed inside.

Before Willis's time most persons who considered the possibility of a concealed director thought he must have been either a child or a dwarf. Both Dutens and Windisch toyed with that idea but concluded that the cabinet and figure were too small to conceal even a child. Thicknesse, on the other hand, deduced, "The real mover is concealed in the counter, which is quite large enough to contain a child of ten, twelve, or fourteen years of age; and I have children who could play well at chess, at those ages," but he did not explain how the child might have been hidden.

One of the first persons to attempt to explain how a dwarf might be concealed in the automaton was Henri Decremps. As previously noted, the chess automaton Decremps described was not Kempelen's Turk but a similar invention in the possession of a M. Van-Estin, who may have been an imitator of Kempelen or simply a character invented by Decremps. According to Decremps, Van-Estin revealed that the director of his automaton was

however, dispensed with the box, and when asked why he no longer used it explained, "The people are now intelligent; then, they were superstitious."

Finally it became clear that the exhibitor was not responsible for the Turk's movements and that there must have been a concealed director. But where and how was the director hidden?

3.

Persons who guessed that a concealed agent was controlling the automaton naturally began to look for his hiding place. Racknitz in 1789 noted that some people "assumed that the machine was directed from outside by pulling strings," but he concluded that it was not possible "because the machine was standing quite freely, it was turned and moved from one place to the other, and it played in rooms where those strings could not have been fixed."

That of course left only the Turk's cabinet as a place of concealment. Willis designated a third class of automaton: those which appear to work mechanically but are really under the control of a concealed human. Some persons have argued that such machines are not automatons at all, but if we

a dwarf, a skillful player, hidden in the cabinet. You cannot see him when the doors are open, because at that time he had his legs and thighs hidden in hollow cylinders which seemed designed to move wheels and levers; the rest of his body is at that moment, outside the cabinet, and is hidden under the cloak of the automaton. When the doors of the cabinet are closed, a crank is turned, under the pretense of demonstrating the springs of the machine, which produce considerable noise; the wheels and catches which are heard, add at the same time an air of plausibility and mystery, and permit the little dwarf to change his place and to reenter the cabinet without being heard.

While the machine is being pushed from place to place on its castors, to prove that it is well isolated, the little dwarf closes the trapdoor through which he passed; then the robes of the automaton are lifted; one is allowed to see into his stomach, to prove that there is nothing deceiving in there. . . .

Decremps explanation is unsatisfactory, at least when applied to Kempelen's chess automaton, for several reasons:

(1) The Turk's cabinet apparently did not contain any hollow cylinders which might have concealed a dwarf's legs and thighs.

(2) The cabinet doors were always left open when the Turk was turned around to reveal the openings in the figure; they were never closed as Decremps said.

(3) The sounds of machinery were never demonstrated by turning a crank; the machinery was

Robert-Houdin's automaton trapeze performer, Diavolo Antonio, was directed from behind the scenes by means of wires in the trapeze. Some persons suspected that the Turk was similarly operated from backstage. COURTESY OF JM.

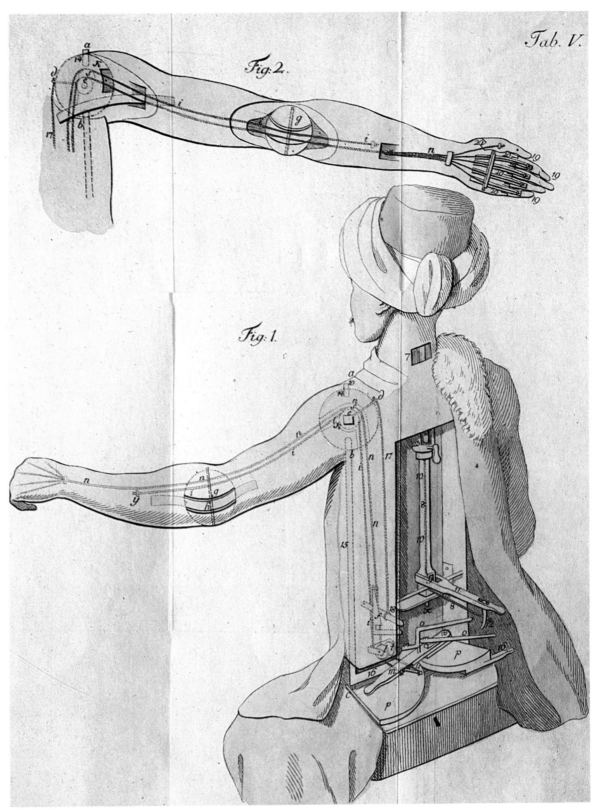

Racknitz's illustrations, though colorful, were inaccurate in some details. COURTESY OF JGW.

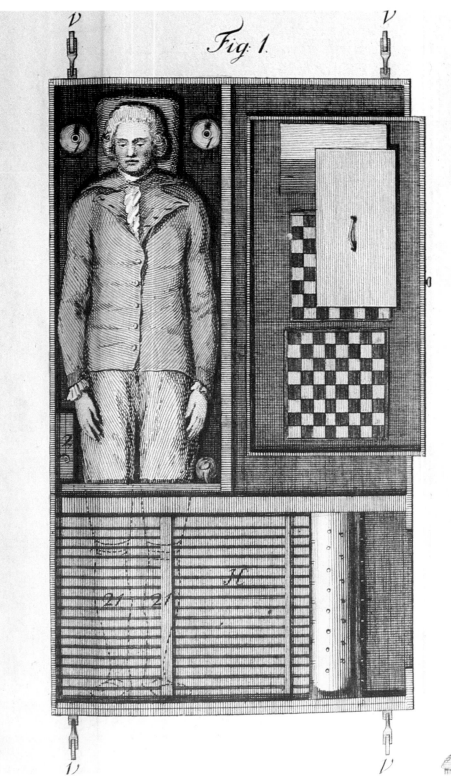

Racknitz supposed that, during inspection of the
cabinet, the Turk's director lay fully extended in a space
below the large compartment and behind the drawer.
That space, however, was not large enough for persons
over four feet high. COURTESY OF JGW.

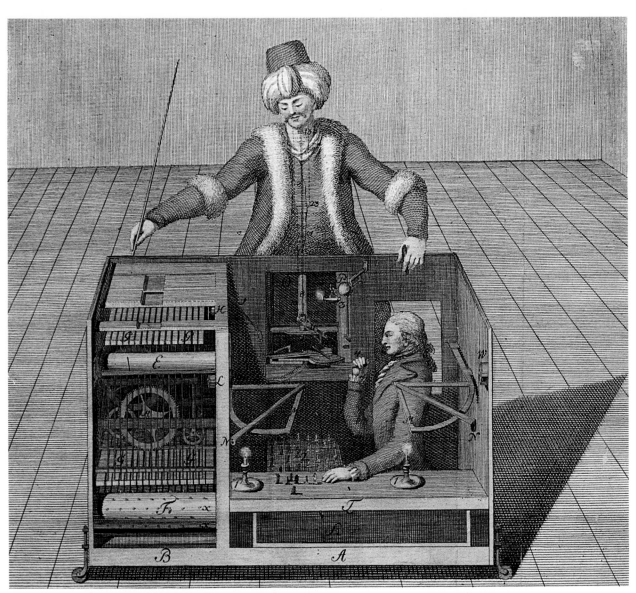

During a game, Racknitz's little man was supposed to have sat up so that he could direct the automaton's head and arms by means of levers, *4.* **He followed the game on a small chessboard,** *2,* **illuminated by two candles,** *1,* **and a lamp,** *3.* COURTESY OF JGW.

wound up with a key at the end of the demonstration.

Racknitz did not actually claim that the Turk's director was a child or a dwarf, but his explanation of how the director was concealed would not have applied to a person of normal stature. According to Racknitz, the director hid in the space behind the drawer of the cabinet during the entire demonstration of the cabinet and figure. He lay there fully extended with his head toward the Turk's left side, which meant that he could not have been taller than the length of the cabinet or about three and a half feet. Racknitz apparently thought that the cabinet was five feet long, but his measurements were very confusing, since he employed the Rhineland foot, the Dresden inch, and the Leipzig inch; and sometimes he did not specify which, if any, of those measurements he was using.

To further add to the confusion, Thomas Collinson, because of his inability to read German, misinterpreted Racknitz's illustrations. Collinson's "well-taught boy, very thin and small of his age," who "agitated the whole" has often been cited to explain how the automaton was operated, sometimes accompanied by Racknitz's illustration of a little person inside the Turk's cabinet.

Besides a child or a dwarf, it has sometimes been supposed that a legless man directed the Turk. That solution had the distinction of being included in several editions of the *Encyclopaedia Britannica* under the article "White Magic," which explained,

The first player was a Polish patriot, Worousky, who had lost both legs in a campaign; as he was furnished with artificial limbs when in public, his

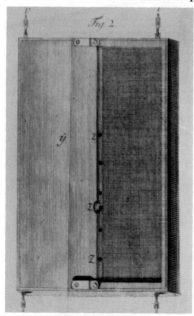

According to Racknitz, there might have been air holes, Z, in the bottom of the cabinet and in the back of the drawer. The cabinet, he thought, was several inches deeper at the rear, Y, to provide more room for the director. COURTESY OF JGW.

appearance, together with the fact that no dwarf or child travelled in Kempelen's company, dispelled the suspicion that any person could be employed inside the machine.

Apparently the legless Worousky was first introduced to the public in the highly romanticized autobiography of the French magician Jean Eugène Robert-Houdin, published in France, England, and the United States in 1859. It has never been proven that Worousky did not once direct the Turk, but it is certain that not all of the fifteen persons who are known to have directed the automaton were legless, nor were they all children or dwarfs. Some in fact were six feet tall. Besides, it has been shown that the automaton's cabinet was capable of accommodating a person of normal size.

Willis in 1821 was apparently the first to clearly demonstrate the possibility of hiding a full-sized individual in the Turk's cabinet. He had never seen the insides of the automaton, a fact he readily admitted, but his solution was based upon careful observation of the exhibition supported by logical reasoning and was clearly illustrated with drawings. The director, he explained, might have assumed two positions while the cabinet was demonstrated, the first when the small cupboard was opened and the second after the rear door to that compartment was closed and locked. The front door remained open, but the director's head and upper body were screened from view by the false machinery in the cabinet. Thus there remained only one question among the Turk's secrets, the question which Kempelen and Maelzel guarded so jealously, and the question which may never be satisfactorily resolved in its entirety: how did the concealed director operate the Turk?

4.

Surprisingly, there were some who did not demand an answer to that question. Bradford, for example, expressed the opinion,

It is not necessary ... to point out the exact manner in which the motions are effected, it is sufficient to show the possibility of the concealment of an individual of ordinary size, which probably will be admitted by every one, who considers the measurements of the space, supposed to be thus occupied.

Also, Jones believed it was "unnecessary to speculate upon the mode in which the individual within may perceive the moves upon the board; several different conjectures have been made upon this point; we think that it presents no great difficulty, and that it might be accomplished in various ways." Anyone agreeing with those views may consider the mystery of the Turk solved and may skip the rest of this was formed by swinging the false back of the large compartment forward and upward.

While the director was thus hidden, the exhibitor began demonstrating the cabinet by opening doors A and B. He then held a lighted candle to door B at the back of the small compartment, allowing the light to be seen through the machinery and thus satisfying the spectators that nobody was hidden in there. He then closed and locked door B, which caused screen I to close automatically. It was necessary to lock door B since the head of the director would soon be placed just behind it and would be seen if the door were to accidentally fly open. Door A was left open to deceive the viewers into thinking they could still see into the small compartment, but in fact they saw only the machinery which occupied a small space near the front as shown in Figure 6. The larger area K was hidden from view behind screen I.

Next, the drawer GG was opened, supposedly to show its contents but actually to allow time for the director to move into his second position of concealment and to replace the false back and partition of the large compartment before it was opened. At that time, the director moved into the position shown in Figure 5. His legs and thighs remained in the space O and were hidden by the drawer GG, while his head and upper body occupied the space K, which was continuous with O as seen in Figure 9. The director remained in that position until it was time to begin a game.

The exhibitor then opened the doors CC and the small rear door D, and the audience was allowed to inspect the large compartment. Those doors were left open, and the keys were left in door D while the exhibitor wheeled the machine around and raised the drapery of the figure to show doors E and F in the Turk's trunk and thighs. Then doors E and F were closed, the drapery lowered, and the Turk was again wheeled around into his original position.

The drawer GG was pushed in, the doors A and CC were closed, and the exhibitor pretended to make some adjustments in the machinery at the rear

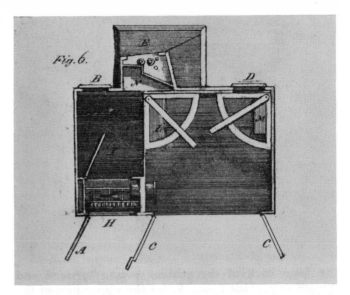

In order to conceal the director's head and upper body in space K, screen I automatically closed when rear door B was shut and locked, as seen in this cutaway view from above. BY PERMISSION OF GRH.

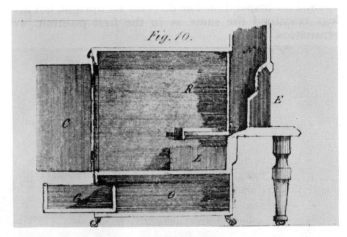

While the director was in the second position, the drawer G, which was only about half as deep as the cabinet, was opened for inspection. The director's legs, in space O, could not be seen. BY PERMISSION OF GRH.

in order to give the director time to slip into his third and final position, as seen in Figures 7 and 8. To accomplish that position, the false back of the large compartment was again pushed forward so that S and N formed one space. When in position the director could see the board through the transparent material of the Turk's clothing and could grasp the pieces with the aid of a string attached to the automaton's fingers. His right hand was free to operate the right arm, the head, and the noisy machinery which was heard during each movement of the Turk. It has often been asked why the Turk played with his left hand rather than his right, and several theories have been advanced to account for it, but the reason may simply have been that the director had more work to do with his right hand than his left.

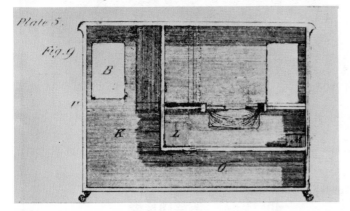

The spaces K and O held the body and legs of the director while in the second position. All doors were open except B.

The third position, as explained by Willis, was the one occupied by the director during the course of a game when all doors to the cabinet were closed. The director's left arm was within that of the Turk, while his head was hidden in the figure's upper torso. He could see the chessboard through the Turk's transparent clothing. BY PERMISSION OF GRH.

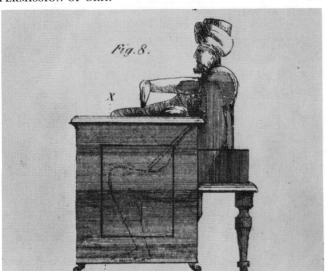

The director assumed a slouching, seated position, as seen in this side view. BY PERMISSION OF GRH.

In order to facilitate the introduction of the director's left arm into that of the figure, it was necessary to draw the Turk's arm backwards. The purpose of that movement was concealed by removing the pipe from the automaton's hand, and for that reason the exhibitor waited until the end of his demonstration to remove the pipe. He then pretended to wind up the machinery to convey the impression that the automaton was run by that means but also to signal the director to put the Turk's head in motion preparatory to the first move.

Willis concluded his explanation by stating:

> The above process is simple, feasible, and effective; showing indisputably that the phenomena may be produced without the aid of machinery, and thereby rendering it probable that the Chess Player derives its merit solely from the very ingenious mode by which the concealment of a living agent is effected.

Evidently Poe, through intermediary sources, derived much of his explanation of the Turk from that of Willis, but he disagreed with Willis on several points:

Willis's drawings have often been copied as in this illustration from Bradford's 1826 booklet on the automaton. COURTESY OF JGW.

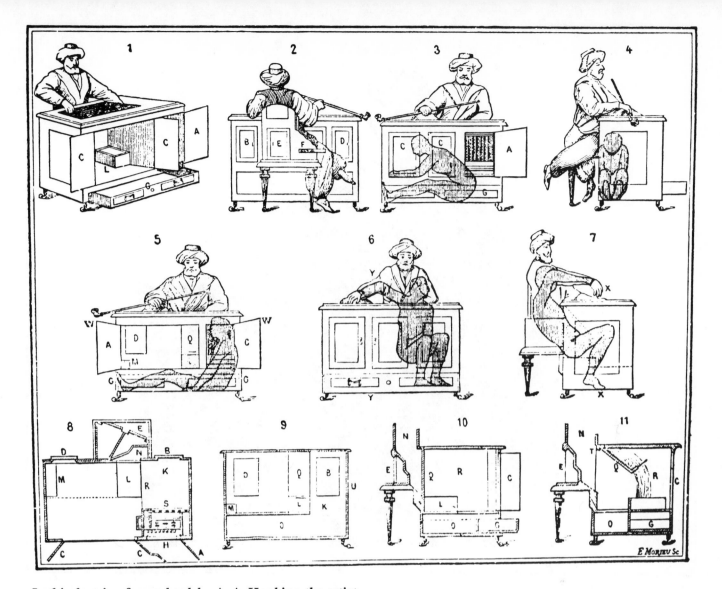

In this drawing from a book by A. A. Hopkins, the artist has reversed everything, thus making the Turk right-handed. COURTESY OF CPL.

(1) Poe rejected the idea of a false drawer, explaining that the legs of the director dropped down behind the drawer only after it was opened.

(2) Poe did not think the director played with his left arm but rather explained, "The right arm of the man within is brought across his breast, and his right fingers act, without constraint, upon the machinery in the shoulder of the figure."

(3) Objecting that Willis's solution had been too detailed, Poe stated,

We have purposely avoided any allusion to the manner in which the partitions are shifted, and it will now be readily comprehended that this point is a matter of no importance, since, by mechanism within the ability of any common carpenter, it might be effected in an infinity of different ways, and since we have shown that, however performed, it is performed out of the view of the spectators.

In that, he somewhat echoed the previously quoted opinions of Bradford and Jones.

Poe, however, agreed with Willis on the three basic elements of his explanation:

(1) The director assumed two positions during demonstration of the cabinet, the first with body flexed forward at the waist, the second seated with feet extended.

(2) During a game, the director occupied a position within the figure of the Turk and viewed the board directly.

(3) The director made his moves directly on the automaton's board.

In 1834, a second and somewhat different explanation, also showing how a full-sized person could have been concealed in the Turk, appeared in the one-page article "Automate Joueur d'Échecs" (Automaton Chess Player) in the *Magasin Pittoresque*. The explanation in the *Pittoresque* article differed with the Willis solution on all of the three basic elements:

(1) The director, according to *Pittoresque*, sat

135

This diagram shows the director in a playing position
such as that described in *Pittoresque*. It is comparable
with the method proposed by Racknitz. *Copyright* ©
American Heritage. BY PERMISSION OF AH.

upon a shelf with castors, with the aid of which he
moved from one compartment to the other while
the cabinet was exposed. The movable shelf would
have been unnecessary—and even a hindrance—if
the director concealed himself according to Willis's
plan.

(2) The *Pittoresque* article explained that in order
to perceive the moves of the adversary, the director
needed a candle and a chessboard whose pieces
were fitted with iron pegs.

That chessboard [the article explained] had all
the squares numbered. Another chessboard,
numbered the same way, formed the ceiling
above his head, and formed the reverse of the
table upon which the automaton played. The
pieces, strongly magnetized, caused to vibrate
little iron balances, which were fitted to the
reverse side of the chessboard, and which thus

indicated to the director, watching their
movements, the move made by his adversary. He
repeated immediately that move on the
chessboard placed under his eyes.

(3) The director played his own move on that
same board,

and then, with the aid of a handle which caused
the arm of the automaton to move, and of an
elastic spring which communicated movements to
the fingers, he made the machine move with a
promptness and precision which rightly incited
the astonishment and admiration of the most
critical spectators.

It has often been stated that the source of information for the *Pittoresque* article, or perhaps even its
author, was Mouret, who was employed by Maelzel
for several years to direct the Turk and who
certainly would have known the automaton's secrets. Since the authenticity of the article seems to be
based upon whether or not Mouret was the source, it

seems that we should examine that question.

It was probably George Walker who, in 1839, first accused Mouret of exposing the automaton. According to Walker, "He burnt out his brain with brandy, and died recently in Paris, reduced to the extremest stage of misery and degradation." But before his death and while in that low condition he had "sold the secrets of his prison-house to the French penny magazine."

Reading those passages, George Allen concluded, "I supposed, therefore, that the article . . . in . . . *Pittoresque* . . . was made up from communications furnished by this very skillful player, who . . . sank into habits of intemperance, and died in 1837."

Those statements have often been cited as proof that Mouret furnished the information in the *Pittoresque* article, but there are some reasons to doubt that he did. George Walker's writings are not free from inaccuracies; for instance, he thought that Eugéne Beauharnais was "King of Bavaria." It is true that Mouret died in Paris in May 1837, but whether he died in the state of degradation pictured by Walker is debatable.

However, it is the *Pittoresque* article itself which causes us most to doubt that Mouret was its source of information. Mouret's name does not appear anywhere in the article, nor is there even any indication that a former director furnished details of the automaton's operation. In fact, the final paragraph of the article makes one suspect that its author was only guessing about his solution to the Turk's secrets:

Furthermore, more than one amateur of the Café de la Régence, and especially of the chess club of Mons. Alexandre, a very distinguished player, must have been told the secret: one of them even, if we are correctly informed, has directed the automaton for awhile, and it is for them to judge the accuracy and truth of our explanation.

As to that paragraph the following points should be noted:

(1) If Mouret had been his source, the author would not have had to express uncertainty with phrases such as "must have been told the secret" and "if we are correctly informed."

(2) Mouret would have known that not just "one of them," but rather several of them—himself, Alexandre, Boncourt, and Weyle—had "directed the automaton for awhile."

(3) If Mouret had supplied the information for the article there would not have been any need "to judge the accuracy and truth of our explanation."

The author of the *Pittoresque* article mentioned Decremps's book, calling it *Magie dévoilée*, and there is thus good reason to believe that it, rather than Mouret, was the source of the article. As we have seen, Decremps incorrectly supposed that the au-

tomaton was directed by a dwarf who sometimes hid under the Turk's robes, and thus it differs with the *Pittoresque* article as to the means of concealment. However, Decremps proposed a means by which the director could see the board and cause the Turk to make his moves that were essentially like those in the *Pittoresque* article. Fifty years earlier Decremps had explained, "One could put in each chess piece a bit of magnetized iron, and under each square of the chessboard a very sensitive little compass needle, so that by its agitation it marks the square which has just been occupied or abandoned." The *Pittoresque* explanation differed only in that it specified "little iron balances" instead of compass needles.

"As to the means employed to give the automaton the necessary movements," continued Decremps, "it is clear that his arm and the interior lever which makes it move, must be considered as a pantograph, of which one extremity moves in unison to enlarge a picture, while the other extremity is traced over the smaller original, thus transferring the traits from the smaller picture." The *Pittoresque* article had not specified a pantograph but merely a "handle which caused the arm of the automaton to move."

Racknitz, although he claimed that he was not influenced by Decremps, had similarly detailed magnetized chess pieces, a chessboard with sus-

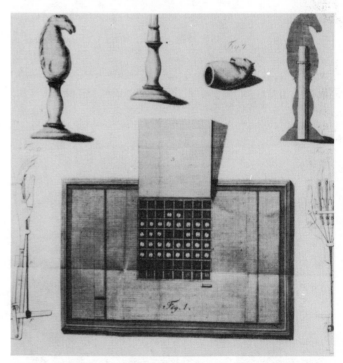

Since the director could not see the chessboard, according to the Racknitz explanation, a magnetic device was employed to inform him of the moves. Each piece, this theory maintained, contained a powerful concealed magnet, which, when placed upon a square, attracted a needle just below it. By noting the position of the needle and its attached piece of paper, the director could follow the movements of the chessmen on the board above. A model showing details of the Turk's hand was included here. COURTESY OF JGW.

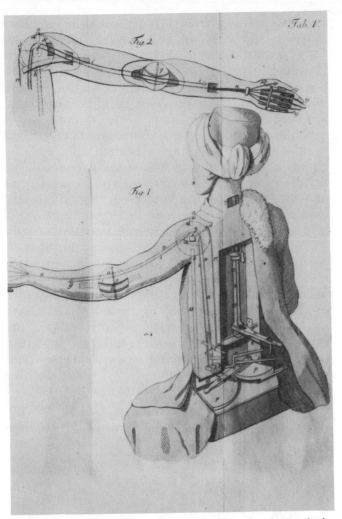

These drawings show a small model which Racknitz constructed to demonstrate how the Turk's arm and head might have operated. COURTESY OF JGW.

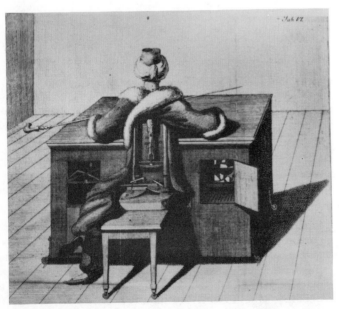

Racknitz also constructed a scale model to demonstrate the fully assembled Turk seated at the cabinet, as seen here in a view from the rear. COURTESY OF JGW.

pended pointers under each square, and a mechanism for moving the arm from within the cabinet. Racknitz, like Decremps, had probably supposed the director to be of less than normal size, and thus his method of concealment was based upon that assumption.

In 1836, two years after the *Pittoresque* article, Mathieu De Tournay's story of the Turk was published in *Palamède*. De Tournay's piece seemed to support the *Pittoresque* explanation to such an extent that George Allen even claimed that the *Pittoresque* article "had been republished, with additional details and a distinct certificate to its authenticity." De Tournay, however, far from providing such a certificate, failed to identify Mouret or anyone else as the source of his explanation.

Moreover, the "additional details" consisted mainly of a confusing account of the positions the director was supposed to have assumed while the cabinet was being displayed. According to De Tournay, he "sometimes took shelter in the torso of the automaton, his legs doubled under him, sometimes bent himself in the opposite direction, his head lowered and his hands forward; he was thus masked by each door which was closed in turn." Since no diagrams illustrated De Tournay's explanation, it is difficult to picture how the movements he described might have correlated with the demonstration of the cabinet and why a "shelf with castors" was needed to accomplish them.

Another version of the *Pittoresque* explanation was included in the 1857 *Chess Monthly* article by Dr. Silas Weir Mitchell. Allen thought that Mitchell's father, Dr. John Kearsley Mitchell, who had been responsible for restoring the Turk in 1840, had furnished materials for the article. The younger Mitchell, however, did not mention his father at all in the article, nor did he claim to be well acquainted with the Turk's construction. "We made no postmortem," stated Mitchell. "Thus, we have nothing left us but to shut our eyes and recall as we may, whatever knowledge we still retain of our lamented friend's most perplexing visceral anatomy."

In spite of that statement, W. K. Wimsatt, Jr. in an article "Poe and the Chess Automaton" in *American Literature*, May 1939, said of Mitchell's piece, "This remains not only the most authoritative but the clearest statement and together with the article in *Magasin Pittoresque*, which it completely corroborates, constitutes the extant evidence of how the automaton actually worked." To begin with, Mitchell's article does not "completely corroborate" the *Pittoresque* explanation but differs with it on several points. Far more damaging to Mitchell's credibility, however, is the fact that his explanation does not correlate with well-confirmed reports of how Maelzel exhibited the Turk. It should be noted that Mitchell was only seven years old in June 1836, the last time he could possibly have seen the Turk exhibited by Maelzel in Philadelphia, and he was only eleven in 1840 when the automaton was restored and then sent to the Chinese Museum. Thus he evidently did not recall how the Turk was exhibited, so that several points of his explanation seem to be in error, as the following analysis should demonstrate:

(1) Mitchell thought the show began with the Turk's director "behind the mock machinery of the smaller apartment, concealed by a door which divided it into two parts." He thought the exhibitor opened the two front doors at once and placed a lighted candle "in front of the smaller apartment." He was wrong; Maelzel always opened the doors *successively,* and he held a candle at the *rear* of the smaller compartment. If the director had been located where Mitchell said he was, he would have been seen.

(2) Mitchell thought both front doors were closed before turning the machine around, and he supposed that the director slid into the large compartment at that time. In fact, Maelzel always left the front doors *open* when he turned the automaton around. Again the director would have been exposed if he had been in the large compartment when Mitchell said he was.

(3) Mitchell explained that the director sometimes slid into the large compartment "before the instrument was turned round and before the front door of the smaller apartment was closed at which time Mr. Maelzel usually held a light at the window in back of it, to show that no one was concealed in it." Wrong again; Maelzel never did it that way either.

(4) According to Mitchell, only the chess pieces of the Turk's adversary were magnetized. The automaton's own pieces did not need magnets, Mitchell reasoned, because the director knew his own moves without having to see them on the chessboard overhead. That supposition, however, is inconsistent with the following incident reported by Allen: "When the automaton had made his move, Maelzel coolly took up the piece and put it back in its place again. The automaton immediately repeated the move, and Maelzel again annulled it. . . .the Turk made the same move a third time." If the director perceived the moves by means of magnetized chess pieces, as Mitchell thought, but the Turk's pieces were not magnetized, as Mitchell also supposed, then how would the director have known that Maelzel had replaced one of those unmagnetized pieces? Again Mitchell's theories are at odds with facts reported elsewhere.

(5) Mitchell thought there were two little books of endgames, one which Maelzel presented to the Turk's adversary, and another which was in the possession of the concealed director. Actually Maelzel did not give the adversary a book of endgames, but rather he presented him with a card showing only *one endgame,* which had been copied from the little green book. The director had to memorize an endgame situation each evening; he did not have a book in the automaton, as Mitchell supposed. The fact that the director lost an occasional endgame, even with the first move, proves he had no book to consult during play.

Dr. Mitchell's version of the solution having thus been disposed of, it might be profitable to look for some evidence which would similarly contradict the whole *Pittoresque* explanation, some verifiable statement which could not be reconciled with the assumption that the director saw the moves through the effects of magnetized pieces on a chessboard over his head. There is such a piece of evidence, and it is found in Poe's essay, "Maelzel's Chess-Player." It should be noted, however, that Poe did not set out to disprove the *Pittoresque* article, and he was probably not even aware of its existence.

When the Automaton is about to move a piece [reported Poe] a distinct motion is observable just beneath the left shoulder, and which motion agitates in a slight degree the drapery covering the front of the left shoulder. This motion invariably precedes, by about two seconds, the movement of the arm itself; and the arm never, in any instance, moves without this preparatory motion in the shoulder. Now let the antagonist move a piece, and let the corresponding move be made by Maelzel, as usual, upon the board of the Automaton. Then let the antagonist narrowly watch the Automaton, until he detect the preparatory motion in the shoulder. Immediately upon detecting this motion, and before the arm itself begins to move, let him withdraw his piece, as if perceiving an error in his manoeuvre. It will then be seen that the movement of the arm, which, in all other cases, immediately succeeds the motion in the shoulder, is withheld—is not made,— although Maelzel has not yet performed, on the board of the Automaton, any move corresponding to the withdrawal of the antagonist. In this case, that the Automaton was about to move is evident; and that he did not move, was an effect plainly produced by the withdrawal of the antagonist, and without any intervention of Maelzel.

Poe thus concluded, "This fact fully proves that [the Turk's] movements are regulated by *mind*—by some person who sees the board of the antagonist."

There we have the proof. If the director had seen the moves in the manner described by the *Pittoresque* article, by De Tournay, and by Dr. Mitchell, he could not have seen the board of the antagonist— only the movements of "little iron balances," which would not have moved because the piece was not moved. If, on the other hand, the director saw through transparent materials in the Turk's torso, as advocated by Willis and Poe, then he could have seen the antagonist's board as well as that of the automaton.

Wimsatt dismissed the above evidence with the statement, ". . . it would appear that Poe's imagination beguiled him," but fortunately we do not have to rely upon Poe's word alone. Philip Thicknesse, whose booklet on the automaton was apparently unknown to Poe, had in 1784 observed, "I saw the ermine trimmings of the Turk's outer garments move once or twice when the Figure should have been quite motionless." Those movements were evidently similar to the ones reported by Poe fifty-two years later.

Further objections to the *Pittoresque* solution came from Charles G. Gümpel, himself the inventor of a mechanical chess player. Gümpel rejected the *Pittoresque* theory because (1) he did not think magnetism could have done what was required of it, (2) the process described would have taken too much time, and (3) the director would have had to assume a very inconvenient position, one quite incompatible with the continuance of good chess play for any length of time.

Despite all of the above objections, one further piece of evidence in favor of the *Pittoresque* explanation must be considered. William Kummer, who was consulted by Dr. Mitchell when the Turk was being reconstructed in 1840, and who later directed the automaton, described his experience inside the mechanism as follows:

> I had a comfortable seat, with my chessmen before me, lighted a lamp (whose smoke was caught by tubes leading through the top of his turban), watching the little balls hanging above me on fine threads, which, by magnetic movements of my adversary's pieces chinkling above, betrayed to me his position, and then, after studying the game on my table and placing my man, took hold of the machine that moved and guided his arm and fingers, and placed my move on the board above."

Does this statement prove the *Pittoresque* explanation to be true? It must be remembered that the Turk Mitchell reassembled was not exactly the same one Maelzel had exhibited. The various pieces of the automaton had been scattered throughout six or seven packing cases and some parts had been completely missing. In addition, Maelzel had packed the Turk in such a manner as to protect the automaton's secrets. Perhaps he had even included false parts to deliberately deceive anyone who, like Mitchell, might attempt to reconstruct the machine.

Kempelen, Maelzel, and others associated with the Turk, guarded the automaton's secrets so well that many of the details of the automaton's inner workings may never be fully revealed. While the explanation of Willis and Poe seems the most reasonable one, it must be remembered that neither of those gentlemen ever saw any more of the Turk's insides than Maelzel intended that they should. Furthermore, the *Pittoresque* solution in one form or another has popped up so often that it cannot be fully discounted. We might just as well admit that this one secret of the Turk remains a mystery.

Before leaving this subject it should be pointed out that there was, even in Maelzel's time, more than one way of building a chess automaton. For example, the chess player constructed in 1825 by the watchmaker Aloys Bayer of Neuburg on the Danube, consisted of a figure about four feet high sitting on a stool. Hidden in the next room, Bayer directed the movements of the automaton's head and right arm by means of rods which entered the body through the stool. From his hiding place he observed the chessboard through a small crack in the wall. During the performance, an exhibitor could disengage the automaton from his seat by secretly pulling on the front feet of the stool. That activated springs that withdrew the rods and concealed from the spectators all evidence that they had been there. Thus the figure of the chess player could be moved about the room, convincing the audience that there was no communication with the stool.

9

The Crystal Palace Automaton; or the Truth About Ajeeb

Ajeeb the chess automaton was first exhibited privately at the home of the inventor, then publicly at the Royal Polytechnic Institution in 1868. COURTESY OF JM.

1.

Throughout the Turk's long career there were various attempts to imitate the invention. After the Turk was destroyed by fire in 1854, still other imitations appeared, patterned more or less after the original chess automaton. Perhaps the most successful of those automatons was Ajeeb, whose long career somewhat paralleled that of the Turk. Ajeeb was constructed in London by Charles Alfred Hooper. (This appears to have been his correct name, although he has been referred to as Charles Edward Hooper, Charles Arthur Hooper, and Charles Arthur Hopper.) Hooper, a native of Bristol, had conceived the idea of the chess automaton in his youth. He had intended to complete the machine in time to display it at the International Exhibition of 1862. He did not, however, get a chance to finish his invention until 1867 after he returned from the Paris Exposition, to which he had been sent as a representative of the Society of Arts.

At first Hooper exhibited Ajeeb privately and was encouraged to discover that the automaton was a source of astonishment and delight to his friends and acquaintances. It had been forty-five years since Maelzel had shown the Turk in London, and few spectators there had seen or remembered the original chess automaton. One of Hooper's friends soon introduced him to Professor John Henry Pepper, the director of the Royal Polytechnic Institution,

At the Polytechnic, Ajeeb was billed alongside such scientific attractions as the great induction coil. FROM ILN.

where it was agreed that the automaton would first be displayed in public.

Early in 1868 Ajeeb's debut at the Polytechnic, on Regent Street, excited great public curiosity, and the automaton was hailed in the London press as "a triumph of mechanical skill not to be surpassed," and an "improvement of Baron Kempelin's [sic] famous invention." As a result, the chess players from various clubs came to match wits with the automaton, but few of the London chess journals seemed to take any notice. *The Chess World* responded somewhat unoriginally to Ajeeb's appearance by republishing Dr. Mitchell's account of the Turk, prefacing it with the remark that a new automaton was now being displayed.

One morning when Hooper entered the Polytechnic, he was shocked to discover that a "flaming big poster" had been erected just inside the doorway proclaiming, "The Automaton Chess Player Challenges the World." Being of a modest and retiring nature, Hooper hurriedly and excitedly sought out Professor Pepper and protested that it would never do to issue such a challenge. "For," he declared, "all the great players will be coming to play, expecting to find Ajeeb win every game."

"Oh, your figure does not say he will win always," replied Pepper, laughing, "he only invites all the world to come and play with him."

Besides Ajeeb, visitors to the Polytechnic Institution could witness popular illustrated lectures, as well as demonstrations of various electrical, mechanical, and optical apparatus once referred to as "side show science." One of the most famous and successful exhibits at the building was Pepper's Ghost, a spectral illusion credited to Pepper but actually the invention of the civil engineer and author Henry Dircks. In one of the many versions of the ghost drama, the spectators viewed a stage with a student in medieval costume studying into the midnight hours. As he gazed from his studies he was suddenly startled by the sight of a ghostly skeleton moving toward him, the fleshless bones assuming the grotesque attitudes of Holbein's "Dance of Death." The student instantly reacted by seizing his sword and aiming a blow at the spectral figure, which vanished but reappeared almost immediately. As each stroke was delivered the elusive vision returned again and again. We now know that the person who manipulated the skeleton was attired from head to toe in black velvet and that the reflection of the skeleton he held could be seen on a large sheet of plate glass set at an angle between the audience and the stage. The ghostly figure could be

Numerous spectators were drawn to the Polytechnic by the ghost illusion, which was exhibited for many years in seemingly endless variations featuring spectral visions that could appear and disappear, float in the air, walk on the walls and ceiling, or allow living actors to walk through them. FROM ILN.

made to dissolve and reappear by dimming the Argand burners that illuminated it. The illusion was very effective from the viewpoint of the audience, and eventually there were a number of variations of the ghost based upon the same principle.

After several months at the Polytechnic Institution, Hooper moved Ajeeb to the Crystal Palace, a magnificent structure of iron and glass near Sydenham, just south of the county of London. The Crystal Palace had originally been erected in London's Hyde Park to house the Great Exhibition of 1851. The following year it was dismantled and reassembled at Sydenham on a slightly smaller but still imposing scale, measuring 1,608 feet in length by 384 feet wide across the transepts. "In the interior is a long and lofty nave," read a contemporary description, "intersected at right angles by three transepts and with aisles on each side, occupied by various fine art, industrial and architectural courts, surrounded by galleries supported by light, airy, and apparently fragile columns, with an

arched roof of glass, extending from north to south upwards of 1,000 feet." On each side of the splendid promenade were "statues, handsome glass cases displaying various works of modern art and industry, and trees, flowers, and plants of the tropical regions, blooming in all the brilliance of their native climes." In addition to the permanent attractions, there were held from time to time special exhibitions, concerts, and other entertainments; and the extensive grounds surrounding the building were often the site of athletic contests and fireworks displays.

The Crystal Palace remained a famous English resort until it was destroyed by fire in 1936. The remains were dismantled five years later because they were being used as a guide for German aircraft which were bombing London during World War II.

Ajeeb first appeared at the Crystal Palace on October 22, 1868, in a special room fitted for the daily reception of visitors. He soon became one of the chief attractions of the palace, which was visited on holidays and other special occasions by as many as seventy or eighty thousand persons, including many foreign visitors. Hooper continued to exhibit Ajeeb there for a period of seven years, during which time he became known as the Crystal Palace Automaton.

143

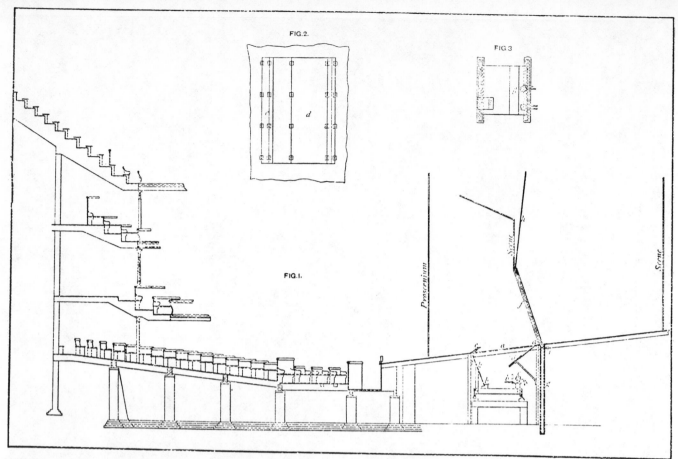

FIG.2.

FIG 3

FIG.I.

Proscenium

Scene

Scene

The ghosts, actually located below the stage, were seen as reflections on a large sheet of clear glass. By dimming the lights that illuminated the actors, they could be made to disappear. BY PERMISSION OF BL.

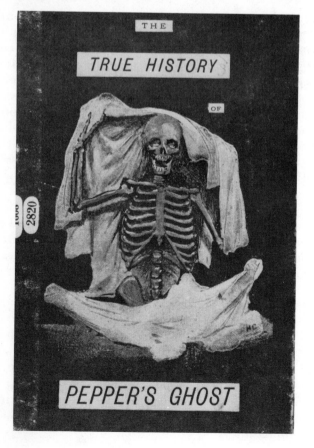

THE

TRUE HISTORY

OF

PEPPER'S GHOST

1063 2820

Those who visited Ajeeb's reception room at the Crystal Palace to see the automaton or to play chess with him beheld a life-size, or perhaps larger, turbaned figure, variously described as Turkish, Moorish, Arabian, or Egyptian. His body was made of papier-mâché, and his head was of wax, but his thick, dark, forked beard consisted of real hair. Dressed in an embroidered oriental costume, Ajeeb sat cross-legged upon a cushion on a rectangular cabinet. At the rear of the cabinet, a small extension resting upon two slender legs provided additional space for the figure to sit. Ajeeb's cabinet had originally rested upon the floor, but shortly after the automaton was installed at the Crystal Palace, the manager of a rival automaton claimed that a concealed player retreated under the floor before the cabinet was displayed, so Hooper elevated the machine upon castors.

Unlike the Turk, Ajeeb moved the chessmen with his right hand, while his left hand, which did not move, held a hookah or water pipe. The chessboard rested upon a slender wooden pedestal and was thus, in contrast to the Turk's board, elevated nearly a foot above the cabinet. Near Ajeeb's right hand was a bowl or basket for depositing pieces that had been removed from the board.

Hooper himself may have sometimes exhibited Ajeeb, but it is known that his wife, once described as

This book by Henry Dircks explained the ghost illusion. BY PERMISSION OF BL.

144

In a French version of the ghost illusion, the audience saw a volunteer from among them transformed into a skeleton. The volunteer could see neither the glass nor the skeleton, but only the startled looks of those gazing at him. COURTESY OF CPL.

The Polytechnic Institution still stands, although Ajeeb and the ghosts have long since departed. FROM AC.

a "large buxom Belgian beauty," also acted as the automaton's exhibitor. During the times Mrs. Hooper was the exhibitor, Mr. Hooper often played the part of Ajeeb's secret director. The Hoopers had a son who for some years directed the automaton, but he eventually grew so fat that he could no longer squeeze himself into the mechanism and was thus forced to retire from those duties.

Before each game the exhibitor would proclaim, "We will now show the mechanism," and would then demonstrate the automaton's interior in much the same way that Maelzel had exhibited the Turk. A door comprising most of the front of the cabinet was opened, revealing what appeared to be a great deal of machinery. That door was left open while two more doors, each six by eight inches, were opened in the front and back of Ajeeb's torso.

A lighted candle was then held at the rear opening, allowing the spectators to see through a tangle of wires and wheels similar to those in a Jacquard loom, a machine familiar to many persons in the audience. They knew that such a loom was capable of weaving elaborate designs according to information on punched metal cards, and they naturally supposed that Ajeeb operated on a similar principle, but the wires and wheels were actually imitation, made of black whalebone and fiber. After everyone had satisfied himself that there was nobody hidden inside, the doors were closed and the exhibitor noisily wound a spring in the automaton with a large key inserted into the figure's right side.

Anyone from the audience who wished to challenge the automaton had to pay sixpence per game

145

THE NEW CRYSTAL PALACE, AT SYDENHAM.—see page 136.

It is still possible in London to catch a Crystal Palace bus, but one finds that only the park remains, the building itself having long since disappeared. FROM AC.

For more than seven years Ajeeb was on permanent exhibition at the Crystal Palace, Sydenham. FROM ILN.

for the privilege, and once those arrangements were made the game began.

The player who undertakes to defend a game against Ajeeb [an observer once reported] is under obvious disadvantages. He is obliged to stand before the railing which separates the spectators, and is hemmed in behind and on either side by lookers-on, whose comments distract his attention and annoy him if he be of a nervous disposition. Whenever his move is not forthcoming with the desired haste, the figure lifts up its hand and the exhibitor calls the player's attention to the fact that it is his turn to move. Taking everything into consideration, the difference of circumstances is equal to the odds of a Knight in favor of the figure.

One opponent complained, "We have played several games with him, usually with the result that, after securing a winning game, some egregious blunder has brought destruction upon us."

Ajeeb's moves, made with his right hand, were said to have been "free and easy," although every movement was made at right angles. Occasionally, when a piece had not been placed exactly in the center of a square, Ajeeb failed to seize it. Like the

146

The Prince of Wales and the Duke of Edinburgh visited the Crystal Palace in 1868, the year Ajeeb was installed there. FROM ILN.

Turk, he never tried a second time to pick it up but continued to make the move as if the piece were in his grasp. Each motion, accompanied by the sound of machinery, was made very rapidly, especially when the agile, quick-witted elder Hooper was directing. It was once said that lady visitors would often exclaim with astonishment, "Why, he does not stop to think!"

The artist and author John Ruskin noted that during one period of an hour and a half Ajeeb played five games, three of them with Ruskin himself. "I never keep him waiting for moves," wrote Ruskin to a friend, "and he crushes me down steadily." Ruskin, however, admitted, "I get quite fond of him, and he gives me the most lovely lessons in chess."

The automaton indicated a check to his opponent's King by nodding his head twice, while checkmate was announced with three nods. "These movements," an eye-witness observed, "always produce a laugh among the spectators."

Ajeeb's response to an illegal move depended upon whether it had been made deliberately or out of ignorance. If it appeared that an adversary had intentionally cheated, the automaton swept the chessmen off the board and the exhibitor declared

Among Ajeeb's visitors at the Crystal Palace was the artist and author John Ruskin, a frequent but satisfied loser to the automaton. BY PERMISSION OF NPG.

Ajeeb the winner by forfeit. When the offending move had obviously been made by accident, however, Ajeeb, would, according to one story, "throw back his head in a gesture of mixed horror and scorn and freeze in that position" until the exhibitor explained the error and corrected the move. It was once reported that an opponent slyly tried to pick up one of Ajeeb's pieces. The automaton's head immediately went back in rage, but then fell off, causing his startled adversary to hastily depart from the exhibition room.

147

Unlike the Turk, Ajeeb apparently did not play composed endgames, nor did he ever force his opponents to play on a separate board. He did, however, after each game perform the Knight's Tour, starting from any square selected by a spectator and returning to that same square in one minute. Before starting another game, the exhibitor permitted the visitors to again inspect Ajeeb's interior.

Ajeeb was usually exhibited from one or two o'clock until five in the afternoon and then again from about seven to ten in the evening, but it was claimed that on one occasion during the Christmas holidays Ajeeb played continuously from eleven in the morning until nine at night. He played, according to Hooper's own estimate, a total of nearly 100,000 games at the Crystal Palace. That figure seems somewhat high, since, to accomplish it, Ajeeb would have had to average during the entire time he was exhibited at the Crystal Palace seven games per hour, which seems unlikely. One visitor, in fact, noted that he once found himself alone with Ajeeb because the theater at the palace was open and the play *Our American Cousin* was being performed.

Hooper also claimed that his automaton won ninety-nine games out of a hundred at the Crystal Palace. Whenever Ajeeb lost a game the inventor blamed it upon mechanical failures, explaining, "A spring may break, a wheel get out of order, in the most perfect of machines."

2.

Many, of course, doubted that Ajeeb was really a machine, and, as in the case of the Turk, there were many attempts to explain how the automaton operated. Spiritualism was popular at the time and had many serious adherents. Spiritualists often visited Ajeeb and, finding no other satisfactory explanation, pronounced him a product of spirit power. Hooper, it was believed, was a medium, capable of calling forth from the "vasty deep" the phantom or spirit of a dead chess player to take possession of Ajeeb during his performances.

Henry Dircks was skeptical of the claims of the spiritualists, hinting in a letter to the London *Times* that he was "acquainted with the diminutive player's physician." Hooper answered Dircks in a letter of his own, in which he stated, "I have no diminutive player, dwarf or little boy to work the apparatus, neither is there any communication with the floor underneath by means of traps, so that the diminutive player could escape before the interior construction is exposed to view." However, Hooper cleverly avoided denying the real truth, which was that a person of normal size concealed himself within the automaton.

Hooper was probably also the author of another letter, which was published in a West London paper. That letter, from "a constant visitor and player," sounded suspiciously like the inventor, again trying to confuse his readers by refuting false theories:

I have myself seen the figure a great number of times, and have remained in the chess department for hours together on most occasions [If Hooper wrote that, it was of course certainly true.], and yet it was not till after frequent and long visits that the full ingenuity of the construction forced itself on my attention. And I feel certain that many of those who flatter themselves that they have written able solutions of the problem are still unaware of the actual key to the position, and have little real perception of the actual difficulty before them. I have been amused by the visitors of the self-satisfied, sharp description who have set to work to explain the whole matter after seeing the figure for five minutes for the first time; and I have observed that they have considered the problem solved at once by the assertion that, of course, someone inside the figure plays the game, and further, as space for a player inside is evidently scanty, they usually settle that such player must be a dwarf or small boy—and this, without even pausing to consider that most certainly no small boy would play the undeniably excellent game which enables the figure to claim victory against all comers. . . . I cannot discover any loophole from which a player inside the figure could see the board. The full difficulty of the automaton seeing the board will not be realised until I point out that the head of the player cannot be inside the head of the figure, for the simple reason that the neck of the figure is too small to allow of a head passing through it.

There was no mention of the possibility of seeing through the figure's torso, which was actually the case. The letter concluded, "I can strongly recommend your readers to pay a visit to the Crystal Palace on purpose to see the extraordinary chess player . . ."

One observer tried to explain how Ajeeb could play by actual mechanical means alone and another how he might have been controlled remotely by electricity, but a writer in *Cornhill Magazine* belittled the automaton both as a chess player and as an illusion, claiming he had beaten him with ease and that "it was tolerably obvious in what part of the figure the chess player was concealed who conducted the games." In another *Cornhill* article Richard Proctor stated,

It is certain that during the play the player is within the figure. Immediately after the last door is closed the frame of the figure vibrates perceptibly, precisely as one would expect it to vibrate as a concealed player squeezed himself, as it were, into the proper position for observing the play of

There were many attempts to explain how Ajeeb was directed, including this one which carried the caption, "The foot pedals worked Ajeeb's right hand and arm in moving the pieces." COURTESY OF JGW.

friend did not catch the suggestion perfectly. So soon as the complete series of moves had been indicated, the automaton's head wagged disapproval, doubtless because the line suggested would have been fatal to the automaton's game. That the suggestion was sound appeared soon, for our friend adopted another move, and in a move or two was compelled to resign, when, by the gracious permission of the automaton, the position was restored, and on examination it was found that a piece must have been captured by the proposed line of play. It is clear, then, that the concealed player, who had been indifferent when indifferent suggestions were made, had caught the drift of the proposed line of play, and objected accordingly. He made no movement until the whole scheme had been indicated. No doubt experience has taught him that in most cases such suggestions are likely to help his game; and in the present case the series of moves began with a sacrifice which, if unsound, would have given him the game at once. The very instant he perceived that it was sound, he set the automaton's head shaking.

Many years later one of Ajeeb's directors explained exactly how he had performed his duties, confirming the suspicions of Proctor. During a game the director was indeed concealed within the figure. He sat upon a small pedestal, his legs hidden within the cabinet, his head at the level of the small door in Ajeeb's torso, just six inches above the chessboard. The space provided was barely adequate to insure the director a minimum of comfort. He could see the board, although not very clearly, through a diamond-shaped network of

opponents and guiding the motion of the figure. It seems to us probable, that at the same moment a portion of the machinery, which during the inspection had seemed to occupy the chest of the figure, may be shifted, so that room is found there for the head of the concealed player.

Proctor conducted a test to confirm his suspicions that the director could both see the board and hear what was said by the visitors, even in low tones.

A friend, who is a tolerably good player [he explained] was conducting a game, and from time to time we suggested a move or two. To this the automaton made no objections, though consultation is forbidden (of which at the time we were not aware), and he might have indicated objection by shaking his head, as when a false move is made. But it happened that at one stage of the game we perceived a line of play by which a noteworthy advantage could have been gained, and whispered accordingly to our friend, giving the series of moves in a low voice; so low, in fact, that our

This diagram, published in 1879, showed the location of Ajeeb's director. BY PERMISSION OF BL.

black and red silk threads making up the facing of the door opening into Ajeeb's interior.

When it was time to open the door so that the audience could look inside, the automaton's attendant signaled the director by announcing, "We will now show the mechanism." The director, upon hearing that warning, quickly bent his body to the right and leaned his head on his right shoulder so that he was no longer visible within the doorway. The false machinery which the spectators saw was then lowered by means of pulleys into the space previously occupied by the director's head, and the door was opened. A black cloth, lining the bottom of the machinery, hid the director from view. After the door was closed, the director raised the machinery by pulling a cord, and he again resumed his position behind the little door.

During play he placed his right arm into Ajeeb's right arm as far as the elbow, where there was a lever which operated the automaton's thumb. By working the lever, the director could cause Ajeeb to grasp and release the pieces seen through the silk facings of the door. The director also had at his disposal a lever which caused the automaton's body to lurch forward, a motion necessary in order to reach the far side of the chessboard.

3.

Although Ajeeb won most of his games against the general public, the London chess community tended to look upon the automaton's play with some scorn. Charles Tomlinson, F.R.S., a noted mathematician and a chess player of considerable ability, once commented:

> Unlike the automaton which plays so badly at the Crystal Palace, Maelzel, with what I think was a true feeling for his trade, saw that, in order to produce the greatest sensation, not only must the automaton be capable of playing chess, but must play well; and not only so well as to beat the best players, but to be in a condition to offer them odds. ... The so-called automaton play, like blindfold play, if bad, is simply abominable. Now that everybody knows the machinery to be merely clever conjuring for concealing a man, the proprietor ought at least to secure the services of a good player.

There were many excellent chess players in London in Ajeeb's time. Wilhelm Steinitz, who in 1866 had won the world chess championship by beating Adolph Anderssen, made his home in the English capital. London had, in fact, become the center of the chess world, "the El Dorado for chess professionals," one writer called it. In those surroundings Hooper and son were comparatively poor players.

There was, however, another reason for Ajeeb's lowly reputation as a player. In addition to the admission fee to Ajeeb's exhibition room, there was a further fee for playing against him. Thus if a group of three or four persons wanted to play, the automaton would quickly lose to the first, or the exhibitor would declare the game a draw, so as not to keep the next player waiting. The result was that when several strong players came to test Ajeeb's abilities, they left with the impression that he lost a majority of his games.

Evidently Hooper discovered, however, that the vast majority of Ajeeb's visitors, something like 99 percent, could be beaten with ease, and he thus saved himself the expense of hiring a master-level player as director, at least during the engagement at the Crystal Palace. Ignored or belittled by the London chess professionals, Ajeeb appealed to those who had learned to play chess, but never very well, and to those who were amazed to find that an automaton could play chess at all.

Besides, Hooper evidently felt that his son would soon join the ranks of the topmost chess players, perhaps even become world champion, "if he only supported his very great talent for the game by the close study of its literature." One visitor in fact suspected that the automaton's director did study the chess literature. "After paying our sixpence," he reported, "we had to wait a few minutes before the door was opened, during which time, doubtless, the player concealed himself within the figure. On entering, we noticed that the handbook was turned down on its open face, and, so far as we could judge, it was opened about where the automaton's favourite opening is dealt with by Staunton. Yet we must admit that there is very little book-work in the automaton's game."

Although scorned by the royalty of chess, the Crystal Palace Automaton was visited by many real monarchs and other notables, among whom were the Shah of Persia; the Empress of Russia, with the Grand Duke Constantine and their suite; Napoleon III, Emperor of the French and the Prince Imperial; the Sultan of Zanzibar; the Nawab of Bengal; the Chinese Ambassador; and the Viceroy of Egypt and his son, Prince Hassan.

Ajeeb remained at the Crystal Palace until January 1876, when arrangements were made to move him to the newly constructed Royal Aquarium at Westminster. The Aquarium's management wished to provide interesting attractions for visitors and thus constructed a room especially for displaying the chess automaton. Beginning in March, Ajeeb was exhibited at the new building daily until the end of 1876, and his reception room attracted many chess players and other visitors, including the Prince (who would become King Edward VII) and Princess of Wales, and Prince Leopold of Belgium.

By the following year the automaton's fame had

In 1876 Ajeeb was moved to the Royal Aquarium shortly after this formal opening by the Duke of Edinburgh. FROM ILN.

become so widespread that Hooper was receiving offers from museums in Paris, Belgium, Holland, and Germany. Plans were made for a tour of Europe, which began on March 1, 1877, at Castan's Panopticum in the Unter den Linden, Berlin.

On the first day of exhibitions in Berlin, reporters from all the German newspapers were on hand to see Ajeeb, and the automaton did not disappoint them. Probably directed by the young Hooper, who had greatly improved since his earlier Crystal Palace days, Ajeeb not only amazed the Germans with the speed of his play, but not even the best challengers were able to beat him on the day of his debut at the Panopticum. Moreover, the Germans were apparently quite mystified as to how the automaton operated, one paper attributing it to a "previously unresearched secret power."

As a result of the favorable publicity, the crowds continued to attend Ajeeb's performances at the Panopticum, and brilliantly uniformed military men of all ranks flocked to the exhibition daily to watch one another being beaten by Ajeeb, to the great delight of all. Princes, grand dukes, and high officers of the Prussian army were especially interested in the automaton and arranged for several special receptions. It was reported by Hooper that nearly 100,000 persons visited Ajeeb during the three months he was shown in Berlin. He played, in addition to chess, the then popular Continental game of "dame," similar to checkers but played on a board of one hundred squares with twenty pieces on each side.

About the first of June the automaton left Berlin and spent the rest of the year 1877 touring the German cities of Breslau (Wroclaw, Poland), Dresden, Leipzig, Hanover, Brunswick, Magdeburg, Cologne, Elberfeld (Wuppertal), Düsseldorf, Frankfurt am Main, and Wiesbaden. Ajeeb continued to attract a great deal of attention and interest throughout the German tour. In Breslau the automaton became the subject of an amusing one-act farce entitled *Ajeeb, der Automatische Schachspieler* (Ajeeb, the Automaton Chess Player), which played as an extra attraction at the Saison Theatre there.

In Dresden the King and Queen of Saxony honored Ajeeb with a visit and played several games with the automaton. The royal spectators were especially interested in and surprised by Ajeeb's rapid performance of the Knight's Tour.

In July Hooper was in Leipzig, where he installed Ajeeb in a large hall in the center of the extensive gardens of the Schützenhaus, a handsome hotel. During the summer evenings, there were illuminations there and an excellent orchestra played in the gardens, which were tastefully laid out with statuary, fountains, and flowers. Ajeeb soon became the center of attraction, especially since there was a chess congress being held at the hotel. In between tournament games, participants in the congress, including some of the best German players, rushed out to Ajeeb's exhibition in the gardens for informal contests with the automaton. Although Ajeeb lost some of those games, he was admired for his style of play. In fact, chess players in every German town demonstrated great interest and pleasure in the exhibitions, always expressing their regret when the time for leaving was announced, and hoping that Ajeeb would soon return.

In Hanover Ajeeb was exhibited at the Tivoli Gardens, a popular resort. One morning Hooper went to the box office and found a letter written in German, which he translated as follows:

To the Proprietor of Ajeeb: With this I am free to send you a drawing and description of Ajeeb's mechanism, with assurance that I have not told anybody about it as yet, but to keep the secret for the future, I request you to pay immediately 3,000 marks, and further 300 marks on the first of every month; and if you are not willing to pay this sum I have no interest to keep the secret, and so you will find next time the mechanism published in all the newspapers. I hope to find tomorrow, Saturday, an answer with your own direct address, and should I find no letter, I do what I have said.
Respectfully,
R. G. 81

In reply Hooper left a message suggesting that the writer meet with him to discuss the matter, but

In the playing position, the director moved the automaton's right hand and operated a cord attached to the head. COURTESY OF JGW.

UN JOUEUR D'ÉCHECS DE 300 ANS A BAT-TU Mme CHAUDÉ DE SILANS CHAMPIONNE DE FRANCE

Was this the Ajeeb that was exhibited at Elberfeld in 1878? The automaton was shown in Paris in 1953 and defeated the French women's champion, Chaudé de Silans. BY PERMISSION OF BN.

155

10
Mephisto and the Insect

1.

Mephisto, billed as a mechanical chess player rather than a chess automaton, was invented early in 1878 by Charles Godfrey Gümpel, a manufacturer of artificial limbs, who was a native of Germany but who had lived for many years in England and spoke perfect English. He was about forty-five years of age when he constructed Mephisto. At that time the West End Chess Club, of which Gümpel was the originator and president, met at his house at No. 49 Leicester Square, London.

Gümpel had evidently built his chess player with the intention of exhibiting him at the Paris Exposition of 1878, the same event which drew Ajeeb to the French capital. Wishing, however, to first test Mephisto, he sent an announcement around to all the London chess clubs, inviting the members to his home to view the figure and to play some games. That challenge naturally aroused the curiosity of many chess players, who went in crowds to Leicester Square.

Gümpel converted one room of his home into a sort of theater, as a place of reception for Mephisto, a slim figure of medium height seated at a chess table.

Mephisto's dress is of a very gorgeous description [reported one visitor], red velvet, trimmed with black; pink hat, with black border and two magnificent pink feathers; and his left hand is covered with a black kid glove, with the object, we suppose of preventing the beholders from

Mephisto's inventor, Charles Godfrey Gümpel, first exhibited the mechanical chess player at his home on London's Leicester Square. BY PERMISSION OF NPG.

entirely forgetting—notwithstanding his on the whole gay appearance—the awful nature of the being before them.

The beautiful smoothness of Mephisto's head has been the subject of much comment, and it is generally supposed to be the result of much study in his perpetual warfare with mankind. His baldness, however, can hardly be called "premature," since he tells us that he has played chess ever since it was invented. The extraordinary merit of

Mephisto was quite different from most other chess players. Gümpel preferred to call him a mechanical chess player rather than a chess automaton. COURTESY OF JGW.

Mephisto caught the fancy of French chess journalist Alphonse Delannoy, who featured the mechanical player in several stories. COURTESY OF JGW.

Mephisto's barber has been observed, and we may add that the excellence of that gentleman as a shaver is only equaled by the skill with which Mephisto "shaves" his opponents over the chessboard.

Mephisto's head was, in fact, made of wax, and it moved in a number of ways: it nodded, moved backwards, and turned around. One observer noted that during some of those movements it was possible to see where the neck terminated behind the ornamental collar clothing the bust.

Mephisto sat at an ordinary chess table of a type then found at the London clubs, and the space beneath the table was clearly open to view. He sat upon a chair which appeared to some to be quite a bit larger than would have been necessary to merely support him. It was large enough, in fact, to conceal a small human figure if the seat and Mephisto's body had formed one enclosure. However, Gümpel attempted to dispel that suspicion by passing a book between the chair and the adjoining portions of Mephisto's anatomy, even during the progress of a game.

Unlike Kempelen's Turk and the various Ajeebs, there was no cabinet in which a hidden player might have been concealed. Gümpel or his assistant showed Mephisto's interior and allowed the figure to be examined, prodded with a stick, and apparently maltreated in general, "as freely and with as little real injury," commented Richard Proctor, "as

the Mephistopheles of Goethe received from the sword of Marguerite's enraged brother." The upper part of the body was, noted Proctor, "open to inspection" even during a game, but he did not specify exactly the manner of inspection.

Mephisto's chessboard was of a peculiar design, which was at first thought to be a clue to the secret of operation. Each square contained a spike upon which it was necessary to press, both in placing a piece on the square and removing one from it. The pieces themselves fitted into shallow circular depressions in the center of each square, and Gümpel was careful to insist that any chessman be set straight if it had not been properly placed in the hollow. In addition, the pieces were of a special unusual design, but later they were replaced by an ordinary Staunton chess set, and a new chessboard was substituted which had depressions but no spikes to push.

Among Mephisto's earliest visitors was Alphonse Delannoy, who wrote for the Paris chess journal *La Stratégie*. Although his fanciful account of Mephisto's first encounters contained more social commentary on the British than facts about the mechanical chess player, there may have been some truth in his report, part of which follows:

They hesitated for several days to accept [Mephisto's] challenge. They doubted, they reflected, each one wanting to try, but none wishing to be first. The first one who dared present himself was an amateur, a member of several aristocratic clubs of the West End, son of a wealthy family, a young man who conformed strictly to all the requirements of English style, with lemon-colored jacket which the maid had allowed to fall in the dust, with a cravat of a frightening mouse-colored shade, with gloves the color of beef blood, with Scottish plaid trousers, the seat of which would have served as a chessboard, with a somewhat golden chestnut head of hair, and with eyes suggesting Cambridge.

That gentleman had all the prejudices of his class and especially that of having accepted as truth the commentary of Boileau, ". . . With his gold, the fool must be a success." Except, however, in the arena of chess, where he was rudely manhandled and rapidly beaten by our hero, to the surprise and applause of the spectators.

That fellow was replaced by a captain of the Horse Guards, with ferocious countenance, assured expression, handlebar moustache, and swelling chest imprisoned in some sort of corset. He appeared certain to impale his impassive adversary with a single thrust of his sword, because he had, in several circles, the reputation of a master. He had, in fact, some talent, remarkable audacity, and knowledge of the openings. His first thrusts were frightening and his impetuosity quite chivalrous. To those passages at arms, which threatened at any time to cleave him

For more than seven years Ajeeb was on permanent exhibition at the Crystal Palace, Sydenham. BY PERMISSION OF BL.

Did a painting such as *A Game of Chess* **by Friedrich
August Moritz Retzsch inspire Gümpel to create
Mephisto?** COURTESY OF JGW.

Señorita Otero—her dancing could stir even the soul of an automaton. COURTESY OF JM.

Robert-Houdin's little automaton pastry cook of the Palais Royale brought out sweets at the command of spectators. The magicians' young son was cleverly hidden inside the tiny building. COURTESY OF JM.

W. N. Potter was one of the first strong masters to succumb to Mephisto's powers. BY PERMISSION OF NPG.

exterminating angel. Mephisto had understood and guessed his plan, allowed him to carry it out, established a countermine under the same subterranean path, opposed the cunning trap, and triumphed over the Dominican, who had been able to save himself with neither his temporizing nor his prudence, nor even with his invocation to Saint Michael.

I saw in turn appear and succumb, a magistrate with rosy complexion, magnificent due to both his health and his wig, but more adroit at entangling a lawsuit than at disentangling a chess position; a monitor captain, whose voluminous projectiles dispersed harmlessly at the breath of Mephisto; an Irish member of the House of Commons, who failed in his attempt to compromise the success of our man by putting him to sleep with one of his discourses; an administrator of a joint stock bank, more skillful at finding the means of giving annual dividends of 15 percent to his shareholders than at the calculations of his game; a Russian prince ending in -off; an Italian excellence ending in -a; an Iman; a Pasha with four pigtails; all of them were wiped out, demolished, pulverized in the twinkling of an eye.

Finally, after trying his strength with amateurs belonging to every class of society, Mephisto encountered some true masters or at least some who had, in the world of chess, a considerable reputation. One of the first, among them, was Mr. [William Norwood] Potter, an amateur who com-

asunder, Mephisto interposed ingenious parries; to the prodigious bounds of his adversary, he replied with calm, patience, and skill. A sardonic smile greeted the flashes of the captain, who, demoralized, impatient, and fatigued by his excessive efforts, soon gave way under his own weight crying, "I surrender!"

The man of battle was followed by one of those individuals with countenance bony and yellowish, mortified by an overly severe abstinence or an excess of passions, one can never know which; a devious-looking personage, equipped with relics and images of saints, and imagining that such strange baggage would protect him against his enemy.

He took his place, head lowered, and the game began. Far from imitating the boldness and petulance of his predecessor, he proceeded with extreme reserve. His pieces, after having made some steps forward, returned by themselves, seeming bound to concentrate in their own territory and presenting some barricades which would have served as models to the rioters of Paris. Then, behind the ramparts, our good friar (he was one), cunningly excavated a subterranean pathway through which he hoped to introduce his Queen, accompanied by her bravest defenders, to penetrate thus unperceived into the camp of the enemy, surprise him, and exterminate him. Moreover, he had prepared a prayer to the

World Champion Wilhelm Steinitz recorded many of Mephisto's games and published them in his chess column in *The Field*. COURTESY OF JGW.

161

bined a deep study and a perfect understanding of the chess books, a great force of will, of patience, and of calculation.

To his listing of the mechanical chess player's victims, Delannoy might have added a verbose French chess journalist, since he himself was among those who succumbed to "the prowesses of Mephisto."

Mechanically, Mephisto was said to be "simply perfect." The actions of his right arm, with which he moved the pieces, were compared with those of a human ball-and-socket joint. During a game, the mechanical player would occasionally appear to take a wide survey of the board, nodding his head thoughtfully, as though taking note of the relative powers of his forces compared with those of his opponent, or considering how some line of play might be pursued. "If he makes a very damaging move," observed Proctor, "he looks up at his opponent with a most sardonic smile."

Mephisto played rapidly and insisted that his adversary do the same. "If his opponent delays over-long," continued Proctor, "Mephisto bestows the same look upon him, but with greater persistency. If a game which has lasted some time seems tolerably equal, Mephisto goes through the movements of counting his own men and his opponent's, and then removes his King to the middle of the board. Nor does this always imply, as some seem to imagine, that in reality he has rather the worst of the game. I have seen him win a game, which he had offered in vain to draw."

Mephisto played with either the white or the black pieces, demonstrating equal skill from either side. When he captured his opponent's pieces, he carefully placed them on the side of the board to his right, and his adversary was requested to do likewise.

2.

There was naturally much speculation as to how Mephisto was operated. Gümpel candidly admitted that the figure was worked by a concealed player, but who was he, and where was he hidden? The director had to be a very strong player, capable of winning game after game played rapidly. On that point, at least, Delannoy did not exaggerate. Mephisto's play was good enough to gain the attention of World Champion Steinitz, who recorded many of the mechanical player's games in his chess column in *The Field*. Steinitz thought, in fact, that the hidden player was handicapped by his condition to the extent of at least a pawn and move, and yet he seldom lost.

One well-known writer and brilliant player suggested that the playing force behind Mephisto

Some persons suspected that Isidor Gunsberg was Mephisto's director—and they were correct. COURTESY OF JGW.

Johannes Zukertort was Mephisto's director for one day only. COURTESY OF JGW.

The Game of Chess by Louis Boilly might have been drawn in the *salle des mazettes* at the Café de la Régence. COURTESY OF JGW.

At the Café de la Régence, Gunsberg's teacher, Rosenthal, seated at far right, contemplates a move in the telegraphic match between Paris and Vienna. COURTESY OF JGW.

The Café de la Régence, here pictured on a 1912 postcard, continued to exist long into the twentieth century, although chess was no longer played there in its latter days. COURTESY OF JGW.

Today, as this recent photo shows, there is no longer even a restaurant located at the old address of the Régence. FROM AC.

might have been Isidor Gunsberg, a twenty-three-year-old Hungarian who had been in London for about two years. When Gümpel heard of that guess, he invited the writer to call and investigate for himself. The writer arrived at Leicester Square and to his amazement found Gunsberg playing a game with Mephisto. To divert suspicion from Gunsberg, who really was the secret director, Gümpel had employed Maelzel's old trick of having the director act as the adversary. In case the skeptical writer had himself wanted to try a game with Mephisto, the nearly invincible Zukertort had been installed for only that one day at the controls of the mechanical chess player.

Mephisto's director, Gunsberg, was born in Budapest on November 2, 1854, but had been taken at an early age to London to prepare for a mercantile career. During the Paris Exposition of 1867, he visited the French capital and was taken by his father to the Café de la Régence. At that time the Régence consisted of two rooms, the larger for smokers and the other for nonsmokers. The smaller room, known as *la salle des mazettes*, was frequented by elderly gentlemen who usually played among themselves. The *mazettes* considered the young Gunsberg a second Morphy, and soon his fame spread to the larger salon, where his delighted father one day introduced him.

Since a major tournament was then in progress at the Exposition, the Régence was the center of activity between hours of play for both competitors and spectators. During one such interval the elder Gunsberg presented the thirteen-year-old for a game with Rosenthal at odds of the Queen. Young Gunsberg easily defeated the French master under those conditions, and he then became Rosenthal's pupil and progressed rapidly.

In 1876 Gunsberg, by then a young man, returned to London, at that time considered the spot most favorable for a chess career.

Britain then had plenty of chess patrons [explained Charles De Vide, a biographer of Gunsberg] but they patronized the talent in a decidedly sportive way. They backed players as they would back a race horse, a pugilist, or a gamecock. In matches they put up the stakes, but half of the winnings went in their own pockets. Or they bought a player's chance for a prize in a tournament; if the player did not belong to the biggest guns of the game, the purchase price, as a rule, did not cover much more than the entrance and very frugal living expenses for the duration of the tourney.

Such was the condition Gunsberg found himself up against in London. There was another source of revenue: playing for shillings at Simpson's Cigar Divan, but here, too, the newcomer confronted difficulties. Leopold Hoffer, somehow or otherwise, managed to rule the waiters at that famous resort and with their aid succeeded in monopolizing all remunerative customers for himself or those under his protection, but Gunsberg did not belong to them.

Gunsberg's opportunity came at last when Gümpel hired him to direct Mephisto. Despite the trick of substituting Zukertort, the secret of who guided Mephisto's play soon leaked out. Thus Gunsberg not only found a means of livelihood but gained a wide reputation for his dashing and brilliant play.

Leopold Hoffer monopolized the customers at Simpson's Cigar Divan. COURTESY OF JGW.

Gümpel had hoped to exhibit Mephisto at the Paris Exposition of 1878 and had announced his intention to do so at performances in his home. Delannoy had even heralded the arrival of Mephisto in Paris by writing for *La Stratégie* a fanciful tale, in which Mephisto's proprietor, called Faustin Lewis in the story, enslaved a chess player named Macfire by a clever trick, exposed him as Mephisto, and then took him to the Paris Exposition. In reality the administrators of the Exposition would not allow Mephisto to be exhibited there, evidently because they did not wish to sanction the presence of a figure so representative of evil.

Undaunted, Gümpel somehow managed to arrange for Mephisto to enter the handicap tourney of the Counties Chess Association, held at King's College, July 29, 1878. That unprecedented entry provoked much unfavorable criticism from the chess journalists.

We have it upon tolerably respectable authority [commented *The Westminister Papers*] that the "Devil" is a gentleman, and presumably, therefore, eligible to take part in a tourney of the "gentle game." But somehow there is a wild suspicion abroad—a lying spirit, no doubt—that the "Devil" admitted to this handicap tourney is occasionally subjected to a mundane influence about whose "gentility" no sort of guarantee can be offered by anyone because it is anonymous. He—the mundane personage we mean—is the great or little Unknown of the Chess world, and, moreover, it is altogether uncertain whether he is not, like Mrs. Malaprop's Cerberus, "three," or indeed any number of gentlemen "at once." Anyhow, the admission of a toy of this kind to a chess tournament is a freak that could not have been expected from a Committee whose gravity is proverbial. . . . If it was at all desirable to admit Mephisto to the lists of the handicap, then the name of the concealed player should have been disclosed, at least to the competitors, if not to the general public.

The Reverend George A. MacDonnell, retired English chess champion, had been entreated to enter the same handicap tourney. To his surprise he was, in the first round, paired against a "foreign professional player," whose entry had caused more consternation than had that of Mephisto. The resulting furor among the entrants, who were all amateurs, caused the foreigner to withdraw. In a later round when MacDonnell, to his great dismay, found himself matched with Mephisto, he withdrew from the tournament, which inspired one spectator to compose the following bit of doggerel:

The Fiend made a grasp, MacDonnell to clasp,
 The latter just lifted his foot, and lo!

The view of the sea from King's Road, Brighton, has changed little since Mephisto was exhibited there. FROM AC.

Joseph Henry Blackburne, caricatured in *Vanity Fair*, was finally defeated by Gunsberg in a match in 1887. COURTESY OF JGW.

In the fall of 1879 Mephisto appeared at Brighton. Still playing brilliantly, he was exhibited there in some rooms at 79 King's Road for the amusement of the local players and those from surrounding towns. Shortly therafter, Mephisto was disassembled and never again operated by Gunsberg, although there is some evidence that the mechanical chess player was later resurrected, with a new director, and exhibited at the Crystal Palace and perhaps elsewhere. At the Paris Exposition of 1889, a Mephisto was exhibited at the Theatre International. Taubenhaus, then chess champion of France, was thought to be Mephisto's director at that time. Mephisto's association with Gunsberg, which probably lasted no more than two years, was over, but Gunsberg's own chess career had scarcely begun.

4.

Still a young man in his middle twenties in 1879, when he retired as the soul of Mephisto, Gunsberg played a match with the formidable Joseph Henry Blackburne, known throughout the chess world as "Black Death." In sharp contrast with the short, mild-mannered, and unassuming Gunsberg, Blackburne was a huge, powerful extrovert who believed that a glass or two of whiskey while playing cleared his brain. Blackburne was also a more experienced player, and when he won the match, although he gave the young challenger odds of two games, Gunsberg retired for a time from public competition and devoted himself to club play.

Gunsberg's career proper began in 1885, when he emerged as first prize winner in the giant City of London Chess Club Handicap Tournament. He soon won another first, this time the initial tournament of the British Chess Association, and without losing a single game. Later in 1885 Gunsberg won first prize at the Hamburg International Tournament, one half point ahead of such international stars as Blackburne, Englisch, Weiss, Tarrasch, and Mason, all of whom tied for second through sixth places. Captain George Henry Mackenzie, the U.S. Champion, was seventh. To top off the year, Gunsberg won a match by the score of 5-1 against the veteran master Henry Bird, originator of the chess opening which bears his name.

In 1886 Gunsberg won first in Purssel's Handicap in London. He met Blackburne again in a match in 1887, that time defeating his old rival 5-2 with two draws. That same year he tied for first with Amos Burn in the British Chess Association National Masters Tournament. In 1888 he won first prizes in Simpson's Handicap, the British Chess Club Handicap, and finally the International Chess Congress at Bradford.

By that time Gunsberg was recognized as the top

In Mephisto's day, Simpson's Cigar Divan was to London what the Régence was to Paris. Leopold Hoffer, with bald head, sits at extreme left, while the Reverend W. Wayte at a nearby table plays Zukertort, as the Reverend MacDonnell leans on the latter's chair. Blackburne, with pipe in mouth, stands near the gentleman with top hat and cigar. Steinitz, at extreme right, removes his overcoat. There is still a Simpson's to this day, but unfortunately chess is no longer played there. COURTESY OF CPL.

British player and a strong contender for the World Championship, and Leopold Hoffer, who had treated him so inhospitably some years earlier at Simpson's, became the champion of his cause. In 1889 the Havana Chess Club invited Steinitz to play a World Championship match in the Cuban capital with any opponent of his choice. Despite the protests of Hoffer, editor of the *Chess Monthly,* Steinitz ignored Gunsberg and chose instead to play the rising Russian star Mikhail Tchigorin, whom he defeated at Havana by a score of 10-6 with one draw.

Tchigorin then played in the Sixth American Chess Congress, where he tied with Weiss for first prize. Gunsberg took third place, but he won both of his games with Tchigorin in that tournament. The following year at Havana Gunsberg met the Russian in a match, which ended in a 9-9 draw. That result won him a chance for a match with World Champion Steinitz.

Steinitz at that time was experimenting with a line in the Evans Gambit, which soon proved to be unsound. When Steinitz made his favorite Queen move in that line during a cable match with Tchigorin, Gunsberg, in his chess column, commented, "Arrant nonsense." The cause of Gunsberg's remark had actually been a mistake in transmission by the Reuter's Telegraph Company, which cabled the moves between the United States and England, but when Steinitz noticed the comment, he was unaware of the error which had caused it, and he thus declared his readiness to play that "nonsense" in the upcoming match with Gunsberg. As a result, Gunsberg won two victories in the match because of Steinitz's stubborn insistence upon playing his unfortunate innovation in the Evans, but Steinitz still won the 1890 match by a score of 6-4 with 9 draws.

Participants in the Masters Tournament of the Counties Chess Association meeting at Hereford, England were caught in this charming Victorian tableau. From left are Gunsberg, Edmund Thorold, James Mason, W.H.K. Pollock, J. H. Blackburne (playing black), Henry E. Bird, Charles Anthony, T. Smith, J. Shallops, Capt. George A. Mackenzie (playing white), Rev. J. Owen, Rev. A. B. Skipworth, and Rev. C. E. Ranken (seated). COURTESY OF JGW.

It was an honorable showing for Gunsberg, who came closer to taking the championship from Steinitz than had Blackburne, Zukertort, or Tchigorin. Some chess historians have considered Gunsberg a "minor star," but his record indicates that, at his best, he was second only to Stienitz.

Gunsberg was never a great chess strategist but rather an ingenious tactician, possessing considerable powers of combination, and it was said that he never played an uninteresting game. "He had," explained De Vide, "a knack of wriggling his pieces into formidable attacking positions; hence his British colleagues bestowed upon him the by no means flattering nickname of 'Insect.'"

Gunsberg lived until 1930, when he was seventy-six years of age. Even in his later years he was considered a most powerful and dangerous opponent in tournament and match play. However, he judiciously devoted himself more and more to journalism and developed chess reporting to a fine point.

By drawing his match with Mikhail Tchigorin, seen here, Gunsberg won a chance at the world championship—but he could not overcome Steinitz. COURTESY OF JGW.

Gunsberg also operated a chess divan near the Strand in London, and in *The Adventure of Chess* Edward Lasker told of meeting him there in 1912. At that time Gunsberg related some of his experiences as the director of Mephisto, including how he compelled women to checkmate the mechanical player. During the conversation, a lady entered, and Gunsberg introduced her to Lasker and suggested that she might like to play a game with him. While she removed her coat, Gunsberg whispered that Lasker should try the suimate with her. As the game progressed, Lasker, noting that the lady played with considerable strength, suspected that Gunsberg was playing a joke on him. She soon won the game, in fact, with no help from Lasker. Smiling, Gunsberg commented, "Oh, I forgot to mention that Mrs. Fagan just recently returned from San Remo, where she won the ladies' world championship."

In 1923, interest in Mephisto was renewed by a series of articles on chess automatons in the chess journal *Our Folder*, which prompted John Keeble of Hastings to seek out Gunsberg and question him about the operation of Mephisto. Keeble then communicated Gunsberg's explanation to *Our Folder* in a letter dated Christmas Day, 1923.

Two rooms were necessary for Mephisto [explained Keeble]. By means of magnetism and electricity the moves made on Mephisto's board were recorded in the other room where Mr. Gunsberg was in charge, and by moving a duplicate arm Mr. Gunsberg could cause his move to be repeated on the board before Mephisto. He could consequently play in great comfort, which was not the case with the other automatons. . . . Mr. Gunsberg had means of seeing who [sic] he was playing against, if he cared to go and look, but, in any event, the fact he was about to meet a strong player, even if known to the person in charge, would be communicated to him.

Although one might wish that Gunsberg had supplied Keeble with more mechanical details, there seems to be nothing in his explanation that is inconsistent with other observations about Mephisto. But was such a complicated arrangement really feasible? Wouldn't it have been simpler to hide Gunsberg in Mephisto's chair? Why was the chair so large as to cause Proctor to observe, "a small human figure could be concealed therein?" Was it a mere coincidence that Gunsberg was "somewhat below the middle height?"

At Cheltenham, England, in 1913, Gunsberg told W. S. Branch that he had directed Mephisto from a cellar below the exhibition room "by a kind of wireless telegraphy." Branch, however, did not understand how he worked the machinery and doubted that it could have been done by wireless "years before Marconi was heard of." Thus the question of how Mephisto was directed still remains somewhat in doubt.

ON THE CHESSBOARD
The Games of Mephisto

More games have survived from the short career of Mephisto than from the much longer careers of both of the Ajeebs. The relative abundance of Mephisto's games is mainly due to the work of World Champion Steinitz, who was then editor of a chess column in *The Field*. Steinitz followed Mephisto's career from the time Gümpel first exhibited him privately until he was retired, and most of the recorded games of Mephisto first appeared in *The Field* with detailed notes by Steinitz.

Game 24

Even before Gunsberg became the director of Mephisto, Steinitz noticed the young Hungarian. At Simpson's Divan the twenty-two-year-old Gunsberg won this miniature game played against the Reverend George A. MacDonnell, who was then champion of England. It appears that MacDonnell underestimated the strength of his youthful challenger.

Philidor's Defense

Simpson's Divan, London, 1876

White	*Black*
MacDonnell	Gunsberg
1 P–K4	P–K4
2 N–KB3	P–Q3
3 B–B4	N–QB3
4 P–B3	B–N5
5 P–Q4	P×P
6 Q–N3	Q–Q2
7 B×Pch	Q×B
8 Q×P	K–Q2
9 Q×R	B×N
10 P×B	Q×P
11 R–B1	P–Q6 and mate in two moves

Game 25

Among the first of Mephisto's victims was Mr. Tinsley, a highly respected London amateur. "White's play throughout," commented Steinitz, "reflects the highest credit on the conductor of the game, whoever he may be."

Two Knights Defense

49 Leicester Square, London, 1878

White	*Black*
Mephisto (Gunsberg)	Tinsley
1 P–K4	P–K4

171

A Retzsch drawing featured Mephisto's chessboard. The form of the King is represented by the Prince of Darkness himself, while the bare-bosomed Queen is Pleasure. Other pieces are the six vices Indolence, Anger, Pride, Falsehood, Avarice and Envy combined, and Unbelief. The Pawns are Doubts. On the right side of the board, the Human Being defends his own soul as King, protected by Queen Religion. The pieces are Hope, Truth, Peace, Humility, Innocence, and Love, while the Pawns are Prayers, represented by winged angels. COURTESY OF JGW.

2	N–KB3	N–QB3
3	B–B4	N–KB3
4	N–N5	P–Q4
5	P×P	N×P
6	N×BP	K×N
7	Q–B3ch	K–K3
8	N–B3	N–N5
9	Q–K4	P–QN4
10	B–N3	B–N2
11	P–Q4	B–Q3
12	P×P	B–B4
13	Q–N4ch	K–B2

Samuel Tinsley was among the many amateurs defeated by Mephisto at Gümpel's home. BY PERMISSION OF NPG.

14	B–N5	Q–K1
15	O–O–O	Q–K3
16	Q–B3ch	K–K1
17	N×N	N×N
18	R×N	Q–KN3
19	P–K6	R–KB1
20	Q–B7ch!	R×Q
21	P×Rch	K–B1
22	R×B	P–KR3
23	B–Q2	Q×NP
24	R–K1	Q×BP
25	R×BP	Q×Rch
26	B×Q	P–N3
27	B–N4ch	K–N2
28	P–B8(Q) mate	

32	R–B1	N–K3
33	R–KB7	P–R4
34	R×QP	N–B4
35	R×P	R–K3
36	R–B1	R–K1
37	B–B6	R–QB1
38	B×P	Resigns

Game 26

The next game is unique in that Gunsberg was Mephisto's adversary rather than his director. For only that one day Zukertort directed Mephisto, so that Gümpel could prove that the mechanical chess player could function without the aid of Gunsberg.

Evans Gambit

49 Leicester Square, London, 1878

White — *Black*

Mephisto (Zukertort) — Gunsberg

1	P–K4	P–K4
2	N–KB3	N–QB3
3	B–B4	B–B4
4	P–QN4	B×P
5	P–QB3	B–R4
6	P–Q4	P×P
7	O–O	P×P
8	Q–N3	Q–KB3
9	P–K5	Q–N3
10	N×P	KN–K2
11	B–R3	P–QN3
12	N–QN5	B–N2
13	N×Pch	K–Q1
14	N×R	N–Q5
15	B×Nch	K×B
16	Q–R3ch	K–Q1
17	N–R4	Q–K5
18	Q–KN3	B×N
19	Q×P	R–K1
20	Q–N5ch	K–B2
21	QR–B1	K–N1
22	B×P	Q×P
23	Q×Q	R×Q
24	QR–Q1	R–K5
25	P–B4	P–N4
26	B–R5	B–N3
27	K–R1	N–K3
28	B–B3	R×P
29	B×B	R×N
30	P–N3	R–R3
31	B–K4	N–Q5

Game 27

Mephisto played the following three games in the handicap tournament of the Counties Chess Association. In the first game he was required to give odds of a pawn and two moves. While most of Mephisto's exhibition games were played quite rapidly, this tournament game lasted four and a half hours.

Irregular Opening

Counties Handicap Tourney, King's College, London, July 1878

White — *Black*

Baxter — Mephisto (Gunsberg)

Remove Black's King Bishop Pawn.

1	P–K4	——
2	P–Q4	P–K3
3	N–KB3	Q–K2
4	P–QB3	P–Q3
5	B–Q3	P–K4
6	O–O	B–N5
7	B–K3	N–Q2
8	QN–Q2	P–KR3
9	Q–B2	P–KN4
10	N–K1	KN–B3
11	P–B3	B–R4
12	R–B2	B–B2
13	N–B1	N–R4
14	P–KN4	N–B5
15	B×N	NP×B
16	R–N2	B–N2
17	P–Q5	O–O–O
18	P–N4	B–B3
19	P–QR4	P–KR4
20	B–K2	P×P
21	P×P	R–R6
22	B–B3	B–N4
23	Q–K2	B–N3
24	R–R2	N–B3
25	P–R5	Q–R2
26	P–R6	P–N3
27	Q–B4	B×P
28	N–Q2	B–N3
29	Q–B6	P–K5
30	N–B4	N×QP
31	Q×N	P×B

32	Q–N7ch	K–Q2
33	N/1×P	B–K5
34	N×B	B×Q
35	N×Q	B×R
36	N–N5	R×BP
37	N×Pch	BP×N
38	K×B	R–KN1
39	N–K4	R×Pch
40	K–B2	R–KR6
41	N–B6ch	K–K3
42	N×R	K–B4
43	R–Q2	K×N
44	R×P	R×Pch
45	K–N1	R–R7
46	P–N5	R–N7
47	R–Q7	R×P
48	R×P	R–R4
49	R–R8	K–B6
50	P–R7	P–N4
51	R–QN8	R×P
52	R×P	R–R8ch
53	K–R2	R–K8
54	R–KB5	R–K2
55	R–B6	R–KN2
56	R–QR6	R–N7ch
57	K–R1	R–Q7
58	R–KB6	K–N6
59	R–N6ch	K–B7
60	R–B6	P–B6
61	K–R2	K–K8 dis ch
Resigns		

Game 28

Playing the next game without giving odds, Mephisto wasted time in the opening but soon made up the loss.

French Defense

Counties Handicap Tourney, King's College, London, July 1878

White	Black
Mephisto (Gunsberg)	Coker
1 P–K4	P–K3
2 P–KB4	P–QN3
3 P–Q4	B–N2
4 B–Q3	P–QB4
5 P–B3	P–KB4
6 Q–K2	P×KP
7 B×P	B×B
8 Q×B	N–QB3
9 N–B3	N–B3
10 Q–Q3	P×P
11 N×P	N×N
12 Q×N	Q–B2
13 Q–Q3	B–B4
14 B–Q2	O–O
15 P–QN4	B–Q3
16 O–O	N–Q4
17 P–N3	R–B4

18	N–R3	P–QR3
19	N–B2	P–QN4
20	P–QR4	N–B3
21	N–Q4	R–R4
22	P×P	Q–N3
23	P–B4	Q–N1
24	P–B5	B–K2
25	R×P	R–Q4
26	R/1–R1	R×R
27	P×R	Q–R2
28	Q–B4	Q–R1
29	P–R7	N–K1
30	B–K3	P–R4
31	Q–N5	N–B2
32	Q–N8ch	K–B2
33	N–N5	
White won.		

Game 29

Mephisto won first prize in the handicap tournament by beating F. S. Ensor in the last round. Steinitz called Mephisto's final moves "an ingenious sorcery."

Ruy Lopez

Counties Handicap Tourney, King's College, London, July 1878

White	Black
Mephisto (Gunsberg)	Ensor
1 P–K4	P–K4
2 N–KB3	N–QB3
3 B–N5	P–QR3
4 B–R4	N–KB3
5 P–Q3	P–Q3
6 P–QB3	B–KN5
7 B–KN5	P–R3
8 B×N	Q×B
9 QN–Q2	P–QN4
10 B–N3	N–K2
11 P–QR4	R–B1
12 P×P	P×P
13 P–KR3	B–R4
14 R–R7	B–N3
15 Q–R1	P–Q4
16 Q–R5	P×P
17 Q×Pch	Q–B3
18 Q–R5	Q–Q3
19 P×P	P–KB3
20 O–O	B–B2
21 B–R4ch	P–B3
22 R–Q1	Q–N1
23 Q–R6	B–K3
24 P–QN4	P–N4
25 N–N3	P–KN5
26 P×P	B×P
27 N–B5	K–B2
28 N–Q7	B×N/Q2
29 R/1×B	R–R2
30 R/Q7–N7	Q–Q3

174

31	R×Nch	B×R
32	Q×R	P–R4
33	N–R4	Q–K3
34	Q×Qch	Resigns

After 34...K×Q, 35 B–N3ch and mate next move.

Game 30

The most interesting encounter on Mephisto's opening day at Westminster Aquarium was this one with Col. James Minchin. Steinitz thought the game should have been a draw, but then on move 20 Mephisto gave up a pawn to throw his opponent off balance. He then offered his Queen, but that gift had to be refused.

Sicilian Defense

Westminster Aquarium, London, October 2, 1878

White	*Black*
Mephisto (Gunsberg)	Col. Minchin
1 P–K4	P–QB4
2 P–KB4	P–K3

3	N–KB3	N–QB3
4	N–B3	P–KN3
5	B–N5	KN–K2
6	O–O	B–N2
7	B×N	N×B
8	P–Q3	O–O
9	N–K2	P–Q4
10	P–K5	P–B3
11	P×P	Q×P
12	P–B3	B–Q2
13	N–N3	QR–K1
14	B–Q2	P–N3
15	Q–B2	Q–K2
16	QR–K1	Q–Q3
17	Q–Q1	P–K4
18	P×P	N×P
19	N×N	B×N
20	B–R6	R×Rch
21	R×R	B×N
22	P×B	Q×P
23	Q–K2	Q–Q3
24	Q–B3	B–B4
25	P–KN4	Q–KB3
26	P×B	P–KN4
27	Q–R5	R–K6
28	R–B3	R–K8ch
29	K–B2	Q–K2
30	R–N3	Resigns

Col. James Innes Minchin was Mephisto's most interesting adversary on the mechanical player's first day at Westminster Aquarium. BY PERMISSION OF NPG.

Game 31

Mephisto did not always win; here he lost to Mr. H. Lee, third board on the Oxford team. "Mr. Lee deserves praise for the conception of this fine sacrifice," commented Steinitz, "and for the manner in which he utilizes its consequences."

King's Gambit Declined

Westminster Aquarium, London, 1878

White	*Black*
Mephisto (Gunsberg)	Lee
1 P–K4	P–K4
2 P–KB4	B–B4
3 N–KB3	P–Q3
4 B–B4	N–KB3
5 P–Q3	P–B3
6 P–B3	P–QR4
7 P×P	P×P
8 N×P	O–O
9 B–KN5	P–KR3
10 B–R4	P–QN4
11 B–QN3	P–R5
12 B–QB2	R–K1
13 N–B3	B–KN5
14 P–KR3	B–R4
15 QN–Q2	P–N4
16 B–KN3	B–K6
17 B×N	Q×B

18	Q–K2	Q–N6ch
19	K–Q1	B×QN
20	K×B	QR–Q1
21	K–B1	Q–B5ch
22	K–N1	P–R6
23	P×P	N–Q4
24	K–N2	N–K6
25	P–N4	B–N3
26	B–N3	R×QP
27	Q×R	Q×N
28	QR–K1	R×P
29	Q–Q8ch	K–N2
30	R–R2	N–B5ch
31	B×N	R×R
32	Q–Q4ch	K–N1
33	B×Pch	

Black threatened mate at QN8. Now Black played Q×B and won.

Game 32

"Of sulphurous subtlety," noted W. N. Potter after Mephisto's sixteenth move in the next game.

King's Gambit Declined

Westminster Aquarium, London, December 1, 1878

White	Black
Mephisto (Gunsberg)	Beardsell
1 P–K4	P–K4
2 P–KB4	B–B4
3 N–KB3	P–Q3
4 B–B4	N–KB3
5 P–Q3	B–KN5
6 P–KR3	B×N
7 Q×B	O–O
8 N–B3	N–B3
9 P–B5	P–KR3
10 P–KN4	N–Q5
11 Q–N2	N–R2
12 P–KR4	P–KN4
13 P×P	N×P
14 R×P	N/5–B6ch
15 K–Q1	K–N2
16 P–B6ch	K×R
17 Q×N	Q–Q2

White mates in three moves.

Game 33

Although Mephisto rarely lost a game, G. H. M'Lennan, "a talented young player," beat him in both the following games. Steinitz thought the mechanical player underestimated his opponent.

King's Gambit

Westminster Aquarium, London, 1879

White	Black
Mephisto (Gunsberg)	M'Lennan
1 P–K4	P–K4
2 P–KB4	P×P
3 N–KB3	P–KN4
4 B–B4	B–N2
5 P–KR4	P–KR3
6 P–Q4	P–Q3
7 Q–Q3	N–QB3
8 P×P	P×P
9 R×R	B×R
10 P–K5	B–N2
11 Q–R7	K–B1
12 Q–R5	Q–K2
13 P–QN3	P×P
14 B–R3	N–N5
15 P–B3?	N–B7ch
16 K–B2	N×B
17 N×N	N–B3!
18 Q–R1	Q×N
19 Q–K1	P–K5
20 N×P	N–N5ch
21 K–N1	N–K6
22 B×P?	Q–N7
23 Q–KB1	N×Q
Resigns	

Game 34

"The devil commits here a ludicrous blunder in grasping at a bishop," declared Steinitz, "and he pays with immediate defeat for his disrespect against the clergy."

King's Gambit

Westminster Aquarium, London, 1879

White	Black
Mephisto (Gunsberg)	M'Lennan
1 P–K4	P–K4
2 P–KB4	P×P
3 N–KB3	P–KN4
4 B–B4	B–N2
5 P–Q4	P–Q3
6 P–KR4	P–KR3
7 Q–Q3	N–KB3
8 P×P	P×P
9 R×Rch	B×R
10 N×P	P–Q4
11 P×P	Q–K2ch
12 K–B1? (Q–K2!)	N–R4
13 N–KB3	B–B4!
14 Q–N3	N–N6ch
15 K–N1	B×Pch
16 N×B?	Q–K8ch
Resigns	

Game 35

Mephisto's reckless attack, though unsound, quickly paid off in this game against J. G. Ascher, secretary of the Montreal Chess Club.

King's Gambit Declined

Mephisto's Chess Rooms, No. 9 Strand, London, April 1879

	White	Black
	Mephisto (Gunsberg)	Ascher
1	P–K4	P–K4
2	P–KB4	B–B4
3	N–KB3	P–Q3
4	B–B4	N–KB3
5	P–Q3	N–N5
6	P×P	N–B7
7	Q–K2	N×R
8	P–Q4	B–N3
9	N–N5	B–K3
10	P–Q5	B–B1
11	P–K6	P–KB3
12	Q–R5ch	P–N3
13	Q–R6	Q–K2

if 13...P×N, 14 B×P wins the Black Queen.

14	N–B7	R–B1
15	Q×RP	R×N
16	Q×P	K–Q1
17	P×R	N–Q2
18	Q–N8ch	Q–B1
19	B–KR6	Resigns

Game 36

In the next game the visitor from Montreal again fell victim to Mephisto's vigorous attack.

Evans Gambit

Mephisto's Chess Rooms, No. 9 Strand, London, April 1879

	White	Black
	Mephisto (Gunsberg)	Ascher
1	P–K4	P–K4
2	N–KB3	N–QB3
3	B–B4	B–B4
4	P–QN4	B×P
5	P–B3	B–R4
6	P–Q4	P×P
7	O–O	P×P
8	Q–N3	Q–B3
9	P–K5	Q–N3
10	N×P	KN–K2
11	N–K2	P–QN4
12	B–Q3	Q–K3
13	Q–N1	N–N3
14	N–N5	Q×P

15	K–R1	P–KR3
16	N×P!	K×N
17	B×Nch	K–N1
18	N–B4	B–B6
19	B–N2!	B×B
20	R–K1	B×R
21	R×Q	B×R
22	Q–B5 (Q–N3ch!)	N–Q1
23	Q×B	N–K3
24	Q–KB5	Resigns

Game 37

White played strongly in this game and won a piece, but Mephisto did not give up. After move 31 Steinitz commented, "Black has defended himself remarkably well under extreme difficulties, and he now forces the game by a fine and well-calculated combination."

Evans Gambit

Mephisto's Chess Rooms, No. 9 Strand, London, 1879

	White	Black
	Mocatta	Mephisto (Gunsberg)
1	P–K4	P–K4
2	N–KB3	N–QB3
3	B–B4	B–B4
4	P–QN4	B×P
5	P–B3	B–R4
6	P–Q4	P×P
7	Q–N3	Q–B3
8	O–O	P–Q3
9	P–K5	P×KP
10	P×P	P×P
11	QN–Q2	KN–K2 (B×N!)
12	N–K4	Q–N3
13	B–Q3	O–O (P–B4!)
14	N/4–N5	B–B4 (Q–R4!)
15	N–R4	Q–B3
16	N×B	N×N
17	P–N4	P–KR3
18	N–K4	Q–N3
19	N–N3	Q×P
20	B×N	Q–R5
21	Q×NP	Q–B3
22	B–QR3	KR–N1
23	Q–R6	R–N3
24	Q–K2	P–N3
25	B–R3	N–K4
26	B–KN2	R–K1
27	B–B5	P–Q6
28	Q–K3	R/3–K3
29	Q×RP	P–Q7
30	K–R1? (N–K4!)	N–N5
31	Q–R3	Q×R!
32	R×Q	R–K8ch
33	N–B1	R×R
34	B–Q4	N×Pch
35	B×N	P–Q8(Q)

36	K–N1	B–N3
37	B×B	RP×B
38	B–B6	Q–Q5ch
39	K–R1	R/1–K8
40	Q–B8ch	K–N2
Resigns		

Game 38

Here White hoped to break through on the King side but soon found his King surrounded by Mephisto's pieces. "A neat finish," remarked Steinitz.

King's Gambit Declined

Mephisto's Chess Rooms, 48A Regent Street, London, 1879

White	Black
Gossip	Mephisto (Gunsberg)
1 P–K4	P–K4
2 P–KB4	B–B4
3 N–QB3	P–Q3
4 N–B3	N–QB3
5 B–N5	N–B3
6 P–Q3	O–O
7 B×N	P×B
8 N–QR4	B–N3
9 N×B	RP×N
10 P–B5	P–R3
11 P–KR3	P–Q4
12 Q–K2	P×P
13 P×P	B–R3
14 P–B4	N–R4
15 K–B2	Q–K2
16 P–KN4	N–B3
17 B–K3	N×KPch
18 K–N2	N–Q3
19 P–N3	P–B4
20 P–KR4?	P–R4!
21 P–B6	Q×P
22 B–N5	Q–K3
23 P×P	P–KB3
24 B–B4	Q–N5ch
25 B–N3	N–B4
26 Q–KB2	B–N2
27 QR–KB1	R×P!
Resigns	

Game 39

Mephisto often employed gambits in order to quickly subdue his challengers, but in the following game, the Allgaier Gambit, named for one of the Turk's directors, took an unexpected disastrous turn for the mechanical chess player.

Allgaier Gambit

Mephisto's Rooms, London, 1879

White	Black
Mephisto (Gunsberg)	Amateur
1 P–K4	P–K4
2 P–KB4	P×P
3 N–KB3	P–KN4
4 P–KR4	P–N5
5 N–N5	P–KR3
6 N×P	K×N
7 B–B4ch	P–Q4
8 B×Pch	K–N2
9 B×P!?	P–B6
10 B×B	Q×B
11 P×P	P–N6
12 Q–K2	N–KB3
13 P–K5	N–R4
14 P–Q4	N–QB3
15 Q–K4	Q–K3
16 P–Q5	Q×KP
17 P×N	Q×Qch
18 P×Q	B–B4
19 K–B1	KR–B1ch
20 K–N2	R–B7ch
21 K–R3	P–N7
22 R–N1	R–B6ch
23 K×P	R–N6ch
Resigns	

Game 40

Mephisto usually made better use of the Allgaier. The tormented victim in this game from the *Leeds Mercury* was one of the best players of the Leeds Chess Club.

Allgaier Gambit

Mephisto's Rooms, London, 1879

White	Black
Mephisto (Gunsberg)	Bennett
1 P–K4	P–K4
2 P–KB4	P×P
3 N–KB3	P–KN4
4 P–KR4	P–N5
5 N–N5	B–R3? (P–KR3!)
6 Q×P	P–Q3
7 Q×P	B×N
8 P×B	B–K3
9 P–Q4	P–QB3
10 N–B3	Q–K2
11 B–K3	N–Q2
12 P–Q5	P×P
13 P×P	B–B4
14 O–O–O	B–N3
15 N–N5!	N–K4
16 B–Q4	P–B3
17 P×P	N×P

18	N×Pch	Q×N
19	B×N	R–QB1
20	B–Q3	B×B
21	R×B	Q–R3
22	B×N	Q×R

White mates in five moves.

Game 41

In this game Mephisto recklessly sacrificed pawns and pieces to get at the Black King, and he finished the game with a brilliant Queen sacrifice.

Cunningham Gambit

Mephisto's Rooms, London, 1879

White	Black
Mephisto (Gunsberg)	Amateur
1 P–K4	P–K4
2 P–KB4	P×P
3 N–KB3	B–K2
4 B–B4	B–R5ch
5 P–N3	P×P
6 O–O	P×Pch
7 K–R1	P–Q4
8 B×P	N–KB3
9 N–B3	N×B
10 N×N	B–R6
11 N×B	B×R
12 Q–N4	O–O
13 N–B5	P–KN3
14 N/B5–K7ch	K–R1
15 P–N3	N–Q2
16 B–N2ch	P–B3
17 R×B!	P–B3
18 Q×N!	Q×Q
19 R×P	P–KR4
20 R–B7 mate	

Game 42

At the seaside resort of Brighton, Mephisto continued to win in spectacular fashion. In this game he sacrificed both Knight and Queen to break through Black's defenses.

Allgaier Gambit

Mephisto's Chess Rooms, 79 King's Road, Brighton, 1879

White	Black
Mephisto (Gunsberg)	Amateur
1 P–K4	P–K4
2 P–KB4	P×P
3 N–KB3	P–KN4
4 P–KR4	P–N5

5	N–N5	P–KR3
6	N×P	K×N
7	P–Q4	P–Q4
8	B×P	N–KB3
9	N–B3	B–N5
10	B–K5	N×P
11	B–Q3	N×N
12	O–Och	K–N1
13	Q–K1	N–K5
14	Q×N	P×Q
15	B–B4ch	K–R2
16	R–B7ch	K–N3
17	R–N7ch	K–R4
18	B–B7ch	K×P
19	K–R2	

White mates in two moves.

Game 43

In this gambit which went astray, Mephisto sacrificed a Knight on move 14, hoping the Black King would move to the Bishop square. His opponent, however, found shelter in the opposite direction.

Evans Gambit

Mephisto's Chess Rooms, 79 King's Road, Brighton, 1879

White	Black
Mephisto (Gunsberg)	Warner
1 P–K4	P–K4
2 N–KB3	N–QB3
3 B–B4	B–B4
4 P–QN4	B×NP
5 P–B3	B–R4
6 P–Q4	P×P
7 O–O	P×P
8 Q–N3	Q–B3
9 P–K5	Q–N3
10 B–R3	KN–K2
11 N×P	P–N4
12 N×P	R–QN1
13 Q–R4	B–N3
14 N–Q6ch?	P×N
15 P×P	N–B4
16 KR–K1ch	K–Q1!
17 B–Q3	Q–B3
18 B×N	Q×B
19 Q–QB4	R–K1
20 B–N2	R–K3
21 QR–B1	B×Pch
22 K×B	R×Bch
23 K–N1	R×QP
24 Q–B3	Q–B3
25 Q–R3	R–N3
26 N–N5	K–B2
27 N–K4	Q–Q5ch
28 K–R1	R–K3
29 Q×Pch	B–N2
Resigns	

179

Game 44

This final Mephisto game was annotated by Steinitz and later by S. G. Tartakover. It featured a double Rook sacrifice, of which Steinitz wrote, "A highly ingenious and brilliant sacrifice, and as beautiful as it is original; to the best of our recollection we have never seen a similar finish in actual play." Tartakover added, "Whether Black accepts it or not, his fate is sealed." Mephisto's adversary, Mr. W., was a member of the St. George's Chess Club.

Scotch Gambit

Mephisto's Chess Rooms, 79 King's Road, Brighton, September 1879

White	Black
Mephisto (Gunsberg)	Mr. W.
1 P–K4	P–K4
2 N–KB3	N–QB3
3 P–Q4	P×P
4 N×P	Q–R5

5	N–KB3	Q×KPch
6	B–K2	P–Q4
7	O–O	B–K3
8	N–B3	Q–B4
9	B–QN5	N–K2
10	N–Q4	Q–N3
11	P–B4	P–B4
12	R–K1	B–Q2
13	N×QP	O–O–O
14	B×N	N×B
15	N–N5	B–B4ch
16	B–K3	B–K3
17	N/N5×BP	B×Bch
18	R×B	B×N
19	N×B	Q–B2
20	P–B4	KR–K1
21	R–QR3	K–N1
22	R–N1	Q–B1
23	P–QN4	N×P
24	Q–Q4	N–B3
25	R×Pch!	K×R
26	R×Pch!	N×R
27	Q–N6ch	K–R1
28	N–B7 mate	

11

Chess, Whist, and the Ladies' Game; or The Games Automatons Play

1.

In 1879 the renowned magician John Nevile Maskelyne explained in a *Leisure Hour* article:

> Some years back I commenced constructing an automatic chess-player of such small proportions as entirely to upset the idea of its even containing a child withinside; a figure, indeed, not weighing more than twelve or fourteen pounds, and . . . perfectly insulated and isolated upon a glass column. . . . This project was laid aside for other, and to the public, more attractive work. The fact is, chess—skilful and beautiful game as it is— cannot be made of a very engrossing character to a general audience, so I prepared other figures with endowments more popular and pleasing, before completing that for chess. I have not therefore abandoned the idea.

Although both Mephisto and Ajeeb were exhibited in London that year, Maskelyne may have been partly correct in evaluating the popularity of chess automatons. Proctor, a few months later, observed that Mephisto's Rooms merited far more numerous visits than they received, and that may have to some extent explained the final demise of the mechanical chess player.

Probably the most celebrated of Maskelyne's "other figures" was Psycho, an automaton whist player first exhibited in 1875 before the Prince of

John Nevile Maskelyne decided that whist would be more popular than chess. COURTESY OF JM.

Psycho, exhibited by Maskelyne, played his card in a game of whist against three startled adversaries. COURTESY OF NYPL.

Wales and a party gathered at Sandringham. Later that year, Psycho performed on stage in London at the Egyptian Hall, Astley's, and also at the London Pavilion.

Psycho, the joint invention of Maskelyne and John Algernon Clarke, was a small Oriental figure sitting cross-legged on a box which was supported by a single large cylinder of clear glass. Originally the cylinder had rested on the carpeting of the stage but was later placed upon a small stool with solid wooden legs.

Maskelyne, in fact, would permit the automaton to be placed in a variety of ways, and it thus seemed impossible that the figure could be influenced by an electric current, a magnetic attraction, or a hydraulic or pneumatic force from outside. There could have been no fine threads or wires attached to Psycho, since they would have been seen by persons from the audience who were permitted to come near the automaton in order to play a game of whist.

The figure of Psycho was much smaller than life-size, only about twenty-two inches tall and thus much too small to contain even a child. Nevertheless, Richard Proctor, a witness at one of Maskelyne's 1875 performances, expressed the opinion that the figure together with the supporting box were "certainly large enough to give room for a small boy." Although the magician made a show of prodding the automaton with a rod, it was noted that there was "room between the rod and the face of the lower enclosure for a boy's legs." Proctor, writing in *Cornhill Magazine,* supposed the boy to be "in a sitting position but somewhat askew posture, with his knees where the legs of the figure appear," and thought he was probably "about four feet in height, and rather thin, but not remarkably so."

When Maskelyne called for volunteers to join Psycho in a game of whist, Proctor was disappointed not to be among the three gentlemen selected to play. He in fact suspected at first that the chosen gentlemen might be confederates of the magician. At a second performance, however, he noted that "a very eminent man of science, president of one of the chief learned societies," was among those selected to go on stage to examine Psycho and eventually to take one of the whist hands. The presence of the scientist, who "most assuredly was not a confederate," convinced the writer that the game was not rigged.

Although Psycho was the best known of the whist players, there had been an automaton whist player in America as early as 1828. Whist was then the leading intellectual card game but has since been largely supplanted by its more challenging off-spring, bridge. Unlike bridge, there is in whist no dummy hand exposed during the play of the cards. Also there is no bidding in whist, the trump suit being determined merely by the turn of the last card dealt.

Psycho did not, of course, shuffle and deal the cards. When those duties had been performed by another player, Maskelyne placed Psycho's thirteen cards in slots in a specially constructed holder, which formed an arc in front of the figure. In so doing, Maskelyne disclaimed all knowledge of the hand, but Proctor thought the magician saw each card and memorized its position. Maskelyne then, Proctor suspected, indicated by prearranged signals the number of the card which his concealed operator was to play. The writer judged Psycho's play to be "not very profound, nor even always sound," chiding the automaton for signaling for trumps without reason, a weakness known as "the Blue Peter." He thought that Maskelyne directed most of Psycho's game but sometimes left the supposed youthful operator to make his own choices.

Psycho's motions were limited to moving his right arm in an arc above the cards, pausing over the selected card, and with thumb and finger plucking that card out of its slot in the rack. In addition, the automaton moved his head as if his eyes were following the actions of his hand.

Besides playing whist, Psycho performed card tricks and mathematical calculations. A spectator was asked to draw a card from the deck. Psycho then indicated the suit and rank of the card by striking a bell. The spectator chose another card, secretly marked it, and shuffled it into the pack. Psycho instantly found the card and held it up. Finally the pack was reshuffled and Maskelyne held it behind his back in full view of the audience. Psycho correctly indicated each card as it was revealed in succession.

It was claimed that Psycho was capable of making all the arm movements necessary to play chess or checkers, and later in his career the automaton may have even played chess, as Maskelyne had originally intended. Albert A. Hopkins, the author in 1901 of a book on magic, evidently thought Psycho played chess and even called him "the automaton chess player." He thought there were "two forms of the 'Psycho,' one which depends upon compressed air, and the other upon a small individual who is secreted in the cabinet." The latter form, however, turned out to be Kempelen's Turk, as was evident from the diagrams copied from those of Willis.

Arprey Vere, in his 1879 *Ancient and Modern Magic,* explained with the aid of diagrams how Psycho might have been operated by means of compressed air. In 1875, the year Psycho was invented, Maskelyne and Clarke had patented a method of controlling the speed of clockwork by compressed air or gas stored in the pedestal of an automaton and controlled remotely by a foot valve. It was not known, however, if the principle was applied to Psycho or to some other invention, or if it was ever used at all.

It is interesting to note that the compressed-air Psycho pictured in Vere's book was obviously designed to play whist and could not possibly have made the more complicated movements required in chess or checkers. Thus, if Maskelyne's Psycho did play chess or was capable of playing chess, it must be concluded that Vere's drawings and explanation are incorrect. If, on the other hand, Psycho was operated by a small person concealed in the figure and box, as Proctor suggested, then the automaton could have played chess as well as whist.

As with Ajeeb and the Turk, there were several imitations of Psycho, some of which may have operated differently from the original. The magician Charles Arbré exhibited a card-playing automaton at the Reichshallen in Berlin in November 1878. That automaton was called "the London automaton, Psycho" and seems to have been patterned after Maskelyne's original invention. A reporter for the *Nationalzeitung* judged that Arbré's Psycho played cards extraordinarily well and thought the figure was directed from a spot behind the curtain, but by what means he could not discover. Arbré also exhibited his fraudulent Psycho in other cities, including Stockholm.

In Paris, Robert-Houdin exhibited Sophos le Savant, a card-playing automaton that appeared remarkably similar to Psycho. When an opponent tried to cheat Sophos during a game, the automaton would ring a bell "in a very comical manner."

Professor Pepper of the Polytechnic Institution also constructed a Psycho imitation and exhibited the figure with the name Synthia. Although very ingeniously contrived, it was said, Synthia's performance fell somewhat short of the original.

Another imitation, named Hanky, was a poorly constructed figure of a man seated on an octagonal box. That automaton was directed by a boy concealed inside who received his instructions by means of signals from the exhibitor, a system that often led to mistakes. Signor Boz eventually acquired Hanky, rechristened him Yorick, and exhibited him in Liverpool and various other towns.

The magician W. H. Cremer exhibited a whist player consisting of a huge complicated mass of machinery that required such careful supervision for a smooth and uninterrupted performance that it could never be relied upon. In those days, however,

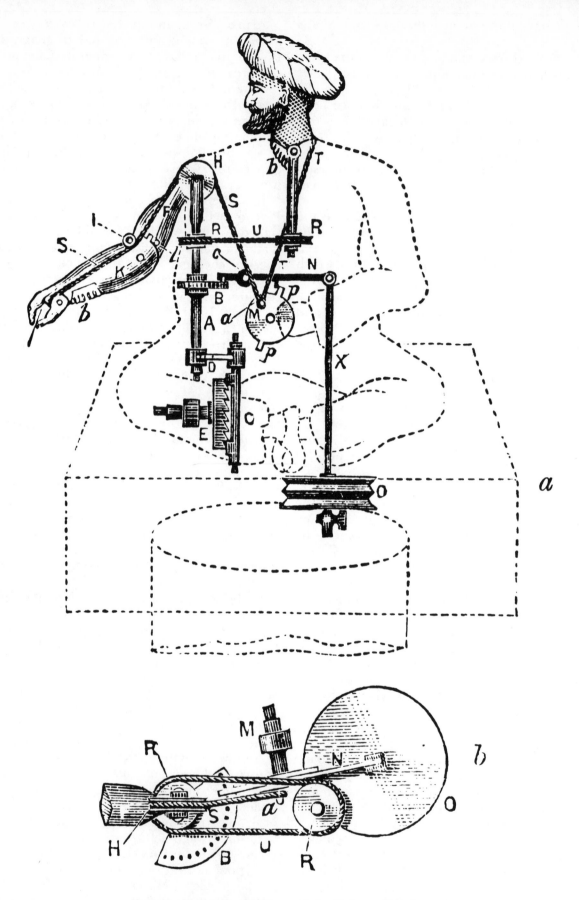

Arprey Vere, in 1879, explained how Psycho was directed from behind the scenes with compressed air which entered the automaton's glass cylinder through a tube beneath the stage. BY PERMISSION OF BL.

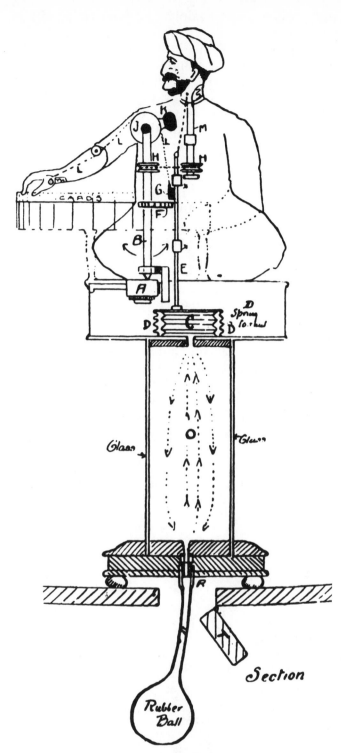

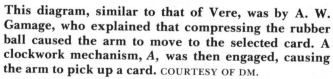

According to Gamage, two assistants were required to direct Psycho from backstage. An expert whist player with binoculars was stationed atop a ladder where he could see the game. By means of a speaking tube he informed the man below stage how to squeeze the rubber ball. The number of squeezes corresponded to the position of the card selected to be played. COURTESY OF DM.

This diagram, similar to that of Vere, was by A. W. Gamage, who explained that compressing the rubber ball caused the arm to move to the selected card. A clockwork mechanism, *A*, was then engaged, causing the arm to pick up a card. COURTESY OF DM.

This automaton card player was invented by Professor Dicksonn in 1900. Like the Turk and Ajeeb, a director was concealed inside. COURTESY OF DM.

no magic act was complete without some sort of whist automaton.

At the time of the Paris Exhibition of 1900, Professor Dicksonn exhibited an automaton card player at his Theatre du Cours la Reine. The figure could be taken apart for the inspection of the audience and placed anywhere upon the stage to prove there were no connections under the floor or behind the scenes. A director was hidden inside the automaton's chair.

A French firm constructed another Psycho imitation for a Mr. Everett. The automaton was eventually taken to America and may have been the same one that was owned by the famous American magician Harry Kellar. That Psycho, a fairly good duplicate of the original, played whist and poker, did calculations, and was said to have been beaten at chess by Benjamin Franklin. After his retirement, Kellar gave his Psycho to Harry Houdini.

There were so many imitations of Psycho that the name became a sort of generic term for any kind of card or chess playing automaton. Thus we see Hopkins calling even the Turk a form of Psycho. But what happened to the real Psycho? An automaton thought to be Maskelyne's Psycho has been exhibited in a London museum. It is difficult, however, to tell if it is the original or one of the imitations.

In addition to Psycho, Maskelyne constructed

Dicksonn's card player was nearly disassembled right in front of the spectators, who could find no director—unless they thought to look inside the automaton's oversized chair. COURTESY OF DM.

On stage at Egyptian Hall, Maskelyne posed with his automatons Psycho, Fanfare, Labial, and Zoe. FROM ILN.

other types of automatons such as Zoe, a figure that wrote and drew at the dictation of the audience. Zoe, devised in 1877, was a nearly life-size but very light doll that sat freely upon a cushioned stand placed on a thick plate of clear glass laid on the carpet of the stage. According to Vere, a real artist under the stage guided her hand by means of a pantograph device.

In 1878 and 1879 Maskelyne invented two musical automatons, Fanfare, a cornet player, and Labial, a euphonium player. Both were said to be operated by mechanisms in the figures and were supplied with wind from separate bellows placed upon the stage. However, Vere claimed that their instruments were connected by hidden tubes to mouthpieces that were played by real musicians under the stage.

Finally, we come to what might be the last word in a game-playing automaton. Maskelyne's Dyno, which played dominoes with a spectator, was nothing more than an artificial hand in a glass case. Explanations of a mechanical nature have been advanced to account for Dyno, but it seems that the trick can be better explained as a variation of the ghost principle of Pepper. In other words, the spectators saw only the reflection of a real human hand whose owner was hidden from view.

2.

At the close of the Paris Exhibition, Ajeeb returned to London and was again exhibited at the Westminster Aquarium, beginning in March 1879, just a few weeks after Mephisto had been moved from the Aquarium to his new rooms on the Strand. It is likely that the Ajeeb shown at the Aquarium at that time was the same that had been at the Crystal Palace.

Ajeeb remained at the Aquarium until November 1880, at which time arrangements were made to exhibit him, or perhaps the other Ajeeb, at the newly opened Castan's Panopticum in Brussels. The Brussels Panopticum, located in the place de la Monnaie, was operated by Maurice Castan, a relative of the proprietor of the Berlin Panopticum. Both buildings housed collections of life-size, costumed wax figures representing noted personages and historical events. Ajeeb remained in Brussels about three and a half years, attracting great interest and curiosity and playing, in addition to chess, the Continental game known as "dame," "*jeu des dames*," or the ladies' game.

The ladies' game was similar to the English game of checkers or draughts, but was at that time played upon a larger board of one hundred squares with twenty pieces on each side. It was then fashionable to consider checkers a form of chess for ladies, and thus it was condescendingly referred to as the ladies'

game, a name which still persists in the names for checkers in various countries, such as *jeu des dames* in France, *Damenspiel* in Germany, *il giuoco delle dame* in Italy, *o jago das damas* in Portugal, and *Daama* in Iran and Turkey.

In 1882, while Ajeeb was being exhibited at the Panopticum in Brussels, As-Rah (or Az Rah), a new chess automaton, appeared at Bordeaux where he drew large crowds at an industrial exposition. The name As-Rah seems to have been derived from the Asrah device used by magicians to counterfeit the shape of an object that is made to vanish. The Asrah, for instance, may be a piece of cardboard shaped like a coin and held under a handkerchief to disguise the fact that the real coin has already been placed elsewhere.

Probably inspired by Ajeeb, the automaton As-Rah sat cross-legged upon a small cabinet, a chessboard on his lap. He was, however, forced to retire from the Exhibition Theatre when the Bordeaux police discovered that he was directed by an eighteen-year-old youth, whose health was being

As-Rah's career was cut short by the Bordeaux police.
BY PERMISSION OF BL.

seriously endangered by long confinements within the mechanism.

When a new exhibition of wax figures, the Musée Grévin, opened in Paris at 10 Boulevard Montmartre in 1882, the museum's directors arranged with Hooper to bring Ajeeb back to Paris as one of the new building's attractions. That Ajeeb, which was first exhibited at the Musée Grévin on May 1, 1884, by a woman with a strong English accent, was almost certainly the Ajeeb originally exhibited at Brighton. It seems likely, in fact, that the Brighton Ajeeb was the one usually exhibited on the Continent, perhaps because he traveled better than the Crystal Palace Ajeeb. Hooper, who always tried to conceal the fact that there were two Ajeebs, probably owned both automatons at that time.

According to Hooper's account, the engagement at the Musée Grévin, which lasted about a year, was a great success.

The reception room was crowded daily [he reported], players at chess and *dame* having to wait for hours in their turn for a chance of playing a game with Ajeeb, so anxious were they not to leave without having the gratification of telling their friends that they had played with the automaton. Often on Sundays and *fête* days hun-

The Musée Grevin, 10 boulevard Monmarte, Paris, is as popular today as it was in Ajeeb's time. FROM AC.

Rosenthal directed the Cercle des Échecs, where he often engaged wealthy gentlemen in simultaneous exhibitions. COURTESY OF JGW.

dreds of visitors were unable to get even a view of Ajeeb, and had to leave the Musée very disappointed at not being able to gratify their excited curiosity at the time of their visit, but determined to do so on the first favorable opportunity.

Rosenthal again visited Ajeeb in Paris and witnessed the automaton's execution of the Knight's Tour. Rosenthal had feuded with his old companions at the Café de la Régence but spent his time profitably directing a private chess club for wealthy gentlemen. Although not considered one of the chess giants of the era, he was formidable at times. In the London Tournament the previous year, he had been awarded a special brilliancy prize for his game with Steinitz and had scored two wins and two draws in his four games against the world champion.

Ajeeb continued to perform at the Musée Grévin until June 1885. The museum's directors were anxious that the automaton should remain another year, but Hooper had already decided that Ajeeb was to visit the United States. He thus dismantled the automaton, packed the apparatus securely in cases, and boarded the Cunard steamer *Etruria* at Liverpool on Saturday, July 18, 1885. As Maelzel had done sixty years earlier, he would seek new audiences for his chess automaton in America. Although he carefully concealed the fact, it seems

quite likely that his cases contained not one but two Ajeebs.

3.

Accompanied by his wife, Hooper arrived in New York on July 25, 1885, and a week later the Ajeeb that had formerly been known as the Crystal Palace Automaton opened at the Eden Musée, 55 West Twenty-third Street. Ajeeb was exhibited at the Musée almost continuously for the next thirty years, and his name became closely associated with that establishment.

The other Ajeeb, the one that had first appeared at Brighton, was exhibited in a booth near the pier on the boardwalk at Atlantic City. Hooper, who remained with the Ajeeb at the Eden Musée, apparently did not exhibit the Brighton Ajeeb in America but rather hired someone else as the exhibitor or perhaps sold the automaton.

Later in 1885 the Brighton Ajeeb was moved from the boardwalk to Hartmann's Hotel, across Atlantic Garden, where he was exhibited every afternoon from two to five and in the evening from seven to eleven. Judging from the language in a program of the exhibition, the exhibitor must have been a foreigner who was not perfectly acquainted with English. "No human being is existing," he

The Ajeeb that had been at Brighton was exhibited in a booth on the boardwalk at Atlantic City in 1885. FROM HM.

AJEEB

the wonderful   automatic

Chess Player.

AJEEB is a figure in oriental dress, which sitting on a case plays chess or draught with his visitors, if they desire so, and wins the game in the most cases.

AJEEB is an original invention. He stays upright on the floor surrounded by the spectators and plays game after game as often as desired.

AJEEB is no optic Illusion. No human being is existing, who could put in motion the apparatus inside of the Automate. After each game the construction of the figure as well as of the case will be shown to the spectators.

AJEEB is a mystery of the science. Thousends of scientific men already have troubled themselves to sound it, but could not. So it will always be a problem Which is the moving power and how is it possible?

AJEEB has won over five thousand games with players of all nations and all joined in saying it is the most wonderful and amusing entertainment of our days.

AJEEB is exhibited every day in the afternoon from 2 to 5 o'clock and in the evening from 7 to 11 o'clock in

Hartmanns Hotel, first floor, across Atlantic Garden.

ADMISSION 25 CENTS.

Everybody is allowed to play one game of chess or draught with Ajeeb.

Jacob Buethe, Printer, 170 Forsyth Street, N. Y.

Later, Ajeeb could be visited at Hartmann's Hotel.
COURTESY OF JGW.

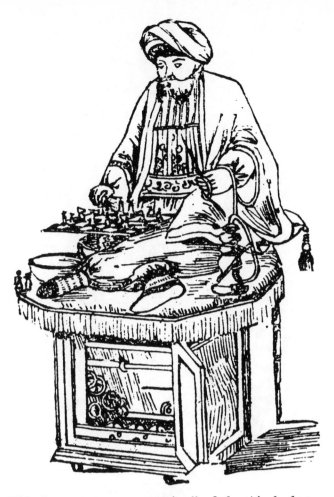

This "accurate representation" of the Ajeeb that appeared in Milwaukee was probably copied from the engraving in *The Adventures of Ajeeb*. COURTESY OF JGW.

proclaimed, "who could put in motion the apparatus inside of the automate. Ajeeb is a mystery of the science." An admission of twenty-five cents allowed each customer to play a game of either chess or checkers with Ajeeb at Hartmann's.

In the spring of 1887, a new Ajeeb made his appearance in Chicago. Evidently constructed in that city, the new automaton was said to be an accurate representation of the original Crystal Palace Automaton, then being shown at the Eden Musée, New York.

The new Ajeeb was exhibited in Chicago during that summer, but his first real showing was at the Milwaukee Exposition in September and October. His performances there aroused intense interest, not only among chess enthusiasts, but among thousands drawn by the mystery of the mechanism. In fact, it was later claimed that the automaton saved the Exposition from a deficit.

Ajeeb was undefeated at chess and his presence at the Exposition was hailed as "the chess sensation of the West." A local paper reported, "None of the boys make any headway with Ajeeb. They are wholly unable to 'solve his delivery.' May, Garner, and other prominent chessists have faced him, and have

struck out every time." At checkers, however, Ajeeb was more vulnerable, sustaining a number of defeats from the Milwaukee players, although his play was said to be clever and rapid.

Among the Milwaukee chess players it soon became an "open secret" that Ajeeb's director was Charles F. Moehle, once described as "one of the most brilliant chess players of America." Moehle was indeed in Milwaukee at the time of the Exposition. He occasionally emerged from his shell to play exhibition games for the local players. As usual, the question was, "How did he direct the automaton?" It somehow became known to some of the local players that certain corners of the chessboard were beyond the director's range of vision. Thus they thought Moehle had to play Ajeeb's games blindfolded. Moehle himself did, in fact, play blindfold exhibitions. Anyone really wishing to completely penetrate the mystery could have done so for a mere $2,500, which was then the asking price for Ajeeb—mystery, figure, and all.

Since no one came forward with the required purchase price, Ajeeb continued to mystify the Milwaukee citizenry until late in October. At that time Ajeeb was embarassed by an accident that occurred during a game with one of Milwaukee's leading clergymen. A local paper reported, "Whether it was the clerical atmosphere, or some other loosening influence which permeated the joints of the machine at that particular time, history

Charles Moehle, a strong American player, directed Ajeeb throughout the Midwest in the 1880s. COURTESY OF JGW.

191

does not recount, but it is said that suddenly and without warning the automaton collapsed and fell apart, disclosing the whole business." Only a few spectators were present to witness the startling revelation, but nevertheless, at the end of that week Ajeeb "silently folded his checkerboard and stole away—to Minneapolis."

Apparently, Ajeeb was successfully put back together, and during November he continued to draw crowds in Minneapolis and St. Paul. Just before leaving that area, Moehle, as himself, gave two simultaneous exhibitions in St. Paul, losing only two games out of twenty-one.

In December, Ajeeb was reported in Toledo and Detroit. It was rumored that the automaton would soon visit Indianapolis, Cincinnati, St. Louis, and New Orleans. By late January 1888, however, Moehle had made "a mysterious reappearance on the streets of Chicago." Ajeeb had suspended his operations to await the end of the blizzard season.

By March things had unfrozen enough so that Moehle was able to visit St. Paul and Minneapolis again. At that time he announced his willingness to back Ajeeb in a chess match against Max Judd, a strong St. Louis player who eventually became U. S. Chess Champion. There is no evidence that the match took place, however.

Ajeeb next made a big public appearance at the Cincinnati Centennial Exposition, first appearing there on Monday, July 16, 1888. At Park Hall on the exposition grounds an elevator carried spectators to the second floor, where Ajeeb was displayed from two to five and from seven to ten. "The silent Turk," reported a visitor, "is surrounded every moment of this time by a curious crowd." There was no extra charge to see or play with the automaton.

As usual, many of the spectators were drawn to the exhibit even though they knew nothing of the game of chess. A bystander tapped one of Ajeeb's opponents on the shoulder and asked what game he was playing. "Chess," was the reply. "Well," said the spectator, "I've been watching you play for half an hour, and I'll be hanged if I understand the game yet."

Ajeeb's manager at that time was a Mr. McNeill, who, it seems, was one of the brashest showmen ever to exhibit an automaton. He was stockily built, weighed about 175 pounds, and had dark eyes and hair. In contrast, Moehle was fair-haired, blue-eyed, and decidedly slight in stature.

Just before the Exposition, one of the German newspapers learned that Moehle was directing the automaton and published a history of Ajeeb, stating that Moehle was inside and did the playing. One day a smart aleck in the audience came up to McNeill and said in a loud voice, "There's a man inside! You can't fool me. His name is Moehle. The *Volksblatt* has given the whole thing away."

Without pausing or seeming the least bit ruffled,

Will Lyons said, "Charley, you have grown a heap since I saw you last, and changed your complexion." COURTESY OF JGW.

McNeill replied, "Sir, my name is Moehle, and as you can see, I am not inside. Any of these gentlemen can readily swear that I could not get inside. I leave it to them."

Fortunately for McNeill, several bystanders who knew better testified that McNeill was Moehle, and the puzzled heckler faded away. After a short pause, Will Lyons, a Newport, Kentucky, dealer in chess supplies, could not resist slipping up to McNeill and quietly saying, "Charley, you've grown a heap since I saw you last, and changed your complexion."

McNeill did not know Lyons, "but very quietly gave a pressing invitation to take a trip to a locality where asbestos credentials are the only ones that have lasting qualities."

Moehle, it appears, was somewhat careless about concealing his role as the director of Ajeeb. One day at the Cincinnati Exposition, a constable called on McNeill to serve a legal notice. Moehle, who was inside the automaton at the time, became so interested in the proceedings that he "popped outside." He was wearing, it was reported, "a decidedly summer costume."

Among Ajeeb's opponents at the Exposition were

AJEEB

THE GREAT AUTOMATIC
CHESS & CHECKER PLAYER

Which created such a great sensation during the Centennial Exposition, will be on exhibition from

2 to 5 o'clock every Afternoon and 7 to 10 every Evening,

For a short time, at

370 ELM ST.

NO ONE SHOULD FAIL TO SEE

The Greatest Wonder of the 19th Century

DON'T FORGET THE PLACE,

370 ELM ST., NEAR TWELFTH

ADMISSION, 25 CENTS

Children Under Fifteen Years of Age, 10 Cents.

Enquirer Job Print, Cincinnati.

The Ajeeb in this 1888 Cincinnati ad was actually an imitation of an imitation of the Crystal Palace Ajeeb. COURTESY OF JGW.

In Chicago, Charles Hefter pronounced Ajeeb "a very sorry checkerist." COURTESY OF JGW.

two very strong players who would eventually become chess champions of the United States. Jackson W. Showalter won his game, and Albert B. Hodges played the automaton to a draw. We will hear more of these two, especially Hodges, in the next chapter.

In all, Ajeeb lost only four games in Cincinnati, with five draws. The wins, of course, were too numerous to count. At checkers he lost somewhat more often, but still won a large majority of games.

After about a month at the Cincinnati Exposition, the exhibitions of Ajeeb ceased as the result of some legal entanglements, and the automaton was moved back to Chicago. During September another new Ajeeb was constructed in Cincinnati by Dowd, a Chicagoan, and Martins, a Cincinnati mechanician and member of the Queen City Chess Club. The new Ajeeb was then exhibited at 370 Elm Street, near Twelfth, the home of Professor Bacharach. It had been hoped that Moehle would direct the new Ajeeb, but Bacharach had to settle for a Cincinnati player, J. Daniels. Although Daniels had drawn a game with Ajeeb at the Exposition, he was apparently not much stronger than the average club player. Thus there was little interest shown in the new automaton. Bacharach, who conducted classes in chess, was a stronger player than Daniels, but he was far too large to get into the machine. Even Bacharach had been easily defeated by the Moehle-directed Ajeeb at the Cincinnati Exposition. In December it was reported that the new Ajeeb constructed in Cincinnati was being exhibited in Boston.

In Chicago, Moehle continued to direct the automaton's play, but Phillip Shaffner replaced McNeill as Ajeeb's manager. One day Ajeeb was visited by some of the Chicago chess experts, accompanied by Charles Hefter, a strong checker player and editor of *The American Checker Review.* When the chess players proved no match for Ajeeb, Shaffner consented to allow Hefter to try a game of checkers with the automaton. "Ajeeb proved himself a very sorry checkerist," Hefter reported later, "and after showing our chess friends the *convincing proof* of the superiority of checkers over chess—which could be most successfully played by machine, while its modest sister required human brain—we departed. A number of subsequent visits failed to show any improvement in Ajeeb's abilities."

After a short stay in Chicago, Ajeeb was taken to the Kansas City Exposition which opened on Monday, September 10, 1888, inaugurating a month and a half of spectacular fall festivities. "This is the time of year," asserted the *Kansas City Times,* "when to live outside of Kansas City is equivalent to being banished to Siberia." Many of those who had been thus banished, however, soon rectified the error by flocking into the city.

The Exposition began at eight in the evening of the opening day with a fireman's parade to the Exposition Hall.

At the Kansas City Exposition, Ajeeb shared the billing with Signor Liberati and the Performing Dogs. COURTESY OF KCPL.

There was [reported the *Times*] a flourish of trumpets, the clanking of sabres, the rattle of machinery, the measured tread of marching, and the parade was in progress. The start was made amid considerable cheering, those who watched it . . . being quick to recognize the procession's more meritorious features.

All along the line of march, . . . the streets were a dense mass of people. This was especially the case on Main Street, where the detachment of mounted police who preceded the parade had great difficulty in forcing a passageway.

The Kansas City Light Cavalry led the parade, followed by military bands and units of infantry and artillery. Then came the Kansas City firemen, who "marched well and were continuously cheered." Their chief, accompanied by his daughter, followed in a gaily decorated carriage surrounded by aides on horseback.

The hose carts and engines, which were next in line, were elaborately decorated, most of them having been transformed into floats. Hose reel No. 3, for instance, represented Liberty enlightening the world. "The goddess was personified by Miss Minnie Fitzpatrick, and the red torch which she held aloft gave to the scene presented a most impressive effect." Other carts, decked in a profusion of flowers and bunting, represented firemen at work on a blazing house, a fiery dragon, and a flowery liberty bell.

Next came groups of Kansas City veteran firemen and visiting firemen from cities in the surrounding

This model of Ajeeb, probably a copy of the Crystal Palace Ajeeb, was exhibited by a man named Mann. COURTESY OF KCPL.

area. Each group of visitors was costumed in colorful distinctive uniforms.

In preparation for the approaching marchers, the exposition building had been flooded with electric lights.

The effect from a distance was superb [the *Times* went on],the snowy roof on the mammoth structure standing out in bold relief against the dark blue sky. Within, the scene was marvelous. Every pillar, every arch, every doorway was handsomely decorated and the brilliant light brought out the coloring most vividly. The scene from the south end of the great auditorium was extremely rich. The monster painting of the surrender of Lee at Appomattox occupied the far end of the hall and formed a magnificent perspective, the gaily decorated galleries and the double row of lights adding immeasurably to the effect. Everywhere there was color, and the people who moved through the various departments expressed their pleasure in various ways.

Long before the monster procession reached the building hundreds of people had passed the doorkeepers and began inspecting the displays contained in the various rooms. From 8 until 10 o'clock the arrivals were continuous. Then came a burst of music from outside, and the head of the procession entered the hall. During the next fifteen minutes a stream of humanity passed through the doors and occupied seats in the auditorium. When Liberati and his musicians mounted to their places fully 3,000 people faced them and bestowed a shower of applause. To pacify those who had waited patiently for the programme to begin, Signor Liberati raised his baton and the band broke forth into a soul-stirring march which resounded throughout the building.

Ajeeb was exhibited on an upper floor of the exposition building by John C. Mann, a new manager who had apparently replaced Shaffner, the exhibitor in Chicago. Nevertheless, Mann claimed to have brought Ajeeb from Europe, to have exhibited the automaton for two years at the Eden Musée, and to have shown him at the Cincinnati Centennial. Although Mann was thought to be a Chicagoan, Hefter, who was well acquainted with all the Chicago checker players, did not know him and suggested that Mann might have been an assumed name. Is it possible that McNeil, Shaffner, and Mann were all the same person? Ajeeb seemed to differ from the original at the Eden Musée in several details, most notably by wearing a veil over the lower part of his face, covering his beard, or perhaps concealing the fact that the beard was absent. It seems likely, however, that he was the same automaton exhibited at the Cincinnati Centennial.

In Kansas City Ajeeb was billed as Ajeeb, the Chess Wonder, but he played only checkers, a strange circumstance in view of the automaton's

humiliation at checkers by Hefter in Chicago. Ajeeb now played a very strong game of checkers, meeting all adversaries for two weeks before losing a single game.

In order to draw attention to the automaton, a man dressed in Turkish attire was sent around the exposition building carrying Ajeeb's advertisement on his back. The automaton was visited by as many as eight hundred spectators a day, many of whom were confident they could beat him. They crowded into his small quarters and demanded many games, but Ajeeb was always the victor.

Finally, A. L. Baird of Kansas City caused a great sensation by defeating the famous automaton. At the close of that game, Mann claimed that Ajeeb had played 225,000 games of chess and checkers in

A man in Turkish attire walked around the Exposition Building with an Ajeeb sign, to which some wag added the sign "Ice Cream Inside." COURTESY OF KCPL.

Europe and America but had suffered only twelve losses. At the Cincinnati Centennial, continued Mann, the automaton had been defeated only once. Actually Ajeeb lost four games in Cincinnati.

"The history of Ajeeb reads like a romance," declared the *Kansas City Times*. Mann was indeed prone to romanticizing. He asserted, for example, that Ajeeb had been "manufactured in Persia" and that the automaton had defeated the Czar in three games of chess at St. Petersburg.

Despite the defeat by Baird, it was quite clear that Ajeeb was directed by a very strong checker player. That fact was made even more evident when the automaton won two games from Frank A. Fitzpatrick, then recognized as the seventh best checker player in the world. The very next day, however, a novice player named White subjected the automaton to his "thirteenth" defeat. White, a contractor, had previously lost two games to Ajeeb. When, in the third, he realized that he had beaten the automaton, he was so astonished that he turned and left the room without exchanging a word with anyone.

Each day at the exposition brought some new feature in addition to the regular attractions. There were baby shows, dog shows, firefighting competitions, and mock presidential elections. There was a German Day, a Scotch Day, an Irish Day, a Babies' Day, a Children's Day, a Young Ladies' Day, and a Candidates' Day. Each afternoon and evening there was a concert by a military band or a string orchestra. As a special feature one day, Ajeeb played a costumed game of checkers on a large board painted on the main floor. Twelve little girls and twelve little boys were the checker pieces.

Since Ajeeb had been playing nothing but checkers, some persons began commenting about his inability to play chess. Finally, Mann announced one evening that, commencing the following night, the last game of each evening would be chess, but there seems to be no evidence that any chess games were actually played as promised.

Ajeeb had been exhibited for about a month at the exposition when the *Kansas City Times* of Sunday, October fourteenth, printed a piece entitled "Ajeeb Not a Machine." The story, by a reporter identified as H. M. S., presented some interesting local theories about Ajeeb:

Having a few leisure moments on an afternoon in the early part of last week, I dropped in on Ajeeb at the exposition, and while playing a game of checkers with him was surprised to hear many and different theories advanced as to the workings of this mysterious attraction. Some were as absurd as they were amusing, and though a few of the better players and one or two of the sound thinking expressed their opinion that there must be a man within, still the majority, and a large one at that, believed it to be a self-working machine, and each had his or her view to express as to how the checkers were manipulated. The electrical theory is the general one, the argument being that each man on the board is coated on the under side with a metal that forms a connection and current when moved from square to square, each move being answered by the machine which is wound up for every player. Others present a far more intricate supposition also based on electricity. It is that the player is not necessarily in the city, but may be hundreds of miles away, where he sits with the board before him and replies to each and every move which is brought to him over the wires with as much ease and precision as if the player was before him. One of the most amusing of explanations for the workings of this machine was given by a lady who had spent the greater portion of the afternoon watching different players taking their turns with Ajeeb. She kept her eyes constantly riveted on Mr. Mann, the manager, who sits near the figure during the progress of a game, and at the close of each [she] looked around in a self-satisfied kind of way that indicated her thorough knowledge of what was a deep mystery to the majority of others in the room. When questioned as to her idea of the playing she answered that she believed, yes, she knew, that the man sitting close to the figure was alone responsible for the losing or gaining of the game, and that his mind had entire control over what moved or caused to move the checker men, whose master was such an enigma to many. Prof. Carpenter or Stevens, the mesmerists, should look into this, for

An article in the *Kansas City Times* was accompanied by a drawing like this to show where Ajeeb's director was thought to be hidden. COURTESY OF KCPL.

if Ajeeb's manager has so powerful and controlling a mind as set forth by this theory, he would be indispensable as an attraction for a museum and coin more money than his curious figure. Others suggested that the most feasible solution was by clockwork alone, and that the many wheels displayed when the doors of the machine were opened plainly showed how the game was played. Scores of speculatists have visited the curiosity to determine whether there was or was not a human hand in some way connected with it, and each one had a different idea as to its motive power; but to those who understand the game as well as Fitzpatrick, Greenwood, and Green, there has never been a doubt as to the existence of a man within, but just how he can stand it boxed up for so long a time and in, as they think, so cramped a position is somewhat of a mystery to even them.

H. M. S. himself was of the opinion there was a man inside. "It's simple enough," he explained. "His feet could be either above or below the clockwork (one foot on either side of the same) in the lower cabinet, while his head and shoulders rested easily within what appeared to be a cushion just back of the figure, then during the noise made by the winding of a ratchet wheel supposed to connect with and start the interior machinery, the man in the case as quietly as possible slips into position for playing, his right arm in the sleeve of the figure's." His explanation, it is now known, was essentially correct.

William Rees, a checker enthusiast from Emporia, Kansas, had heard that Ajeeb was in Kansas City and, in a letter, asked Hefter for his opinion of the automaton. Judging from his own experience in Chicago, Hefter unhesitatingly pronounced Ajeeb "a *scrub* checker player." Rees, however, hearing that Ajeeb was scheduled to play a match with Fitzpatrick, decided to go to Kansas City and see for himself.

After returning to Emporia, Rees wrote his friend Hefter on October eighteenth, saying,

I have tackled the wonderful Ajeeb and will say that in my opinion you were never more mistaken in your life when you called him a scrub player. He puts up the finest game I have ever witnessed across the board—his endings being especially brilliant. I have played him six games, losing the first three and drawing the last three; I will also say that the draws were about the hardest games I ever played in my life. Of course you know that any one playing it is handicapped by having to stand up; also the checkers look like chess queens; also he *always moves first,* and has the White men each game. I don't think I could win a game in a month, and would have to play fine for draws. I do not wonder much at losing the first three, not being accustomed to the conditions, and they were in reality easier games than those I have drawn, but he plays harder each game, and takes a fearful long time to move. Let me hear from you if

you are acquainted with the name and history of the occupant, as I believe he is one of the world's greatest. He has beaten Fitzpatrick two games and drawn four.

A few days later Rees again wrote Hefter, reporting,

I am anxious to know something about the man in this machine, as I think he is very fine. I think I saw him on the street and he looks like an Englishman, has a full face, rather red, also reddish mustache, and weighs probably 150 pounds; he is below medium height. I am told that Fitzpatrick claims it is an English player named Terrell.

Hefter knew of no English player named Terrell

American Checker Champion Charles Francis Barker directed Ajeeb in Kansas City. COURTESY OF JGW.

but recognized the man that Rees had described. The "Englishman" was in fact a Bostonian named Charles Francis Barker and was the champion checker player of America and Great Britain. For the Kansas City engagement of Ajeeb, Barker had replaced Moehle, while the latter played in the Cincinnati Chess Tournament, in which he shared first prize with Major Hausman of New York.

Soon after leaving Kansas City, Barker, accompanied by his brother Isaiah, went to England, where he defeated the English champion James Smith. He had hoped to remain in Great Britain to play matches with some of the other English and Scottish players, but the negotiations were going so slowly that the Barkers could not afford to maintain themselves abroad and had to return to America before the matches were arranged.

Barker wanted to play a match for the world checker championship with the famous James Wyllie, known as Herd Laddie, but Wyllie was in the Antipodes at the time of Barker's visit to England. When Barker was fifteen he had met World Champion Wyllie in a match in which the youth won three games, lost ten, and drew twelve. Then in October 1882, at the age of twenty-four, Barker played Wyllie for the world championship. The match was

When Barker drew a match with World Champion James Wyllie, pictured here, many persons thought he had a legitimate claim to the title, but Wyllie never allowed a rematch. COURTESY OF JGW.

closely contested but finally resulted in each player winning one game with forty-eight games drawn. In 1885 Barker lost the American championship by a score of 6-3 to Clarence H. Freeman, a Pequod Indian from Rhode Island and the only person ever to defeat Barker in a match. Barker, however, regained the title the following year from A. J. Heffner, who then held it.

For many years after the Kansas City Exposition, Barker directed Ajeeb at Austin and Stone's Museum, Tremont Row, Boston. He also held a position as advertising manager of Star Mills Company of Cambridge, Massachusetts. During that same period he again visited Great Britain, defeating Robert Martins, ex-champion of the world. Then, until his death on July 5, 1909, Barker continued to operate Ajeeb in Boston. He was "in the harness," reported a checkers publication, right up to the last few days before his rather sudden death at the age of fifty-one. In fact, it seems likely that Barker might have owned Ajeeb at that time. Isaiah Barker, himself a capable checker player, continued to manipulate Ajeeb and it was said that he worthily upheld the reputation of the "Barker Boys of Boston."

Evidently the Ajeeb directed by the Barkers in Boston was the same one constructed in Cincinnati in 1888, just after the Cincinnati Exposition. In Kansas City, however, Barker had directed the Ajeeb usually directed by Moehle. In November 1888 Moehle left Cincinnati and went back to Chicago to join the Ajeeb that had just returned from Kansas City. At that time Ajeeb was installed as one of the attractions at the Eden Musée in Chicago. Moehle and Mann then took Ajeeb to Augusta, Georgia, where, on December 21, 1888, the automaton assisted in an exhibition of living chess. On January fifth, Ajeeb was reported to be in Atlanta and was planning to go next to St. Augustine, Florida. During 1889, Ajeeb was in Kansas City again in March and at Portland, Oregon in October. It was also reported that a "new Ajeeb" would be featured at the Piedmont Exposition in Atlanta during October 1889. By 1890 Moehle and his Ajeeb had settled down for a stay at the Eden Musée, Chicago.

4.

During the time Ajeeb was exhibited as a checker player in Boston, there appeared several other automaton checker players, including Ali, Akimo, and Mazam. Beginning in 1899, Mazam the Marvel, also called the Egyptian Marvel, was exhibited in London by George Benson, the brother of a noted expert checkerist. At the exhibition hall, located at 61 Regent Street, W., the center of London's fashionable quarter, a black gentleman in red turban

Vol. V.   AUGUST, 1893.   No. ...

AMERICAN
CHECKER REVIEW.

DEVOTED TO THE INTEREST OF THE GAME OF DRAUGHTS.

JAMES WYLLIE   CHAS. F. BARKER.

ISSUED MONTHLY
CHICAGO.
→ PRICE 15 CENTS ←
$1.50 A YEAR.

American Checker Review featured Barker along with Wyllie on the cover. COURTESY OF JGW.

"Fold up the board; lay by the men;
One player needs them not again.
The match is o'er, Grim Death has won,
And Dameh mourns her brilliant son."
        —New York *Tribune* on the death
        of Charles F. Barker.
    COURTESY OF JGW.

This group of prominent checker players included Isaiah Barker, rear, second from left, a noted composer of checker problems who directed Ajeeb after his brother's death in 1909. A third brother, William R. Barker, front, second from left, was also a celebrated checker player. Dr. August Schaefer, rear, far right, directed Ajeeb at the Eden Musée, New York. COURTESY OF JGW.

announced, "Show now on; no waiting." After paying half a shilling each, the spectators were ushered into the presence of Mazam. One visitor, who had seen Ajeeb in Boston, said that Mazam was superior. Mazam was visited by "the very pick of the London experts," but lost only ten games of checkers out of about three thousand played in less than a month. Benson claimed that the automaton would beat any player in London.

Professor Hermann, who was said to be the inventor of Mazam, was supposed to have stated that his automaton was really worked by mechanism and that the machine was capable of "no fewer than 64,000 different moves in combination." Most of the better checker players did not believe that claim, but their curiosity was greatly aroused as to who was directing the automaton. Some of them supposed that Charles Barker had come to England to operate

Harry Jacob, runner-up for the English checker championship, directed Mazam, the Marvel, in London. Jacob was deaf as the result of a fall at the age of six. COURTESY OF JGW.

Mazam, while others suspected it was James P. Reed, another strong American checker player, who had not been heard of for some time. The English checker players were apparently unaware that Ajeeb had originated in England as a chess player, and thus it was thought that the idea of an automaton player was an American novelty and that an American must have been imported as the concealed director. Actually, the brains of Mazam was an English player named Harry Jacob.

One interesting theory about Mazam was advanced by W. S. Branch, who thought it barely possible that Mazam was actually the rechristened and refurbished figure of Mephisto. However, Branch offered no details to further support that idea.

In November 1899 Mazam was exhibited in Manchester, the first stop on a proposed tour of England and Scotland. The success of the tour, however, did not measure up to the expectations of the promoters, and by December Mazam was back in London, where arrangements were made for the automaton to hold receptions at the Sultan's Café, 136 Cheapside, London, E.C. The Sultan's was the headquarters of the Wonderers, a London checkers club. Jacob died October 18, 1905, after an illness of over three years, and thus W. D. Witt of Philadelphia thought that Mazam "probably went out of commission about 1902."

12
Did Ajeeb Kill Pillsbury?

1.

At New York's Eden Musée on August 1, 1885, the Ajeeb who had formerly been known as the Crystal Palace Automaton opened an engagement that would last about thirty years. During that period out-of-towners coming to see the sights of New York felt as much obligated to visit the Musée at 55 West Twenty-third Street as they did to see the Statue of Liberty, which was unveiled two years after the Eden opened. "All out for the Muse-*ee!*" cried the horsecar conductors, resolutely ignoring the acute accent over the first *e*. Visitors who got out there, in the middle of the block between Fifth and Sixth Avenues, were confronted with three stories of gilded columns, arches, and statuary which might have been patterned after those of the Paris Opera.

The Eden, an American cousin of the Musée Grévin in Paris and Madame Tussaud's in London, had first opened its doors on March 29, 1884, and was thus a comparatively new building when Ajeeb arrived a little over a year later. Like its European counterparts, the Musée exhibited "the wonders of the world in wax," some sixty tableaux ranging from "The Life of Our Saviour" to "The Rulers of the World" to "The Chamber of Horrors." The latter was a downstairs section too grisly for the younger children but favored by amorous couples, who liked to hold hands among scenes depicting the tortures of the Spanish Inquisition and the annihilation of early Christian martyrs.

Hoping to diversify the attractions, the Musée's president, Richard G. Hollaman, had imported Paul

The Eden Musée, 55 West Thirty-third Street, New York, was Ajeeb's home for thirty years. COURTESY OF NYPL.

Olah's Hungarian band for the daily promenade concerts. He also cabled an attractive offer to Hooper, who was then exhibiting Ajeeb at the Musée Grévin.

When Ajeeb arrived at the Eden, which at that

202

Wax figures at the entrance to the Eden Musée portrayed a visiting couple intent upon a pickpocket warning, the truth of which could hardly be doubted. COURTESY OF NYPL.

EDEN MUSEE, 23d-st., between 5th and 6th-ave.
Open from 11 to 11. Sundays from 1 to 11.
The sensation of the day,
THE LIFE OF OUR SAVIOUR
in six wonderful tableaux.
OUR DEAD HERO, GEN. GRANT.
New Wax Groups and Stereoscopes.
GRAND SACRED CONCERTS.
Admission, 25c.
First appearance in America of
"AJEEB,"
the great European chess automaton, who defeats
and bewildered the entire European chess world.
SPECIAL ADMISSION, 25 CENTS.

A *New York Times* ad of August 2, 1885 announced Ajeeb's first appearance in America. FROM AC.

time happened to be featuring a display honoring the recently deceased General U. S. Grant, he was installed in a small second-story room facing a balcony. Hooper hired a barker to direct patrons up the stairway to Ajeeb's reception room, where Mrs. Hooper acted as the automaton's exhibitor. Hooper himself directed Ajeeb's play, since the younger Hooper had by then grown too large to fit inside the automaton and apparently did not operate the automaton in America.

Simon Lipschuetz headed a delegation of visitors from the New York Chess Club. COURTESY OF JGW.

An Eden Musée advertisement in the *New York Times* announced the "First appearance in America of Ajeeb, the great European chess automaton, who defeated and bewildered the entire European chess world." A number of players from the New York Chess Club, then quartered at 49 Bowery, evidently regarded the ad as a challenge and visited Ajeeb in a body that same week. Some of the club members lost their games, but others succeeded in defeating the automaton, and Simon Lipschuetz, the club champion, won both of his games.

Despite those losses on the chessboard, Ajeeb soon became a financial success. To help publicize the automaton, Hooper had published a twenty-four page pamphlet, *The Adventures of Ajeeb*, telling of Ajeeb's career—Hooper's version of it, at least—up to his debut at the Eden Musée. Visitors paid a special admission of twenty-five cents just to view Ajeeb, with an additional fee of ten cents to play checkers or twenty-five cents to play chess. Hollaman charged one hundred dollars a week for the use of the second-floor exhibition room and the barker's salary had to be paid, but after deducting those expenses, the Hoopers were left with about a thousand dollars a month profit.

E. L. Torsch, president of a Baltimore badge company, recalled that, while on his honeymoon in New York in 1885, he played Ajeeb at the Eden Musée. He inspected the wiring in the cabinet and waited while Mrs. Hooper wound up the figure and set it going. Torsch then began playing with great care and without the least bit of haste.

"Hurry up, hurry up," Mrs. Hooper implored

THE ADVENTURES

OF

AJEEB

THE WONDERFUL

CHESS AUTOMATON.

Hooper published his own version of *The Adventures of Ajeeb*. COURTESY OF JGW.

Visitors to the Eden Musée could purchase postcards bearing a likeness of Ajeeb. COURTESY OF JGW.

Seeking a director for Ajeeb, Hooper wrote to U. S. Champion Max Judd. COURTESY OF JGW.

him, "if you keep the automaton waiting that long with your moves, he will have gray hair in a very short while."

Torsch noted that the lady's own hair was turning the color of which she spoke and thought perhaps she made the remark through sympathy. He was naturally disconcerted, then annoyed, and finally lost the game through poor play. However, he saved the color of Ajeeb's hair.

By 1889 Hooper had grown weary of life inside Ajeeb and decided to hire a director for the automaton. He had to proceed with caution, however, so as not to give away any secrets. Thus he discreetly wrote to U. S. Chess Champion Max Judd of Saint Louis, whom he knew he could trust, and offered a position to an expert chess and checker player at a salary greater than a chess professional could reasonably hope to achieve in those days. Judd passed the letter on to his friend and chess companion Albert Beauregard Hodges, who for the past two years had held a low-paying job in Saint Louis as a government clerk. Hodges, then twenty-nine years of age, told Judd to write Hooper that he would be

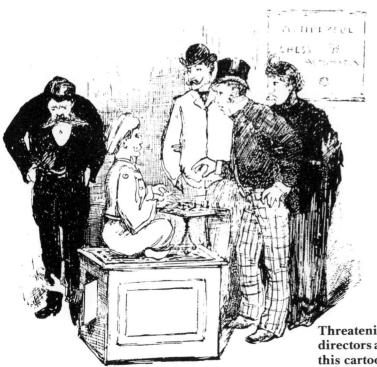

Threatening Hooper with exposure, one of Ajeeb's directors at the Eden demanded an immediate reward in this cartoon of 1886. COURTESY OF JGW.

Judd recommended his friend Albert Beauregard Hodges. COURTESY OF JGW.

Zukertort's head was a hatmaker's nightmare, a phrenologist's dream, and a perfect delight for the cartoonist. COURTESY OF JGW.

glad to accept the offer. Hooper then sent Hodges his traveling expenses to New York along with explicit directions for their secret meeting upon his arrival.

Hodges, who was born at Nashville, Tennessee, on July 21, 1861, during the early days of the Civil War, had learned to play chess at the age of nineteen and had won the state championship a few years later. At about that time Hodges made a special pilgrimage to New Orleans to see the great chess player Paul Morphy, but when he arrived he found that he was not permitted to speak to Morphy. He had to settle for a distant view of his enigmatic hero, who had retired completely from chess play.

Hodges did, however, get a chance to play against Zukertort, whom he met at Louisville, Kentucky, in the early 1880s. "When Zukertort started to play," Hodges later recalled, "he placed his hat on the window casing. I remarked that it was a big hat. Zukertort told me he had brought it from England, that it was a size 9½, and that it would be difficult to find one here large enough to fit him. Then and there I thought how absurd it was for me to try to win from a man with a head like that. I was right—he beat me."

While working in Saint Louis in 1888 and 1889, Hodges had greatly improved his game by playing informally with Max Judd, so that by the time he arrived in New York in January 1890 he was a very strong chess player and was also an expert at

checkers. Following Hooper's written instructions, Hodges appeared at the specified hour on the northeast corner of Broadway and Twenty-third Street, half a block from the Eden Musée. He was wearing a red carnation which Hooper had insisted upon for purposes of identification. Ajeeb's proprietor met his new director as planned and led him up a back stairway to the balcony of the Musée and into the small room where Ajeeb was exhibited.

It was not the first time Hodges had seen a chess automaton. Two years earlier in Cincinnati he had visited another Ajeeb and had even met the automaton's director, Charles Moehle, who had shown Hodges the secrets of how Ajeeb was operated. "This figure," Hodges later explained, "was not so well made as the one I afterwards played in at the Eden Musée, but was evidently a good imitation." One peculiarity of the Ajeeb which Hodges had examined in Cincinnati was that it was very difficult for the director to see Black's Queen Rook square.

Hooper required his new director to sign a contract in which it was stipulated that Hodges would conceal his identity from the chess players and that under no circumstances was he to visit any chess club. The slender young Hodges was then asked to divest himself of all his outer garments and crawl into the wooden cabinet that supported the figure for an immediate lesson in the manipulation of Ajeeb's machinery. After several hours of practice, Hodges was ready to start his new career, which began the very next day.

At the opening of the exhibition, Hodges was concealed within Ajeeb and could hear the barker crying, "Step this way, ladies and gentlemen. Buy your tickets here. Only twenty-five cents to see Ajeeb, the Automaton, a wax figure that plays chess and checkers. Plays with anyone and beats everybody. Don't fail to see this mechanical wonder!"

Although most of the players who challenged Ajeeb were novices, master chess and checker players sometimes came in to test the automaton's skill. Hodges was much better at both chess and checkers than Hooper, a fact which was soon discovered by the better players, and Hodges could hear their comments about a "new man inside." One afternoon a strong player from the Manhattan Chess Club came in with several friends, "evidently cock-sure," reported Hodges, "that he could win from Ajeeb. He became so exasperated at losing in the presence of his friends that he said in a loud tone, so that I might hear him, though a block distant, that he could not play his game standing up and in so crowded a place, but if I would visit his club he would give me odds of pawn and move for $5.00 a game. And several years later I did go to his club and had the satisfaction of beating him decisively on even terms. But he never knew my secret, for I still felt under obligation to Mr. Hooper not to reveal it."

Hodges usually worked Ajeeb for a two-hour session in the afternoon and another in the evening, with one day off during the week. He found that the chess and checker play became monotonous after a while, but he enjoyed the sounds of the Hungarian band and of the celebrated vocalists, who could be heard entertaining visitors in the theater on the ground floor.

In October Señorita Carolina Otero, a Spanish dancer, caused quite a stir at the Eden Musée, drawing the largest crowds the auditorium had ever held. "She appears to dance all over, so to speak," commented the *New York Times*. "Every muscle, from her dainty toes to the crown of her shapely head, is brought into play, and the consequent contortions are wonderful and at times startling.... When she stomps upon the stage it seems as though the boards must give away." While putting Ajeeb through his paces upstairs, Hodges enjoyed the "musical patter" of Otero's heels on the stage below.

"Often the expressions of the visitors amused me," declared Hodges, "except on one evening, when a very hilarious party of Wild Western men came in, and one of them said he would pay the damage if his friends would let him shoot a hole through the dummy, reaching for his hip pocket as he shouted his contempt for the ignorance of the onlookers. I did not feel at ease until his friends forced him to leave the room."

While Hodges was directing Ajeeb he felt obligated to Hooper to keep the automaton's secrets, but by November 1923 he thought that Ajeeb no longer existed and that it was safe to reveal the mystery. At that time Hodges presented the following interesting picture of how Ajeeb worked and what it was like to direct a chess automaton:

The handicap that the player inside the figure had to bear was much greater than the inconvenient or discomforting position of his opponent who merely had to stand up and play, whereas I could make use of but one eye, as I was compelled to sit in a sidewise position, and also I did not have a clear view of the chess board, as my vision was intercepted by a network of diamond shaped squares of silk threads, colored black and red. Those squares composed the facing of the small door which opened so that the interior of the body of the figure was exposed to view. Looking through the silk facing was much like seeing through a heavy veil. I attribute a slight defect in my left eye to the strain which this experience in my chess career counted. When in the figure I was seated on a small pedestal, my lower limbs concealed in a narrow base, and just enough space to sit in without being cramped. My head was just about six inches above the level of the chess board. The arm of the figure was made of papier-mâché, and draped with folds of colored silk, so light in weight that I could lift it with ease, and move the thumb of the hand with a lever, operated from its elbow, which was as far as my hand penetrated into the arm. Moving this lever opened the thumb so that the chess pieces to be moved could be grasped, and removing the pressure on the lever released the piece.

Also at times in the game, when I was required to reach the far side of the board, by operating another lever, I could cause the body of the figure to lurch forward, which gave me just sufficient reach. The greatest handicap of all, of course to me, was the lack of ventilation, for when in the figure, and the front and rear doors closed, there was no fresh air, and all that saved me from suffocation was the frequent and timely showing of the interior to the curious onlookers. This announcement was always made in a clear voice by the attendant, usually Mr. Hooper or his wife, and when I heard the signal, "We will now show the mechanism," there was a quick action on my part. It required but a second for me to lean so that the right side of my face rested on my shoulder, my body bent sideways, so that there was just enough space to allow the wires and wheels to drop from over my head, where they were fastened by a pulley arrangement, the bottom of this network of *machinery* was lined with black cloth, which served to cover and conceal me from view. These wires and wheels were imitation, made of black whalebone and fibre. When the doors were again closed, the attendant proceeded to wind up a spring at the side, which made a rachet-like noise, and was my signal to get ready for play. By pulling a cord the wires were raised above my head, and I was released from a very uncomfortable and crowded position. . . . It was so very warm inside the figure that I was clothed, even in the coldest weather, with the thinnest underwear, for during the winter season the interior of the theatre was always uncomfortably heated by steam, and the crowded room did not improve the atmosphere.

Ajeeb was strangely fascinating to certain chess devotees, several of whom came so often that the Musée admitted them at a reduced rate. One of them, a fairly good player, knew the secrets of the automaton but kept returning anyway with the hope of someday beating him. Once, when Hodges was outside Ajeeb, he happened to make the acquaintance of that gentleman, who invited the director to be his guest, on any of his days off, at a very exclusive club. After several such visits, the gentleman one day offered Hodges a sum of money as payment for the pleasure he had received. Hodges politely declined the remuneration, and his friend then asked him if he could be of any other service. Hodges was beginning to realize that his work in the automaton would be detrimental to his health and thus inquired if it would be possible for the gentleman to assist him in obtaining a mercantile position. "You write me an application and I think I can help you," replied the friend, who was a Wall Street multi-millionaire.

A few days later, when Hodges visited his friend's office, the broker took the application from his desk and wrote on it, "Charlie, this is the young man I spoke to you about," and said to take it over to the president of the Chamber of Commerce. The following day Hodges took up duties as secretary of Sailors' Snug Harbor, a position which ended his job as Ajeeb's director, although later he occasionally substituted as the automaton's operator.

In 1894 Hodges, who was by then champion of New York State and of the Manhattan Chess Club, won the United States Chess Championship by defeating Jackson W. Showalter, "The Kentucky Lion," by a score of 5-3 with one draw. Showalter challenged Hodges to a rematch, and in 1895 Harry Nelson Pillsbury also challenged him, but Hodges never defended the title. It would have meant giving up his business career for the precarious life of a chess professional, but in order to give others a chance at the title Hodges announced his retirement

From Jackson W. Showalter, shown here, Hodges won the U. S. Chess Championship. COURTESY OF JGW.

as U. S. Champion in 1896, the year he married Miss Laura I. Robinson of Stapleton, Staten Island. Hodges did, however, participate in all thirteen of the famous cable matches with Great Britain without losing a single game.

Hodges remained an official of Sailors' Snug Harbor until his retirement in 1913 after over twenty years of continuous service. He then became part-time auditor for a railroad, devoting the rest of his time to chess activities. He founded the Staten Island Chess Club and served twelve years as its president.

Hodges in his later years also continued his interest in checkers and while on vacation trips always looked up the local champion at the game. He once played five games with the New England champion, winning the majority.

"Who are you?" asked the checker player.

Hodges introduced himself, but the champion responded, "No, your name isn't Hodges. I know all the good checker players in the United States, but I don't know that name."

"That's quite possible," replied Hodges, "I quit playing checkers before you were born."

On February 3, 1944, Hodges died of a heart attack at his Staten Island home at the age of eighty-two. Over a period of sixty years he had competed against several generations of the greatest grandmasters of chess, everyone, in fact, from Z to A—from Zukertort to Alekhine.

Constant Ferdinand Burille, a Bostonian born in Paris, directed Ajeeb in the 1890s. COURTESY OF JGW.

After Hodges left Ajeeb, the post of director was filled by Constant Ferdinand Burille, a Parisian-born Boston player in his mid-twenties who had come into prominence in 1889 by defeating both Steinitz and Pillsbury when given odds of pawn and move. That same year he was a competitor in the Sixth American Chess Congress in New York. Burille, it was once claimed, conducted Ajeeb in nine hundred games of chess, of which he lost only three, and at checkers it was said that he never lost any of the countless games he played.

The Englishman William Henry K. Pollock, also a participant in the 1889 Chess Congress, lived in Baltimore a number of years afterward. He once told a friend there that he had directed Ajeeb at one time.

Around 1895 Ajeeb's director was Dr. August Schaefer, a famous checker player who was also good at chess. Schaefer, it was said, was a fairly competent director but occasionally would doze off in the middle of a game. When that happened a Musée employee was called in to make repairs, which consisted mostly of banging on Ajeeb's cabinet until the startled occupant resumed his duties.

Schaefer was working Ajeeb one day when a chess expert came in and gave the automaton a sound beating in a series of games. Schaefer was outclassed as a chess player but continued to perform his obligations as best he could until finally the expert

William Henry K. Pollock admitted that he had at one time directed Ajeeb. COURTESY OF JGW.

Dr. August Schaefer specialized in checkers and had a very private practice. COURTESY OF JGW.

Pillsbury was, if we can believe various accounts, a combination of Apollo, Abraham Lincoln, and Sherlock Holmes. COURTESY OF JGW.

closed the session with the remark, "Oh, I don't know—this automaton isn't so hard to beat!"

With that, a gruff voice exclaimed from the bowels of the figure, "The hell he ain't—you wait till Pillsbury gets back!"

That indiscreet outburst may have been the first indication that Harry Nelson Pillsbury, America's strongest chess player, was directing Ajeeb, at which times the automaton was naturally a much improved chess player. After the incident with the chess expert, in fact, only Pillsbury was allowed to direct the automaton's chess games, and Ajeeb was restricted to checkers during the times when Schaefer was directing. Schaefer died a short time later and Pillsbury, who was also a very fine checker player, became the automaton's principal director.

Pillsbury was born December 5, 1872 at Somerville, Massachusetts, and on Thanksgiving Day 1888, when almost sixteen, he first learned the game of chess. In Boston, where he went to study for a commercial career, he found himself attracted to the Deschapelles Chess and Whist Club, the Y.M.C.A. Club, and Van Doren's Chess Divan on Tremont Street, where he improved rapidly in encounters with the best Boston players, including C. F. Burille, who would also be one of Ajeeb's directors.

In 1892 young Pillsbury played a match with John F. Barry, the strongest player in New England, who won the first four games and needed only one more point to win the match. He never got it. Pillsbury

At Hastings in 1895, Harry Nelson Pillsbury startled the world by riding a dark horse to victory. COURTESY OF JGW.

210

won the remaining five games, defeating Barry 5-4.

Steinitz visited Boston in April of that year and played three games with Pillsbury, giving him odds of pawn and move. Pillsbury won two of the three games and then another one when the World Champion played twenty games simultaneously, and thus Pillsbury was convinced that he should abandon his business studies for a chess career.

In 1893 Pillsbury went to New York, entered several tournaments, and continued to improve. The following year, in a tournament arranged for the leading American players, he finished in first place, followed by Hodges and Showalter. Then in 1895 he attracted many admirers in New York by leading the Brooklyn Chess Club to the championship of the Metropolitan Chess League. As a result, a fund was raised to send Pillsbury as the American representative to the great international congress of the world's masters at Hastings, England in 1895.

Hastings was the greatest tournament of the nineteenth century and the field of contenders was truly impressive. Dr. Emanuel Lasker had just taken the world championship from Steinitz, and both were among the participants at Hastings, as were the champions of Austria, England, France, Germany, Italy, and Russia. Nobody expected much of a showing from the relatively unknown American

Gunsberg was still active in international chess. COURTESY OF JGW.

representative except Pillsbury himself. "I mean to win this tournament," he declared and chose a quiet hotel which would be free of distractions.

After a first-round loss to Tchigorin, it appeared that Pillsbury was indeed outclassed, as had been expected, but in the next round he surprised everyone by defeating the formidable Dr. Siegbert Tarrasch. Pillsbury then continued to win, so that by the twenty-first and final round he led the field by half a point. As the last game progressed, it appeared that the young American was trying for only a draw, content to tie for first place. His twenty-seventh move, however, initiated a brilliant winning combination which remains a classic of endgame play. Pillsbury's opponent, who lost after a hard struggle, was none other than Isidor Gunsberg, the soul of Mephisto. Gunsberg had directed the mechanical chess player sixteen years earlier in London and was now forty-one years of age and still quite active in international chess.

When Pillsbury returned to America from Hastings, the winner of the great tournament and its thousand-dollar first prize, he was greeted as a national hero and was given a reception that had not been equaled since the days of Morphy. He was, in fact, often compared with Morphy and was known as "the Morphy of the North."

Few figures in chess or other fields have had more praise heaped upon them or have been more deserving of popularity than Pillsbury. "With a resolute Abraham Lincoln cut in countenance," wrote Leopold Hoffer in London, "Pillsbury is of a kindly and modest disposition. He has made many friends in this country, and he will carry with him the good wishes of all who came in contact with him."

Writing in the St. Paul *Dispatch*, George B. Spencer commented that Pillsbury was "blessed with a handsome and friendly presence" and possessed "characteristic Grecian features that Apollo might have envied."

Armin Fieldman, writing in the Hungarian journal *Pester Lloyd* added, "His profile is cameo-like, nobly cut, every movement is dignified and gentle elegance. For such a youth to acquire so much self-restraint, deliberation, and coolness is wonderful and could only have been obtained by occupation at the chessboard. When Pillsbury sits at the board he has an absolute stony calmness in his face; not a single muscle moves, only now and then will he wink a bit faster, when he feels himself slowly and satisfactorily nearing the goal, so finely calculated and elaborated."

It has even been suggested, although perhaps not seriously, that Pillsbury was actually Sherlock Holmes and that the great detective was the real winner at Hastings.

After the Hastings tournament Pillsbury was invited to play against Lasker, Steinitz, and Tchigorin in a tournament at St. Petersburg. The American scored 3½–2½ against Lasker, but did so poorly against Steinitz that Lasker won the tournament. Pillsbury finished third ahead of Tchigorin.

In 1896 Pillsbury again finished third in tournaments at Nuremberg and Budapest. At Nuremberg, however, he defeated Lasker, Steinitz, and Tchigorin on three successive days.

Returning to America in 1897, Pillsbury played a match with Showalter, who, after Hodges retired, had become the United States Champion by beating Lipschuetz, Barry, Kemeny, and Albin. Pillsbury was naturally expected to win, but after thirteen rounds Showalter actually led by a score of 6-5 with two draws. Pillsbury had to make an extra effort in the final rounds to win the match 10-8.

The U. S. Championship seemed to hold little interest for Pillsbury, whose real ambition was to win the world title from Lasker. In fact, there had been no mention of the championship during arrangements for the match with Showalter. "I was not seeking the match," explained Pillsbury, "and even if I should win I shall leave Showalter in possession of the title; I am not in search of any title but one." In the return match with Showalter in 1898, however, the title was at stake, and Pillsbury again won, this time 7–3, to become the second director of Ajeeb holding the title of U. S. Champion.

Pillsbury had no means of supporting himself other than chess, so that while not playing in tournaments, matches, or exhibitions, he directed Ajeeb at the Eden Musée, which was perhaps his most dependable source of income.

In 1896 or 1897, the two Hoopers, who had accumulated a considerable sum of money by exhibiting Ajeeb, returned to Europe and opened a hotel in Brussels. Hooper, the automaton's inventor, had exhibited Ajeeb almost continuously for twenty-eight years and had himself acted as director for much of that time. Even during times when others directed the automaton, Hooper had been obliged to substitute on their days off. So it was not surprising that he was ready to retire.

When they left New York, the Hoopers sold Ajeeb to Pillsbury, who intended to continue exhibiting the chess player. However, Pillsbury was not able to obtain the concession to show Ajeeb at the Eden Musée and was thus forced to remove the figure from the museum.

After that, Pillsbury planned to take Ajeeb "out west" and it is known that he exhibited the automaton for several weeks in 1898 at the Dime Museum at Ninth and Arch Streets in Philadelphia. While there, Charles J. Newman, an international cable chess player, went one day to play the automaton. "I should have beaten him," reported Newman, "if after lifting a Rook he had not put it back and played another piece. 'Can this automaton take moves back?' I asked indignantly. 'Yes,' said the lady

In 1898 Pillsbury directed Ajeeb at the Dime Museum, Ninth and Arch streets, Philadelphia. COURTESY OF FLP.

attendant, 'he can.' And worse luck he did!"

Pillsbury, without Ajeeb, toured America five times, giving performances of blindfold chess and other amazing feats of memory.

His specialty [reported the *American Chess Bulletin*] was to combine checkers, at which he became very expert and was classed as one of the best twenty draughts players in this country, with chess, playing say twelve chess, six checkers, taking at the same time a hand in a game of duplicate whist. While conducting the card game with all the precision of a fairly good player, he would keep the ever-changing chess and checker positions at his back clearly in his mind's eye and call off his moves at each board in succession with an accuracy and promptness that looked little short of miraculous. He could break off a séance for an intermission and upon resumption readily call up the positions on every board at will and, when requested, would announce the moves made in any particular game from the beginning, correcting possible errors made by the scorer.

Pillsbury's feats of memory seemed to border upon the mystic. He could flip through a shuffled deck of cards and then recite the order of cards from memory. He began one popular stunt by requesting the audience to write five-word sentences on each of fifty numbered slips of paper. He would then read the slips, drop them in a hat, and ask a spectator to randomly draw them out one at a time and read the numbers. As each number was read, Pillsbury would reel off its accompanying sentence, and he would then conclude the performance by reciting each sentence backwards.

No list of words, it seemed, was too difficult for Pillsbury to memorize instantly. Hoping to baffle him, two professors in London presented him with the following list which has since been often quoted:

Antiphlogistine, periosteum, takadiastase, plasmon, ambrosia, Threlkeld, streptococcus, staphylococcus, micrococcus, plasmodium, Mississippi, Freiheit, Philadelphia, Cincinnati, athletics, no war, Etchenberg, American, Russian, philosophy, Piet Potgelter's Rost, Salamagundi, Oomisillecootsi, Bangmamvate, Schlecter's Nek, Manzinyama, theosophy, catechism, Madjesoomalops.

Pillsbury scanned the list, returned it, and then continued his exhibition, which included blindfold chess and card playing. To conclude the performance, he correctly repeated the list both forwards and backwards, and he again recited the list the following day when he met the two gentlemen who had composed it.

Although his record in blindfold play has since been surpassed, Pillsbury's ability to simultaneously play twenty-two blindfold games of chess was unprecedented at the time. While competing in a tournament at Hanover in 1902, he amused himself between rounds by taking on twenty-one opponents in an exhibition of blindfold play, not against ordinary players but eighteen competitors of master-level strength from the Haupt Tournament Section A and the three best from Section B. As an incentive for best play, the tournament committee offered the participants monetary prizes for beating or drawing Pillsbury. The exhibition lasted from two in the afternoon until past two the following morning with a half hour break at six. During that time Pillsbury sat with his back to the players, announcing his moves in German notation. He generously allowed his opponents to consult with one another and to move the pieces, yet he lost only seven games.

The following day he appeared for his regular tournament game, looking none the worse for his exertion. "How far Pillsbury damages his chances by exhibition play is difficult to say," observed Hoffer; "the constant effort must affect his nerves, though he is not conscious of it as yet."

There have been several attempts to account for Pillsbury's extraordinary feats of memory. During childhood he had been in charge of the paper route for his father's newspaper and had built a foundation for accurate memory by memorizing all the addresses where papers were to be delivered. Pillsbury himself, just prior to a 1900 blindfold performance, told chess columnist Rhoda A. Bowles that he would mentally group the twelve boards into three groups of four, planning to play a certain opening in each group. As play progressed, he would regroup and subgroup the boards until each game took on its individual characteristics and thus became "as clear before me as you are at this moment." "The critical stage of the game," said Pillsbury, "is quite in the opening moves, for one stitch dropped there would spoil the whole fabric." Dr. Louis Miller, writing in the *Illinois Medical Journal*, October 1914, expressed the opinion that Pillsbury visualized several squares at a time, keeping other squares in his peripheral memory.

Unfortunately, none of Pillsbury's startling mental accomplishments were financially successful, and, as Hodges once noted, "it was a continual struggle for him to make both ends meet." One by one he had to sell the trophies he had won in the great tournaments in order to meet the necessities of day-to-day living. Yet he never became bitter or lost his sense of pride. One afternoon Pillsbury and Hodges were invited to the home of a powerful captain of industry to play an exhibition game. After

Frank J. Marshall succeeded Pillsbury as U. S. Champion. COURTESY OF JGW.

a hard-fought contest in which Pillsbury was the victor, both participants were invited to remain for dinner, but neither the host, his family, nor even Hodges could persuade Pillsbury that he should accept the hospitality, and the two friends departed together. On the way home Hodges expressed his disappointment that they could not have stayed, to which Pillsbury replied, "He paid me $100 and I did not feel that I was on the plane of a guest."

At Chicago on January 17, 1901, Pillsbury was married to Mary Ellen Busch of Monticello, New York, and evidently for that reason he confined his tournament play that year to America. In August at the Chess Congress in Buffalo, he took first prize ahead of Frank J. Marshall, who would succeed him as U. S. Chess Champion. It has been claimed that the first encounter between Marshall and Pillsbury occurred while Pillsbury was directing Ajeeb, but Marshall himself reported that he first played Pillsbury at a simultaneous blindfold exhibition in Montreal in 1893. Marshall, who won the game, was sixteen at the time and Pillsbury was twenty-one.

In 1902 and 1903 Pillsbury again visited Europe to compete in international tournaments, and although he did not win any first prizes, he was always among the prize winners. In May 1904 an international tournament at Cambridge Springs, Pennsyl-

vania, attracted many foreign masters including World Champion Emanuel Lasker. Despite Pillsbury's reputation, the American had never succeeded in arranging a match for the world title because Lasker had been occupied with his studies for a doctorate in mathematics. Pillsbury went to Cambridge Springs to help represent the Americans and perhaps to show Lasker that he was ready for the long awaited attempt at the world championship. It was Marshall, however, who upheld the American reputation by winning first prize, two points ahead of Lasker. Pillsbury, six points below Marshall, did not even make the prize list, and it was the only tournament in which he lost more games than he won.

Throughout the tournament Pillsbury suffered from insomnia and restlessness, yet he did defeat Lasker in one remarkable game. For a long time Pillsbury had been saving an original variation of the Queen's Gambit for just such an encounter with Lasker. Evidently Pillsbury's poor showing at Cambridge Springs was caused by paralytic dementia, a chronic degenerative disease of the brain, resulting from a previous syphilitic infection. Steinitz, in 1900, had died of the same disease.

Pillsbury, accompanied by his wife, went to Bermuda in November 1905. He was suffering still more mental and physical deterioration and thus had played no serious chess since the Cambridge Springs tournament except for two annual matches between the Franklin and Manhattan Chess clubs. Despite his condition, he had in the first of those defeated Marshall, thus avenging his loss to him at Cambridge Springs.

Soon after his return from Bermuda in January 1906, Pillsbury entered a hospital at Frankford, Pennsylvania, where on March seventh he suffered an attack of apoplexy and was reported to be on the point of death. In June, however, he sent a message to the *American Chess Bulletin,* saying, "I am very much alive, although, as I understand, reported out of chess for all time—and other sensational stories about me. I had a very close call, no doubt, but my 'rough and ready' bringing up has given me something of a constitution."

Unfortunately, the very next issue of the *Bulletin* had to report "the sad demise of Harry Nelson Pillsbury," which occurred on Sunday, June 17, 1906, during his thirty-fourth year. Although he never had the opportunity of playing Lasker for the world title, many felt that Pillsbury could have won it. His overall tournament record with the World Champion was 7-7. Like Boncourt, Lewis, Gunsberg, and Barker, a slight shift in his fortunes might have given him the world title, but it was not to be. Pillsbury had competed in eighteen major tournaments in the decade from 1893 to 1904 and had finished or tied for first or second in ten. Only in his first and last two had he finished lower than third.

Could Pillsbury have beaten World Champion Emanuel Lasker, pictured here? Unfortunately, there was no title match. COURTESY OF JGW.

There were many tributes to Pillsbury, but also some speculation as to the cause of his death. A theory was prevalent at the time that chess produced insanity and morbid tendencies among its greatest practitioners. Steinitz, after all, had gone insane and died in 1900, and Morphy too had shown signs of mental derangement during his last ten years, although he had not played chess for thirty years before his death in 1884.

Some, such as Hoffer and Lasker, blamed Pillsbury's decline and death upon the overtaxing of his memory, combined with other bad habits. "Unfortunately, Pillsbury made it his business to give blindfolded performances," explained Lasker. "During the trying hours of his exhibitions, in which he often gave also feats of memory and played checkers and whist, Pillsbury would smoke and partake of whiskey. Thus little by little his health was undermined."

"Such a strain," agreed Hoffer, "however little it may have taxed his mental powers, . . . could not fail to react injuriously on a man of his delicate physical organization, combined as it was with an inordinate craving for tobacco, which led him to smoke perpetually the strongest cigars."

Hodges, however, offered another explanation for Pillsbury's untimely death. "Our friendship was enduring," he declared, "and when he was in control of the chess automaton, it was my privilege, on a number of occasions, to relieve him from the steady monotony by taking his place, and I have always felt, from my own experience, that this strenuous work and the unhealthy environment of the chess figure, must have to a great extent undermined his health and was the primary cause of his physical breakdown." In Pillsbury's own words, "It was a pretty tight squeeze and not at all a pleasant duty, for I often played ten to fifteen games a day."

"How he stood it for so long a period," continued Hodges, "I cannot understand, and I am sure it contributed to his early demise. My waking dreams of Ajeeb recall to my present thoughts that story of the Arabian Nights Entertainment, of the bad man of the sea who fastened himself on the shoulders of Sinbad; and so the ponderous bulk of Ajeeb looms over me, and I thank that kind Providence, who has ever looked over our destinies, for releasing me from an ignominious bondage."

Did Ajeeb really kill Pillsbury, or at least hasten his death from the brain disease? No one, of course, can say for sure, but it is interesting to recall that other persons who directed chess automatons seem to have suffered a similar fate. Dr. Adolph Schaefer died after directing Ajeeb at the Eden Musée for several years. Charles F. Barker died at the age of fifty-one after directing another Ajeeb in Boston for about twenty years. Mazam's director, Harry Jacob, died at the age of only thirty-three after a long and painful illness. He left a wife and two-year-old child totally unprovided for. As-Rah was closed at Bordeaux because the health of his youthful director was compromised. Kempelen's twelve-year-old daughter, it was claimed, had to stop directing the Turk due to "her health declining, from the confinement to which she was subjected." Schlumberger died of yellow fever in Havana after a tenure of twelve years as the Turk's director.

On the other hand, several persons, like Hodges, have directed automatons for short periods of time, retired to some other line of work, and then lived to a fairly advanced age. These include Allgaier, Alexandre, Boncourt, Lewis, and Gunsberg. Is it merely a coincidence that those who directed automatons the longest died the youngest? Or was there really something deadly about the close confinement and lack of fresh air in the machines?

3.

Some newspapers reported, when Pillsbury died, that Ajeeb's head had been found among his effects. That story seems difficult to reconcile with the fact that Ajeeb continued to be exhibited at the Eden Musée until one recalls that the original automaton was removed from the Musée after the Hoopers departed. At that time, Miss Emma Haddera (or Hattara), the ticket-seller at the Musée, obtained the automaton concession and had a duplicate Ajeeb constructed. Shortly thereafter, Miss Haddera married James Smith, assistant manager of the Musée. She died a few years later, and thus Smith became the proprietor of the new Ajeeb. The automaton continued to be exhibited at the Eden until bankruptcy caused the place to close its doors in 1915, thirty years after the original Crystal Palace Ajeeb had made his debut there.

Peter J. Hill directed the new Ajeeb at the Eden Musée from about 1899 to 1908. He was later joined in his duties by Jesse B. Hanson, who continued to operate the automaton until the closing in 1915. Hill directed Ajeeb as a chess player, while Hanson operated the automaton when checkers was called for. A patron who wished to play chess once complained of having been kept waiting at the door of Ajeeb's chamber. The delay, he presumed, was due to the need to switch directors.

Hill was "a mild-mannered, unobtrusive chap" who had received his chess training in Boston in the company of Pillsbury, Burille, and Barry. Directing Ajeeb, he found, could be quite hazardous at times. One woman, angered at having her Bishop captured, ran her hatpin into Ajeeb's mouth, stabbing Hill sharply. On another occasion, Hill was wounded in the shoulder when an irate Westerner emptied his six-shooter into the automaton. Hodges had once feared that such a thing would happen to himself.

Hanson, a native of Santa Cruz, California, was also modest and unassuming and was very popular

**After Pillsbury removed Ajeeb from the Eden Musée,
this new Ajeeb was constructed to replace him. Note the
special checkers, which were designed to be picked up
easily.** COURTESY OF JGW.

Jesse B. Hanson was probably Ajeeb's last director.
FROM AC.

among checker players, to whom he was known, appropriately, as "the mystery man of checkers." He had a distinguished career in checkers, nearly winning the U.S. Championship at Chicago in 1929. His biggest handicap in directing Ajeeb was his height, which was nearly six feet. He weighed, however, only a hundred pounds and, improbable as it may seem, was able to coil snakelike inside the automaton.

Smith owned Ajeeb for nearly twenty years, but shortly before he died of tuberculosis of the bones, he presented the automaton to his lifelong friend and co-worker, Mrs. Hattie Elmore, who had cared for him during his final days. Mrs. Elmore, a divorcee, had sold catalogues at the Musée and had later become a costumer for the wax figures. It was she who owned Ajeeb in 1915, when the Musée was closed prior to being torn down to make way for a sixteen-story commercial building.

By that time the Musée had become a New York landmark, but most of the theaters had moved uptown, leaving it stranded in a commercial district. Women who had visited the Musée as children

The Eden Musée lobby in 1899 displayed an ad for the pioneer moving picture *The Passion Play*. It is difficult to determine which figures in the scene were living and which were wax. COURTESY OF NYPL.

brought their own youngsters to the box office, and there were many other loyal patrons, but they were too few to keep the place in business. James Gibbons Huneker, writing in the *New York Times*, considered the waxworks a link between stereopticons and the movies, observing that "After seeing for years the figures 'in the round,' they now enjoy them in crazy flickering motion." But the Musée could not compete with the new movie industry.

Ironically the Eden Musée had itself pioneered in moving pictures. In 1898 it had produced a cinema version of *The Passion Play* which enjoyed a run of nine months. That film was 2,200 feet long, a remarkable production at a time when the usual fare was a 500-foot "sidesplitting comedy" showing in reverse a man eating a chicken. Henry E. Abbey had originally planned *The Passion Play* as a theatrical production at Booth's Theatre in 1885, but after spending a fortune on costumes, Abbey was confronted by so much indignation from the local clergy that his production was forbidden by the authorities. Nobody seemed to object, however, when three years later the play was filmed on the roof of the old Grand Central Palace and then shown in its new form at the Eden Musée.

Other highlights which the Musée had presented over the years included the first Hungarian band New York had known, a troupe of eight young Viennese women fencers, and, in 1887, New York's first orchid exhibition at a time when that flower was practically unknown to society.

Among the notables who were said to have played Ajeeb at the Eden Musée and were invariably defeated at chess or checkers were Emperor Mutsuhito of Japan, Admiral Dewey, Theodore Roosevelt, William Jennings Bryan, Bob Fitzsimmons, Marie Dressler, Sarah Bernhardt, the ballplayer Christy Mathewson, and Harry Houdini. O. Henry, who lived in the neighborhood, used to visit the Musée for an occasional game with the automaton and would, according to one story, slip the director a bottle of whiskey during the course of an especially arduous game.

When the Musée closed, Mrs. Elmore moved Ajeeb to Hamid's Museum on Surf Avenue, Coney Island, and later to the nearby World of Wax. By that time Ajeeb had become exclusively a checker player, and most noteworthy among those employed by Mrs. Elmore to direct the automaton was Samuel Gonotsky, who would win the U. S. Checker Championship at Chicago in 1929. Gonotsky, it was said, worked part time as a Western Union messenger and often wore his uniform while directing Ajeeb.

About 1925, Mrs. Elmore retired and took Ajeeb to her home at 2018 Avenue U in Brooklyn, where the automaton remained for about ten years. During that time she received several attractive offers from persons wishing to purchase Ajeeb, but Mrs.

U. S. Checker Champion Samuel Gonotsky, who directed Ajeeb at Coney Island, has been favorably compared with Barker and Wyllie. COURTESY OF JGW.

Elmore preferred to keep him at her home, where, although elegantly wardrobed in a newly embroidered oriental costume, he remained inactive.

There have been reports that Ajeeb perished in a fire at Coney Island on March 15, 1929. It seems unlikely, however, that the Ajeeb from the Eden Musée could have been thus destroyed, since he was at Mrs. Elmore's house at that time. Of course there were other Ajeebs, but it is difficult to establish that a fire even occurred at Coney Island on that date.

On January 25, 1929, the *New York Times* printed the editorial "Ajeeb Is Dead." However, it was not the automaton that had died, but rather it was Peter J. Hill, who had directed Ajeeb's play for nine years at the Eden Musée. Nearly forgetting poor Hill, the editorialist lapsed into a reminiscence about the Eden Musée, and he even included a history of waxwork exhibitions in New York ranging back to the days of George Washington.

In 1934 Ajeeb was resurrected through the efforts of Frank Frain, who was finally successful in persuading Mrs. Elmore to, in his own words, "give Ajeeb back to the world once more." Frain, along with his partner Jesse Hanson, purchased the automaton from Mrs. Elmore for a reported one thousand dollars. Hanson had manipulated Ajeeb's checker playing at the Eden Musée and was happy to resume his old role.

John Kobler, who wrote a "Where Are They Now?" article for the *New Yorker* in November 1943, looked up Frain in his apartment in Queens and found that Ajeeb was at that time stored in the back of a Cadillac touring car. Frain, however, kept the automaton's head in a trunk in his apartment. Kobler reported, "I found Frain to be a slight man with a wedge-shaped head that was bald three-quarters of the way back, at which point a shock of gray hair rose from his skull like a fright wig." Frain attributed many supernatural qualities to Ajeeb, claiming that the automaton sometimes shoved him down when he attempted to affix the figure's head.

Born in Passaic, he had moved with his family to Manhattan at the age of nine. There he had sold evening newspapers in front of the Eden Musée and had thus become friendly with James Smith and Jesse Hanson. Eventually Hanson revealed to the boy the secrets of Ajeeb. In the years that followed, Frain worked at various journalistic jobs while Hanson traveled around playing checkers until the chance arose to acquire Ajeeb.

Under Frain's guidance Ajeeb was reintroduced to the world in early January 1935. At that time the automaton, "rigged out anew in resplendent oriental regalia," posed for a newsreel troupe at the Marshall Chess Club with U.S. Champion Marshall himself. Frain later claimed that Marshall "encountered Ajeeb at chess, and went away shaking his head after a draw."

Contending that he had made "considerable research" regarding Ajeeb's history, Frain asserted that Ajeeb was the original chess automaton invented by Kempelen in 1769. He brushed aside the fact that Kempelen's Turk was destroyed by fire in Philadelphia, insisting that Maelzel, "then in the twilight of his life," had sold the Turk to Hooper, who had rebuilt the automaton and given him the name of Ajeeb.

Frain further seemed to believe that Ajeeb was possessed of some vague supernatural powers. "The apparatus is all so mysterious," he told Kobler, "that even genuine scientists don't ask questions for fear of embarrassing themselves."

After bringing Ajeeb out of retirement in 1935, Frain and Hanson toured the country for several years, carrying the automaton in the Cadillac and exhibiting him at clubs, state fairs, and chess and checkers tournaments. In 1936 they signed a contract with RCA to travel around and advertise the Magic Brain radio. Ajeeb, fitted out with a new Magic Brain head, was shown in department stores, amusement parks, and hotels, where the radios were offered as prizes to anyone who could defeat

A resurrected and refurbished Ajeeb, complete with new clothing and stuffed cockatoo, was exhibited in 1935 by Frank Frain. COURTESY OF JGW.

the automaton. With Hanson at the controls, however, there were no radios won, but eight persons had draws and were thus awarded credit slips of twenty-five dollars each toward the purchase of Magic Brain radios. The partners, who split three hundred dollars a week and ten cents a mile expenses, considered it a prosperous year.

During that period Ajeeb appeared at the President's Birthday Ball and at an Aid to Britain party at the Hotel Astor. During World War II, however, it was difficult to obtain gasoline, so that by 1943 the Cadillac touring car, still containing Ajeeb, was stored on blocks in a parking lot, and apparently the automaton's career ended at that point. Or is Ajeeb still hidden away somewhere, waiting to be rediscovered and exhibited again to a new generation?

Can this be Ajeeb? It is, except for the Magic Brain head and radio cabinet. COURTESY OF FLP.

Under the watchful eye of Frank Frain, the Magic Brain Ajeeb defeated Kathryn McCool, Miss Philadelphia and Miss Radio of 1935. The match took place at the Electric and Radio Show in Convention Hall, Philadelphia.
COURTESY OF FLP.

ON THE CHESSBOARD
The Games of Ajeeb and His Directors

Compared with the Turk and Mephisto, relatively few of the games of Ajeeb have survived. At the Crystal Palace, it was reported, Ajeeb usually took White and played the following opening moves of the Giuoco Piano:

White	Black
Ajeeb	Opponent
1 P–K4	P–K4
2 N–KB3	N–QB3
3 B–B4	B–B4
4 P–Q3	N–B3
5 O–O	O–O
6 P–KR3	

The purpose of Ajeeb's sixth move, explained one of his opponents, was that "first it prevents his King's Knight from being pinned, and next it gives that piece a square to move to, which . . . affords a retreat whence the Knight can be very effectually brought out at the right moment." In addition to that maneuver, Ajeeb usually pinned the Black King Knight with his Bishop, "after which, if his opponent was a weak player, the Automaton made very short work of him." When playing Black, Ajeeb tried to avoid accepting the well-known gambits, such as the King's Gambit and the Evans Gambit, which were often played at the time.

In addition to the actual games of Ajeeb, there are, of course, many games which Ajeeb's famous directors played outside the automaton. From those games we may obtain some idea of how Ajeeb might have played while under their direction.

Game 45

Ajeeb had been at the Eden Musée less than a week when a group of players from the New York Chess Club came in to try out the automaton's abilities. Hooper, who was directing, defeated some of the club members but lost a pair of games to Simon Lipschuetz, winner in 1892 of the U. S. Chess Championship. The following is one of those games. Except for the order of moves, it appears that the automaton is employing the same opening used at the Crystal Palace.

Bishop's Opening

Eden Musée, New York, August 7, 1885

White	Black
Ajeeb (Charles A. Hooper)	Lipschuetz
1 P–K4	P–K4
2 B–B4	B–B4
3 N–KB3	N–QB3
4 P–Q3	P–Q3
5 P–KR3	N–B3

6 B–KN5	P–KR3
7 B–R4	O–O
8 N–B3	B–K3
9 B–Q5	N–QN5
10 P–R3	N/5×B
11 P×N	B–B4
12 P–KN4	B–KN3
13 P–N5	P×P
14 B×P	P–B3
15 N–Q2	Q–N3
16 O–O	N×P
17 N×N	P×N
18 Q–N4	Q×P
19 N–N3	Q×BP
20 N×B	Q×N
21 P–KR4	Q–B1
22 Q–N3	Q–KB4
23 K–R2	QR–B1
24 QR–Q1	P–B3
25 B–K3	K–B2
26 P–B4	R–B7ch
27 B–Q2	R–KR1
28 R–B2	Q×QP
29 P×P	P×P
30 Q×P	R×Pch
31 K–N1	B–K5
Resigns	

Game 46

Ajeeb was supposed to have played this charming little gem in Milwaukee. The same game has been published often throughout the history of chess, the author usually claiming to have won it himself. It was first recorded by Gioachino Greco in 1619. Did Ajeeb really play the game? Or was its publication just a hoax? In either case, the game is still quite amusing.

Queen's Fianchetto Defense

Milwaukee Exposition, September 1887

White	Black
Ajeeb (Charles Moehle)	Professor Baez
1 P–K4	P–QN3
2 P–Q4	B–N2
3 B–Q3	P–KB4
4 P×P	B×P
5 Q–R5ch	P–N3
6 P×P	N–KB3? (B–KN2!)
7 P×P dis ch	N×Q
8 B–N6 mate	

Game 47

While Hooper operated Ajeeb at the Eden Musée, Charles Moehle directed another version of Ajeeb at the Cincinnati Centennial Exposition, where the following game was recorded.

Evans Gambit

Cincinnati Centennial Exposition, July 1888

White	Black
Ajeeb (Charles Moehle)	Amateur
1 P–K4	P–K4
2 N–KB3	N–QB3
3 B–B4	B–B4
4 P–QN4	B×P
5 P–B3	B–B4
6 P–Q4	P×P
7 O–O	P–Q3
8 P×P	B–N3
9 N–B3	N–R4
10 B–KN5	N–KB3
11 P–K5	N×B
12 P×N	P–N3
13 Q–R4ch	Q–Q2
14 KR–K1ch	K–B1
15 B–R6ch	K–N1

White mates in two moves.

Game 48

Even with Hooper directing, Ajeeb won most of his games, but losses such as the following must have convinced the automaton's proprietor that he needed to hire a strong director.

Bishop's Opening

Eden Musée, New York, 1888

White	Black
Ajeeb (Charles A. Hooper)	Charles Devidé
1 P–K4	P–K4
2 B–B4	N–KB3
3 N–KB3	N–B3
4 N–N5	N×P
5 N×BP	Q–R5
6 Q–K2	B–B4
7 P–KN3	Q–B3
8 Q×N	Q×Pch
9 K–Q1	P–Q4
10 B×P	B–B4
11 B×Nch	P×B
12 Q×KPch	K×N
13 Q×BPch	K–N1
14 Q–B4	Q×Q
15 P×Q	B–N5ch
16 K–K1	R–K1ch
17 K–B1	B–R6 mate

Game 49

Hodges directed Ajeeb for about a year, during which time he pledged to Hooper "to conceal my identity from the chess players, and under no

circumstances to visit any chess club." No longer under that obligation when this game was played, Hodges was the first player to defeat Lasker when the World Champion visited America.

Ruy Lopez

Exhibition Game, New York, March 24, 1892

White	Black
Emanuel Lasker	Albert B. Hodges
1 P–K4	P–K4
2 N–KB3	N–QB3
3 B–N5	P–Q3
4 N–B3	B–Q2
5 O–O	KN–K2
6 P–Q3	N–N3
7 B–K3	B–K2
8 P–Q4	O–O
9 B–QB4	B–N5
10 P–Q5	N–N1
11 P–KR3	B×N
12 Q×B	P–KB4
13 P×P	N–R5
14 Q–N4	N×BP
15 B–Q2	N–Q2
16 B–Q3	P–KN3
17 N–K4	R–B2
18 QR–K1	Q–KB1
19 N–B3	P–QR3
20 N–Q1	Q–N2
21 B–B3	QR–KB1
22 P–N4	B–Q1
23 B–N2	N–B3
24 Q–QB4	N–R4
25 P–B4	P–QN4
26 Q–B6	N–K2
27 Q×RP	N×BP
28 Q×NP	Q–R3
29 N–B2	Q–N4
30 B–K4	N–B4
31 Q–B4	N–N6
32 B–KB3	N×R
33 R×N	Q–R5
34 Q–K4	N×Pch
35 N×N	Q×Q
36 B×Q	R×Rch

Black won.

Game 50

In the New York Impromptu Tourney, which Lasker won without losing a game, Hodges met and defeated a young player named Harry Nelson Pillsbury. Within a few years Pillsbury would be recognized as one of the four strongest chess masters in the world and would secretly become Ajeeb's director.

Ruy Lopez

Impromptu Tourney, New York, 1893

	White	Black
	Hodges	Pillsbury
1	P–K4	P–K4
2	N–KB3	N–QB3
3	B–N5	P–KN3
4	B×N	QP×B
5	P–QN3	B–N2
6	B–N2	Q–K2
7	P–Q3	P–QB4
8	QN–Q2	P–QB3
9	N–B4	P–B3
10	O–O	B–K3
11	K–R1	O–O–O
12	KN–Q2	P–KN4
13	P–QR4	P–KR4
14	P–R5	B–B1
15	Q–K2	P–R5
16	P–R3	N–R3
17	N–K3	N–B2
18	N/2–B4	R–R2
19	B–B3	N–R1
20	QR–N1	N–N3
21	P–QN4	N–B5
22	Q–K1	Q–Q2
23	P×P	B×P
24	B–N4	B×B
25	Q×B	P–N5
26	P×P	B×P
27	Q–B5	K–N1
28	P–R6	Q–K3
29	N–R5	P–N3
30	N×Pch	K–B2
31	N×R dis ch	K×N
32	Q–KB8ch	K–Q2
33	Q–QN8	K–B3
34	R×Pch	P×R
35	P–R7	R×P
36	Q×R	B–K7
37	R–QN1	K–B4
38	Q–B7ch	Q–B3
39	Q–K7ch	K–Q5
40	N–B5ch	K–B6
41	Q–N4ch	K×P
42	R–N2ch	K–B8
43	Q–Q2 mate	

Game 51

Besides Hodges and Pillsbury, Ajeeb was directed in the 1890s by C. F. Burille, a strong player who was sometimes capable of defeating even Pillsbury. In this game, in fact, he finished him off with great brilliance.

Evans Gambit

From a manuscript of Burille, date not recorded

	White	Black
	Pillsbury	Burille
1	P–K4	P–K4
2	N–KB3	N–QB3
3	B–B4	B–B4
4	P–QN4	B×P
5	P–B3	B–R4
6	O–O	Q–B3
7	P–Q4	KN–K2
8	P–Q5	N–Q1
9	Q–R4	B–N3
10	B–KN5	Q–Q3
11	N–R3	P–QB3
12	QR–Q1	Q–N1
13	B×N	K×B
14	P–Q6ch	K–B1
15	N×P	P–B3
16	N–B3	B–B4
17	P–K5	P–QN4
18	B×P	P×B
19	Q–KB4	N–K3
20	Q–B5	B×N
21	P×P	P–N3
22	Q–K5	B–N2
23	N–N5	Q–Q1!
24	P–B7	Q×N
25	Q×Rch	K×P
26	Q×Pch	N–N2
27	Q–R3	N–B4
28	P–KB4	B–B4ch
29	K–R1	Q×Pch
30	Q×Q	N–N6ch
31	P×N	R–R1 mate

Game 52

In the 1895 Hastings tournament, the final round game between Pillsbury and Gunsberg determined whether Pillsbury would win the tournament or only tie for first, but the contest also had a special significance of which the spectators—and perhaps even the players—were unaware: it was, so to speak, Ajeeb against Mephisto.

Queen's Gambit Declined

Twenty-first Round, Hastings International Tournament, 1895

	White	Black
	Pillsbury	Gunsberg
1	P–Q4	P–Q4
2	P–QB4	P–QB3
3	P–K3	P–KN3
4	N–QB3	B–N2
5	N–B3	N–B3
6	B–Q3	O–O
7	N–K5	P×P
8	B×BP	N–Q4
9	P–B4	B–K3

10	Q–N3	P–QN4		26	NP×B	N–N1
11	B×N	B×B		27	P–B5!	P–N4
12	N×B	Q×N		28	N–N4	P–QR4
13	Q×Q	P×Q		29	P–B6	K–Q3
14	N–Q3	N–Q2		30	P×P	N×P
15	B–Q2	KR–B1		31	N×N	K×N
16	K–K2	P–K3		32	P–K4!	P×P
17	KR–QB1	B–B1		33	P–Q5ch	K–Q3
18	R×R	R×R		34	K–K3	P–N5
19	R–QB1	R×R		35	K×P	P–R5
20	B×R	B–Q3		36	K–Q4	P–R4
21	B–Q2	K–B1		37	P×P	P–R6
22	B–N4	K–K2		38	K–B4	P–B4
23	B–B5	P–QR3		39	P–R6	P–B5
24	P–QN4	P–B3		40	P–R7	Resigns
25	P–N4	B×B				

Confronted by the massive figure of Ajeeb, few adversaries could play their best games. COURTESY OF JGW.

13

The Myth of the Supermechanical Chess Player: Computer Chess

1.

In November 1915, just after the closing of the Eden Musée ended Ajeeb's long engagement there, a new mechanical chess player attracted much interest when introduced to the public at the Sorbonne in Paris by the Spanish inventor Leonardo Torres y Quevedo. Unlike the chess automatons, the Torres machine had no exotic name, nor was it made to represent an Oriental person or any other human figure. It looked, in fact, like nothing more than a machine consisting of pulleys, weights, wheels, wires, electric lamps, and electromagnets, all attached to the top of a table. Mounted in an upright position amid the mass of machinery was a small chessboard. The Torres machine was not capable of playing complete games of chess and was indeed limited to the performance of only a single endgame. In that ending, which is known even to beginning chess players, the machine played with the White King and one White Rook against the lone Black King moved by a spectator. No matter how the human adversary moved his King, he was invariably checkmated by the machine, which, despite the simplicity of its task, had to provide for a very great number of possible combinations. The Torres machine was the first purely mechanical chess player, an automaton of the first class, since there was no human director either concealed inside or operating it remotely from elsewhere.

The older automatons, explained Torres, imitated the appearance and movements of living beings. The new class of apparatus which he proposed to create left out the mere visible gestures of a human being and attempted to accomplish the results which a living person obtains, thus replacing man with a machine. Torres had, in fact, constructed the chess player to demonstrate certain of his ideas relating to automatic mechanisms of a very complex character. He wanted to prove that there was scarcely any limit to what an automatic apparatus could do, and he felt that once the principle of his chess machine was examined anyone would be convinced of the truth of his ideas.

Along with the chess machine Torres exhibited various other automatic devices, such as a wireless apparatus for steering boats. He had previously invented a machine for solving algebraic equations and an airship known as the Astra-Torres.

A spectator who was selected to play against the chess machine began by moving his King from the starting square to any square he chose. The pieces were in the form of jack plugs which fitted into receptacles in each square of the chess board. When the Black King was inserted into the receptacle in the selected square, an electrical circuit was completed which resulted in a reply by the machine based upon certain rules built into its mechanism. The mechanical player first responded to the move by testing to determine if it was legal, and if not it

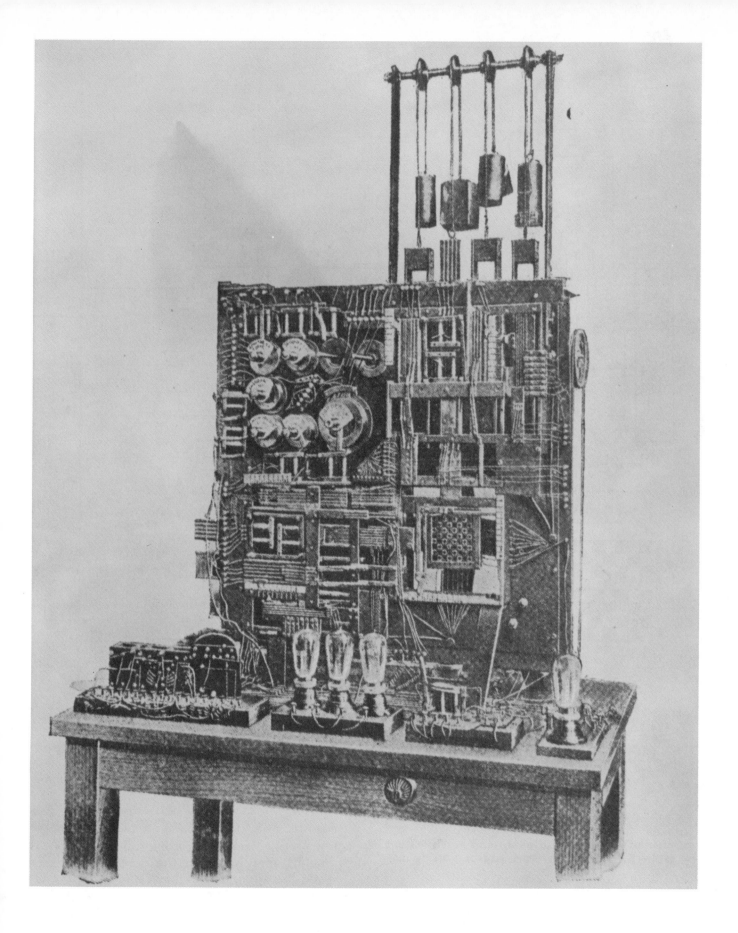

Señor Torres aimed to replace man with a machine, and he thus built the first authentic mechanical chess player.
COURTESY OF SA.

227

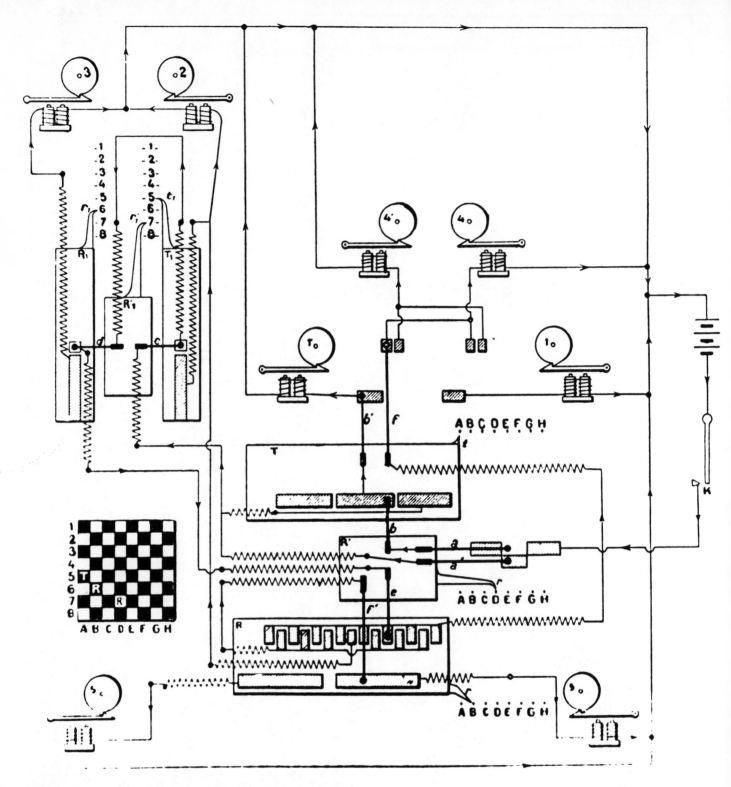

This diagram revealed the scheme of electrical connections of the Torres machine along with the starting position of the chessboard, on which T = White Rook, R = White King, and R′ = Black King. COURTESY OF SA.

protested by lighting one of the lamps at its base. If the move was permissible according to the rules of chess, the machine, after taking into account the positions of the three pieces, decided upon a reply. The machine's decision, however, was in no sense a voluntary one, having been determined in advance by the manner in which the inventor had constructed the apparatus. It was, in fact, the human opponent who really caused the machine's moves, which were merely responses to moves by the Black King.

Having thus selected a reply, the machine made the move with one of the two arms at the top and left of the board. The appropriate arm grasped the

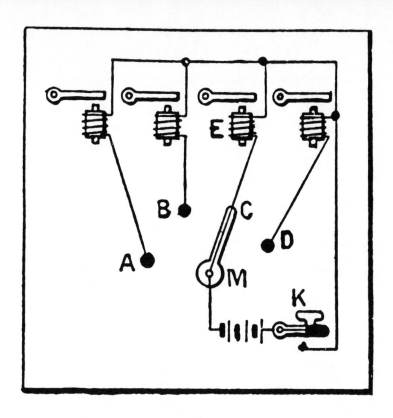

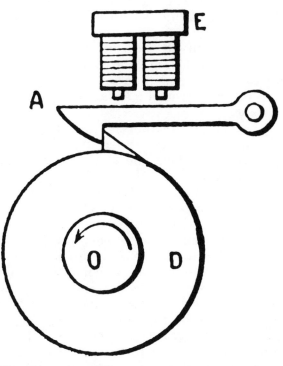

The Torres machine played chess with the aid of switches and electromagnets. COURTESY OF SA.

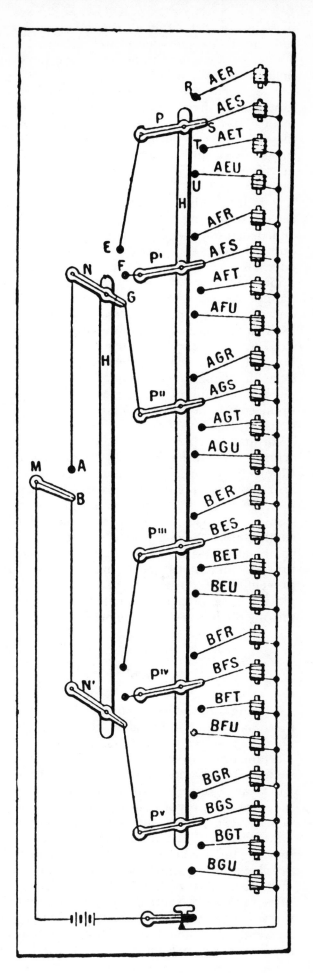

piece by the neck, lifted it from the board, transferred it to the proper square, and deposited it there. The game continued until the mating position was finally reached.

The machine allowed its adversary only three false moves, lighting a lamp each time one was made. After all three lamps were lit, the mechanical player refused to continue and a new game had to be started by closing a special switch which caused the machine to turn off its lights and set the pieces in their initial places again.

It is interesting to note that the machine was capable of playing only in the lower half of the board and that the upper half of the board was present only for the sake of appearance. If the machine's adversary were to move the Black King into the upper half of the board, it would have to cross the path of the Rook, an illegal move that would cause one of the warning lamps to be lit. The machine itself had no mechanism for moving its own King or Rook upward, since such operations would contribute nothing toward the checkmate and could only delay the game.

The operation of the Torres machine was based upon commutators working in various combinations, which allowed the machine to select one move according to rules determined in advance. The actual moves were initiated by escape wheels which were released when electromagnets attracted the armatures holding them in place.

In theory it would have been possible to construct a more complicated chess machine, using more commutators and escape wheels to accomplish more combinations with a larger number of pieces. The practical limitations of size, however, would have prevented the construction of a machine capable of playing more than a very limited endgame, such as the one the Torres machine performed.

2.

Throughout the history of the chess automatons, there has been considerable speculation about the possibility of constructing a real chess playing machine of the first class. Some of the early writers, such as Dutens and Windisch, thought Kempelen's Turk was a pure machine, but others were more skeptical and provided arguments supporting their belief that such a machine was impossible, or at least impracticable. Racknitz, for example, pointed out that a true machine would have to calculate the possible movements of both partners and the necessary movements of the Turk for each move. The wheelwork seen inside the automaton, he felt, was not sufficient to perform such a task, nor could it have been completed during the six-month period in 1769 in which Kempelen constructed his chess automaton. Racknitz and other writers of his day, knowing no other technology, reasoned that if a true chess machine were to be devised, it would have to be based upon clockwork, aided perhaps by magnetism.

By 1804 the French inventor Joseph Marie Jacquard (1752-1834) had perfected his loom, a machine which would weave any pattern automatically by employing a series of metal cards with holes punched in them. Gümpel, as noted in Chapter Eight, compared the mechanism of a true chess-playing machine with that of a Jacquard loom and reasoned that if a real chess machine were to be constructed it would require the lifetime services of about 5×10^{23} workmen. Proctor added that the completed machine would "require a space about a million times larger than the whole of the space within the glass walls of the Crystal Palace." Charles Tomlinson, a mathematician and chess writer, also hypothesizing a chess machine employing the Jacquard principle, estimated that "the surface of a moderately-sized London square would be required for its accommodation." He, like Gümpel, Proctor, and others who had considered the problem, thought a genuine chess machine was theoretically possible but for practical reasons could never be constructed.

The idea that a chess machine was possible only in theory continued to be accepted until the late 1940s at which time several large-scale electronic computers were put into operation. The new technology occasioned a re-examination of the feasibility of constructing, or rather programming, a machine to play a full game of chess. The British mathematician Claude E. Shannon, who is generally credited with being the first to outline a workable method for programming electronic computers to play chess, conceived his ideas in 1948 and presented them the following year in a talk before the National Institute of Radio Engineers, and then in 1950 published articles on the subject in the *Philosphical Magazine* and in *Scientific American*.

Shannon's ideas were important in that they not only explained how a computer might be programmed as a chess player, but they also dispelled the longstanding concept of what former World Chess Champion Mikhail Botvinnik once called a "supermechanical chess player." When Poe thought about a true chess machine he could conceive of it only as a supermechanical chess player, as when he wrote, "The Automaton does not invariably win the game. Were the machine a pure machine, this would not be the case—it would always win. A little consideration will convince anyone that the difficulty of making a machine beat all games is not in the least degree greater, as regards the principle of the operations necessary, than that of making a machine beat a single game." When Gümpel, Proctor, Tomlinson, and others considered the possibility of a true chess machine, they also had in mind the supermechanical chess player, capable of analyzing every move up to the completion of the game and thus playing the perfect game of chess. It was the supermechanical chess player which they pronounced unfeasible because of the size it would have to be and the time it required to construct it.

Shannon, however, rejected the concept of a machine which could play perfect chess. In an average game, he explained, such a machine might have to consider about 10^{120} possible variations. Even if it were to calculate a million such variations each second, it would still require over 10^{95} years to decide its first move. Instead, Shannon proposed a machine which would play a reasonably skillful game, choosing its moves according to certain rules, but often selecting a line of play that was less than perfect, just as a human player might do.

In preparing a computer to play chess, explained Shannon, there were three basic problems, the first of which was to devise a system of numbers that would represent each of the chess pieces and their positions on the board. This would allow the game to be translated into a form which could be analyzed by the computer and stored in its memory. Shannon proposed that each square on the chessboard be assigned a two-digit number, the first digit representing a rank or horizontal row of squares, the second a file or vertical row. Both digits would range from 0 to 7 starting in the lower lefthand corner of the board, and thus the squares would be numbered from 00 to 77. The system was similar to algebraic notation, which is used by many players to record chess games. For instance, the square 00 in Shannon's system would be *a1* in the algebraic system.

Shannon also suggested that each piece be assigned an arbitrary number. A pawn, for instance, might be number 1, a Knight 2, a Bishop 3, a Rook 4, a Queen 5, and a King 6. White pieces would be given positive numbers and Black pieces negative ones. Thus any position on the chessboard could be recorded as a series of numbers that could be stored in the computer's memory.

The second step in Shannon's plan involved deciding on a strategy for choosing the moves to be made, the most difficult part of the program. As an approach to the problem, Shannon suggested that a method be established for the numerical evaluation of any given chess position. Actually, such a method was already available and was known to virtually every chess player from beginner to grandmaster. Experience has shown that a Bishop or Knight is worth about three pawns, a Rook is worth about four and a half or five pawns, and a Queen is worth nine, while the King's value cannot be measured in pawns. Shannon proposed that other variables such as mobility and placement of the pieces, safety of the King, and arrangement of the pawns would also have to be numerically weighed and combined in the evaluation, so that the computer could review a number of possible positions and select the one with the highest numerical rating for its own side.

After setting up a method for the numerical evaluation of each position, the machine's programmer would have to decide upon a method for selecting a move. Assuming that the opponent had just moved, the computer would have several promising moves from which to select. Each of those moves would lead to several more possible moves by the opponent, which in turn would lead to more possible computer moves. The resulting branched pattern of possible moves has come to be known as a tree. It is at this point that the computer's task would become impracticable if it were required to examine too many branches of the tree. To overcome that difficulty, Shannon suggested a compromise by examining only the important possible variations, as a human player might do. Thus the computer would investigate forcing moves, captures, and main threats with enough depth to make clear the possible consequences of each, but a line of play would be abandoned as soon as it was clear that it showed no promise of gain. Eliminating such useless variations would permit the computer to analyze more promising lines in greater depth. Shannon felt that the computer would be somewhat less efficient at selecting important variations than a human chess master, but that the size of the tree could still be reduced to manageable proportions.

The last problem, Shannon explained, involved reducing the strategy to a sequence of orders in computer language. To accomplish that, the complete program would consist of a master program and nine subprograms. The master program would correlate and supervise the subprograms, six of which would deal with the movements of the six kinds of chess pieces, one would make hypothetical moves in the memory, one would list such moves, and one would evaluate positions.

Shannon was of the opinion that a computer that was programmed as he described would play "a fairly strong game at speeds comparable to human speeds." One peculiarity of the machine, he thought, would be that it would always make the same move in any given position. Once the opponent had won a game, he could continue to win that same game over and over again simply by making the same moves. To overcome that problem, Shannon suggested that the program should contain a statistical element to randomly select moves whenever the numerical evaluations of several possible moves were nearly the same.

Although Shannon's ideas eventually became the basis for all successful computer chess programs ever written, Shannon himself never wrote a chess program. Soon, however, there were several attempts to put his theories into practice, and the public began to read about chess-playing computers. The Computer Research Corporation of Torrance, California, was reported by the newspapers to have claimed that the company's high-speed electronic digital computer could play chess and "would always win." On November 11, 1951, Donald H. Jacobs, president of Jacobs Instrument Company of Bethesda, Maryland, responded to the claims by offering to bet a thousand dollars that he could beat the California computer in a twenty-game chess match. The challenge was accepted that same day by Richard E. Sprague, a director of Computer Research Corporation, who declared that his machine, the CRC-102, could "outthink any being" and suggested that Shannon himself act as arbiter for the match. However, it appears that no such contest took place, and it is very doubtful that there was even a successful computer chess program at that time.

The person usually credited with first designing a workable computer chess program is Alan M. Turing of the University of Manchester, England. It was Turing who in 1951 first staged a chess game between a computer program and a human opponent. In that game, however, Turing did not actually employ a computer, but rather he himself hand-simulated each move of the machine, laboriously performing each calculation just as a computer would. Although matched against a very weak human opponent, Turing's hand-simulated program played like a beginner and soon lost the game as the result of a serious error.

By coincidence, that same year Gonzales Torres y Quevedo exhibited his father's electromagnetic chess player at the Congress of Cybernetics in Paris. The machine had not changed much except that a loudspeaker had been added which cried out in Spanish, "Check to the King!" and "Mate!" at the appropriate occasions. A few years later Professor van der Poel, working with a small computer named "Ptera" at a Dutch laboratory, produced a program that played the same endgame as the Torres machine—King and Rook against King.

Another program which played a limited game was devised by a group working at Los Alamos Scientific Laboratories in 1957. The Los Alamos program played on a chessboard of 6×6 squares instead of the usual 8×8, no Bishops or Bishop Pawns were used, and the game was further simplified by eliminating castling and initial two-square Pawn moves. As a result, the computing time for each move was shortened to about ten minutes and the computer, known as "MANIAC I," was able to look ahead two complete moves, but the program was hampered by the lack of a proper method for selecting the variations to be analyzed at each move. Despite that discrepancy, MANIAC I beat a beginner who had been taught the game the week before just to test the computer's playing level. A good player, however, could easily beat the machine.

Clearly a method was needed to limit the variations which the computer was to examine so as to enable the machine to play chess on a normal 8×8 square board and at the same time to speed up its playing time. The problem was solved in 1958 by Alexander Bernstein and others, who programmed an IBM 704 computer to play a normal game of chess. Bernstein's program, like the one at Los Alamos, looked ahead two complete moves—two moves by the computer and the opponent's possible replies to those moves. Bernstein, however, limited his program to selecting the seven most promising moves after answering eight questions, such as whether the King was in check, whether a piece was attacked, whether it was adequately defended, and several others. After listing the seven chosen moves, the computer analyzed the seven best replies, then the seven best replies to each reply, and finally the seven best replies to those, thus limiting the positions examined to $7 + 7^2 + 7^3 + 7^4 = 2,800$. To evaluate each of the 2,800 positions in the tree, the program had to perform about 7,000 operations, so that about 20,000,000 operations were required to decide upon a move. At the speed of the IBM 704, a move could be made in about eight minutes, which was slower than the time usually allowed for an average move in chess tournaments but was not unreasonably long.

Although the Bernstein program could play a proper game of chess, it played at the level of a beginner. Nevertheless, as noted by International Master David Levy, an authority on computer chess, the computer drew much more publicity in the United States than did the world championship matches that were played between Botvinnik and Smyslov at about the same time. As a result of the interest, there were renewed efforts to program computers to play chess. However, progress was slow and the new programs that were developed were not much more skilled than the Bernstein program.

3.

On January 21, 1967, participants arriving for the Massachusetts Amateur Championship in Boston discovered that there would be an extraordinary entrant among the competitors. An electronic computer named "Mac Hack VI" would actually compete along with the usual human players who enter such an event. Mac Hack VI would observe all the rules pertaining to time limit, pairings, touch-move, and other formalities imposed upon its human opponents. In short, it would be treated, as nearly as possible, just like any other entrant in the tourney. The Mac Hack VI program, which had been written for the PDP-6 computer by Richard Greenblatt and Donald Eastlake of MIT, played all five rounds of the tournament and finished with a score of ½–4½. "It was able to pull off a couple of pretty combinations," commented Tournament Director Benjamin Landey, "but is very weak in the endgames." Despite Mac Hack's weaknesses, it was an important landmark for computer chess.

Mac Hack VI was allowed to become specially registered in the United States Chess Federation (USCF), so that for the first time a computer could be objectively rated and compared with human players. All participants in USCF tournaments receive numerical ratings based upon their performances against previously rated players. The ratings determine a player's class, which may range from Class E players, who are rated below 1200, to Senior Masters, who have over 2400 rating points. Based upon Mac Hack's first tournament result, it was awarded a provisional rating of 1239, making it a Class D player.

Greenblatt improved Mac Hack VI and soon entered other USCF tournaments, so that by June 1967 the computer's rating had climbed nearly a hundred points to 1338. In September of that year Mac Hack became a Class C player with a rating of 1493. After that, progress was slower, and in January 1969 the program's rating had risen to only 1529. One year at the Massachusetts Amateur, Mac Hack scored a respectable 3-2 despite the fact that it lost one game because of illness: it was down for repairs and had to forfeit the game. However, the rating list for December 1972 showed that Mac Hack had actually dropped to a rating of 1512, and at about that time the program was retired from the tournament scene.

Besides entering human tournaments, computer programmers began entering their machines in competitions with other computers. The most famous series of computer tournaments began in 1970 at the annual conference of the Association for Computing Machinery (ACM), which has sponsored a computer chess championship at its meeting every year since. Most of the computers are not actually present at the conferences, but rather remain at their home bases, relaying their moves to the playing site by special telephone connections. An impartial observer at each computer site makes sure that it is really the computer that is sending the moves.

At the first ACM tournament, which was held in New York, six programs were entered in a three-round Swiss System event, which means that players with similar scores were paired. The winner of the tournament was a program known as "CHESS 3.0," which had won all three of its games. CHESS 3.0 had originated in 1968 at Northwestern University, Evanston, Illinois, where David J. Slate, Lawrence R. Atkin, and Keith Gorlen wrote the program for a CDC 6400 computer. Later versions of the program won the ACM championships in Chicago in 1971,

Boston in 1972, and Atlanta in 1973.

By that time the field had grown from six to twelve entrants, the number of rounds had been enlarged to four, and the tournament had become the U. S. Computer Chess Championship. During the first four championships, CHESS 4.0 (the number is increased each time the program is revised) had not lost a single game and had allowed only one draw.

Like Mac Hack VI, CHESS 4.0 entered tournaments with humans and by January 1972 had become a Class C player with a provisional rating of 1452. By May 1974 CHESS 4.0 had played a total of fourteen tournament games with human opponents and was rated 1579. In the Northwestern University Winter Swiss that year, the program scored a respectable 4½–1½ game points against human adversaries, matching the abilities of a strong Class B human player. More recently at the Paul Masson American Class Championships in July 1976, CHESS 4.5 actually scored an incredible 5-0 against Class B human competition, to the surprise of everyone including programmer Slate. The result in the Paul Masson earned the program a performance rating of 2184. CHESS 4.5 also won the Minnesota Open the next year with a performance rating of 2271. The December 1975 rating lists showed that the computer programs Dartmouth (1210), DUCHESS (1333), and TECH II (1323) had also entered human tournaments that year, but all three were provisionally rated Class D players.

At the Fifth U. S. Computer Chess Championship in San Diego in 1974, CHESS 4.0 finally lost its title when it was beaten in the decisive last round by TREEFROG (also known as RIBBIT), a Canadian program. The next year in Minneapolis, however, CHESS 4.4 scored a perfect 4-0 to regain the title from TREEFROG, which tied for second with 3-1.

Chess has never been an important spectator sport in the United States, yet the U. S. Computer Chess Championships have drawn audiences of up to 200 for some rounds. Such crowds are probably comparable to those that flocked to see the Turk or Ajeeb. They are more interested in seeing a machine play chess than they are in the game itself. This time, however, there is no deception; the machines really are playing the game.

4.

Since the Soviet Union has long dominated world chess, it is not surprising that they have also been in the vanguard of computer chess. In 1961 former World Champion Botvinnik quoted a prominent Soviet cybernetics expert as saying that "in principle, a chess robot could be built, but its size would be commensurable with the new University of Moscow." However, only a little over five years later the Soviet computer M-20, which was nowhere near the size of the university, began an international chess match with a U. S. computer from Stanford University. During the match, Grandmaster Yuri Averbakh commented, "That a machine is capable of playing chess is a fact that is now no longer able to astonish anyone." After over a year of play the match was won by a score of 3-1 in favor of the Soviet M-20, which had been programmed by scientists at the Insitute of Theoretical and Applied Physics in Moscow.

That same M-20, however, was defeated by the citizens of eighty towns in the Urals, who, in 1968, competed with the machine by means of letters to a local newspaper. Each week the paper printed the move sent in by a majority of the readers along with the computer's reply to it.

The strongest Soviet computer chess program is KAISSA, written at the Institute for System Studies in Moscow, by Drs. M. V. Donsky and V. Arlazarov. At the First World Computer Chess Championship in Stockholm in 1974, KAISSA scored a perfect 4-0 to win against four U. S. programs, three British programs, and one program each from Austria, Canada, Hungary, Norway, and Switzerland. KAISSA was never matched against the second-place CHESS 4.0 during the tournament, but the two were paired in an exhibition game that followed. After a long struggle KAISSA won a pawn, but the game still ended in a draw.

KAISSA was favored to win the Second World Computer Chess Championship at Toronto in August 1977, but of course CHESS 4.6 was expected to put up a good fight. Unfortunately for the defending champion, its programmers reshuffled its program shortly before the tournament, causing it to lose in the first round to DUCHESS. Thus CHESS 4.6, playing in top form, won all of its games and captured the world championship. Again, by chance, the two top contenders were not paired, but CHESS 4.6 won the inevitable exhibition game after the tournament, establishing itself clearly as the top computer program.

In the audience were former World Correspondence Chess Champion Hans Berliner, left center, and International Master Edward Lasker, to his left. Earlier in the year both masters had lost games to CHESS 4.5, the eventual winner of the tournament. FROM AC.

In 1960 Lasker had been the first master to play against a computer. FROM AC.

What were these people watching? It was a computer chess tournament—the Second World Computer Chess Championship, in fact, held in Toronto in August 1977. FROM AC.

Computer chess tournaments are much noisier affairs than those in which humans participate. International Master David Levy, as he often does at such events, delivered a running commentary on the games in progress. He observed that the increasing number of draws indicates a higher level of computer play than in the past. FROM AC.

Demonstration boards mounted on a stage provided the audience a clear view of all games. FROM AC.

Computers matched against each other shared a table with a chessboard between the two terminals. By each board a chess clock recorded the time for each player. Telephones provided verbal communications between the tournament site and the computer location. FROM AC.

The participants, in the form of computer terminals, were arrayed between the demonstration boards and the audience. Most of the computers were far from the tournament site, their moves relayed by means of telephone lines. FROM AC.

The Russian computer KAISSA, winner of the First Computer Championship, experienced programming difficulties and lost to DUCHESS, the Duke University program. FROM AC.

Aglow with activity, this terminal printed out the eagerly awaited next move. Eventually the opponent's reply was entered on the keyboard. FROM AC.

David Slate, talking on the phone, and Larry Atkin, looking on at his left, were the programmers of the undefeated champion, CHESS 4.6. As at the first championship, CHESS 4.6 and KAISSA did not happen to be paired. However, in an exhibition game following the tournament, the American program proved victorious. FROM AC.

A breakdown in one of the terminals called for a hurried repair job. The smoothly organized tournament was a part of the 1977 Congress of the International Federation for Information Processing (IFIP). FROM AC.

Besides commenting on the games, Levy was often called upon to arbitrate disputes. Betting that KAISSA would win, Levy lost $50.00 to Monty Newborn, the author of *Computer Chess*. FROM AC.

5.

Will computers soon be playing master-level chess? Will they defeat the strongest human players? When one recalls the gloomy predictions of Gümpel, Proctor, and Tomlinson only one hundred years ago, it appears that chess machines have made remarkable progress. However, David Levy, who acts as tournament director at the ACM tournaments, thinks that it will be at least the year 2000 before computer programs will play well enough to earn the title of International Master. Levy, who is himself an International Master, made a famous bet in 1968 that no computer would beat him in a chess match by the end of August 1978. The initial wager was five-hundred British pounds, but it was later increased to 1,250 pounds. Levy won his bet after defeating, in late August 1978, a pair of challenges

by a Mac Hack-CHEOPS program (2–0) and CHESS 4.7 (3½–1½). Since then the stakes have increased dramatically. The Fredkin Foundation of Cambridge, Massachusetts has offered a $100,000 prize to the first computer program to win the world chess championship.

Levy, of course, has made a study of chess-playing computers and knows their weaknesses. Most human players when playing against computers suffer a psychological disadvantage comparable to that felt by persons who played against chess automatons.

One form of chess at which the best computers are especially adept is blitz chess, in which each opponent must complete all of his moves in five minutes. In order for the computer to play blitz, the rules must be modified. The program is allowed five seconds per move and must either mate its opponent or announce mate by move 60 or it loses on time. Its human adversary plays in the usual manner, losing by time forfeit after five minutes have elapsed on his clock.

At such speeds the program's tactical abilities prove to be a decided advantage. Employing the phenomenal speed of the CDC Cyber 176 computer, CHESS 4.6, with a performance rating of about 2100 in normal tournament games, plays blitz at a 2300 rating, somewhat above the master level. Thus, in a four-game match, the program held Levy to a score of 2-2. CHESS 4.6 has outblitzed several masters and even at normal speeds has scored eight wins, one draw, and only one loss in a simultaneous exhibition against ten human players of considerable strength. To top off this impressive record, in August 1977 the program won a blitz game against Michael Stean, the first computer victory over a grandmaster.

Playing against human competition, CHESS 4.6 entered and won the Twin City Open in St. Paul, April 29–30, 1978. With a top-seeded rating of 1936, the computer scored a perfect 5-0 result.

A new electronic chessboard, known as Chesstor, was used for the first time at the Twin City Open. Chesstor's microprocessor magnetically sensed the opponent's move, transmitted it by telephone to Cyber 176, and indicated the computer's response by illuminating the square of the piece to be moved and the square to which it was to be moved. Chesstor also sensed when the clock was hit, thus recording the time used.

During the tournament, U. S. Champion Walter Browne, a grandmaster, simultaneously played forty-four games, including one against CHESS 4.6. Browne began quite rapidly, but he was soon slowing down at the computer's table. He eventually offered CHESS 4.6 a draw, which was declined, and finally had to resign. In fairness to Browne, it must be added that he played the game in twenty-six minutes while the computer used just over four hours.

The next step in the rapid evolution of computer chess was to make available to the average chess player a small, reasonably-priced chess computer for his personal use. One such microcomputer device, Chess Challenger by Fidelity Electronics, was widely advertised in 1977. The first model of Chess Challenger, about the size and shape of a large notebook, was easy to beat. It was soon replaced by a model that played at three levels of difficulty. The highest level, however, played at the strength of only a Class E human player.

Another microcomputer, named Boris, was soon competing for the market. Boris could play at several levels depending upon the amount of time allowed for each move. In addition, Boris had a display that flashed comments about the game, although these were not always entirely pertinent.

It was not long before a new Chess Challenger with ten levels of play was in the field. There were also two models of Checker Challenger. Probably by the time this book appears there will be available a new model of Boris and perhaps other brands of chess microcomputers. It seems that they might follow the trend of pocket calculators and digital watches, in which case their size and price will diminish while their level of performance will improve. This, of course, will depend upon the market. Even today, anyone with a few hundred dollars can have his own chess computer. It is also possible to purchase a microcomputer and program it to play chess.

The First Microcomputer Chess Tournament was held in the Convention Center in San Jose, California, March 3–5, 1978. Entrants were limited to computers based on 8-bit microprocessor chips,

In September 1977, the Chess Challenger, a miniature chess computer, was entered in a Kansas City tournament, winning only one half point. Jack Winters, owner of the device, entered the moves and scored the games. Since then, the United States Chess Federation has ruled the Challenger ineligible for USCF events. FROM AC.

with less than 32K bytes of memory, and small enough to attend "in person." It was the first computer chess competition without terminals hooked up by telephone to multimillion-dollar machines far from the playing site. Entrants ranged from an $85 "homemade metal box" to an outfit priced around $6,000. Three of the computers, including Chess Challenger and Boris, were off-the-shelf consumer products.

The winning microcomputer, SARGON, scored 5-0, two points ahead of the field. SARGON was programmed by husband and wife Dan and Kathe Spracklen for a Z-80 computer. Boris and Chess Challenger tied for second place with Commodore Chessmate, the prototype of a consumer product soon expected on the market. Each ended with three points.

The quality of play in the First Microcomputer Chess Tournament was rather poor by both human and computer standards, but considering that most contestants were little more than slightly overgrown pocket calculators, they did remarkably well. Furthermore, microcomputers are rapidly expanding their capabilities.

The USCF has ruled that commercial microcomputers, such as Chess Challenger, are not eligible to play in its rated tournaments. Thus the machines do not have USCF ratings. Other computer programs must at present be evaluated by the USCF Ratings Committee. If acceptable, the programs are issued a certificate for rated play. Changes in the program or computer require reregistration.

So computers now have their own world championship, microcomputers vie for their own little championship, and under certain conditions the top computer occasionally overpowers a human grandmaster. What next? The supermechanical chess player?

ON THE CHESSBOARD
Some Computer Games

What is it like to play a game of chess with a computer? It is not much like playing against the Torres machine and nothing at all like playing a chess automaton. Before the game can begin it is necessary to dial a telephone number which connects a teletypewriter with the computer. Then the chess program is activated by typing in the proper password. The machine is then ready to play, and its human opponent may begin by typing in his first move. After checking the move's legality, the computer calculates a reply and types it out. The machine makes no moves on the chessboard, which is present only for the convenience of the human player. If the human opponent requests it, the computer will produce a printout of the chessboard, which is stored in its memory.

A computer age chessboard displayed the position in a game at the World Championship. Computers can also type out the position when called upon to do so. FROM AC.

The human player may at first be startled by the rapidity of the computer's replies, which seem to be made almost instantly. This is because the machine has stored in its memory several hundred sequences of moves covering the most popular openings. Soon, however, the computer slows down as it encounters moves that are not in its book of openings. The mathematical impossibility of storing more than a few of the possible opening sequences has often been demonstrated.

Of the computer's style of play, C. H. O'D. Alexander, Ireland's strongest player, once wrote, "You cannot easily tell a computer from a human player by the style of its game. One sees exactly the characteristics the layman would least expect. The computer is not mechanically accurate and dull, but wild, ingenious and undisciplined. It is at its best in thinking up tricky short-term manoeuvres; its weakness is long-term planning. As yet I have seen nothing that looks like depth of thought."

Grandmaster William Lombardy once analyzed a game between a computer and a human chess master without knowing which was which. By move 4 Lombardy suspected the identity of the computer, and he was positive of the identification after move 5. However, he apparently based his decision upon the quality of the computer's play rather than upon its style. The following selection of games should allow the reader to judge the style of computer play. Additional computer games may be found in *Computer Chess*, by Monroe Newborn, and *Chess and Computers* and *1975 U.S. Computer Chess Championship*, both by David Levy.

Game 53

The first program capable of playing a game of chess was designed by Alan Turing in 1951. The Turing program played only one game, however, a tedious hand-simulation in which Turing himself performed the calculations instead of a computer. One peculiarity of the program was that it tended to weaken its position by advancing pawns.

Vienna Game

University of Manchester, England, 1951

White	Black
Turing Program, hand-simulated	Human
1 P–K4	P–K4
2 N–QB3	N–KB3
3 P–Q4	B–N5
4 N–B3	P–Q3
5 B–Q2	N–B3
6 P–Q5	N–Q5
7 P–KR4	B–N5
8 P–R4	N×Nch
9 P×N	B–KR4
10 B–N5ch	P–B3? (N–Q2!)
11 P×P	O–O
12 P×P	R–N1
13 B–QR6	Q–R4
14 Q–K2	N–Q2 (B×P!)
15 R–KN1	N–B4
16 R–N5	B–N3
17 B–N5? (B–QB4!)	N×NP
18 O–O–O	N–B4
19 B–B6	KR–B1? (N–K3!)
20 B–Q5	B×N
21 B×B	Q×P
22 K–Q2? (P–R5!)	N–K3
23 R–N4? (B×N!)	N–Q5? (N–B5!)
24 Q–Q3	N–N4
25 B–N3	Q–R3
26 B–B4?	B–R4
27 R–N3	Q–R5
28 B×N	Q×B
29 Q×P??	R–Q1
Resigns	

Game 54

Alex Bernstein and his associates are credited with developing the first feasible chess program for a computer, an IBM 704. Averaging about eight minutes per move, the computer played against "a skillful opponent" in this game which appeared in *Scientific American*, June 1958. "We have deliberately chosen a game which the machine lost," explained the programmers, "because we want to emphasize the point that a machine is not infallible and also because it is more instructive to watch the computer lose than to watch it win."

Bishop's Opening

1958

White	Black
Bernstein Program, IBM 704	Human
1 P–K4	P–K4
2 B–B4	P–QN3
3 P–Q3	N–KB3
4 B–KN5	B–N2
5 B×N	Q×B
6 N–KB3	P–B3
7 O–O	P–Q4
8 P×P	P×P
9 B–N5 ch	N–B3
10 P–B4? (N×P!)	P×P
11 B×Nch	Q×B
12 P×P? (R–K1!)	P–K5
13 N–N5	Q–N3
14 N–KR3	P–K6
15 P–B3	B–B4
16 R–K1	O–O
17 N–B3??	P–K7 dis ch
18 N–B2	B×P
19 P–KN3	P×Q(Q)
20 N×Q	Q–B7
21 P–N3	QR–Q1
22 P–KR4	R×N
Resigns	

Game 55

"A History Making Tournament!" proclaimed *Chess Life* when, in January 1967, Mac Hack VI entered the Massachusetts Amateur Championship on equal footing with human players. Mac Hack was unable to win any games in that contest but later defeated a human opponent in the Massachusetts State Championship, the first tournament in which a computer program ever won a game.

Sicilian Defense

Massachusetts State Championship, 1967

White	Black
Mac Hack VI, PDP-6	Human, USCF 1510
1 P–K4	P–QB4
2 P–Q4	P×P
3 Q×P	N–QB3
4 Q–Q3	N–B3
5 N–QB3	P–KN3
6 N–B3	P–Q3
7 B–B4	P–K4
8 B–N3	P–QR3
9 O–O–O	P–QN4
10 P–QR4	B–R3ch
11 K–N1	P–N5
12 Q×QP	B–Q2
13 B–R4	B–N2

14 N–Q5	N×P
15 N–B7ch	Q×N
16 Q×Q	N–B4
17 Q–Q6	B–KB1
18 Q–Q5	R–B1
19 N×P	B–K3
20 Q×Nch	R×Q
21 R–Q8 mate	

Game 56

International chess competition between computers began November 23, 1966 with a four game match between computers from the U. S. and U. S. S. R. The four games, which were played simultaneously, took more than a year to complete and ended with the Soviet computer winning two games and drawing two. The following game shows that the Soviet machine deserved the victory.

Three Knights' Game

Game Three, Moscow-Stanford Match, November 23, 1966 to March 10, 1967

White	Black
Program of the Institute of Theoretical and Experimental Physics, M-20 Computer	Kotok-McCarthy Stanford University Program, IBM 7090
1 P–K4	P–K4
2 N–KB3	N–QB3
3 N–B3	B–B4
4 N×P!	N×N
5 P–Q4	B–Q3
6 P×N	B×P
7 P–B4	B×Nch
8 P×B	N–B3
9 P–K5	N–K5
10 Q–Q3	N–B4
11 Q–Q5	N–K3? (P–Q3!)
12 P–B5	N–N4?
13 P–KR4!	P–KB3
14 P×N	P×NP
15 R×P!	R–B1
16 R×P	P–B3
17 Q–Q6	R×P
18 R–N8ch	R–B1
19 Q×R mate	

Game 57

In 1972, the Soviet computer program KAISSA played a simultaneous two-game match against the readers of the newspaper *Komsomolskaia Pravda*. Moves made against the computer were those receiving the most votes in weekly letters from the readers. One game was drawn, while the other, reproduced below, was won by the readers.

Queen's Fianchetto Opening

U.S.S.R., January to November, 1972

White	Black
Komsomolskaia Pravda Readers	KAISSA, ICL 4/70
1 P–QN3	P–K4
2 B–N2	N–QB3
3 P–QB4	P–B3
4 N–QB3	B–N5
5 N–Q5	KN–K2
6 P–QR3	B–Q3
7 P–N3	O–O
8 B–N2	N–N3
9 P–K3	P–B4
10 N–K2	R–K1
11 Q–B2	P–K5
12 P–Q3	P×P
13 Q×P	R–B1
14 P–B4	B–K2
15 P–KR4	P–KR3
16 P–R5	N–R1
17 P–K4	P–Q3
18 O–O–O	R–B2
19 N×Bch	Q×N
20 N–B3	B–K3
21 N–Q5	Q–Q2
22 N–K3	P×P
23 B×KP	N–K2
24 B×QNP	R–N1
25 B–K4	N–B4
26 N–Q5	P–R4
27 P–KN4	N–K2
28 N×Nch	R×N
29 P–N5	P×P
30 P–KB5	N–B2
31 P×B	Q×P
32 B–Q5	Q–K6ch
33 Q×Q	R×Q
34 QR–B1	Resigns

Game 58

The strongest American chess program is CHESS 4.0 (or various later versions of the program with higher numbers). At the Northwestern University Winter Swiss in 1974, CHESS 4.0 held up well against average human tournament players, scoring a creditable 4½–1½. In the following game the program defeated a Class D player in twenty-four moves, taking a total of only seventeen minutes and forty-one seconds to calculate the moves. More amazing, however, was the way CHESS 4.0 launched an attack on the weakened Black King side.

Sicilian Defense

Northwestern University Winter Swiss, Evanston, Illinois, January 1974

White	Black
CHESS 4.0, CDC 6400	Human, USCF 1226
1 P–K4	P–QB4
2 N–KB3	N–QB3
3 P–Q4	P×P
4 N×P	N–B3
5 N–QB3	P–Q3
6 B–KN5	P–K3
7 Q–Q2	B–K2
8 O–O–O	O–O
9 P–B4	N×N
10 Q×N	P–KR3
11 B–R4	P–R3
12 B×N	P×B
13 B–K2	B–Q2
14 K–N1	B–B3
15 Q–Q3	R–B1
16 P–KR4	Q–N3
17 Q–B3	K–R2
18 P–KN4	R–KN1
19 P–N5	P–B4
20 Q–R5	R–N3
21 KP×P	P×P
22 KR–K1	B–K5??
23 N×B	P×N
24 P–B5	Resigns

Game 59

Among U. S. computer programs, CHESS 4.0 has been a consistent winner. The following game decided first place at the ACM tournament in Atlanta.

Queen's Gambit Accepted

Round Four, U. S. Computer Chess Championship, Atlanta, August 28, 1973

White	Black
CHAOS, UNIVAC 1108	CHESS 4.0, CDC 6400
1 P–Q4	P–Q4
2 P–QB4	P×P
3 N–KB3	N–KB3
4 P–K3	P–K3
5 B×P	P–B4
6 O–O	P–QR3
7 Q–K2	P–QN4
8 B–N3	B–N2
9 N–B3	QN–Q2
10 B–Q2	B–Q3
11 KR–K1	P×P
12 P×P	O–O
13 B–N5	Q–N3
14 B–B2	B×N
15 Q×B	Q×P
16 QR–Q1	Q–QN5
17 P–KN3?	Q×P
18 R–K2	Q–R6
19 Q–B6	B–N5
20 R×N?	QR–B1

21	R–B7	R×R
22	Q×R	Q×N
23	Q–N7	Q–B5
24	B–Q1	R–Q1
25	R–K5	R×Bch
26	K–N2	Q–B8ch
27	K–B3	Q–R8ch
28	K–K2	R–K8ch
29	K–Q3	Q–B8ch
30	K–Q4	Q–B5 mate

Game 60

CHESS 4.0 won all of the U. S. Computer Chess Championships until RIBBIT (later known as TREEFROG) won the title at San Diego in 1974 by winning the following game.

Sicilian Defense

Round Four, U. S. Computer Chess Championship, San Diego, 1974

White	Black
RIBBIT, Honeywell 6060	CHESS 4.0, CDC 6400
1 P–K4	P–QB4
2 P–QB3	P–Q4
3 P×P	Q×P
4 P–Q4	P×P
5 P×P	N–QB3
6 N–KB3	B–N5
7 N–B3	Q–Q3?
8 P–Q5	N–N5
9 B–N5ch	B–Q2
10 B×Bch	K×B
11 B–K3	Q–QR3?
12 N–K5ch	K–K1
13 P–QR3	Q–Q3
14 Q–R4ch	N–B3
15 P×N	P×P
16 N×QBP	P–K4
17 N×RP dis ch	Q–Q2
18 Q×Qch	K×Q

White won.

Game 61

Although CHESS 4.0 and KAISSA were not paired in the First World Computer Chess Championship, they met in an exhibition game the day after the final round, a contest which David Levy called "the Fischer-Spassky match of the computer world." However, the game demonstrates the weaknesses of the best chess programs at that time.

Center Counter Defense

Exhibition Game, Stockholm, August 9, 1974

White	Black
CHESS 4.0, CDC 6400	KAISSA, ICL 4/70
1 P–K4	P–Q4
2 P×P	N–KB3
3 P–Q4	N×P
4 N–KB3	P–KN3
5 B–K2	B–N2
6 O–O	O–O
7 R–K1	B–B4
8 N–R4	P–K4?
9 N×B	P×N
10 P×P	N–N5
11 Q×Q	R×Q
12 B–KN5	R–Q2
13 N–R3	B×P
14 P–QB3	N/5–B3
15 N–B4	P–QR4
16 B–B3	P–B3
17 B–R6	P–R5
18 QR–Q1	R×R
19 R×R	K–R1
20 B×N	N×B
21 P–B4	P–N4
22 P×B	P×N
23 P×P	R–Q1
24 R–KB1	K–N1
25 R×P	R–Q8ch
26 K–B2	N–Q1
27 B–B4	P–B3
28 K–B3	R–KB8ch
29 K–K4	R–QR8
30 P–QR3	R–K8ch
31 B–K3	R–K7
32 R–B2	R–K8
33 R–Q2	N–K3
34 R–Q6	N–B4ch
35 K–B3	N–Q6
36 B–Q4	P–B4
37 B–K3	K–B2
38 R–Q7ch	K–N3
39 R–KN7ch	K×P
40 R×P	N–K4ch
41 K–B4	N–Q6ch
42 K–K4	N×P
43 P–N4	N–Q8
44 P–N5ch	K–N3
45 R–R6ch	K–N2
46 K–Q5??	R×B
47 K×P/4	R×Pch
48 K–N5	R×P
49 P–R4	R–R6
50 K×BP	N–N7
51 P–R5	P–R6
52 R–KN6ch	K–B2
53 R–KB6ch	K–N1
54 R–KN6ch	K–B2
55 R–KB6ch	K–K2
56 P–R6	N–R5ch
57 K–N4	P–R7
58 R–B1	N–B6

241

59	K–N3	P–R8(Q)
60	R×Q	N–K5 dis ch
61	K–B4	N×P
62	R–R6	N–B2
63	R–R7ch	K–K3
64	R–R6ch	K–B4
65	K–Q4	N×P

Draw

Game 62

At the 1975 ACM tournament Levy played a simultaneous exhibition against twelve computer programs. Although exhausted after a difficult day as director of the tournament, Levy won ten of the games with two draws. Here we see one of the two games he played with CHESS 4.4, the winner of the tournament. "I was particularly amused," commented Levy, "when my opponent pointed out after the game that I could have mated it one move earlier."

Bird's Opening

Simultaneous Exhibition, Minneapolis, October 19, 1975

White	Black
CHESS 4.4, CDC 6400	David Levy, International Master

1	P–KB4	P–Q4
2	N–KB3	N–KB3
3	P–K3	B–N5
4	P–QN3	P–B3
5	B–N2	QN–Q2
6	B–K2	B×N
7	B×B	Q–B2
8	O–O	P–K4
9	P×P	N×P
10	B–K2	B–Q3
11	N–B3	P–KR4
12	P–KR3	N/4–N5!
13	P×N	B–R7ch
14	K–R1	P×P
15	B×P	B–N8 dis ch
16	K×B	Q–R7ch
17	K–B2	Q–R5ch
18	K–B3	N×B
19	R–R1	Q–B7ch!
20	K×N	P–B4ch
21	K–N5	Q–N6ch
22	K×P	O–Och (R–KB1ch!)
23	K–K6	R–B3ch
24	K–K7	Q–Q3 mate

Game 63

Scoring 5–0, CHESS 4.5 beat all of its opponents in the Class B section of the 4th Annual Paul Masson

Class Championships. In this exhibition game played at the rate of 30 moves in 30 minutes, the program defeated a Class A player.

Modern Benoni

Exhibition Game, Saratoga, California, July, 1976

White	Black
A. Hough, USCF 1886	CHESS 4.5, CDC Cyber 176

1	P–Q4	N–KB3
2	P–QB4	P–B4
3	P–Q5	P–K3
4	N–QB3	P×P
5	P×P	P–Q3
6	N–B3	P–KN3
7	P–KN3	B–N2
8	B–N2	O–O
9	O–O	B–N5
10	N–Q2	Q–K2
11	P–KR3	B–Q2
12	P–QR4	N–R3
13	N–B4	N–K1
14	Q–N3	N–N5
15	B–B4	P–KN4
16	B–Q2	P–KR3
17	K–R2	N–B2
18	P–R5	P–B4
19	P–B4	QR–N1
20	P–K4	BP×P
21	N×KP	N/5×P
22	P×P	Q–K3
23	N/K×QP	P×P
24	QR–K1	Q–N3
25	N–K3	Q×N
26	N×N	B–K3
27	R×B	N×R
28	R–K1	R–B7
29	R×N	Q×R

White time forfeit

Game 64

At the Minnesota Open, CHESS 4.5 took first place with a surprising 5–1 score. An example of how the program dealt with an expert follows.

Sicilian Defense

84th Minnesota Open, Minneapolis, February 1977

White	Black
CHESS 4.5, CDC Cyber 176	C. Fenner, USCF 2016

1	P–K4	P–QB4
2	N–KB3	P–K3
3	P–Q4	P×P
4	N×P	P–QR3
5	P–QB4	N–KB3

6	B–Q3		Q–B2
7	O–O		B–B4
8	N–N3		B–R2
9	N–B3		N–B3
10	B–N5		N–K4
11	B×N		P×B
12	Q–K2		P–Q3
13	K–R1		B–Q2
14	P–B4		N×B
15	Q×N		O–O–O
16	QR–Q1		B–B3
17	P–KB5		B–N1
18	P–N3		P–KR4
19	P×P		P–R5
20	R×P		RP×P
21	Q×NP		QR–N1
22	P×P		Q×P
23	R×Q		R×Q
24	N–Q5		B–K1
25	N–N6ch		K–Q1
26	R×P		B–B3
27	R×Bch		K–B2
28	R–B8ch		R×R
29	P×R		B×Pch
30	K–N1		R–KR1
31	N–Q5ch		K–B3
32	N–R5ch		Resigns

Game 65

Edward Lasker was, in 1960, the first master to play and defeat a computer. Thus, this victory by CHESS 4.5 marks something of a turning point in computer chess. At the time the game was played, Lasker was ninety-two years old.

Ruy Lopez, Schliemann Defense

Simultaneous Exhibition by CHESS 4.5, New York, March 29, 1977

White	Black
CHESS 4.5, CDC	Edward Lasker,
Cyber 176	International Master

1	P–K4	P–K4
2	N–KB3	N–QB3
3	B–N5	P–B4
4	N–B3	N–Q5
5	P×P	N–KB3
6	N×N	P×N
7	N–K2	P–B3
8	B–B4	P–Q4
9	B–Q3	B–Q3
10	N×P	O–O
11	O–O	P–B4
12	N–K6	B×N
13	P×B	P–B5
14	B–B5	P–KN3
15	B–R3	N–K5
16	P–Q3	N×P

17	R×N		Q–N3
18	P–Q4		B×Pch
19	K–B1		R×Rch
20	K×R		R–B1ch
21	K–K2		P–B6
22	P×P		Q–B2
23	B–R3		R–B5
24	Q–Q3		R–K5ch
25	K–Q1		B–N6
26	Q–B3		R–K8ch
27	K–Q2		Q–N1
28	Q–B7ch		K–R1
29	B–B8		Q–B5ch
30	Q×Q		Resigns

Game 66

Levy would have lost 1,250 British pounds if he had allowed CHESS 4.5 to defeat him in this game.

Sicilian Defense

Carnegie Mellon University, Pittsburgh, April 1, 1977

White	Black
CHESS 4.5, CDC	David Levy,
Cyber 176	International Master

1	P–K4	P–QB4
2	N–KB3	P–Q3
3	P–Q4	P×P
4	N×P	N–KB3
5	N–QB3	P–KN3
6	P–B3	B–N2
7	B–K3	O–O
8	Q–Q2	N–B3
9	B–QB4	P–QR3
10	N×N	P×N
11	O–O	N–Q2
12	P–B4	N–N3
13	B–K2	B–K3
14	P–QN3	N–B1
15	P–QR3	Q–R4
16	P–QN4	Q–B2
17	P–B5	B–Q2
18	B–R6	Q–N3ch
19	K–R1	Q–Q5
20	Q×Q	B×Q
21	R–B3	B–N2
22	B×B	K×B
23	R–QN1	N–N3
24	R/3–B1	KR–QN1
25	QR–Q1	P–B3
26	P–QR4	P–QR4
27	P–N5	BP×P
28	RP×P	R–QB1
29	R–Q3	R–B4
30	R–N3	R/1–QB1
31	R/1–B3	P–R5
32	P–R4	P–R6
33	P×P	P×P
34	R–K3	B–K3
35	P–R5	P–N4

36 N–Q5 P–R7
37 R–QR3 B×N
38 P×B R×BP
39 B–Q1 R–Q7
40 K–R2 R–B8
41 B–N3 P–R8(Q)
42 R×Q R×R
Resigns

35 Q×B R–B3
36 Q–K5 R–QN3
37 Q×BP R×P
38 Q–QB8ch K–R2
39 Q×P Resigns

Game 67

This blitz game was the first victory ever scored by a computer over a grandmaster.

Queen's Fianchetto Defense

Exhibition Blitz Game, London, August 1977

White	Black
CHESS 4.5, CDC Cyber 176	Michael Stean, International Grandmaster

	White	Black
1	P–K4	P–QN3
2	P–Q4	B–N2
3	N–QB3	P–QB4
4	P×P	P×P
5	B–K3	P–Q3
6	B–N5ch	N–Q2
7	N–B3	P–K3
8	O–O	P–QR3
9	B×Nch	Q×B
10	Q–Q3	N–K2
11	QR–Q1	R–Q1
12	Q–B4	N–N3
13	KR–K1	B–K2
14	Q–N3	Q–B3
15	K–R1	O–O
16	B–N5	B–R1
17	B×B	N×B
18	P–QR4	R–N1
19	Q–R2	R–N5
20	P–QN3	P–B4
21	N–KN5	P×P
22	N/3×P	R×BP
23	R×QP	Q×R
24	N×Q	R×P/N7
25	N/5–K4	R–N5
26	P–B4	N–B4
27	P–R3	N–N6ch
28	K–R2	R×N
29	Q–KB2	P–R3
30	N×R	N×N
31	Q–B3	R–N1
32	R×N	R–KB1
33	Q–N4	B×R
34	Q×KPch	K–R1

Game 68

For want of a better example of a game between a chess microcomputer and a human, the following is presented. Although the human was heard to say that he found the game highly amusing, it appears that he was very careless with his pieces. White, in fact, had a Rook en prise for ten moves, while a Bishop was left hanging for fourteen. On move 24, White had four of his pieces en prise. Apparently, the poor computer, allowed a minute for each move, could not in that time adequately examine the consequences of so many possible captures.

Stonewall Opening

Cleveland, Ohio, July 1978

	White	Black
	B. Ewart, USCF 1737	Boris
1	P–Q4	P–Q4
2	P–K3	N–QB3
3	P–KB4	N–B3
4	N–Q2	P–K3
5	P–B3	B–Q3
6	KN–B3	N–KN5
7	Q–K2	P–KR4
8	P–KR3	N–R3
9	P–K4?	B×P
10	P×P	B–N6ch
11	K–Q1	Q×P
12	N–K4	N–B4
13	B–N5	P–R3
14	K–B2	N–R4
15	R–Q1?	Q×RP
16	N/3–Q2	P–KB3
17	N×B?	N×N
18	Q–K1	Q–R5ch
19	K–B1	N–N6ch?
20	N×N	P–R5?
21	N–B5	Q–R8ch
22	K–B2	Q–R7
23	P–Q5	P–QN3
24	B–N5ch!	P×B
25	N×P	B×N
26	Q×Bch	K–B1
27	R–R1	Q×R
28	R×R	R–K1
29	Q–Q7	P×B
30	R–R7	

White won.

14

Catherine the Great and the Chess Automaton; or Chess Automatons in Fiction

1.

"Everybody has heard of that famous automaton, the 'chess-player of Kempelin [sic],' by means of which the little Russian officer escaped from his enemies, and beat them at chess at the same time." When readers of *Frank Leslie's Popular Monthly* read that line which began the story "In Love with an Automaton" in the November 1878 issue of the magazine, they probably agreed with that statement, although some may have recalled that the officer was Polish rather than Russian, and that it was the enemies who were Russian. In those days anyone who had heard about chess automatons probably knew the story and regarded it as the true history of Kempelen's Turk. Even the *Grande Encyclopédie Larousse* and the *Encyclopaedia Britannica* carried the tale, the latter explaining that the automaton's first director "was a Polish patriot, Worousky, who had lost both legs in a campaign; as he was furnished with artificial limbs when in public, his appearance together with the fact that no dwarf or child travelled with Kempelen's company, dispelled the suspicion that any person could be employed inside."

The story of Worousky, Kempelen's chess automaton, and Catherine the Great had first appeared in the 1858 memoirs of the French conjurer Jean-Eugène Robert-Houdin, and, although it was basically a work of short fiction, it was woven into the autobiography as if it were a true story. Robert-

The great French conjurer Jean-Eugene Robert-Houdin wrote a spurious history of Kempelen's Turk. That tale spawned two novels, two plays, two movies, and at least one short story. COURTESY OF NYPL.

245

Houdin introduced the narrative by stating that he had seen the chess automaton at the house of the mechanician Cronier in Bellville. He then related the automaton's supposed history, claiming to have learned it from a Monsieur Hessler, the nephew of Dr. Osloff.

The tale began at Riga in 1796 when the Polish officer Worousky led an ill-fated revolt against his Russian oppressors. Both his legs having been shattered by a cannon ball, the fugitive dragged himself to Dr. Osloff's house, who saved his life, but in the process had to amputate the gangrenous limbs.

At that time Kempelen visited his friend Osloff in order to gather materials for his book on human speech. Noting that the crippled Worousky was a strong chess player, Kempelen invented the chess automaton as a means of concealing the Pole but still permitting him to earn a living. The mechanician planned to tour the Russian cities with the automaton and thus work his way to the frontier of Germany so that Worousky could escape.

In Vitebsk, however, Kempelen received a letter from the Empress Catherine, requesting that he immediately bring the chess player to St. Petersburg to play a game with her at the imperial palace. Although Kempelen was greatly alarmed, the impetuous Worousky was delighted at the prospect of not only deceiving Catherine by his presence in the automaton, but of beating her at chess. Since Worousky was unable to travel rapidly, it required fifteen days to reach St. Petersburg, but Kempelen explained that he had been delayed in order to make some additions to the automaton that were indispensable for so important a game.

The Empress demanded a game the evening of Kempelen's arrival. The contest began, and she quickly found herself in difficulty and attempted to cheat. The Turk responded by striking the cushion violently and putting back the piece that had been moved. Unwilling to admit her indiscretion, Catherine repeated the dubious move, but then the automaton knocked over the pieces with a sweep of his hand.

"Ah, ah! My good automaton! your manners are rather rough," said the Empress, adding that a fear of losing the game had undoubtedly prompted the Turk to act as he did. Kempelen tried to apologize, but Catherine was more amused than angry and announced that she wished to purchase the automaton. The mechanician managed to dissuade her by arguing that the Turk was unable to operate without him, and thus he could not sell the machine.

After escaping from Russia, the automaton was sold to Anthon, then to Maelzel, and finally arrived at the home of Cronier, where Robert-Houdin claimed to have seen him.

The story is so far from the truth that it is hard to

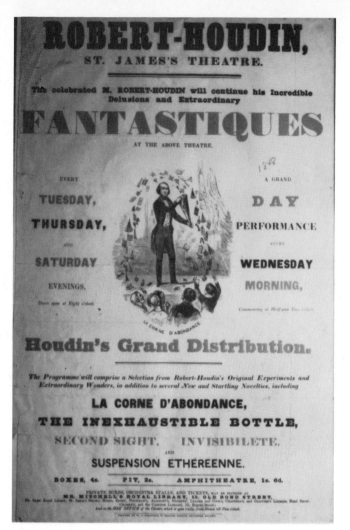

believe that Robert-Houdin ever intended that anyone take it seriously. In fact, the conjurer may have inserted certain incongruities as clues to the spurious nature of the passage. For example, the story began by saying that the year was 1796, but only two paragraphs later the reader was informed that Kempelen was gathering information for a book published in 1791. Later one reads that Kempelen and Worousky wanted to reach the Prussian frontier, less than 200 miles from their starting point in Riga. However, they are soon found in Tula, nearly 500 miles from Riga and in almost the opposite direction from the frontier. Even if those errors could be blamed on carelessness or absent-mindedness, the story is still at odds with nearly every other detail of the known history of Kempelen's automaton.

Yet despite its lack of authenticity, Robert-Houdin's story of the Turk was widely read and—give or take a few subplots—it became the basis for a large body of fiction. Robert-Houdin first published his memoirs, including the account of the automaton, in his home town of Blois in 1858. Editions of the popular book were soon published in Paris, London, and Philadelphia. It was in an 1859

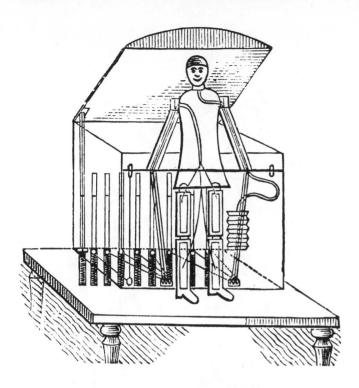

For his performances, Robert-Houdin created several automatons of his own. This diagram indicates how his little *Harlequin* was made to jump out of his box and move about by means of springs and compressed air. COURTESY OF JM.

Philadelphia edition that Dr. R. Shelton Mackenzie, the editor and translator, warned his readers that the automaton section was "entirely wrong," citing mistakes in dates, places, and events. However, it appears that Mackenzie's comments were largely ignored while the story became for many—perhaps for most—the official history of Kempelen's Turk.

Probably the first fictional work to be based upon Robert-Houdin's story was *La Czarine,* a play in five acts and eight tableaux by Jules Adenis and Octave Gastineau. It was first staged in 1868 at L'Ambigu in Paris. Robert-Houdin himself constructed an automaton chess player for that production, and he offered the use of the mechanism to anyone wishing to stage the play in other parts of France or in foreign countries.

The conjurer also devised for the play a spectacular ghost illusion based upon the principle invented by Dircks and popularized by Professor Pepper. In one of the final scenes, the ghost of Czar Peter III appeared to denounce the impostor Ymélian Pougatscheff, who resembled the dead Czar, and who, under the influence of Prince Orloff, sought to win the throne from Catherine.

In spite of Robert-Houdin's close association with the play, its plot followed the original story less closely than some later versions did. Count Christian Vorowski, unlike his counterpart in the original

The play *La Czarine* featured the game of chess between Catherine and the automaton. COURTESY OF JGW.

In H. J. Chaytor's short story "Guioco (sic) Piano," the Russian Jew Petroff revealed his chess automaton to the Frenchman Tarant. Both were anarchists hoping to escape from Russia to England, Petroff as the exhibitor of the machine and Tarant hidden inside as director. COURTESY OF JGW.

While Petroff observed, Chief of Police Diansky opposed the automaton. Later, Diansky discovered Tarant and demanded one more game, in which the stakes were the freedom of the two anarchists. COURTESY OF JGW.

version of the story, was an aide-de-camp of Catherine. Also in the play, there was no occasion to amputate his legs, a circumstance which most theatergoers might have regarded as a bit extreme. Vorowski became a fugitive because of his love for Kempelen's daughter Marie, which aroused the ire of the jealous Catherine. That gave him the opportunity to hide inside the chess automaton and play a game with the Empress. In the end Catherine retained her throne mainly through the exploits of Kempelen and Vorowski. Marie had meanwhile married and become the widow of one of the villians, the result of a plan by Catherine to insure the girl's safety in case the Empress lost her throne.

In the play Kempelen was the inventor who could accomplish nearly anything with his machines. In real life Robert-Houdin could stage the baron's feats by means of his stage magic. Besides inventing the chess automaton and the ghost in the play, Kempelen created an echo device that allowed persons to overhear conversations at a distance without themselves being heard, thus anticipating the bugging devices of this century.

H. J. Chaytor's short story "Guioco [sic] Piano" derived its name from the chess opening Giuoco Piano, which, however, had very little significance in

At the climax of *The Turkish Automaton*, Worouski held a pistol on Chechkofski, the sinister head of the Russian secret police. Our hero, it seemed, would have to kill his dreaded adversary when suddenly Rudolph de Kempelen burst in exclaiming, " 'Victory, victory! Oh, dear Worouski, we are saved! The Empress forgives, fully and freely. She is the grandest woman in the world, the noblest queen. And the Osloffs are pardoned, both of them. Glory! Glory!"

"Worouski lowered his pistol and bowed ironically. 'You can go now, Monsieur Chechkofski,' he said."

After leaving Russia, Worouski and the automaton settled in London. At the Café de la Régence in Paris, they vanquished the great Philidor, who, after their two-and-a-half-hour game, gallantly presented the Turk a diamond to wear in his turban.

Another novel, *Le Joueur d'Échecs* (The Chess Player), was written in 1926 by the French author Henry Dupuy-Mazuel. Although quite different from the earlier work by Braine, Dupuy-Mazuel's

Sheila Braine's novel *The Turkish Automaton* was based upon Robert-Houdin's story of the Turk. COURTESY OF JGW.

the story. The piece was written in, and apparently took place in, 1894, the heyday of anarchism. It was therefore a pair of anarchists who planned to escape from Russia, one of them concealed in a chess automaton, while the other acted as the exhibitor of the machine. The story was obviously patterned after the original version of Robert-Houdin, but was not nearly as interesting or imaginative.

In 1899 Sheila E. Braine transformed Robert-Houdin's story of the Turk into a novel, *The Turkish Automaton*. It may surprise some readers to learn that Kempelen's chess automaton has been the subject of at least three novels, a trilogy of exactly 1,001 pages. The plot of *The Turkish Automaton* was basically the same adventure that Robert-Houdin invented but was padded with additional characters and incidents. Dr. Michael Osloff had a brother Vassili and a son Sacha who both figured in the action at the court of Catherine, and there was also a Rudolph de Kempelen, son of the familiar Baron Wolfgang de Kempelen. Worouski, whom Robert-Houdin had supplied with neither rank nor first name, was commissioned and christened Captain Casimir Worouski.

In *The Turkish Automaton* the eyes of the superintendent of police "nearly started out of his head" when the automaton replaced a false move. COURTESY OF JGW.

249

Rudolf de Kempelen and his servant Joseph discovered the dwarf Zenko spying on them in the Turk's exhibition hall. COURTESY OF JGW.

The giant Count Alexis Orloff caught up a spy who had attacked the automaton during a game with Princess Daschkoff, while Baron de Kempelen, at right, looked on. COURTESY OF JGW.

story also drew upon Robert-Houdin's tale of the chess automaton. In the French novel Catherine was not as kind and generous as in the earlier versions of the story. When the Turk, directed by the novel's hero, this time known as Boreslas Vorowski, swept the pieces from the chessboard, the Empress ordered the chess automaton to be shot. A dancer named Wanda secretly took the place of Vorowski inside the automaton and died in Vorowski's arms after the Turk was executed by a firing squad.

Le Joueur d'Echecs was evidently much more successful than Braine's novel. It was translated into Dutch, German, Italian, Portuguese, and Spanish, but apparently not into English. It was made into a French play by Marcel Achard and into two French films, one version silent and the other in sound.

The 1926 silent film *Le Joueur d'Échecs* was directed by Raymond Bernard. It starred Pierre Blanchar as the hero, Colonel Boleslas (rather than Boreslas as in the novel) Vorowski. The character

actor Charles Dullin played Kempelen and his wife played Catherine. In the cinematic version it was Kempelen who took the place of the hero in the automaton and died before Catherine's firing squad.

The sound version of the Dupuy-Mazuel novel was directed by John Dréville in 1938. The film was awarded a prize at the Venice Film Festival. Françoise Rosay was the Empress Catherine, while Kempelen was portrayed by the famous actor Conrad Veidt, known for such diverse roles as Cesare in *The Cabinet of Dr. Caligari* and Major Strasser in *Casablanca*.

2.

Although a large body of chess-automaton fiction was based upon the story by Robert-Houdin, such works make up only about one third of the total literature on the subject. In another popular cate-

250

Captain Casimir Worouski trained his pistol on Chechkofski, sinister head of the Russian secret police. COURTESY OF JGW.

Attacked on the road by ruffians, Baron de Kempelen was rescued by the mysterious Xavier Dmitrich Stenka, supposedly a tea merchant but actually the Polish Count de Zaleska, an escapee from Siberia. COURTESY OF JGW.

Henry Dupuy-Mazuel wrote the novel *Le Joueur d'Échecs*, which enjoyed much greater success than *The Turkish Automaton*. COURTESY OF KB.

Raymond Bernard directed the first of two French films based upon the novel of Dupuy-Muzuel. COURTESY OF KB.

251

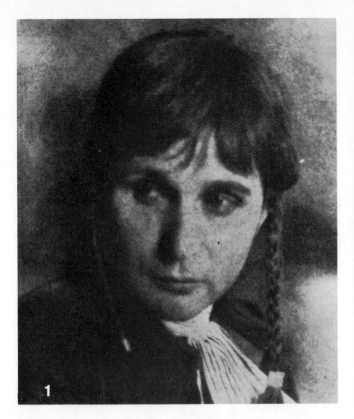

In the 1926 silent version of *Le Joueur d'Echecs,* Pierre Blanchar played Count Boleslas Vorowski, colonel of a Russo-Polish regiment garrisoned at Vilna in 1776, just after Poland was annexed by Russia. COURTESY OF KB.

The Russian nobleman Prince Serge Oblonsky, played by Pierre Batcheff, was Vorowski's friend and second-in-command. He realized the Pole planned to head a revolt at the first opportunity. COURTESY OF KB.

Charles Dullin as Siegfried Wolfgang, Baron de Kempelen, inhabited a lonely old dwelling, where he constructed automatons in his laboratory. COURTESY OF KB.

gory of fiction, the person who hid the automaton, rather than trying to escape from Russia, was usually attempting to sneak into the home of his lover. As one might suspect, these were all light comedies or farces, and were mostly nineteenth-century plays. The first fictional work featuring a chess automaton was probably *Die Schachmaschine* (The Chess Machine) by Heinrich Beck, first published at Leipzig in 1797 and popular for many years.

The play *Le Joueur d'Échecs,* written by Marseiller and Charet and staged in 1801, seems typical of this type of work. As described in *A History of Chess,* by Jerzy Gizycki, a young officer had unsuccessfully sought the hand of the daughter of an elderly chess enthusiast. He fooled the old gentleman by entering his house concealed in a chess automaton, the gift of an anonymous friend. Soon the daughter developed an unusual passion for chess and began spending many hours playing with the automaton. Growing suspicious, the father surprised the lovers "at a game bearing little resemblance to chess." The

Kempelen was constructing, for the Empress Catherine II, an automaton figure in the image of Wanda, star of the Petersburg Imperial Ballet. The real Wanda, played by Jacky Monnier, served as a model. COURTESY OF KB.

Kempelen often visited the palace of Count Vorowski, whom he had raised after the Countess Vorowski left the boy in his charge. The Baron had also brought up Sophie Vorowska, entrusted to him at birth by the Empress. Sophie, played by Edith Jehanne, was in love with Oblonsky, despite his being a Russian. COURTESY OF KB.

drama ended happily, as such things always do, when the father finally consented to the marriage, thus gaining not only a son-in-law but also a fairly good chess companion.

While Maelzel was exhibiting the Turk in Philadelphia in July 1831, news reached him that in the wake of his latest visit to New York there was being staged a new comedy, *The Automaton Chess Player,* at the Bowery Theatre, then under the management of a Mr. Hamblin. The play's author was the same J. Walker who, along with his brother, had constructed the American Automaton Chess Player. For purposes of the stage production, another chess automaton was constructed "on a more simple principle," and that automaton was also exhibited privately in New York for several years thereafter.

The New York production of the play was apparently not very successful. Having opened on July 8, 1831, it closed on the twelfth. But in 1866 J. Walker published the three-act play in London under the title of *Modus Operandi; or The Automaton Chess Player.*

The drama was set in the city of New York where Captain Check and Squire Dashwood were rival lovers of Caroline. She was the niece of Gambit, an

6

Trouble began with a tempestuous game of chess between Boleslas Vorowski and the wicked Russian Major Nicolaieff, portrayed by Camille Bert. COURTESY OF KB.

The revolt lasted two days, but finally the badly outnumbered Poles were defeated by the Russian forces. COURTESY OF KB.

8

Later, Wanda came to dance at the military club, some Russian officers insulted her, Boleslas drew his sword, and the revolt began. COURTESY OF KB.

The Cossacks patrolled the ancient streets of Vilna searching out the last remnants of Polish resistance, but Boleslas had disappeared and was believed to be dead. COURTESY OF KB.

Actually Boleslas had been wounded and had fallen in the swampy region surrounding the city, where Kempelen had rescued him at nightfall. Sophie nursed the fallen revolutionary in a secret room. Although both his legs were fractured by a bullet, no amputation was performed as in the original story. COURTESY OF KB.

11

12

For Boleslas, escape seemed hopeless, but Kempelen had a sudden inspiration. He rushed to his laboratory and sketched the plans for a new automaton in the form of a Turk seated at a chessboard. COURTESY OF KB.

Working feverishly, the Baron quickly completed his invention and then sent Sophie to post a placard announcing the exhibitions of the automaton chess player. COURTESY OF KB.

13

14

The automaton was a great success and was soon summoned to Warsaw to play before King Stanislas Pontiatowski, portrayed by Pierre Hot. COURTESY OF KB.

Each evening when the performances were over, Kempelen and Wanda would help the wounded Boleslas out of his hiding place in the automaton, whose play he directed. COURTESY OF KB.

256

In Warsaw King Stanislas received Kempelen and his Turk with great honor and suggested that he play a game with Major Nicolaieff. The villainous major was soon defeated but during the game he learned that Boleslas was inside. COURTESY OF KB.

Kempelen's party was escorted to Petersburg by troops under Prince Oblonsky. Sophie was happy to be reunited with Serge, but she hesitated to reveal the hidden Boleslas, who had to remain in the automaton throughout the journey. COURTESY OF KB.

Inspired with a fiendish scheme, Nicolaieff suggested that the King send the automaton to play a game with Catherine, who fancied herself the Empire's greatest chess player. COURTESY OF KB.

In Petersburg the whole court assembled for the game between the Empress and the automaton. Having been warned by Nicolaieff, Catherine planned a cruel fate for Boleslas. COURTESY OF KB.

In order to save Boleslas, Kempelen took his place in the automaton. The Baron himself was about to slip out when guards came and carried the Turk to his place of execution in the Court of Honor. COURTESY OF KB.

When Catherine, played by Mme. Charles Dullin, tried to cheat the automaton, he responded by knocking down the pieces. Furious, the Empress turned to Kempelen and declared that the Turk had committed treason and must be shot that night after the masked ball. COURTESY OF KB.

21

When the order was given to fire, there arose the shocked cry, "The automaton is bleeding." The Empress approached to savor her revenge, but was surprised when Kempelen emerged mortally wounded. "Your majesty," he whispered, pointing to Sophie, "I return to you the child you once confided to me. In exchange I beg that you pardon Boleslas Vorowski." COURTESY OF KB.

22

Meanwhile, Nicolaieff had gone to Kempelen's house in Vilna seeking Sophie's birth records. Uncovering a figure, he found an automaton in the form of Kempelen. COURTESY OF KB.

Moved by Kempelen's sacrifice, Catherine pardoned Boleslas, whereupon he and Sophie, realizing they were in love, fell into one another's arms. COURTESY OF KB.

Suddenly the Major heard the sounds of a whole regiment of automaton soldiers advancing with sabers drawn. Vainly he tried to escape but was cut down. COURTESY OF KB.

old gentleman extremely fond of chess. Captain Check hid inside the automaton chess player and sent his Irish servant Pat, disguised as Dr. Philidorus, to exhibit the machine at the home of Gambit. Gambit, the Squire, and Lucy looked on in amazement while Pat exhibited the automaton and invited Gambit to play a game. When Gambit, at Pat's request, made a false move, the automaton shook his head and rapped on the cabinet. Then after a few more moves the automaton bowed his head as a sign he had won the game. Gambit was greatly impressed, and Pat agreed to sell him the machine for $1,500.

When they left the room for a few minutes, Caroline pretended to exhibit the automaton for her maid, but when she opened the cabinet, she saw the Captain inside and fainted. After she had been revived, Captain Check climbed out and asked her to marry him and the two left together.

In their absence the Squire discovered the secret of the automaton and showed Gambit the insides of the machine. There they found a letter from Captain Check to Caroline, explaining how he planned

to trick Gambit. The old gentleman was outraged, and Lucy told him that she saw a man get out of the automaton and run into the street, saying he would return at three o'clock. Gambit, planning to play a trick of his own, told Lucy to allow the man to enter the machine when he returned.

Before Captain Check returned, however, Lucy tricked the Squire into getting inside the automaton. She told him that Caroline's lover was going to hide in the automaton and that Philidorus, an Irish priest in disguise, was going to marry the couple. The Squire planned to say "No, I'll be hanged if I do!" when asked if he'd have her. Gambit then entered with a small pan of fire, which he set inside the cabinet, causing the occupant to cough and shout. The Squire got out of the automaton and threatened to thrash Gambit, but Captain Check returned in time to save the old fellow, and the Squire left amid laughter. Caroline announced that she had married the Captain, Pat admitted that he had been Philidorus, and all ended happily.

Another amusing stage production was occasioned by Ajeeb's 1877 visit to Breslau, where the Saison Theatre featured, in addition to the automaton, the added attraction of a one-act play entitled *Ajeeb, der Automatische Schachspieler*. As the curtain opened, an old gentleman who was very fond of chess had just returned from playing a game with the wonderful Ajeeb. Nothing would satisfy him except to become the owner of the marvelous automaton, and he was obsessed day and night with the idea.

When a young suitor appeared to ask for his daughter's hand, the old fellow refused to consent to it unless the young man would obtain for him, no matter what the cost, the cherished mechanical figure that would be the only solace to his peace of mind. Faced with the utter impossibility of complying with the father's extravagant demand, the lovers formulated a novel plan. They persuaded one of the young man's friends to impersonate Ajeeb. A cabinet and chessboard like the original were constructed, the friend was costumed in Turkish dress, and the fraudulent automaton was assembled for the deception of the old gentleman. According to the plan, the father was to be invited to play a game

with Ajeeb, and in return he was to immediately bestow his blessings upon the marriage.

Of course the old gentleman was overjoyed when he was ceremoniously ushered into the presence of what he believed to be the real Ajeeb. The young suitor immediately proceeded to wind up the mechanism, causing the automaton to grimace and contort his body, as if each turn of the key produced the most excruciating torture.

After Ajeeb won the first game, the old gentleman requested another, during which he indulged himself with a cigar. In the excitement of the contest he sometimes brought the cigar too close to Ajeeb's nose, causing the figure great annoyance and ruining the automaton's game because of the violent efforts required to suppress sneezes and coughs.

Finally, no longer able to restrain himself, Ajeeb exploded with a loud sneeze, surprising the father and greatly alarming the lovers. Thinking quickly, however, they explained to the old gentleman's

"In Love with an Automaton" ended happily when Francis Pinkerton pulled Ollie Conway from the automaton George Washington after a coal stove toppled over. COURTESY OF JGW.

satisfaction that this new accomplishment had been added to make the automaton a more perfect and complete representation of a living chess player. The father was not only surprised but delighted, for he soon won the second game and immediately joined the hands of the lovers in consent to their betrothal.

Ajeeb had meanwhile suffered cramps in his legs and could no longer maintain his position. He leaped from his cabinet and ran out of the room as the curtain closed.

In the previously quoted short story "In Love with an Automaton," one finds the familiar characters: a father, his daughter, a would-be suitor, and a chess automaton. There, however, ended the similarity between the story and others of this type, since the father was the proprietor of the automaton, the daughter was the director, and the automaton himself was the figure of George Washington. Francis Pinkerton, a bank clerk, played chess with the automaton every day during his lunch hour and found himself strangely attracted to the figure.

One day when Pinkerton was alone with the automaton, he made a foolish move on the board and heard the sound of girlish laughter from within the machine. Then a young girl's voice pleaded with him to keep the secret and he promised to do so. Pinkerton soon realized that he was in love with a young lady he had never seen. The next time he found himself alone with the automaton he asked the mysterious voice if they might become better acquainted, but Ollie, the young lady inside, said that her father would never allow it.

On the last day that the automaton was to be exhibited in the city, the room was crowded with visitors, and Pinkerton had some difficulty getting a final game. Before the game was completed a coal stove was accidentally overturned, and, as the flames spread, everyone ran out of the room except Pinkerton. Tearing open the figure, he removed Ollie and carried her to safety. Ollie, of course, became Mrs. Pinkerton, and her father had to rebuild the automaton and find himself a new director.

3.

A number of chess stories have been devised to present a problem, which usually appears at the climax. The reader is thus challenged, as is a character in the story, to solve the problem. Unless the context were known, one might not recognize the following story as an automaton piece at all, since in the tale itself no mention was made that Mephisto was a mechanical chess player. When Gümpel first exhibited Mephisto at his home in London, one of the earliest visitors was Alphonse Delannoy, a writer for the French chess journal La Stratégie. At that time it was thought that Mephisto would be exhibited at the Paris Exposition later that year, and accordingly Delannoy in April 1878 wrote "Méphistophélès à L'Exposition Universelle de Paris de 1878" (Mephisto at the Paris Exposition of 1878).

The story began at Inverness in the Highlands of Scotland, where Dr. Faustin Lewis, an enthusiastic but mediocre player, organized a chess tournament that attracted the best players from all over Scotland. Just before the great event was about to begin, a mysterious visitor appeared carrying a letter that introduced him as Mr. Macfire, a great chess amateur. Dr. Lewis welcomed him and invited him to participate in the tournament.

Macfire was victorious, and the doctor so admired his play that he invited him to supper at his home that evening. After the meal, Macfire told his host that he could himself become a first-class chess player if only he would agree to accompany Macfire for ten years and play chess for him. In order to prove that his promise was true, Macfire instructed the doctor to go the next day to the chess club and play with the strongest players. Macfire would then return the next night for his final reply.

After Macfire had departed, Dr. Lewis, thinking over the day's events, concluded that Macfire was Satan himself. The doctor then formulated a plan to outwit the Prince of Darkness. The next day Dr. Lewis went to the chess club and challenged a player who was very much stronger than he. Just as Macfire had predicted, he won the game and several that followed, winning over two hundred pounds in bets.

That evening Macfire returned and asked the doctor if he had considered his proposition.

"Yes, but I myself have a condition to propose to you."

"What?"

"You must find it easy to solve chess problems?"

"It is child's play for me."

"Well, I have one to challenge you, a checkmate in four moves. If you can mate the Black King on this chessboard in four moves, I accept your offer; I am yours. In case you cannot perform that mate, then for ten years you shall be my servant; you shall obey me."

"Accepted."

"You swear it?"

"I never swear. My word suffices. I cannot break it."

"Agreed. As for me, I swear to keep mine."

"Let's get it over with."

The doctor placed the chessmen in the following manner:

White

author of the piece was Charles Godfrey Gümpel, the inventor of Mephisto. Gümpel had written the legend in 1878 and had submitted it to Delannoy to be translated into French. Delannoy liked the idea but felt the framework of the story was unsuitable for the French taste. He thus obtained Gümpel's consent to rewrite the story in his own style as "Mephisto at the Paris Exposition of 1878."

In Gümpel's original story, as it appeared in *Brentano's*, the narrator called himself "A." Mephisto bargained to play a match of three games of chess for the soul of A. If A was able to at least draw any one of the three, he would be the winner of the match.

Mephisto easily won the first two games, each of which reached a position in which he announced mate in seven moves. In the third game Mephisto also announced mate in seven, but A insisted that they play the game to its conclusion. As Mephisto was about to make his final move, he discovered that to do so would form a cross. He was thus unable to win the match, and he became the slave of A.

Gümpel's cross problem was:

Macfire examined it or rather looked it over nonchalantly. He rapidly executed the first three moves, but then he stopped. The mocking smile which pinched his lips changed suddenly to a horrible grimace. His eyes sank under the thickness of his brows, his features distorted, his forehead inclined as if burdened by the most sinister thoughts. His body, immobile and frozen, revealed the trouble which shook his spirits. A power superior to his enchained his hand. He was not able to execute the cross which represented checkmate! Dr. Lewis had succeeded.

Thus Mephisto was enslaved, although, as we have seen, the real mechanical chess player was not exhibited at the Paris Exposition after all.

The solution to Dr. Faustin Lewis's problem is as follows:

White	*Black*
1 Q–R4	Q–Q5
2 Q×Qch	P×Q
3 N×P/6	P–K4
4 R×P mate	

In *The Gentleman's Magazine*, September 1881, there was published anonymously "How Mephisto Was Caught, a Chess Legend." That story was also condensed in the *Chess-Player's Chronicle*. Finally, in 1882, *Brentano's Chess Monthly* printed "How the Devil Was Caught, a Chess Legend," a somewhat expanded version of the story in *The Gentleman's Magazine*. At that time it was revealed that the

Black (Mephisto)

White		*Black*
1		R×Nch
2	K–B3	Q×Rch
3	R×Q	R×Rch
4	Q–K3	R×Qch
5	P×R	N–B7
6	P–K4	N×Pch
7	K–Q3	

Mephisto could not play 7...R–K7 mate, but he should have realized there were many ways to win the game without forming a cross. He must have had his heart set on mate in seven.

Another story based on a chess problem was "The Rival Automata, a Tale of Two Turks" in the *Columbia Chess Chronicle* of 1889. The two rivals, Ty-Foo and Azrael, played a match to determine which was the better automaton. Each automaton won a game. The third game was to decide the winner of the match.

Just as the game reached a critical point, the director of Azrael discovered that both he and his rival director had mistakenly entered the other's automaton. Thus, if he won the game, Ty-Foo would be the victor of the match. He noted that in the following position Ty-Foo had an easy win by playing Q×Pch, followed by B–Q3ch.

Black (Ty-Foo)

White (Azrael)

Thinking quickly, Black devised the following suimate, forcing Azrael to mate Ty-Foo.

White	Black
1	R×P
2 Q×R	Q×Pch
3 K×Q	B–Q3ch
4 B–K5	B×Bch
5 Q×B mate	

Thus, although his director had been inside the wrong figure, Azrael won the match.

Who could resist a game of chess with the Devil himself? "Satan Playing with Man for His Soul" by Theodore von Holst appeared in *The People's Journal*, February 20, 1847. COURTESY OF JGW.

4.

In another category of chess automaton fiction, which might be called "tales of terror," there was usually some mysterious force or being associated with the automaton. The classic work of that type was Ambrose Bierce's story "Moxon's Master," which, in fact, made its appearance under somewhat mysterious circumstances. The story was not included in Bierce's original 1893 edition of *Can Such Things Be?* but was added, apparently by Bierce, to a later volume of the work.

"In 'Moxon's Master,'" wrote Bierce's biographer Richard O'Connor, "Bierce seemed to be anticipating the age of cybernetics. It has been oddly neglected by those considering the brief history of science fiction, yet it created a situation which can be considered contemporary by readers of seven decades later. It was also one of the few instances in which Bierce set up shop as a prophet." O'Connor compared Bierce's chess automaton with the Frankenstein legend, but it seems likely that Bierce owed as much to Poe and his "Maelzel's Chess Player" as he did to Mary Shelley's monster.

Quite simply stated, "Moxon's Master" was the story of a chess automaton that rose up and strangled his inventor. To make such a plot believable to any degree, Bierce had to build up a certain mood. He wrote the story in the first person as if the storyteller had visited the inventor Moxon, who, employing various examples and philosophical arguments, sought to convince the skeptical visitor that a machine was capable of thinking.

At one point, the conversation was interrupted by a noise from Moxon's workshop in an adjoining room, as if someone were pounding with an open hand upon a table. Moxon went into the room, there were sounds of a scuffle, and the inventor returned saying, " 'Pardon me for leaving you so abruptly. I have a machine in there that lost its temper and cut up rough.' "

Noting four bloody marks on Moxon's left cheek, the storyteller said, " 'How would it do to trim its nails?' "

Moxon ignored the jest and continued to advance his arguments at length, concluding with " 'Do you happen to know that Consciousness is the creature of Rhythm?' "

Unconvinced, the visitor departed into the stormy night, but as he groped his way through the dark and muddy streets, Moxon's final words haunted him like a revelation. On a sudden impulse the storyteller returned to Moxon's house. He found the inventor in the workshop completely absorbed in a game of chess with a mysterious stranger, only the back of whom was visible.

He was apparently not more than five feet in height, with proportions suggesting those of a gorilla—a tremendous breadth of shoulders, thick, short neck and broad, squat head, which had a tangled growth of black hair and was topped with a crimson fez. A tunic of the same color, belted tightly to the waist, reached the seat—apparently a box—upon which he sat; his legs and feet were not seen. His left forearm appeared to rest in his lap; he moved his pieces with his right hand, which appeared disproportionately long.

As the storyteller continued to observe the game he realized—and the naive reader learned for the first time—that Moxon's opponent was a chess automaton. Were all of Moxon's philosophical arguments merely building up to the eventual exhibition of this mechanical device? But then Moxon checkmated the figure. In response the automaton sprang up and seized his inventor by the neck, overturning a candle.

The storyteller sprang to Moxon's aid as the blazing room burned into his memory a nightmarish picture of the combatants on the floor. Then blackness and silence closed in. After three days in a hospital the storyteller regained consciousness and discovered that Moxon was dead. He himself had been rescued from the flames by Moxon's workman, Haley. Thanking Haley, he asked if he had also rescued the murderous chess automaton.

The man was silent a long time, looking away from me. Presently he turned and gravely said:

"Do you know that?"

"I do," I replied; "I saw it done."

That was many years ago. If asked to-day I should answer less confidently.

Welcoming in the new century, "The Automaton," by the pseudonymous-sounding Reginald Bacchus and Ranger Gull, appeared in *The Ludgate* for January 1900. The automaton in the story, like Moxon's invention, did not exactly fit the description of any real chess automaton. As depicted by Bacchus and Gull,

Stuart Dryden, "the leading chess player of England," reluctantly agreed to a match with "The Automaton" in the story of that name by Bacchus and Gull. COURTESY OF JGW.

265

Fearing defeat in the match, Dryden consulted his friend the Reverend Henry Druce, who suspected that the automaton's director was Philip Murray, an elderly librarian. COURTESY OF JGW.

Just before the match, Dryden confronted Murray, threatening to expose the automaton unless he were allowed to win. When Murray refused, Dryden impulsively murdered the old man, whose body rolled into the river and was swept away. COURTESY OF JGW.

As the match approached, excitement grew in Bristol, the site chosen for the great contest. COURTESY OF JGW.

The machine consisted of a large figure of wood, roughly hewn and painted to resemble a man. It was about twice the size of a full-grown human being, and when playing was seated in a chair made on a very open design. It was quite motionless, except for the jerky movements of its arm and of the two long steel pincers that served it for fingers. It made no sound save the one word "check," that rasped out from its wooden throat, and the final "check-mate," pitched in a higher and more triumphal key.

Little attempt had been made to conceive more than the roughest image of man. The forehead sloped backwards, and the long crooked nose that rose above thin tight-set lips and a hard chin had a flavor of the American Indian, while the whole aspect of the morose, seated figure, one arm clasped to the body and one poised forwards with half-bent elbow, conveyed a haunting suggestion of some hawk-faced god of Babylon.

A Polish Jew named Greet exhibited the automaton, but the machine's inventor was the stage magician Edouard Roulain, a character very likely patterned after Robert-Houdin. The figure was opened before and after each game, revealing, as one might expect, nothing but machinery. This was accomplished, the story disclosed, "by an elaborate

Dryden went coolly to the theatre to collect his prize money, which, with Murray out of the way, he expected to win by default. The game began and to Dryden's horror the automaton was moving. Moreover, he sensed that Murray was his opponent. When the automaton's exhibitor, Greet, approached, he discovered that Dryden was dead and that no one was inside the automaton.
COURTESY OF JGW.

system of mirrors, some improvement on the Pepper's Ghost idea."

At the climax of the tale, Stuart Dryden had murdered the automaton's director, Philip Murray. Yet he sensed that somehow Murray was inside the machine.

He hastily stretched out his hand and made a rapid, unconsidered move. As he did so his fingers came for a brief moment in contact with the iron paw of the Automaton, and he knew who his adversary was. He felt so strange and terrible a message flash to his brain that his whole body became cold and rigid in a moment. He could not keep his eyes from the lens-like eyes of his adversary, and he felt rather than saw the intelligence that looked out at him, for he knew he was playing with no earthly opponent.

It was soon discovered that Dryden was dead. After his body was removed, attention centered again upon the automaton.

Greet opened the panel of the figure and called in hoarse, agitated tones to Mr. Murray to come out. There was no answer, and Roulain fetched a candle and they looked into the hollow in surprise. There was no one there!

A third story in this category was "Szach i Mat" (Check and Mate), by the nineteenth century Polish author Ludwik Niemojowski. Portions of that tale were quoted in Jerzy Giżychi's *A History of Chess*. "Szach i Mat" was the story of the Italian chess genius, Bartolomeo, who was impoverished, driven insane, then killed by his pathological passion for the game. After undergoing several misfortunes, Bartolomeo was invited to Marseilles to play a series of exhibition games for a large fee. Upon his arrival he found himself under the control of a clever English impresario, the inventor of a chess automaton.

The automaton that Bartolomeo was compelled to direct differed from most others because it was operated remotely from an adjoining room, as some persons have reported that Mephisto was. The Englishman ushered Bartolomeo into a small, square, empty room, in the middle of which stood a chessboard. There was at the right of the chessboard a keyboard with chess pieces inscribed on the keys. A network of wires, issuing from behind the keyboard, disappeared into the wall opposite.

While directing a game, Bartolomeo had to lie down so that he could view the chessboard in the room below through a hole that was concealed in the stucco work of the ceiling. To begin the game the director pressed a blank key that caused the automaton below to nod and raise his hand. Then, by touching a numbered pawn key, the chess player was compelled to move the pawn that the key controlled.

Bartolomeo had no alternative but to accept the Englishman's proposition to direct the automaton. The mechanical chess player soon attracted many spectators and, guided by Bartolomeo, defeated every opponent. As the money poured in, the Englishman organized more and more exhibitions, forcing Bartolomeo to play day and night. Under the intense strain of physical and mental exhaustion, Bartolomeo began to lose his mind and his play deteriorated.

Finally reaching the breaking point, Bartolomeo lost several games. Early the following day, a huge throng of curious spectators packed the hall, eager to witness the inglorious defeat of the once marvelous chess automaton. Although in a state of collapse, Bartolomeo was dragged from his bed by the automaton's inventor and told to play.

The next thing Bartolomeo remembered was regaining consciousness a long time afterward in a hospital. He learned that the Englishman had lost his entire fortune and had disappeared from Marseilles. The experience had, however, permanently damaged Bartolomeo's mind. His last act was a violent, feverish game of chess with himself, ending in the final checkmate, death.

John Dickson Carr, in his 1938 mystery novel *The Crooked Hinge*, introduced an automaton known as the Golden Hag. Although that automaton was not really a chess player, Carr admitted in a footnote that he had gotten the idea from the *Encyclopaedia Britannica* article quoted earlier in this chapter. Also, in one of his section headings, he quoted a line from "Moxon's Master."

According to Carr, the Golden Hag played the cittern, thumbed her nose at the spectators, and made other indecorous gestures. Patterned after one of the ladies in the court of Charles II in 1676, the nearly life-size automaton had once been a beauty, but had decayed considerably with age. Half of her wax face, including one glass eye, was missing, and the remaining portion of her visage was badly cracked. The painted iron hands and fingers of the automaton were raised "with burlesque and rather horrible coquetry." The Hag sat upon a faded oblong box resembling a small couch.

Betty Harbottle, a maid in the manor house where the story was set, had a frightening experience with the automaton. To reveal the details of this or to explain how the Golden Hag was directed might spoil the story for readers who desire to search out the novel and read it for themselves. The work was reprinted in 1969 and may be available to those who search for it. However, it would probably not reveal too much to state that the principle upon which the automaton operated has already been outlined elsewhere in this book.

Kingkill by Thomas Gavin, the most recent of three novels based upon the Turk, follows a recent trend toward "what-if" writing. For example, what if

Lee Harvey Oswald had not been killed? Or what if General Custer had survived the massacre at the Little Big Horn? In this case it is what if Schlumberger had not succumbed to yellow fever in Havana? What if he had written a journal detailing his relationship with Maelzel and the Turk? Following the style some editors call "the new history," Gavin has transformed Maelzel into a thoroughly despicable scoundrel, manipulating and destroying the lives of everyone within his grasp, and particularly that of Schlumberger.

As the plot of *Kingkill* progresses it becomes clear that the Gavinized Maelzel had been so wicked that he must be done away with. Did the Turk rise up like "Moxon's Master" and throttle him? Certainly not! Did the ghost of Schlumberger haunt the Turk in the manner of Bacchus and Gull? Not exactly. Was Schlumberger driven mad as Bartolomeo had been? Very likely, but for the real story it is necessary to read the novel itself. Since it was published in 1977, the book should be more readily available than *The Turkish Automaton* or *Le Joueur d'Échecs*, both of which are quite rare. Gavin writes very well, being especially adept at evoking the atmosphere of nineteenth-century America, although at times the reader is overwhelmed with images of chamber pots that might better be forgotten. Another possible lament is that many of the most interesting real-life characters are missing from *Kingkill*. Where, for instance, are the Duchess de Berry and her courtly guests, Eugène Robertson and his balloon, and Signor Blitz and his magic show? On the whole, however, Gavin's novel should please anyone interested in the lore of the chess automaton. But do not expect it to be the true history of the Turk any more than its predecessors were.

In addition to the three chess automaton novels mentioned above, several others have been at least partly about chess automatons. *The Blue Wall*, a 1912 novel by Richard Washburn Child, was a mystery in which a chess automaton played a minor role.

Jermyn Estabrook, one of the narrators in the novel, visited the old Natural History Museum for a game of chess with the Player of the Rolling Eye, also called the Sheik of Baalbec. That fictitious automaton was unique in being entirely coin-operated, without the need for any human exhibitor.

The representation of a squatting Arab, robed in red Oriental swathes and with a chessboard fastened to its knees, sat cross-legged on a boxlike structure. Upon dropping a coin into a slot in the flat top, two folding doors in front of this box would open for a few moments, showing a glass-covered interior, which, as far as the back of the box, was filled with a tangle of wheels and pulleys, seeming to preclude the possibility that a human being could hide therein. As soon as these doors closed, a flat space in the chest of the Sheik opened, with a faint purr of machinery to expose internal organs of metal levers and gears.

The effect of this last exposure was extraordinary, and in all the time I knew the Sheik, I never got over it. The moment this cavity in his chest opened, he was an impersonal piece of mechanism; the moment it closed, however, the soul, the personality of a living being returned, and it seemed to me that the brown, wax skin of his nodding head, the black hair of his pointed beard, the red of his curved, malicious lips, the whites of his eyes, which showed when he moved with a squeak of unoiled bearings in his neck, and even the jointed fingers of his hand, with which he moved the pawns in short, mechanical jerks about the board, all belonged to a human body, containing an individual intelligence.

While playing the automaton, Estabrook felt that he had gained an advantage. In a few moves, however, he found that he had lost the game.

And at the same moment the infernal Sheik lifted his head with the clicking of gears, stared at me, drew down one papier-mâché eyelid in a hideous wink and rolled the other glassy eyeball in a complete orbit of the socket, and as soon as this evil, mechanical grimace had been accomplished, the head fell forward, the doors in the being's chest opened once more, showing the moving wheels, and again the creature seemed to become soulless.

As the story progressed, the heroine discovered that she was not the daughter of the judge she had always regarded as her father, but of a criminal. That discovery and her fear that she would inherit criminal tendencies disrupted her life and that of her family. Eventually the criminal father was flushed from his hiding place, which was the chess automaton, of course.

In the Hungarian novel *A Noszty Fiú Esete a Tóth Marival* (The Affair of the Noszty's Son with Mary Tóth) by Mikszáth Kálmán, Kempelen's Turk was the subject of an argument between the hero, Noszty, and Palásthy, a nephew of Kempelen. Since, according to the novel, not even Kempelen's relatives knew the secrets of the automaton, Palásthy was angered when Noszty said that he thought a human was hidden in the machine. Palásthy interpreted the remark as an insult to his uncle, and he thus developed an animosity to Noszty.

Still another novel that was partly about a chess automaton was *This Way to Byzantium!* by J. G. Sarasin, a pseudonym for Geraldine Gordon Salmon. The book was published in London in 1940.

Other authors whose works have mentioned or been influenced by chess automatons include Honoré de Balzac, E. T. A. Hoffmann, and Ralph Waldo Emerson.

5

As might be expected, chess-playing computers have had roles in many science fiction stories and especially in films. Unlike their real counterparts, the science fiction computers are nearly always unbeatable master chess players. In some fictional world of the future the supermechanical chess player has become a reality.

As early as 1926, the Soviet author Abramov wrote a novel, *Gibel' Shakhmat* (The Ruin of Chess), in which a chess machine was always victorious against even the strongest human players. The machine caused such a sensation that it threatened to destroy the game of chess, a cliché often connected with the myth of the supermechanical chess player. The crisis was resolved when the machine's inventor went mad and died, never revealing one essential key to the mathematical formula. Thus the world was saved from "the ruin of chess."

The notion that computers would discover the perfect game and thus destroy chess has persisted throughout the literature of science fiction, and the problem has been solved in various ways. Pierre Boulle, the author of *Bridge on the River Kwai* and *Planet of the Apes,* wrote the short story "Le Robot Parfait" (The Perfect Robot), in which the brilliant Professor Fontaine invented a series of remarkable machines. Among them was a chess robot that in every possible position was capable of finding the one correct move involving no risk of losing the game. The chess player was, of course, quite a formidable opponent until some rival researchers working on the same principle, developed an automaton as ingenious as the original. The result was the perfect game of chess, always running the same identical course and always resulting in a draw. Eventually, however, Professor Fontaine realized that something was lacking in his chess player and in his other faultless machines. He then put them out of order, supplying the final human attribute: the ability to bungle.

Perhaps as a result of such stories, some people really believe that computers will someday play perfect chess and will thus bring about the downfall of the game. Recently, in his column in *Chess Life and Review,* Grandmaster Larry Evans quoted the mathematician Dr. Nathan Divinsky as saying, "As soon as machines completely solve the mysteries of chess . . . the game will vanish. It will have become another mathematical theorem locked away in a cold book. In fact, few will look at the body as it is buried. Few will know the details of the inhuman calculation. They will only know that a good and warm friend has vanished."

In a later column, however, Dr. Hans Berliner, who has himself written a computer chess program, commented, "There will not be enough time left in the life of the universe for all computers that will

A popular theme in computer chess fiction is echoed in this cartoon. The computer scientist, losing to his own creation, makes a few adjustments, thus producing a more satisfying result. *Copyright © February 1950 by Scientific American, Inc. All rights reserved.* BY PERMISSION OF SA.

ever be built even to begin to probe the real mysteries of chess, so let's cut out all that nonsense of 'losing a dear friend' when computers solve chess." Evans added that he did not think computers would do away with chess any more than automobiles did away with track meets.

The science-fiction writer Fritz Leiber has sometimes alluded to chess automatons in his stories. He once described a desk as containing "space enough

270

for a couple of life-size girls if they were doubled up according to one of the formulas for the hidden operator of Maelzel's chess-playing automaton."

In Leiber's "Poor Superman" the computer was much more than a mere chess player—it was a post World War III super computer thinking machine, a great electronic brain named Maizie that "remembered by cutting delicate notches in the rims of molecules." The president of the United States thought that perhaps Maizie was the Second Coming, an incarnation in metal rather than flesh, but a group of physicists became suspicious. They wanted to know if Maizie stood for Maelzel.

Puzzled by the question, the secretary of space wondered who Maelzel might be. Then he remembered having read as a child "Maelzel's Chess Player" by Edgar Allan Poe. It had been about an automaton that played chess, and Poe had proved there was a man inside. But what did this have to do with Maizie?

As Leiber's readers soon discovered, the answer lay inside the computer itself where, in a small room, "a suave fat man in shorts sat drinking beer." It was he who was the brain of Maizie.

6.

Somewhere among the novels, short stories, farces, dramas, films, mysteries, and science fiction about automaton chess players it seems almost inevitable that someone would write a poem. It may be argued that a piece of poetry does not belong in a chapter on fiction. Nevertheless, there seems to be no better place to put it, nor better way to end this book. So, without attempting to analyze or criticize, here is the poem entitled . . .

A sudden shuddering seized my frame;
With feeling that defies a name,
Of wonder, horror, doubt and shame,
    The *tout ensemble*,
I deemed thee formed with power and will;
My hair rose up—my blood stood still,
And curdled with a fearful chill,
    Which made me tremble.

I thought if, e'en within thy glove,
Thy cold and fleshless hand should move
To rest on me, the touch would prove
    Far worse than death;
That I should be transformed, and see
Thousands and thousands gaze on me,
A living, moving thing, like thee,
    Devoid of breath.

When busy, curious, learned and wise
Regard thee with inquiring eyes
To find wherein thy mystery lies,
    On thy stiff neck,
Turning thy head with grave precision,
Their optic light and mental vision
Alike defying, with decision,
    Thou giv'st them *"check!"*

ADDRESS TO THE
AUTOMATON CHESS PLAYER

Thou wondrous cause of speculation,
Of deep research and cogitation,
Of many a head and many a nation,
    While all in vain
Have tried their wits to answer whether,
In silver, gold, steel, silk or leather,
Or human parts, or all together,
    Consists thy brain!

When first I viewed thine awful face,
Rising above that ample case,
Which gives thy cloven foot a place,
    Thy double shoe,
I marvelled whether I had seen
Old Nick himself, or a machine,
Or something fixed midway between
    The distant two!

Some say a little man resides
Between thy narrow, bony sides;
And round the world within thee rides:
    Absurd the notion!
For what's the human thing 't would lurk
In thine unfeeling breast, Sir Turk,
Performing thus thine inward work,
    And outward motion?

Some whisper that thou 'rt he, who fell
From Heaven's high courts down, down, to dwell
In that deep place of sulphury smell
    And lurid flame.
Thy keeper then deserves a pension,
For seeking out this wise invention
To hold thee harmless, in detention,
    Close at thy game.

Now, though all Europe has confessed,
That in thy master Maelzel's breast
Hidden, thy secret still must rest,
    Yet, 't were great pity,
With all our intellectual light,
That none should view thy nature right,—
But thou must leave in fog and night
    Our keen-eyed city.

Then just confide in me, and show,
Or tell, how things within thee go!
Speak in my ear so quick and low
    None else shall know it.
But, mark me! if I should discover
Without thine aid, thy secret mover,
With thee for ever all is over,
    I'll quickly blow it!

—Hannah Flagg Gould, *Poems,* 1835

Bibliography

Abramov, Al. *Gibel' Shakhmat* (The Ruin of Chess), a fanciful story. Moscow, 1926.

"Account of an Automaton Chess Player, Now Exhibiting at No. 4., Spring-Gardens, London." *Blackwood's Magazine* 4 (February 1819): 579–81; *Sporting Magazine*, n.s. 4, no. 19 (April 1819): 17–20.

Adenis, Jules, and Gastineau, Octave. *La Czarine*, drama in five acts. Paris, 1868, 1869.

The Adventures of Ajeeb, the Wonderful Chess Automaton. New York, 1885[?].

"Ajeeb." *The Kansas City Star*, September 17, 1888, p. 1; also related article October 9, 1888, p. 1.

"Ajeeb Comes to Life." *The New Checkergram* 2, no. 12 (February 1935): 195, 198–99.

"Ajeeb Is Dead." *New York Times*, January 25, 1929, p. 22.

"Ajeeb Not a Machine." *The Kansas City Times*, October 14, 1888, p. 14.

Allen, George. "The History of the Automaton Chess-Player in America." *The Book of the First American Chess Congress.* Philadelphia, 1859, pp. 420–84.

Allen, Hervey. *Israfel: The Life and Times of Edgar Allan Poe.* New York, 1926, 1934.

"American Automaton." *The Philadelphia Monthly Magazine* 1, no. 4 (January 15, 1828): 199–200.

Anderson, Emily, ed. *The Letters of Beethoven*, 3 vols. New York, 1961.

"An Attempt to Analyse the Automaton Chess Player of M. De Kempelen." *Edinburgh Philosophical Journal* 4 (April 1821): 393–97.

"De Automaat Schaakspeler." *Het Leeskabinet* 4 (1835): 216–22.

"Automata." *The New Monthly Magazine* 1 (1821): 524–32.

"Automata." *Chamber's Journal*, February 5, 1876, pp. 87–90.

"Of Automata." *The Weekly Entertainer*, n.s. 3, no. 18 (Monday, April 30, 1821): 335–38.

"Automate Joueur d'Échecs." *Magasin Pittoresque* (Paris), 1834, p. 155.

"The Automaton Chess Player." *The Hive* (London) 1, no. 4 (September 1822): 81–83.

"The Automaton Chess-Player." *The Youth's Monthly Visitor* 3, no. 15 (April 1, 1823): 203–8.

"Automaton Chess Player." *The Popular Magazine* 1 (1836): 43–54.

"The Automaton Chess Player." *The Chess Player's Chronicle* (London), n.s. 1 (1841): iii–xviii, 10, 40.

"The Automaton Chess-Player." *Littel's Living Age* (New York), no. 784, 3d ser., no. 62 (June 4, 1859): 585–92; *Blackwood's Magazine* 4: 584 ff.; *Penny Magazine* (London) 6: 28 ff.

"The Automaton Chess Player." *Cornhill Magazine* (London), n.s. 52, no. 27, old ser. no. 309 (September 1885): 299–306; *Eclectic Magazine* (New York), n.s. 42, no. 5 (November 1885): 649–53; *Leisure Hour* (London) 28: 198 ff.

"Automaton Chess Player." *Bibliotheca Van der Linde—Niemeijeriana*, a catalogue of the chess collection in the Royal Library. The Hague, 1955, pp. 165–68.

"The Automaton Chess Player Redivivus." *The Illustrated London News*, December 20, 1845, pp. 389–90.

Bacchus, Reginald, and Gull, Ranger. "The Automaton." *The Ludgate*, n.s. 9 (January 1900): 201–14.

Bachaumont, Louis Petit de. *Mémoires Secrets Pour Servir à l'Historie de la Republique des Lettres en France depuis 1762 Jusqu'à Nos Jours.* London, 1777–89. Vol. 22, pp. 249–50, 262–64, 305–7; Vol. 23, pp. 3–6, (April–June, 1783).

Barker, Charles Francis. *The American Checker-Player.* Boston, 1880.

Beck, Heinrich. *Die Schachmaschine.* Comedy in four acts. Leipzig, 1797; Vienna, 1797; Berlin, 1798; Venice

(Italian), 1806; Milan (Italian), 1845; The Hague (Dutch), 1803; Vienna, 1826.

Bell, Alexander Graham. "Prehistoric Telephone Days." *The National Geographic Magazine* 41, no. 3 (March 1922): 233–37.

Bell, J. D. "Famous Automata." *Appleton's Journal*, n.s. 3, no. 15 (September 1877): 254–57.

Bernstein, Alex, and Roberts, Michael de V. "Computer v. Chess-Player." *Scientific American*, June 1958, pp. 96–105.

Beste, H. P. *Personal and Literary Memorials.* London, 1829.

Bierce, Ambrose. "Moxon's Master." *Collected Works of Ambrose Bierce,* 12 vols. New York, 1909–12. Vol. 3, *Can Such Things Be?; The Collected Writings of Ambrose Bierce.* Edited by Clifton Fadiman. New York, 1946; *The Complete Short Stories of Ambrose Bierce.* Edited by Ernest Jerome Hopkins. Garden City, N. Y., 1970.

Blind, Adolphe. *Les Automates Truqués.* Geneva and Paris, 1927.

Blitz, Signor Antonio. *Fifty Years in the Magic Circle.* Hartford, Conn., 1871.

———. *Life and Adventures of Signor Blitz.* Hartford, Conn., 1872.

Boeckmann, Johann Lorenz. "Hypothetische Erklärung des Berühmten Schachspielers des Herrn von Kempelen." *Magazin für Aufklärung.* Kehl, 1785. Also in *Macklots Hofbuchdruckery* and *Kleine schriften physischen Innhalts.* Carlsruhe, 1789.

Botvinnik, Mikhail Moiseevich. *Computers, Chess, and Long-range Planning.* Translated by Arthur Brown. New York, 1970.

Boulle, Pierre. "Le Robot Parfait." *Contes de l'Absurde.* Paris, 1953; New York, 1966 (English).

Bradford, Gamaliel. *The History and Analysis of the Supposed Automaton Chess Player of M. de Kempelen.* Boston, 1826.

Braine, Sheila E. *The Turkish Automaton, a Tale of the Time of Catherine the Great.* London, 1899.

Brewster, Sir David. *Letters on Natural Magic.* London, 1832, 1833, 1834, 1838, 1845, 1882, 1883; New York, 1832.

Brion, Marcel. *Daily Life in the Vienna of Mozart and Schubert.* Translated by Jean Stewart. 1962.

Busch, G. C. B. "Schachspieler." *Versuch eines Handbuchs der Erfindungen.* Eisenach, 1794.

Buck, Robert J. "The Emperor and the Turk." *Chess Review* 15 (January 1947): 16.

Byard, Stanley. "Robots Which Play Games." *Penguin Books Science News,* 16. Harmondsworth, 1950.

"At the Café de la Régence." Translated from the *Petit Journal,* April 9, 1894. *The Chess Monthly* 15 (May 1894): 264-68.

Carr, John Dickson. *The Crooked Hinge.* New York, 1938, 1964, 1969.

Carroll, Charles Michael. *The Great Chess Automaton.* New York, 1975.

Chapuis, Alfred. *Les Automates dans les Oeuvres d'Imagination.* Neuchâtel, 1947.

Chapuis, Alfred, and Droz, Edmond. *Les Automates.* Neuchatel, 1949; Translated by Alec Reid, 1958 (English).

Chapuis, Alfred, and Gélis, Edouard. *Le Monde des Automates.* 2 vols. Neuchâtel, Paris, 1928.

Chaytor, H. J. "Guioco [sic] Piano." *In Town,* no. 3 (September 1894): 41–43.

"A Chess Humbug." *Harper's Weekly,* supplement, September 27, 1879, pp. 779–80.

" 'The Chess-Player': A Dramatic French 'Robot' Film of 18th Century Poland to be Seen in London." *The Illustrated London News,* April 16, 1927, pp. 674–75.

"The Chess Player Discovered." Baltimore *Federal Gazette,* June 1, 1827, p. 2; also related articles June 5, p. 2; June 6, p. 2.

Child, Richard Washburn. *The Blue Wall.* Boston and New York, 1912.

Christopher, Milbourne. *The Illustrated History of Magic.* New York, 1973.

Cochrane, John. *A Treatise on the Game of Chess.* London, 1822.

Cohen, John. *Human Robots in Myth and Science.* London, 1966.

Cooke, Conrad William. *Automata Old and New.* London, 1893.

Crankshaw, Edward. *Maria Theresa.* New York, 1969.

Dann, Stephen. "Pillsbury: the Unknown American." *Chess Life and Review* 27, no. 11 (November 1972): 712-13.

Davidson, Henry A. *A Short History of Chess.* New York, 1949.

"Death of Pillsbury." *American Chess Bulletin* 3, no. 7 (July 1906): 121-29.

Decremps, Henri. *La Magie Blanche Dévoilée.* Paris, 1784, 1785, 1788, 1789, 1792-93; London, 1785 (English); Rome, 1827 (Italian).

———. *Cinque Sessioni.* Padua, 1788.

Delannoy, Alphonse. "Méphistophélés a l'Exposition Universelle de Paris de 1878." *La Stratégie* 11, 2d ser., no. 4 (April 15, 1878): 98–111.

———. "Les Prouesse de Méphisto." *La Stratégie,* 11, 2d ser., no. 11 (November 15, 1878): 325–31.

Depping. "Maelzel's Automaton Chess-player." Translated from a French journal. *New York Mirror,* January 19, 1839, pp. 236-37.

De Tournay, Mathieu-Jean-Baptiste Nioche. "La Vie et Les Aventures de l'Automate Joueur d'Échecs." *Le Palamède* 1, no. 3 (1836): 81-87.

De Vide, Charles. "Isidor Gunsberg—Last of Victorians." *American Chess Bulletin* 27, no. 5 (May–June 1930): 96-97.

de Waard, Romke. *From Music Boxes to Street Organs.* Translated by Wade Jenkins. New York, 1967.

"Die in London restaurirte von Kempelen'sche Schachmaschine." *Morgenblatt für gebildete Stände.* Stuttgart, 1819.

Dircks, Henry. *The Ghost!* London, 1863.

Douglas, J. R. "GM Walter Browne vs. CHESS 4.6." *Chess Life and Review* 33, no. 7 (July 1978): 363.

Drake, Samuel Adams. *Old Landmarks and Historic Personages of Boston*. Boston, 1900.

Dupuis-Delacourt, Jules-François, *Nouveau Manuel Complet d'Aérostation*. Paris, 1850.

Dupuy-Mazuel, Henry. *Le Joueur d'Echecs,* Roman. Paris, 1926; Berlin, 1927 (German); Paris, Madrid, 1927 (Spanish); Oporto, 1927 (Portuguese); Antwerp, 1927 (Dutch); Milan, 1928 (Italian).

Dutens, Louis. "A Presbourg, ce 24 Juillet, 1770." *Mercure de France; Gentleman's Magazine* (English), January 24, 1771, pp. 26-27; *Lettres sur un Automate, qui Joue aux Échecs.* 1772; *Oeuvres mêlées.* Geneva, 1784.

————. "A Vienne, ce 18 Janvier, 1771." *Journal Encyclopédique; Lettres,* 1772; *Oeuvres,* 1784.

————. "A Vienne, ce 21 Janvier, 1771." *Mercure de France; Lettres,* 1772; *Oeuvres,* 1784.

Ebert, Johann Jakob. *Nachricht von dem berühmten Schachspieler und der Sprachmaschine des Herrn von Kempelen.* Leipzig, 1785.

Eco, Umberto, and Zorzoli, G. B. *The Picture History of Inventions.* Translated by Anthony Lawrence. New York, 1963.

"The Eden Musée is Thirty Years Old." *New York Times,* April 5, 1914, section 8, p. 7.

Egan, Pierce, *Sporting Anecdotes.* London, 1820.

————. *Life in London.* Vol. 2. London, 1821.

"Enthüllung des Geheimnisses des schachspielenden Automaton des Baron von Kempelen." *Blätter aus der Gegenwart.* Vol. 9. Leipzig, 1838.

"Etwas über den Schachspieler, und die Sprachmaschine des Hrn. Hof-Kammerraths von Kempele." *Magazin für das Neueste aus der Physik und Naturgeschichte,* 3 (1875): 183-92.

Evans, Henry Ridgely. *The Old and the New Magic.* Chicago, 1906.

————. *History of Magic and Conjuring.* Kenton, Ohio, 1930.

————. *Edgar Allan Poe and Baron von Kempelen's Chess-Playing Automaton.* Kenton, Ohio, 1939.

"The Festival Season Begins." *The Kansas City Times,* September 11, 1888, p. 3; also related articles September 12, p. 5; Sept. 18, p. 5; Sept. 19, p. 5; Sept. 22, p. 8; Sept. 24, p. 8; Sept. 26, p. 8; Sept. 27, p. 8; Sept. 29, p. 5; October 9, p. 8.

Fétis, F. J. "Maelzel." *Biographie Universelle des Musciens.* Paris, 1870. pp. 396–97.

Feudge, Fannie Roper. "Some Wonderful Automata." *St. Nicholas* 7, no. 4 (February 1880).

Fiske, Willard. *Chess Tales and Chess Miscellannies.* New York, 1912.

Friedel, Johann. "Nachricht meines Freundes über den Schachspieler." *Briefe aus Wien.* Leipzig and Berlin, 1784. pp. 481–86.

Frost, Thomas. *The Lives of the Conjurors.* London, 1881.

The Games of Gunsberg's Matches with Tchigorin and Steinitz. London, 1891.

Gavin, Thomas. *Kingkill.* New York, 1977.

Geyler, Johann Samuel Traugott. "Automat," *Physi-*

kalisches Wörterbuch. Vol. 1 (A and B). Leipzig, 1825. pp. 649–60.

Gibson, Walter. *Secrets of Magic, Ancient and Modern.* New York, 1967.

Gilmor, Robert. "The Diary of Robert Gilmor." *Maryland Historial Magazine* 17, nos. 3, 4 (September and December 1922): 330–41.

Gizychi, Jerzy. *A History of Chess.* Translated by A. Wojciechowski, D. Ronowicz, and W. Bartoszewski. London, 1971. First published in Polish in 1960.

Gooch, G. P. *Catherine the Great and Other Studies.* Hamden, Conn., 1966.

Gould, Hanna Flagg. *Poems.* Boston, 1835.

Grimm, Friedrich Melchior Baron, et Diderot, Raynal, Meister, etc. *Correspondance Littéraire, Philosophique et Critique.* Vol. 13 (September 1783). Paris, 1880.

Grover, Kenneth M., and Wiswell, Tommie. *Twentieth Century Checkers.* Philadelphia, 1946.

Gümpel, Charles Godfrey. "How Mephisto Was Caught, a Chess Legend." *The Gentleman's Magazine,* n.s. 27 (September 1881): 330–49.

————. "How the Devil Was Caught, a Chess Legend." *Brentano's Chess Monthly* 1 (1882): 427–33, 487–93.

Hagedorn, Ralph K. *Benjamin Franklin and Chess in Early America.* Philadelphia, 1958.

Hale, Philip et. al. "The 'Battle' Symphony, Opus 91," *The Beethoven Companion,* Edited by Thomas K. Scherman and Louis Biancolli, New York, 1972. pp. 906–18.

Halle, Johann Samuel. *Magie.* Berlin, 1785.

Harkness, Kenneth, and Battell, Jack Straley. "This Made Chess History." *Chess Review,* February–November 1947.

Hefter, Charles. "Ajeeb, the Automaton." *The American Checker Review* 1, no. 15 (November 1, 1888): 169–70; no. 17 (November 23, 1888): 193.

————. "Barker's Return." *The American Checker Review* 1, no. 24 (February 16, 1889): 286–88.

Heltai, H. Istvan. "Az önmüködö sakkozó-gép" (The Automatic Chess Machine). *Magyar Sakklap* 5, no. 3 (March–April 1909): 4–15.

Hindenburg, Carl Friedrich. *Ueber den Schachspieler des Herrn von Kempelen, nebst einer Abbildung und Beschreibung seiner Sprachmaschine.* Leipzig, 1784, 1785; in *Leipziger Magazin zur Naturkunde, Mathematik und Oekonomie.* Leipzig, 1784.

"A History-Making Tournament!" *Chess Life* 22, no. 2 (February 1967): 23.

"Hodges Celebrates 80th Birthday." *Chess Review* 9, no. 6 (June–July 1941): 135.

Hoffer, Leopold. "Our Portrait Gallery: Isidor Gunsberg." *The Chess Monthly* 10 (September 1888): 1–2.

Hopkins, A. A. *Magic: Stage Illusions and Scientific Diversions.* New York, 1901.

Huneker, James Gibbons. "Passing of the Eden Musée." *New York Times Magazine,* June 20, 1915, pp. 15–16.

Hunneman, W. *A Selection of Fifty Games from Those Played by the Automaton Chess Player.* London, 1820; in Walker,

Chess Studies, chap. 6, pp. 59–67.

Hunt, Douglas and Kari. *The Art of Magic.* New York, 1967.

Huon (E. E. Hulfish). "The History of a Certain Chess Player." *The Philadelphia Monthly Magazine* 6 (1859): 131–37, 153–61.

Hutton, Charles. "Automaton." *A Philosophical and Mathematical Dictionary.* 2 vols. London, 1815. Vol. 1, pp. 193–95. First published in Supplement, 1796.

"In Love with an Automaton." *Frank Leslie's Popular Monthly* 6, no. 5 (November 1878): 567–70.

Jenness, George A. *Maskelyne and Cooke, Egyptian Hall, London, 1873–1904.* London, 1967.

Jones, Thomas P. "Observations upon the Automaton Chess Player, Now Exhibiting in This City, by Mr. Maelzel, and upon Various Automata and Androides." *The Franklin Journal, and American Mechanic's Magazine* (Philadelphia) 3, no. 2 (February 1827): 125–32.

"Le Joueur d'Échecs," *La Petite Illustration Cinématographique* (Paris), no. 8 (February 1927).

Joveyn, Jorge. "Robot's Gambit." *New York Times Magazine,* May 4, 1952, pp. 48–49.

Julia de Fontenelle, Jean-Sébastien-Eugène. *Manuel Complet des Sorciers.* Paris, 1829.

Kempelen, Wolfgang von. *Le Mécanisme de la Parole.* Vienna, 1791; Vienna, 1791 (German).

Kennedy, Captain Hugh A. *Waifs and Strays, Chiefly from the Chess-board.* London, 1862, 1876.

Kobler, John. "Where Are They Now? The Pride of the Eden Musée." *The New Yorker* 19, no. 40 (November 20, 1943): 30 ff.

Köszega, I. and Pap, J. *Kempelen Farkas.* Budapest, 1955.

Kramm, C. "De Automaat Schaakspeler." *De Navorscher* (Amsterdam) 15, no. 12 (1865): 382.

Kummer, William F. "Maelzel's Automaton Chess-Player." *Philadelphia Sunday Dispatch,* February 1859.

Labourdonnais, Louis Charles Mahé de. "Napoléon, Amateur d'Échecs." *Le Palamède* 1, no. 1 (1836): 12–13.

———. "L'Automate Joueur d'Échecs," *Le Palamède,* 4, nos. 2, 3 (1839): 54–70.

Lardin, Jules. "Philidor Peint par Lui-meme." *Le Palamède,* 2d ser. 7, no. 1 (January 1847): 12–13.

Lasker, Edward. *The Adventure of Chess.* New York, 1949, 1959.

"Leben und Abenteuer eines Schachspielenden Automaten." *Der Sammler.* Vienna, 1837.

Leiber, Fritz (Francis Lathrop). "Poor Superman," *The Best of Fritz Leiber.* New York, 1974.

Lettera Sopra il Famoso Automa o Giucatore di Scacchi de Kempelen. Rome, 1786.

Levy, David. "Computer Chess—Past, Present and Future." *Chess Life and Review* 28, no. 12 (December 1973): 723–26.

———. *1975 U. S. Computer Chess Championship.* Woodland Hills, Calif., 1976.

———. *Chess and Computers.* Woodland Hills, Calif., 1976.

Lewald, August. "Kempelen's Schachmaschine." *Ein Menschenleben.* Vol. 7. Leipzig, 1845. pp. 320–24.

Lewis, William. *Oriental Chess.* London, 1817.

Liddell, Donald M. *Chessmen.* New York, 1937.

Lienard, J. S. "La Machine Parlante de Kempelen." *Bulletin du Groupe d'Acoustique Musicale* (Paris), no. 34 (March 28, 1968).

Lindner, Ernö. "Kempelen Farkas és Viszonylásai a Nyelvtudományhos." *Nyelvtudomanyi Kozlemények.* Pest, 1870. pp. 325–480.

"Lipshuetz and the Automaton." *American Chess Bulletin* 4 (1907): 14.

"Machine That Played Chess." London *Sunday Express,* January 27, 1946.

"Maelzel, Johann Nepomuk." *Grove's Dictionary of Music and Musicians.* 5th edition. Vol. 5 (L–M). New York, 1964.

"Maelzel's Conflagration of Moscow." *The Philadelphia Monthly Magazine* 1, no. 4 (January 15, 1828): 200.

Magee, James F., Jr. "The Chess Automaton, de Kempelen's." *The Good Companion Chess Problem Club, Our Folder* 4 (October 1916): 41–44, 46.

———. "Matter Relative to Maelzel's Automaton." *The Good Companion* 4 (November 1916–April 1917): 66–72, 83–84, 141–43, 168.

———. "More Automaton Dope and Knight Tricks." *The Good Companion* 4 (March 1917): 134–40.

———. "Café de la Régence." *The Good Companion* 5 (January 1918): 119–22.

———. "Ajeeb, Automaton Chess Player." *The Good Companion* 5, no. 7 (March 1918): 133.

———. "Automaton Echoes." *The Good Companion* 9 (January 1922): 73–77.

———. "Ajeeb, the Automaton Chess Player." *The Good Companion* 11 (November 1923–January 1924): 26–27, 68–71, 78–82.

———. "Mephisto, the Mechanical Chess Player." *The Good Companion* 11 (November 1923, April 1924): 27–29, 181–82.

Malo, Charles. *Bazar Parisien.* Paris, 1824.

Marek, George R. *Beethoven, Biography of a Genius.* New York, 1969.

Marshall, Frank J. *My Fifty Years of Chess.* Philadelphia, 1942.

Maskelyne, John Nevile. "Automata," part 4, *Leisure Hour,* March 29, 1879, pp. 198–200.

"Mazam, the Automaton." *The Draughts World* 13 (September–December 1899): xlvi, 664, 686, 703.

"Mephisto." *The Chess Player's Chronicle* 2 (1878): 114–15, 257–58.

"Mephisto." *The Westminster Papers* 11 (September 1878, March and April 1879): 93–94, 230, 253.

Miller, J. W. "Ajeeb the Chess Automaton" and numerous related articles. The *Cincinnati Commercial Gazette,* 1885–91.

Miller, Louis. "Mental States in Famous Chess Players." *Illinois Medical Journal* 26, no. 4 (October 1914): 414–18.

Mitchell, Silas Weir. "The Last of a Veteran Chess Player." *The Chess Monthly* (New York) 1 (January and

February 1857): 3–7, 40–45; *The Chess World* (London) 4 (April and May 1869): 1–4, 41–45.

Murray, H. J. R. *A History of Chess.* Oxford, 1913.

"Musical Notes on Prince Bernard's Trip to America, 1825." *The American-German Review* 10, no. 3 (February 1944): 27.

Napier, William Ewart. "Lest We Forget: A. B. Hodges." *Chess Review* 2, no. 12 (December 1934): 222.

"Napoleon and the Automaton." *American Chess Magazine* 3 (1899): 164.

Nettl, Paul. *Beethoven Encyclopedia.* New York, 1956.

Newborn, Monroe. *Computer Chess.* New York, 1975.

"The New Spanish Dancer." *New York Times,* October 2, 1890, p. 5.

Observations on the Automaton Chess Player Now Exhibited in London at 4, Spring Gardens, by an Oxford Graduate. London, 1819.

O'Connor, Richard. *Ambrose Bierce: A Biography.* Boston, 1967.

O'Dell, George C. D. *Annals of the New York Stage.* 15 vols. New York, 1940, 1970.

Oman, Carola. *Napoleon's Viceroy, Eugène de Beauharnais.* 1966.

Ord-Hume, Arthur W. J. G. *Clockwork Music.* New York, 1973.

Ostertag, Johann Filipp. *Etwas über den kempelischen Schachspieler.* Frankfurt am Main, 1785; in *Auswahl aus den kleinen Schriften des verstorbenen Johann Filipp Ostertag,* vol. 1. Sulzbach, 1810.

"Le Panharmonicon." *Journal de l'Empire,* March 9, 1807.

"Une Partie d'Échecs Gagnée par Napoléon." *Le Palamède,* 2d ser. 5, no. 7 (July 15, 1847): 328–30.

Pasquiez, Jean-Claude. *Automates et Robots.* Paris, 1961.

Pepper, Professor John Henry. *The True History of the Ghost; and All About Metempsychosis.* London, 1890.

"Pillsbury's Chess Career." *American Chess Bulletin* 20, no. 5 (May–June 1923): 89–91.

Poe, Edgar Allan. "Maelzel's Chess-Player." *Southern Literary Messenger* 2 (April 1836): 318–26; *The Complete Tales and Poems of Edgar Allan Poe.* Edited by Hervey Allen. New York, 1938; *The Portable Edgar Allan Poe.* Edited by Philip Van Doren. New York, 1945.

Poppe, Johann Heinrich Moritz von. *Wunder der Mechanik.* Tübingen, 1824.

Portal, Camille, and de Graffigny, Henri. *Merveilles de l'Horlogerie.* Paris, 1888.

Powers, Patrick. "The Automaton Chess-Player." *Chamber's Journal,* 7th ser. 13, no. 654 (June 9, 1923): 433–36.

"Problème du Cavalier." *Le Palamède* 2d ser., no. 13 (December 15, 1842): 268–77.

Proctor, Richard. "Automatic Chess and Card Playing." *The Cornhill Magazine,* 32 (November 1875): 584-96; *Eclectic Magazine,* 86: 46 ff. *Science Byways,* Philadelphia, 1876.

———. "Mechanical Chess Players." *Belgravia,* 39, no. 153 (July 1879): 71-90; *Rough Ways Made Smooth.* New York, 1880.

Racknitz, Joseph Friedrich, Freyherr zu. *Ueber den Schachspieler des Herrn von Kempelen und dessen Nachbildung.* Leipzig and Dresden, 1789.

Randi, The Amazing, and Sugar, Bert Randolph. *Houdini: His Life and Art.* New York, 1976.

Rémusat, Claire de. *Memoirs of Madame de Rémusat.* Translated by Mrs. Cashel Hoey and John Lillie. New York, 1894.

"The Resurrection of Ajeeb." *American Chess Bulletin,* 32, no. 1 (January 1935): 17

Richter, Johann Paul Friedrich. "Unterthänigste Borstellung unser, der sämtlichen Spielerund redenden Damen in Europa entgegen und wider die Einführung der Kempelischen Spiel– und Sprachmaschinen." *Auswahl aus des Teufels Papieren.* Gera, 1789. pp. 70–99.

"The Rival Automata, a Tale of Two Turks." *Columbia Chess Chronicle* 4 (1889): 94-95, 105-8.

Robert-Houdin, Jean Eugène. *Confidences d'un Prestidigitateur.* Blois, 1858; Paris, 1859; Translated by R. Shelton Mackenzie, Philadelphia, 1859 (English); Translated by Sir Frederick C. L. Wraxall, Philadelphia, 1859 (English); Translated by Sir Frederick C. L. Wraxall, London, 1860, 1942.

———. *Confidences et Révélations, Comment on Devient Sorcier.* Paris, 1868.

Roch, Eugène. *Essais sur les Voyages Aériens d'Eugène Robertson.* Paris, 1831.

Roget, P. M. "Description of a Method of Moving the Knight over Every Square of the Chess-board, without Going Twice over Any One; Commencing at Any Given Square, and Ending at Any Other Given Square of a Different Color." *Philosophical Magazine,* 3d ser. 16 (1840): 305 ff.

Ruskin, John. *Letters of John Ruskin to Charles Eliot Norton.* Cambridge, Mass., 1905. 2:71-72.

Saint-Amant, Pierre de. "Automate Joueur d'Échecs," *Le Palamède* 2d ser. no. 5 (April 15, 1842): 236–37.

Sarasin, J. G. (Geraldine Gordon Salmon). *This Way to Byzantium!* London, 1940.

"De Schaakspelende Automat." *Europa.* Dordrecht, 1838. pp. 416–27.

"Das Schachspiel." *Das Pfennig-Magazin* 2, no. 70 (August 30, 1834): 559-60.

Schindler, Anton Felix. *Beethoven as I Knew Him.* Edited by Donald W. MacArdle. Translated by Constance S. Jolly. London, 1966.

Scholes, Percy A. "Mechanical Reproduction of Music, 8. Maelzel's Inventions." *The Oxford Companion to Music.* 9th ed. London, 1956.

Schonberg, Harold C. *Grandmasters of Chess.* Philadelphia and New York, 1973.

"Schreiben über die Kempelische Schachspiel– und Redemaschine." *Hessische Beiträge zur Gelehrsamkeit und Kunst.* Vol. 1. Frankfurt am Main, 1785. pp. 475–87.

Sergeant, P. W., and Watts, W. H. *Pillsbury's Chess Career.* New York and London, 1922; Philadelphia, 1937.

Shannon, Claude E. "A Chess-Playing Machine." *Scientific American,* February 1950, pp. 48-51.

Shipman, Walter J. "America's Chess Champions." *Chessworld* 1, no. 2 (March–April 1964): 34-39.

Simmen, René, ed. *Der Mechanische Mensch.* Zurich, 1967.

Strunk, William, Jr. "Ajeeb." *Columbia Chess Chronicle,* 3 (July 14, 1888): 59.

Svendsen, Kester. "Chess Fiction in English to 1945: A Bibliography." *The Southwestern Journal* 5, no. 4 (1950).

Taruffi, G. A. *Lettre sur un Automate qui Joue aux Échecs.* Pressburg and Vienna, 1770.

Taylor, Joseph. "Automaton Chess Player." *Curiosities for the Ingenious.* London, 1821. pp. 29–32.

Thayer's Life of Beethoven. Revised and Edited by Elliot Forbes. 2 vols. Princeton, N.J., 1967.

Thicknesse, Philip. *The Speaking Figure, and the Automaton Chess-Player, Exposed and Detected.* London, 1784.

Thomas, Rowland. "Solved: Mystery of Ajeeb, Chess Automaton." *The New York Herald,* December 16, 1923, p. 3.

Tilton, Theodore. "Café de la Régence." *The Chess Monthly,* December 1886; *Chessworld,* 1, no. 2 (March–April 1964): 2-7.

Timbs, John. "The Automaton Chess Player." *Stories of Inventors and Discoverers in Science and the Useful Arts.* New York, 1860. pp. 88–92.

Tomlinson, Charles. "The Automaton Chess-Player." *The Saturday Magazine* 19 (1841). A series of five articles.

———. *Amusements in Chess.* London, 1845.

———. "Chess." *Quarterly Review* 85 (June 1849): 89–91.

———. "Chess-Playing Automata." Quoted from an article in *Notes & Queries. The Field* 36, no. 927 (October 1, 1870): 8.

"Torres and His Remarkable Automatic Devices." *Scientific American Supplement,* no. 2079, November 6, 1915, pp. 296-98.

"Le Trompette Automate." *Journal de l'Empire,* October 12, 1808.

Twiss, Richard. *Chess,* 2 vols. London, 1787–89.

———. *Miscellanies,* 2 vols. London, 1805.

"Ueber Herrn von Kempelens Schach-Spieler und Sprach-Maschine." *Der Teutsche Merkur,* October 1784, pp. 91-96; November 1784, pp. 178-82.

Van der Linde, Antonius. *Quellenstudien zu Geschichte des Schachspiels.* Berlin, 1881. pp. 294-96.

Vandermonde. "Remarques sur les Problèmes de Situation." *Mémoires de l'Académie Royale des Sciences.* Paris, 1771.

Vere, Arprey. *Ancient and Modern Magic.* London, 1879.

Wagner, Larry and Benson, Alan. "1st Microcomputer Chess Tournament." *Chess Life and Review* 33, no. 6 (June 1978): 311.

Walker, George. "Anatomy of the Chess Automaton." *Fraser's Magazine* 19 (June 1839): 717-31. In *Chess and Chessplayers.* London, 1850. pp. 1–37.

———. "The Café de la Régence." *Fraser's Magazine* 22 (December 1840): 671-77; *Littel's Museum of Foreign Literature,* n.s. no. 51 (March 1841): 360–60. In *Chess and Chessplayers.* London, 1850. pp. 247–90.

———. *Chess Studies: Comprising One Thousand Games.* London, 1844.

Walker, J. *Modus Operandi; or the Automaton Chess-Player,* a play in three acts. London, 1866.

Weber, Carl Maria von. "Der Trompeter." *Allgemeine Musikalische Zeitung,* no. 41 (October 7, 1812): 663–66.

Wellmer, Arnold. "Die Schachmaschine." *National Zeitung* (Berlin) 30, no. 113 (March 8, 1877).

White, Alain C. "A Problemist Who Might Have Been: Edgar Allen [sic] Poe." *The Good Companion Chess Problem Club* 11 (December 1923): 50–55.

"White Magic." *Encyclopaedia Britannica.* 9th ed. (1883). 15:208-10.

Willing, Charles. "Beethoven and Chess." *The Good Companion Chess Problem Club* 4 (May 1917): 169-81.

Willis, Robert. *An Attempt to Analyse the Automaton Chess Player, of Mr. de Kempelen. With an Easy Method of Imitating the Movements of That Celebrated Figure. . . . To Which is Added, a Copious Collection of the Knight's Moves Over the Chess Board.* London. 1821.

Wimsatt, W. K., Jr. "Poe and the Chess Automaton." *American Literature* 11, no. 2 (May 1939): 138-51.

Windisch, Karl Gottlieb von. A report in *K. K. Privil. Anzeigen Sammtlichen K. K. Erblandern.* Vol. 3. Vienna, 1773.

———. *Geographie des Koenigreichs Ungarn.* Pressburg, 1780.

———. *Briefe über den Schachspieler des Herrn von Kempelen.* Basel, 1783; Pressburg, 1783; Basel, 1783 (French); London, 1784 (English); Amsterdam, 1785 (Dutch); London, 1819 (English).

Wisker, John. "The Mystery of the Automaton." *The Popular Recreator* 1 (1873): 145-47.

Witt, W. D. "Chess and Checker Playing Automatons." *The Good Companion Chess Problem Club* 11 (June 1824): 208-10.

Wittenberg, Ernest. "Échec!" *American Heritage* 11, no. 2 (February 1960): 34-37, 82-85.

Zobrist, Albert L., and Carlson, Frederic R., Jr. "An Advice-Taking Chess Computer." *Scientific American,* June 1973, pp. 92-105.

General Index

Page numbers in *italics* refer to illustrations.

Chess Index

Games